ANALYZING SHORT STORIES

Ninth Edition Revised Printing

Joseph Lostracco

Austin Community College

George Wilkerson

Columbia State Community College

David Lydic

Austin Community College

Kendall Hunt

publishing company

For Supporting Material and Resources
VISIT

◀D℞WRITE▶

WWW.DRWRITE.COM

Cover image © "Blue Swallow Motel," Artist: Kerry Awn. Reprinted by permission.

Kendall Hunt
publishing company

www.kendallhunt.com
Send all inquiries to:
4050 Westmark Drive
Dubuque, IA 52004-1840

CONTENTS

10 Sample Essays

11 Analyzing Other Forms of Literature

Contents

The Philosophy Behind This Book

The approach used in this book is classic. We take a tried and true approach to the study of Literary Narration which has the following characteristics:

- **A Special Use of Language** How something is said is more important than what is said.
- **Probability** The characters and events have the appearance of reality.
- **Entertainment Value** The writing evokes an emotional response.

Our goal is to teach a basic approach to analyzing works of literature. We have chosen the short story as a basis for analysis because our teaching experience shows that it's the easiest place for students to begin learning the concepts of analysis and evaluation. The structure and elements are generally the same; each story contains a conflict, characters, a setting, an emphasis on language, and a clear distinctive voice.

While oral discussions of prose are valuable, the most common approach to evaluating the understanding of a work of literature is through an analytical essay which discusses a story's elements and explains their interrelationship, especially as they work together to produce a single effect.

The separate parts of an automobile engine can't make the car go; only by operating together can they accomplish that goal. To explain how an engine works, we need to know how each piece works in relation to each other piece. The same is true of analyzing literature. We need to understand how each of the elements works with the others to achieve the single effect that is central to the story.

Writing that performs this analytical function must be objective, present valid evidence, and draw reasonable conclusions that follow from the evidence. Emotional words and exclamatory terms are inappropriate. So are words which are ambiguous or confusing. Formal grammar and punctuation are important, especially as they contribute to the clarity of the writing, and the organization of the writing must conform to the traditional format for academic papers: an introduction (interpretation), body (evidence), and conclusion.

In this book, we provide the basic information needed to understand literary writing and promote the following basic format for writing a paper about a short story.

Part I.

A brief summary of the story is followed by a statement of the central idea (your interpretation of the story's meaning).

Part II.

A discussion of each element of the story as it relates to or supports the interpretation.

- Character
- Conflict
- Point of view
- Setting
- Language
- Tone

Part III.

A brief review of the elements of the story and their contribution to the central idea.

Once this basic approach has been mastered, a student can modify it to suit other needs. Compare and contrast one story with another or using the analysis as a basis, evaluate the story.

We have found that mastering the analytical process enhances the appreciation of literature and increases the ability to objectively judge a story's quality. Furthermore, this skill can be generalized and extended to nonliterary subjects, providing a basic methodology for writing about subjects in science and the humanities.

CHAPTER ONE

The Central Idea

"God has no need to justify His actions to man. He who built the universe can destroy it when He chooses. It is arrogance; it is perilously near blasphemy; for us to say what He may or may not do. This I could have accepted, hard though it is to look upon whole worlds and peoples thrown into the furnace. But there comes a point when even the deepest faith must falter, and now, as I look at the calculations lying before me, I know I have reached that point at last."

[from "The Star" by Arthur C. Clarke]

Some stories merely ask a question—the central idea may be to raise questions about how people live or behave. Life is complicated and messy—and so may be the process of inferring a story's meaning. This chapter deals with the basic concepts of central idea, interpretation, and the various types of ideas authors often write about.

THE CENTRAL IDEA

The central idea is the author's implied comment on the subject of the story. It reveals the author's view of some aspect of life. As such, the central idea is an organic part of the story and grows naturally from it. And while the story may do no more than ask a question about life (e.g., why do bad things happen to good people?), it rarely provides an answer.

Through the central idea, a story gives us insight into ourselves and increases our awareness of the part of our world that is presented by the story. When we have finished reading it, the attitude we feel toward the subject of the story is an indication of the central idea.

Kate Chopin's "Desiree's Baby" is about love and hate. The author's presentation of those conflicting human emotions gives the story its significance. We come away from it with the feeling that people who let hatred (born of bigotry), rather than love, guide their lives often invite tragic, self-destructive consequences. That's the central idea, and the way it is conveyed is what causes the story to stick in our minds.

THE CENTRAL IDEA AS THE GUIDING FORCE

As authors work to create a story, the central idea, or theme, drives their choices: what characters to create, where to place the conflict, what point of view is best, where and when the story takes place (the setting), and what words and phrases are best (the language). An author may not have a clearly defined central idea in mind when writing the story; he or she may not be consciously aware of the force behind it, but the central idea is there nonetheless. The author may clearly conceive it or it may form during the writing process. In fact, a critical reader, in the process of analyzing a story, may develop a clearer sense of the central idea than the author did. That awareness results from the reader working after the fact with the story as a whole.

The Central Idea and the Elements of Fiction

Analyzing a story requires a thorough examination of how each piece (character, conflict, setting, and so on) contributes to the whole, how they work together to achieve the central idea. Each element influences the central idea and, in turn, is influenced by it. And very often, a specific element communicates the theme, especially when change occurs within one or more of the elements, i.e., a change in the character, a change in the conflict, a change in the setting, a shift in tone. In some instances, a particular element may be so essential to the central idea that it dictates the form of one or more of the other elements.

THE CENTRAL IDEA AS THE INTERPRETATION

Interpretation is the process of deriving a generalization from a set of specifics. An interpretation makes a general statement about the meaning of a story based on the specific evidence within it. That generalization is the statement of the story's central idea or theme; the evidence that produced it consists of the specifics of each element (character, conflict, point of view, setting, and language).

Because our own experiences can give us a deeper understanding of ourselves, of other people, and of life in general, we can also gain insights vicariously through literature. In a well-written story, the central idea grows naturally out of the unique combination of narrative elements, and that idea is inseparable from the narrative that embodies it.

An essay analyzing a short story always contains an interpretation which is the thesis of the essay. Such an analysis should always state the interpretation in the introductory paragraph following a brief summary of what happens in the story. (This is for the benefit of someone who may not have read it.) The summary includes only the events essential to understanding what the story is about. Subsequent paragraphs, analyzing each of the story's elements and the relationship between those elements and the central idea, should include more details and provide support for the interpretation.

During the analysis, some evidence may be found that cannot be supported by the central idea. When this occurs, the central idea needs to be modified to account for this evidence. To be valid, the central idea must be supported by all of the available evidence. All of the elements of the story—character, conflict, setting, and so forth—must fit. Nothing should be out of place or extraneous.

One way we deduce the central idea of a story is to ask, "What is the story submitting as evidence?" Consider John Steinbeck's "The Chrysanthemums." If Steinbeck had been a scientist interested in the behavior of people living in a particular set of circumstances (i.e., farm wives who are childless), he might have conducted experiments, studying such people and collecting information about them. And, eventually, he might report that nine out of ten women who live in isolated areas for an extended period of time and are childless are more apt to be frustrated and easily misled than those who have children and live in urban areas. With that evidence, he might have then made the general observation that isolation and childlessness create circumstances that make women vulnerable.

But Steinbeck was a writer, not a scientist, so he chose the literary method to illustrate the idea. His approach to defining a truth of human nature is the opposite of that of the scientist. He relied on the human tendency to generalize on the basis of emotion rather than scientific evidence. Knowing this, he created a story that *seems* real. He created characters for whom we could feel emotions like those we feel toward real people. Then he simply allowed us to make inferences based on the fictitious experience in the same way we make inferences based on real experiences.

We must also remember that a story must entertain us. In fact, that's all that some stories do. They simply stir our emotions for the entertainment value. They don't mean to direct that emotional response toward some kind of central idea statement about life. For example, a good mystery story is meant to create suspense, an adventure tale produces excitement, horror stories generate fear, and comical stories produce smiles and laughter. That's primarily what they do.

SOURCES FOR CENTRAL IDEAS

Central ideas are commonly found in stories that continue to be read long after they are first published. They're common because great writers deal with the truths about life that don't change. The statements they make are universal and they often fall within the following categories.

Psychological Stories

Stories that make a statement about individual human behavior, psychological motives, the way our minds work and "what makes us tick," have a psychological basis. They make statements that are not value judgments (telling us what's right or wrong), but simply an observation about behavior that is part of the human condition; it's just the way some of us behave. A central idea of Updike's "A & P," that teenage boys are apt to act like fools when smitten by a pretty girl, is simply a fact of life. It's not likely to change.

Sociological Stories

The behavior of humans in groups (nationalities, small town folk, city dwellers, country folk, or those in regions like the American South or Northern Ireland) is the domain of the sociological central idea. A story with a sociological basis points out a truth about groups rather than individuals. Showing us that people tend to go along with the crowd, as in "The Lottery," produces a sociological story.

Philosophical Stories

When a story points out a limitation of human perception, like the inability to distinguish fantasy from reality, it has philosophy at its core. Such stories address questions of existence, like

- *Why are we here?*
- *Is life worth living?*
- *Is there life after death?*
- *Do the ends justify the means?*
- *What is the truth?*
- *What is our duty to one another?*

While the story may raise questions like these, they do not necessarily provide an answer. Check out "The Star" and "The Possibility of Evil" for stories that ask some of these important questions.

Didactic Stories

Those stories that take a clear position on an issue (e.g., *abortion is wrong*, *capital punishment is right*) and try to change the reader's mind, are called *didactic* (some might say *preachy*.) While the philosophical story might raise a moral or ethical question without proposing an answer, didactic stories do give an answer. The writer wants the reader to accept his or her particular view of the world and/or life. In such stories, everything is aimed at promoting that view. And discussions of such stories often refer to "the moral." If your inclination is to say "The moral of the story is . . ." you are very likely dealing with a didactic story. "Son in the Afternoon" might be considered a didactic story, one making obvious how wrong it is to judge people by the color of their skin.

Escapist Stories

As explained earlier, some stories are aimed solely at providing us with an escape from our everyday life. They are simply meant to generate an emotional response (laughter, sorrow, fear, anger, horror, repulsion, surprise, or shock) for its own sake. Many of us enjoy those responses, and some stories are written simply to evoke them. If some kind of meaning is inferred, it may be that you feel the need for a meaning, not that the story was designed to produce it. (As children, we are often taught to look for the "moral" of a story and that can be a hard habit to break.)

Nonetheless, a writer knows that a good story will evoke an emotional response and a boring story doesn't succeed in eliciting a response. For example, Edgar Allan Poe's "The Cask of Amontillado" is primarily a horror story. The central idea is to entertain us by generating an emotional reaction: horror. If that's all the story does, then the central idea of the story is "to entertain," and the only issue our analysis has to settle is what emotion the story aroused. Of course, Poe's story may also show the darker side of human nature, the possibility of responding out of proportion to a real or imagined insult.

But if the reader comes away from a story like Steinbeck's "The Chrysanthemums" with a feeling of sadness about Elisa's situation, it should be clear that sadness is not the central idea because the story goes for something beyond that. The sadness we feel has been aroused to support the story's central idea: how isolation and childlessness can make women easy prey for exploitation.

IF THE CENTRAL IDEA ISN'T A MORAL, WHAT IS IT?

Students often begin their study of literature by looking for "the moral to the story." But a serious literary analysis requires that we reach a higher level of understanding. Learning the difference between a central idea and a moral is critical. A moral tells us how to live (or not live) and it's often in the form of an 'If . . . then . . .' statement. (*If you don't think before you act, then you'll get into trouble.*) A central idea, on the other hand, says *Insensitive people who act without thinking sometimes get into trouble.*

A moral is absolute. The moral says that not thinking before you act will *always* produce trouble. There are no exceptions. But the central idea says that insensitive people who act before they think sometimes get into trouble. The moral tells us what to do: *don't act without thinking*, but the central idea tells us about *insensitive people who act without thinking*.

John Updike, author of "A & P," wants us to see adolescence as an impulsive age. He created Sammy, an adolescent, who seems very real. Perhaps he reminds us of someone we know. Updike then lets us in on the way Sammy thinks and acts. He tells the story in such a way that when we have finished reading it, we don't just say *That adolescent boy acted foolishly*. Instead, we take that idea to another level and say *Adolescent boys can be impulsive*. But there is no moral in that; the story does not admonish adolescents about the dangers of being impulsive.

Notice in that last paragraph the difference between *adolescent*, which is specific and *adolescents*, which is general. The central idea of "A & P" lies in the general statement about adolescence: adolescents are often impulsive. Sammy is simply a specific example; he's a piece of evidence created by the writer to support his case that adolescents can be impulsive.

rushing =

WRITING THE ANALYSIS

A brief summary, a single paragraph of about one hundred fifty words (or fewer) that tells the reader the major details of the story (the main characters, the setting, and the major events) should open any analysis. This summary should include only the major highlights of the story; the details are saved for later. And the last sentence of this summary should be a statement of the central idea.

This is a standard approach to writing an analytical essay. The central idea is usually a single sentence at the end of the summary. The sentence with the central idea should leave no room for doubt. So a safe way to be sure it's clear is to begin the sentence this way: *The central idea of this story is that . . .*

Since in your discussion you are proving that your interpretation is a reasonable one, you must give evidence to support it. Explain clearly, explain where in the story your evidence occurs, and provide a generous number of brief direct quotations.

Being placed as it is at the end of the essay's first paragraph, the central idea statement functions as a thesis statement.

SAMPLES

Before reading the following examples, you might want to read the stories they were written about. These examples, written by students, are of introductory paragraphs for analytical papers.

The Central Idea in "A & P"

"A & P," by John Updike, is the story of a significant event in the life of Sammy, a nineteen-year-old grocery store checker. One summer day, three girls dressed in bathing suits come into the store. Before Sammy can ring up their purchase, Lengel, the store manager, sees the girls and informs them that their attire is inappropriate and that they must be decently dressed the next time they come in. Embarrassed for the girls, and in an attempt to impress them, Sammy tells Lengel that he is quitting. Lengel, recognizing Sammy's resignation for what it is, gives him an opportunity to change his mind, but Sammy is determined to follow through with his gesture even though he realizes "how hard the world was going to be to me hereafter." Updike's Central Idea suggests that youthfulness and immaturity contribute to impulsive decisions, and that the consequences of such decisions contribute to our growth.

The Central Idea in "I Want to Know Why"

"I Want to Know Why," by Sherwood Anderson, is a story about an adolescent who has a passion for race horses, and the dilemma he faces when confronted with the shocking reality of his role-model horse trainer. The boy, who narrates the story, takes a trip with three friends to Saratoga to see a horse race. Before the race, the boy spots his favorite horse, Sunstreak, and Sunstreak's trainer, Jerry Tilford, whom the boy admires. The night after the race, the boy goes alone to search for his hero and is enraged to find him in a house full of prostitutes, leaving the boy to wonder how a man of such valor and beauty could be found with "bad women." Anderson's story reveals how the actions and morals of role models have a strong influence on those who admire them. The Central Idea also touches on the pain associated with the loss of innocence.

The Central Idea in "Like a Bad Dream"

Heinrich Boll's "Like a Bad Dream" is the story of a dutiful husband striving to get ahead in the business world. The questionable ethics involved in negotiating a contract, and the willingness of the participants (including his wife) to support these practices, is somewhat shocking to the protagonist. When he sees how easily he becomes a willing participant in the affair, it all seems like a bad dream to him, leaving the reader and the protagonist wondering if the pursuit of material gain is worth the agony of compromising one's moral convictions. The Central idea of the story is that there is an inherent conflict between moral values and material success.

The Central Idea in "A Worn Path"

"A Worn Path," by Eudora Welty, is the story of an aged black woman's difficult cross-country journey from her rural home to a distant town where she must go to get her grandson's medicine. In spite of her age and frailty, and because of her determination and courage, she overcomes physical and human obstacles to accomplish her task. Welty's Central Idea is that despite indignities, suffering, and prejudice, the nobility of the human spirit can prevail.

The Central Idea in "Miss Brill"

Katherine Mansfield's "Miss Brill" is the story of a shy schoolteacher who spends her Sundays sitting in a public park imagining herself and others around as actors in a stage play. A young couple's rude remarks shatter her illusion of belonging to the group in the park and put an end to her satisfying self-deception. The story's Central Idea reveals how lonely, shy people can be deeply hurt when their illusions of "belonging" are shattered and they must face the lonely singularity of their lives.

You may have noticed in these examples that while some of the central idea statements do not begin with the phrase "The central idea of the story is that . . ." you had no problem understanding the interpretation. Beginning students would do well to stay with the "formula" approach, but once you become comfortable with the central idea concept you will be able to modify the way you state it. Notice in the following how each of these central ideas could be phrased using the formula approach.

Instead of . . .

The central idea of this story is that youthfulness and immaturity contribute to impulsive decisions, and that the consequences of such decisions contribute to our growth

. . . we could say

Anderson's story reveals how the actions and morals of role models have a strong influence on those who admire them.

Instead of . . .

The central idea of this story is that there is an inherent conflict between moral values and material success.

. . . we could say

> Boll's theme is that there is an inherent conflict between moral values and material success.

Instead of . . .

> The central idea of this story is that dignity is its own reward and that, despite indignities, suffering, and prejudice, the nobility of the human spirit can prevail.

. . . we could say

> Welty implies that dignity is its own reward and that, despite indignities, suffering, and prejudice, the nobility of the human spirit can prevail.

Instead of . . .

> The central idea of this story is that lonely, shy people can be deeply hurt when their illusions of "belonging" are shattered and they must face the lonely singularity of their lives.

. . . we could say

> The story reveals how lonely, shy people can be deeply hurt when their illusions of belonging are shattered and they must face the lonely singularity of their lives.

COMMON INTERPRETATION PITFALLS

Whether you read for pleasure or as part of an assignment, you should remain aware of the guiding principles of interpretation. The goal is to identify the central idea and explain how you determined it without falling into the pitfalls that trap many beginners. Don't look for the one correct interpretation or reject an obvious interpretation because it conflicts with your own values. Interpretations differ from one reader to the next; some central ideas are complex and some may conflict with your own view of the world. Consider the following common errors.

Differing Interpretations

Because everyone's experiences are unique, no two readers respond to and interpret a story in exactly the same way. Likewise, there is no single best way to express the central idea of a story. There is only a range of ideas. The best stories have multiple levels of meaning, so they are open to various interpretations. And serious readers know that most stories require more than one reading before the central idea becomes clear.

Complex Ideas

Sometimes you may sense the central idea, but you're unable to put it into words. Don't give up; analysis involves finding the words to express the sensed meaning of a story. In other cases, the central idea may be too complex to reduce to a single-sentence statement, so you may need to use the entire analysis to elaborate and clarify your interpretation.

Ideas That Conflict with Your Own

You can't ignore or deny the theme of a story merely because you don't agree with it. Keep in mind that authors are only showing us how they see some aspect of life. You shouldn't bend the story to fit *your* view. A story is the expression of an author's vision or experience. While that vision or experience may differ from yours, it cannot be ignored. After all, a major function of literature is to entertain, and one way an author may entertain us is to challenge our way of looking at life, at other people, or even at ourselves.

"The Lottery" has been one of the most challenged American short stories since its appearance in *The New Yorker* in 1946. It unsettles readers because it questions the propensity of people to blindly follow tradition. But just because readers don't like what it says doesn't mean the story doesn't say it.

Meaning Beyond the Story

Because a story's theme is a generalization about people and life, the interpretation must not be limited to the specific characters and situations of the story. They represent something larger. Sometimes we must probe beneath the surface to discover what the story can reveal. To interpret a story correctly, focus on what the action means rather than on the action itself.

Reading Exercise:

See if you can determine the central idea in Arthur C. Clarke's "The Star." After you've read the story, try writing a Central Idea statement. Remember to begin the statement this way: *The Central Idea of "The Star," by Arthur C. Clarke, is that . . .*

CHAPTER TWO

Character

> "Paul was tall for his age and very thin, with high, cramped shoulders and a narrow chest. His eyes were remarkable for a certain hysterical brilliancy, and he continually used them in a conscious, theatrical sort of way, peculiarly offensive in a boy. The pupils were abnormally large, as though he were addicted to belladonna, but there was a glassy glitter about them which that drug does not produce."
>
> **[from "Paul's Case" by Willa Cather]**

Analyzing a short story requires a careful examination of the characters and the parts they play in the execution of the story's central idea. Characters can be defined as round or flat and static or dynamic. And authors use a variety of ways to present and develop them. Once you can identify the characteristics and understand how and why writers develop them as they do, you will be well on the way to a solid analysis of the story.

CHARACTER TYPES

The characters in a story are created by the author to advance the action. They're usually human, but animals can be characters too (as in Liam O'Flaherty's "The Hawk" or the husky dog in Jack London's "To Build a Fire."). Once in a great while a natural force, like nature or time, is just as much a character as a human being because they play a major part. Sometimes they are as much a hero or villain as the other players. Jack London used a force of nature as a character in "To Build a Fire" and there has been a spate of films (*Twister*, *Volcano*, *Typhoon*, etc.) where the main "character" driving the story forward is a natural force. However, if human beings or even animals are key to the story, they usually are a better choice to discuss as characters, while natural forces probably work better as a type of conflict (see Chapter 3).

Round and Flat Characters

A character is called flat if he or she has only one dimension. For example, the porter in "The Bride Comes to Yellow Sky" is described this way:

> . . . he surveyed them [the newlyweds] from afar with an amused and superior grin. On other occasions he bullied them with skill in ways that did not make it exactly plain to them that they were being bullied. He subtly used all the manners of the most unconquerable kind of snobbery. He oppressed them; but of this oppression they had small knowledge . . .

That is all we are told about this man and, so far as the story goes, it's all we need to know. His job is to give the reader a sense of how others reacted to the couple on the train. He is one-sided: flat.

But when we say characters are round, we're saying they have many sides to their role. We see their complexity and we are given many details of their personality. We see that they are not black and white, completely perfect or completely flawed; there's a "a gray area."

Character development is relative. The central/major character will always be rounder—more thoroughly developed—than the supporting minor character(s) in the same story, even though the central character of one story may not be as round as the central character of another story. For example, Tess Hutchinson is the central character of "The Lottery" because the story focuses on her throughout its telling. However, Tess is not nearly as developed, not nearly as round, as Paul in "Paul's Case" or Sammy in "A & P." We know much more about each of those young men than we know about Tess.

Details

Unique physical and behavioral details make a character seem more realistic. Some of these details may concern the character's physical appearance; others might focus on how the character acts. Notice the careful selection of details in this description of Paul from "Paul's Case" by Willa Cather:

> Once, when he had been making a synopsis of a paragraph at the blackboard, his English teacher had stepped to his side and attempted to guide his hand. Paul had started back with a shudder and thrust his hands violently behind him. The astonished woman could scarcely have been more hurt and embarrassed had he struck at her. The insult was so involuntary and definitely personal as to be unforgettable. In one way and another, he had

made all his teachers, men and women alike, conscious of the same feeling of physical aversion. In one case he habitually sat with his hand shading his eyes; in another had made a running commentary on the lecture, with humorous intent.

The character is carefully drawn. One of the unique things we learn about him is that he made all of his teachers uncomfortable by doing things like commenting on a lecture or sitting with his hand shading his eyes. He's clearly not like others his age.

The "Gray Area"

Real people are rarely all good or all bad. Their personalities are multifaceted. They may show one side to their family, another side to their friends, and yet another side to their co-workers. A good story makes a character real by revealing his or her many sides. The author gives them rich, complex, and even ambiguous personalities to make them seem real. (Read Katherine Mansfield's "Miss Brill" for a good example of a complex, concisely drawn character.)

Complexity

Rather than giving us simplistic descriptions ("Everyone loved him" or "She was a warm and loving person") a good writer spends some time telling us things about the character that will make us feel as if we know him or her. The writer doesn't have to tell us that the character is a warm and loving person; we can see it in the character's words and actions.

Major and Minor Characters

The most common structure for a short story includes a major character and one or more minor characters. The focus of the story is usually on the major character and the role of the minor characters is to enhance that focus.

Major Characters

The central (or major) character is who the story is about. He or she is crucial to the story and the action; the story revolves around what that character says and does. This character is usually "round." Without him or her there would be no story.

Minor Characters

The remaining characters in a story are never as fully developed as the major character. (This is in contrast with a novel, where a writer has the space to develop even minor characters; short stories don't usually allow that luxury.) Minor, supporting characters may contribute to the action, add to the story's meaning, or serve as a complement or a contrast to the central character. They are usually flat, lacking complexity, and are portrayed in broad strokes, with little attention to detail.

Stereotypes

A stereotype is a special type of flat character. A stereotype conforms to a pattern that has already been established in other works of literature. The personality is recognized easily and quickly; we already know it, so the author doesn't have to provide much. Often, the personality of a stereotype can be summed up in a single phrase: the miserly money-lender; the sweet, lovely heroine waiting to be rescued by another stereotype, the brave, wholesome and handsome hero. And that hero may have to confront the refined, but totally evil villain and his dim-witted, but loyal servant. (Read Richard Connell's "The Most Dangerous Game" for examples of those last two stereotypes.)

A writer who lacks the skill or imagination to invent a new, unique character may use a stereotype. It might be done for a humorous effect or to save time, but stereotypes generally weaken a story's impact and deprive it of "newness." If we know the character type, we can anticipate what he or she will do, so there are no surprises. Nonetheless, even a skillful writer may occasionally use a stereotype. If it suits the central idea or produces a needed effect (especially if the effect is humor or satire), a stereotype may be called upon to play a trivial part, but never to serve as the main character. Occasionally, a good writer may even use a stereotyped character as a central one. For example, Dorothy Parker's "Big Blonde" uses Hazel Morse, a stereotypical "dumb blonde," a "bimbo," as the central character. Hazel is financially supported by a series of salesmen for their pleasure, as their "party girl" when they come into New York City. As she ages and realizes that getting older increases her limitations, she attempts suicide. Parker uses Hazel to show the depth of human feelings present behind the superficial, stereotyped image seen by others.

Sometimes an inexperienced reader may describe a character as a stereotype without realizing that the character is actually the source, not the result, of stereotyping. Stephen Crane's "The Bride Comes to Yellow Sky" includes Scratchy, the town drunk. When the story first appeared (in 1898), the "western" was still a new genre and Scratchy was an original. But since then his character has been repeated frequently in westerns. Rather than being a stereotype, Scratchy is the prototype, the original from which others were copied.

Static and Dynamic Characters

Characters are defined as static or dynamic on the basis of whether or not they stay the same from the beginning to the end of the story. Those who undergo some important personality or behavioral change are considered "dynamic;" characters who remain the same are called "static."

The Static Character

Static characters do not change in any basic way during the course of a story. They have the same values, the same attitudes, and the same behavior patterns at the end of the story as they had at the beginning. Because short stories are compact, most focus on the personalities of static characters. Walter Mitty is the main character in James Thurber's "The Secret Life of Walter Mitty." He is an excellent example of a static character. He never changes from the beginning to the end of the story. This is because Thurber's central idea is about that type of character; Mitty's static nature is essential. If he changes (from a meek daydreamer to an active "go-getter"), the entire story changes and so does the central idea.

The Dynamic Character

Dynamic characters undergo a fundamental change in their nature. The experiences depicted in the story result in an alteration of the character's personality in a significant way. In John Updike's "A & P," Sammy, the main character, is a dynamic figure. At the beginning, and throughout most of the story, he is immature and foolish, but at the end of the story he realizes he can't act that way anymore. We can tell that his values and attitudes have changed when he says, "My stomach kind of fell as I felt how hard the world was going to be to me hereafter." He has begun to mature.

With the exception of stories that are fantasies, we expect plausible motivations for changes in a character's personality. If a character is to be credible, the changes in their behavior must also be credible. Mystical revelations and sudden insights are not realistic causes for change.

CHARACTER PRESENTATION OR EXPOSITION

The way the author defines develops, and reveals a character to the reader is called "presentation" or "exposition." Character presentation may be either direct or indirect. In a direct presentation, the author uses explicit statements to tell what a character is like. ("Jack was a nervous boy, easily frightened by the slightest noise and not comfortable in strange places.") In an indirect (or "dramatic") presentation, the author shows us a character's personality by presenting the character's actions, words, or thoughts. ("When the school bell rang, Jack was surprised, nearly jumping out of his seat. Later, when his family moved to their new house, he stayed in the car. At least that had not changed.")

An author may choose from four methods of exposition:

- What the narrator of the story says, (direct)
- What the character does (the character's actions), (indirect)
- What the character says (the character's words), (indirect)
- What the character thinks (the character's thoughts), (indirect).

What the Narrator Says (Direct)

What the narrator of the story says directly about a character is usually reliable. After all, it is the author's story and the characters are the author's creations. Notice how much the narrator of this passage from Sherwood Anderson's "Brother Death" reveals about the children in the story:

> They were both children, but something had made them both in an odd way. Mary was fourteen and Ted eleven, but Ted wasn't strong and that rather evened things up. They were the children of a well-to-do Virginia farmer named John Grey in the Blue Ridge country in Southwestern Virginia . . . Ted had some kind of a heart disease, a lesion or something of the sort, the result of a severe attack of diphtheria when he was a child of eight. He was thin and not strong but curiously alive. The doctor said he might die at any moment, might just drop down dead. The fact had drawn him peculiarly close to his sister Mary. It had awakened a strong and determined maternalism in her.

We know that Ted is thin, not strong, and close to his sister Mary. These are facts provided directly by the writer. They are the "givens" of the character.

Another example is from Jack London's "To Build a Fire." Early in the story the narrator says about the central character that "he was quick and alert in the things of life, but only in the things, not in the significances." From this direct characterization we know he is practical but shortsighted. We realize later, therefore, that if he were more thoughtful and looked at the world in a deeper way he might not have gotten himself into the predicament we see later.

What the Character Does (Indirect)

A character's actions help define the personality in the same way people's actions define them in real life. Behavior under certain circumstances or in a given situation provides clues to the character's true self. In this and other dramatic methods of characterization, the author involves the reader by setting up situations that force the reader to make inferences. We learn about the character by what the author *shows* us rather than what the narrator tells us. Here's a description of the main character of John Steinbeck's "The Chrysanthemums" getting ready to go out with her husband. Notice what her actions tell us about her.

> In the kitchen she reached behind the stove and felt the water tank. It was full of hot water from the noonday cooking. In the bathroom she tore off her soiled clothes and flung them into the corner. And then she scrubbed herself with a little block of pumice, legs and thighs, loins and chest and arms, until her skin was scratched and red. When she had dried herself she stood in front of the mirror in her bedroom and looked at her body. She tightened her stomach and threw out her chest. She turned and looked over her shoulder at her back.
>
> After a while she began to dress slowly. She put on her newest underclothing and her nicest stockings and the dress which was the symbol of her prettiness. She worked carefully on her hair, pencilled her eyebrows, and rouged her lips.

[handwritten margin note: angry women]

She didn't simply get undressed; she tore off her clothes and flung them into the corner. That the author chose those words to describe her undressing is his way of revealing her state of mind. She now feels frustrated with her limitations. She is ridding herself of some part of her former doubts with energy and decisiveness.

What the Character Says (Indirect)

What characters say is often more revealing than their actions; however, in order to draw valid conclusions about a character's personality, the reader must consider the character's words in relation to the character's mood, the situation the character is in, the character's relationship to others in the story, and whether or not the character's behavior is consistent with the words.

The Character's Mood: Does the character seem to say one thing, but mean another? If so, the author may be showing us something about the character's state of mind.

The Situation: Is there something ironic about the circumstances or something that the character does not know, but we do? Writers will often let the reader know about a character's circumstances so we are "in on" it.

The Relationship Between Characters: Is there an unspoken understanding between the characters that changes the nature of the remarks or affects the way they are to be taken? If a character speaks one way to one character and differently to another, the author may be telling us something important about them.

The Consistency Between the Character's Words and Actions: What is the character doing while speaking? Is that action consistent with the words? Did he say "I love my dog" but then kick him?

Notice in this passage from Kate Chopin's "Desiree's Baby" how the author lets Desiree speak and how her own words tell us much about her.

"Oh, Armand is the proudest father in the parish, I believe, because it is a boy, to bear his name; though he says not, that he would have loved a girl as well. But I know it isn't true. I know he says that to please me. And mama," she added, drawing Madame Valmonde's head down to her, and speaking in a whisper, "he hasn't punished one of them—not one of them— since the baby is born. Even Negrillon, who pretended to have burnt his leg that he might rest from work—he only laughed, and said Negrillon was a great scamp. Oh, mama, I'm so happy; it frightens me."

Desiree tells us about a difference between what Armand says ("that he would have loved a girl as well") and what she knows to be true ("he says that to please me.")

What the Character Thinks (Indirect)

The ability to tell us what a character thinks is one of the unique aspects of fiction. In real life, we can never truly know what someone else thinks, but in a story we can. And it is often the best clue to a character's personality. A character's thoughts constitute the most intimate part of his or her nature; they are the most revealing. A glimpse inside a character's mind provides a more reliable basis for making inferences about his or her personality-even more than actions or words.

In this second passage from "Desiree's Baby," Kate Chopin makes us privy to one of the character's thoughts:

> He thought Almighty God had dealt cruelly and unjustly with him; and felt, somehow, that he was paying Him back in kind when he stabbed thus into his wife's soul. Moreover he no longer loved her, because of the unconscious injury she had brought upon his home and name.

Without this "inside look" at what the character thinks, we would never know so much about Armand and we would never see that he does not even entertain the thought that the situation may have been caused by his genes, not hers. We might assume that knowing what characters think is direct characterization since we see directly into their mind. But seeing Armand's thoughts still requires us to surmise what kind of person he really is, so what the character thinks is still indirect.

Reading Exercise:

See if you can determine the central idea in Willa Cather's "Paul's Case." After you've read the story, try writing a central idea statement. Then look at what happens to the main character (for whom the story is named) and determine how this ties in to the central idea.

CHAPTER THREE

Conflict

"The two men faced each other at a distance of three paces. He of the revolver smiled with a new and quiet ferocity. 'Tried to sneak up on me' he said. 'Tried to sneak up on me!' His eyes grew more baleful. As Potter made a slight move-ment, the man thrust his revolver venomously forward. 'No; don't you do it, Jack Potter. Don't you move a finger toward a gun just yet. Don't you move an eyelash. The time has come for me to settle with you, and I'm goin' to do it my own way, and loaf along with no interferin'. So if you don't want a gun bent on you, just mind what I tell you.'

Potter looked at his enemy. 'I ain't got a gun on me, Scratchy,' he said. 'Hon-est, I ain't.'"

[from "The Bride Comes to Yellow Sky" by Stephen Crane]

A story's action consists of a sequence of events called the "plot." Most authors present these events in chronological order, but occasionally they may choose to present them in a non-chronological sequence, out-of-time order. Conflicts, which occur when two or more forces collide, drive the plot. A conflict results from a cause and effect relationship between events. The first event in "Jack and the Beanstalk" is his mother's request that he take the cow and sell it at the market. In the second event, Jack is duped into trading the cow for some beans. This sets up the conflict. In the third event, Jack's mother, on learning what Jack has done, becomes angry and throws the beans out of the window. This causes the next event; the beanstalk begins to grow . . . and you know the rest.

DEVIATING FROM CHRONOLOGICAL ORDER

In John Steinbeck's "The Chrysanthemums," the narrative unfolds chronologically. Steinbeck begins with the first event: Elisa Allen, work-ing in her flower garden, and looking down across the yard at Henry, her husband, who is talking to two men in business suits. From there the story moves forward through time to the last event, which occurs as the wagon Elisa and her husband are riding in heads into town and we read that Elisa "turned up her coat collar so he could not see she was crying weakly like an old woman."

If it serves a special purpose (usually determined by the central idea), the writer can take the reader back and forth in time, telling the last event first and saving the first event to be told last. This can be utilized for a surprise effect or for a suspense that's created when an event is concealed until the end of the story, even though it occurred earlier. For example, in a mystery, beginning the story with the details of the murder may rob it of the suspense it would hold if that were saved for last.

Here's the plot—the sequence of events—in Kate Chopin's "Desiree's Baby:"

1. Armand's mother writes the letter that tells of Armand being African American.
2. The Valmondes find Desiree, an orphan.
3. Desiree grows up into a beautiful girl.
4. Armand rides by and falls in love with her.
5. Armand and Desiree are married.
6. The baby is born.
7. Armand is proud; he does not punish his slaves.
8. Madame Valmonde comes to visit.
9. Armand's behavior changes (baby is about 3 months old).
10. Desiree recognizes that the baby is African American.
11. She writes to Madame Valmonde.
12. Madame Valmonde replies, *Come home*.
13. Desiree goes to Armand with the letter.
14. He tells her to go.
15. Desiree takes the baby and leaves (commits suicide).
16. Armand burns all remnants of Desiree and the baby.
17. Armand finds the letter his mother wrote.

When Kate Chopin tells the story, she changes the order; she begins with the eighth event. So, as you read it, the events are presented in the following sequence:

8. Madame Valmonde comes to visit.
2. The Valmondes find Desiree, an orphan.
3. Desiree grows up into a beautiful girl.
4. Armand rides by and falls in love with her.
5. Armand and Desiree are married.
6. The baby is born.
7. Armand is proud; he does not punish his slaves.
9. Armand's behavior changes (baby is about 3 months old).
10. Desiree recognizes that the baby is African American.

11. She writes to Madame Valmonde.
12. Madame Valmonde replies, *Come home*.
13. Desiree goes to Armand with the letter.
14. He tells her to go.
15. Desiree takes the baby and leaves (some believe she commits suicide).
16. Armand burns all remnants of Desiree and the baby.
17. Armand finds the letter his mother wrote.
 1. Armand's mother writes the letter that tells of Armand being African American.

THE MAJOR ELEMENTS OF A PLOT

Whether or not they are presented chronologically, the events of a story have a cause-and-effect relationship which leads to a possible resolution of the conflict. An author may present the events in a piecemeal fashion, letting us build the plot ourselves as the story progresses, or the climax and resolution may occur in a single event.

If the author wants to shock us or suggest that some conflicts have no resolution, the story may end at the moment of climax. And some experimental fiction dispenses with the elements of plot altogether, forcing the reader to create a story out of a series of seemingly unrelated events.

CONFLICT AND PLOT

Of all of the elements of fiction, conflict is the most essential to the progression of the plot. Most stories consist of characters who face or must work out a conflict. The conflict engages the reader. The clash and resulting struggle is the force that drives the story. It stimulates our curiosity and helps us understand the significance of the story. We want to know how it "turns out."

Conflicts are classified as internal or external and are always defined as being *between* two forces. An external conflict involves a struggle between characters, or between a character and social or physical forces. An internal conflict involves the struggle between elements within the psyche, like beliefs or emotions that are within the character.

EXTERNAL CONFLICTS

There are three types of traditional external conflicts: Character vs Character, Character vs Nature, and Character vs Society.

In a Character vs Character conflict characters interact with one another. The story has many interactions; some may be negative, some may be neutral, some may be positive. For example, in "Paul's Case" Paul interacts with his father, with his teachers, with his classmates, and briefly with a number of strangers. While Paul's interaction with his father is the most revealing of these and therefore the more important, each of these conflicts helps us understand Paul's character more thoroughly.

In a Character vs Nature conflict a character battles against natural environmental forces, such as the jungle (*Tarzan*), the desert (*Flight of the Phoenix*), a deserted island (*Cast Away*), or in space (*The Martian*). Natural processes, such as aging or illness, are also natural conflicts. How the character copes with these forces tells us about the type of person he or she is.

In a Character vs Society conflict a character has to deal with traditions or other social forces such as social class ("Paul's Case"), racial prejudice ("Desiree's Baby" and "Son in the Afternoon"), gender expectations ("The Chrysanthemums" and "The Story of an Hour"), religion ("The Star"), or abuse of government power ("Harrison Bergeron").

INTERNAL CONFLICTS

In an internal conflict characters struggle with emotional issues; their beliefs are challenged or they need to make a tough decision. An internal conflict usually occurs within the mind of the central character, so it is usually the central conflict. It may not be the first conflict to appear and it may not have the greatest number of words devoted to it, but it is usually the most important one. For example, "The Story of an Hour" begins with an external description of Mrs. Mallard's friends and relatives and how they are preparing to break the news of her husband's death. Only after several paragraphs do we see her internal emotional struggle.

A classic example of an internal conflict occurs in Mark Twain's *The Adventures of Huckleberry Finn*. Huck is helping his friend Jim, a runaway slave, escape to the North. Jim is out of sight inside a tiny structure on a raft they've built for his escape when a boat filled with men looking for the runaway slave comes by. They ask Huck if he's seen anything of the slave. Huck now has an internal conflict because of these two competing elements: (1) he's been told that it's a sin to lie and if he lies he will go to hell, but (2) he also knows that if he tells the truth the men will take his friend Jim and return him to slavery.

This conflict (to lie or to tell the truth) goes on for a while, but it's finally resolved when Huck reasons to himself that his Aunt Polly is going to heaven and he has so much trouble being around her now, when she's alive, that he couldn't stand having to put up with her after they're dead. So he lies. Usually, as with Huckleberry Finn, an internal conflict requires that the character resolves some kind of emotional or ethical dilemma.

Some stories can have more than one conflict. Very often there is an internal conflict as well as an external one. In Harry Sylvester's "Going to Run All Night," for example, Pete Nilson, a former marathon runner now serving in the army, is selected to run through enemy lines to summon help for his besieged unit. The reader is interested in the obvious external conflict between Nilson and the enemy soldiers because it raises the question of his physical stamina: Can he make it through the enemy lines? Of equal—or perhaps even greater—interest, however, is Nilson's internal struggle to overcome his self-doubt. So the reader also wants to know if he has the internal fortitude to make it.

Sometimes, as in Ring Lardner's "Haircut," an author creates a conflict between the values of a character in the story and those of the reader to make the reader a more active participant in the story.

For a story to succeed, the conflict should be plausible and the opposing forces must be balanced. Otherwise, the consequences of the conflict hold little interest or significance, and the reader cares little about the outcome and gains nothing from the story.

CONFLICT RESOLUTION

A major factor in the analysis of the conflict is discussing whether it is resolved. Sometimes a resolution provides a satisfactory conclusion. For example, by the end of "A & P" Sammy understands something important about growing up and becomes a little more mature; a resolution ends the conflict with some small satisfaction. In "The Chrysanthemums" Elisa tries to be satisfied with her life as a farm wife who is removed from the larger world, but at the end of the story, though her internal conflict is resolved, she is not satisfied. She cries "weakly like an old woman." She is now fully aware that her life is constrained and stifled.

CONFLICT AND THE CENTRAL IDEA

Regardless of how many conflicts occur in a story, there is usually one that is central. This central conflict is often the key to the central idea. In "Desiree's Baby," an important though largely implied conflict involves an emotional dilemma: Armand is torn between his love for his wife and child and his hatred of blacks. How he decides to deal with this conflict and the results of his decision are crucial to the central idea of the story (that is, the potentially tragic and self-destructive power of hatred and bigotry). However, the central conflict may be Desiree's emotional struggle. Can she go on with her life once she and the child are rejected by Armand? Her suicide shows her decision and the unfortunate resolution of this internal conflict.

In the following example, taken from a student's analysis of Heinrich Boll's "Like a Bad Dream," the relationship between the conflict and the central idea are described:

> The basic internal conflict in "Like a Bad Dream" involves moral values or choices of action. Even though both Bertha and her husband desire wealth and success, she senses his reluctance to indulge in bribery and graft in order to reach these goals. Determined to bring him around to her moral standards, Bertha places her husband in a dilemma; he can either admit to Bertha's autonomy and dominance or he can pretend to have given his consent and take credit for the action. Bertha knows that her husband's pride and strong ambition will not allow him to take the former course; therefore, she has manipulated him to act as her surrogate. Working his way through the dilemma, Bertha's husband thinks of the events as a bad dream or a nightmare, signifying his mental anguish. These events and the emotions they evoke are appropriate to the central idea that an imperceptive but ambitious person can be deceived and manipulated to act contrary to his moral convictions.
>
> Central and supporting conflict are similar to central and supporting character. Just as the most important job of the supporting character is to help us understand the central character, the main job of the supporting conflict is to help us understand the central conflict. Sometimes the supporting conflict actually causes the central one. For example, the social conflict of Paul resisting social expectations and traditions for a boy of his class, education, and age causes his internal conflict of how to be fulfilled and happy in the world.

CONFLICT AND CHARACTER

The reaction of the story's central character to the conflict provides an important clue to the central idea. The point the author is making is often tied to whether the character succeeds or fails, whether the character's personality, values, or beliefs are reinforced or permanently altered.

In this second example from a student analysis, the relationship between the character and the conflict is explained to form the basis for the central idea. The paper follows the basic analytical structure: a summary paragraph (concluding with a statement of the central idea), a paragraph discussing character, and a paragraph discussing conflict. In the analysis of this particular story, that sequence is perfect for using the link between character and conflict to underscore the central idea.

"The Story of an Hour" by Kate Chopin tells of Louise Mallard, a woman who receives news that her husband has been killed in a train wreck. Her sister and a friend break the news gently, for she has a heart condition. Upon hearing of the tragedy, Louise weeps and then retires to the solitude of her room. While staring out her window, she comes to the conclusion that she has been freed. A wave of understanding overwhelms her, and she sees that she can now live on her own terms. She joins her sister and triumphantly heads downstairs. At this instant, her husband, who was not on the train that crashed, enters the house. Upon seeing him Louise dies suddenly of a heart attack. Chopin's theme is that triumph and tragedy may be defined only in the mind of the beholder.

At the outset, Louise seems to be a passive person; however, she quickly deals with the grief caused by her husband's "death," which indicates that she has cared for him, but now accepts his death. She revels in the knowledge that, with him gone, she can now live life on her own terms. Her sudden realization suggests that her marriage was a veil concealing her true feelings from herself. The ending of the story is a classic example of life's irony: her husband dies, she achieves self-awareness, and when he arrives unharmed, she dies because her heart now is unable to accept a lifetime with him. The doctor's assertion that she died of "joy that kills" represents life's injustice; her true feelings will never be known. Her character embodies the reaction to triumph and tragedy that is the central idea.

The central conflict in "The Story of an Hour" is an internal one between Louise's grief over her husband's death which conflicts with her joy over her new-found freedom. She has never considered living life for herself, but she is suddenly presented with the chance to do so. This blinding realization shows that she has repressed this conflict for a long time, and the author's description of her internal change suggests that she has no control over it. She has always desired freedom, but has allowed her marriage to take precedence over her true sentiments. Now that her husband is gone, her long-suppressed desire possesses her and she experiences true joy. In fact, she is so elated to be "Body and soul free" that she dies when she discovers that she is not free at all. So, in a sense, her free-spirited side has won—choosing death over a dull, loveless lifetime. Thus, the conflict is resolved; triumph is followed by tragedy.

Sometimes not all conflicts in a story are resolved. In the sample analysis of "The Story of an Hour" (above), the student clearly describes the resolution of Louise's internal conflict but overlooks an important social conflict: In a male-dominated world, men have the advantage and the only way a woman can acceptably escape marriage is by becoming a widow. This social conflict remains unresolved. Louise's death does not change the "rules" of her society.

Reading Exercise:

See if you can determine the central idea in Stephen Crane's "The Bride Comes to Yellow Sky." After you've read the story, try writing a central idea statement. Then, look at the conflict and try to determine how it represents the central idea of the story.

CHAPTER FOUR

Point of View

"They're so damn cocky,' thought Walter Mitty, walking along Main Street; 'they think they know.' Once he had tried to take his chains off, outside New Milford, and he had got them wound around the axles. A man had to come out in a wrecking car and unwind them, a young, grinning garage man. Since then Mrs. Mitty always made him drive to a garage to have the chains taken off. 'The next time,' he thought, 'I'll wear my right arm in a sling; they won't grin at me then.'"

[from "The Secret Life of Walter Mitty" by James Thurber]

A major decision the writer must make is who will tell the story. Will it be the main character? A minor character? Or someone who is not a part of the story at all? This choice is closely related to the element of character. The narrative voice that an author chooses to tell the story determines how and what the reader sees and hears, and this, in turn, has an impact on the reader's understanding and emotional response to the story.

The point of view takes one of three distinct forms: first person, omniscient, or dramatic. The author's choice of which to use depends on (and should be consistent with) the story's central idea. This chapter considers these different types of narrative voices, their advantages and disadvantages, and how they affect an interpretation. Once you can identify the point of view and understand how and why the writer chose it, you will have defined another piece in the analysis.

THE FIRST PERSON POINT OF VIEW

When the story is told by one of the characters within it, the narration is in the "first person." The author uses the pronouns "I" and "me." In these instances, the narrator is most often the central character or an active participant in the action, as in Sherwood Anderson's "I'm a Fool" and John Updike's "A & P." Occasionally, the first person narrator is a minor character or a mere observer of the action. (Read William

Faulkner's "A Rose for Emily" for an example.) Of the three types of narration, first person point of view is the most restrictive. It limits the presentation to those things that the chosen character knows and his or her interpretation of the things other characters do and say. It also prohibits comments from the author. Furthermore, the author must be careful to assure that the narrative voice (the character's awareness, speech, and attitudes) are consistent with the details of the character's personality and background.

The First Person Narrator's Perspective

Despite its limitations, the first person narrator appears in many variations. In one common use of the first person, the narrator, speaking as an adult, tells of an experience from his or her childhood. This allows the author to show how the passage of time has affected the character's attitudes. And because the adult can reflect on the reactions he or she had as a child, the author is able to include comments on the events. The distinction is this: a story told to you by a ten-year-old child is very different from the same story told twenty-five years later by that child who is now an adult. The events may be the same, but the level of understanding and insight are very different.

In this example from Poe's "The Cask of Amontillado," the first person narrative reveals the twisted mind of a man driven by revenge. Poe chose to have the main character speak and, through his remarks, reveal his tortured feelings. Notice how Poe not only reveals Montresor's feelings, but lets us in on how he rationalizes them.

> "Fortunato!"
> No answer. I called again. "Fortunato!"
> No answer still. I thrust a torch through the remaining aperture and let it fall within. There came forth in return only a jingling of the bells. My heart grew sick; it was the dampness of the catacombs that made it so. I hastened to make an end of my labour. I forced the last stone into its position; I plastered it up.

"My heart grew sick" (Montresor's admission of his feelings) is immediately followed by "it was the dampness of the catacombs that made it so" (a denial). Because Montresor can describe what he thinks and feels as well as what he sees and hears, this first person narrator creates a sense of realism and immediacy a "you-are-there" feeling. In this way, the first person point of view creates a personal bond with the reader. Consequently, an author can use the first person point of view to capture our interest and increase our involvement with the narrator.

Because Poe's narrator is intelligent, he provides some clever, even witty, observations. A sharp contrast to this and the sense of immediacy in Poe's story occurs when the narrator is ignorant and unreliable. Rather than a sense of insight, the result is irony. (Read "Haircut" by Ring Lardner for a good example of first person narration.) Instead of closeness, a distance is created between the narrator's values and those of the reader.

Confusing the Narrator with the Author

There is a tendency to confuse the first person narrator with the author of the story. This can lead to invalid assumptions. We should never lose sight of the fact that the narrator is fictional. It's not the author speaking. If the author's attempts to involve us in the story are successful, we may believe, for a while at least, that the voice we're hearing is that of a real person, but that's an illusion created by a skillful writer. The story never really happened; the characters never existed; the narrator is not real. Poe never walled up his friend in the catacombs. The fictional character named Montresor did that.

Contributions the First Person Makes to a Story

When police officers speak to someone who has witnessed an auto accident, they don't say, "Go tell someone what you saw and have them come tell me." The officer asks the witness: "What did *you* see?" Similarly, the first person narrator in a story is our witness. Readers feel as if they are being spoken to directly by a character involved in the story. That character has *eyewitness accountability*. When someone in the story is describing what they see, we feel that we should believe them.

But we often have to ask whether the narrator is a *credible* witness. Eyewitnesses don't always get it right. They are susceptible to the same flaws as anyone. So we need to question everything the witness says. For example, Poe often forces readers to ask whether the narrator's revenge is justifiable. In "The Cask of Amontillado" the narrator says "The thousand injuries of Fortunato I had borne as I best could," but we must ask if those "injuries" were real or imagined.

Likewise, in "The Tell-Tale Heart" the narrator makes a point of telling us he is not mad: "The disease had sharpened my senses—not destroyed—not dulled them. Above all was the sense of hearing acute. I heard all things in the heaven and in the earth. I heard many things in hell. How, then, am I mad? Hearken! and observe how healthily—how calmly I can tell you the whole story."

Sometimes, we even must ask whether the events he describes are actually happening, as in "The Fall of the House of Usher":

"There grew in my mind a strange fancy—a fancy so ridiculous, indeed, that I but mention it to show the vivid force of the sensations which oppressed me. I had so worked upon my imagination as really to believe that about the whole mansion and domain there hung an atmosphere peculiar to themselves and their immediate vicinity—an atmosphere which had no affinity with the air of heaven, but which had reeked up from the decayed trees, and the gray wall, and the silent tarn—a pestilent and mystic vapor, dull, sluggish, faintly discernible, and leaden-hued."

The basic premise of the First Person is that we tend to trust those who are speaking directly to us. The First Person creates a level of *intimacy*, a sense of a personal connection between the narrator and the reader. This intimacy may draw us into a story, making us feel more integral to the action. In some cases, however, we may feel pushed away as we realize the untrustworthy or deranged nature of a first person narrator, as with many of Poe's storytellers.

One caution, then—while the First Person Point of View uses the pronouns "I" or "we," these pronouns also appear in the conversation of characters that do not indicate first person. In Richard Connell's "The Most Dangerous Game," we see this:

"I've read your book about hunting snow leopards in Tibet, you see," explained the man. "I am General Zaroff."

In this quote, "I" is part of the conversation. One character is speaking to another, not to us. This is a Dramatic Point of View because the reader has an outsider's perspective; we are simply listening to them talk.

THE OMNISCIENT POINT OF VIEW

People conceal many of their thoughts and feelings. Even if someone tells us what they're thinking or feeling, we cannot be completely certain it's the truth. Fiction, on the other hand, allows us inside a character's mind. This is accomplished through the use of an omniscient narrator, one who knows everything, including the true thoughts and feelings of a character. This adds a dimension to characterization that goes beyond anything in reality.

Of the three points of view, an omniscient narration gives an author the greatest flexibility. The omniscient narrator is credible and reliable;

the reader accepts the narrator's revelations as true and accurate. This allows an author to control the reader's attitude toward the story. If the author tells us that a character's thoughts are evil, we accept the premise that the character is evil, regardless of what the character says or how he or she acts toward others. We know what they really think.

In the following quote from "Desiree's Baby," we have no reason to doubt the omniscient narrator. When the narrator says that Armand's nature had softened and Desiree loved him desperately, we know it's true because the narrator is omniscient and therefore knows the character's true feelings:

> What Desiree said was true. Marriage, and later the birth of his son, had softened Armand Aubigny's imperious and exacting nature greatly. This was what made the gentle Desiree so happy, for she loved him desperately.

Later in the story, Chopin reveals Armand's true feelings by telling us his thoughts.

> He thought Almighty God had dealt cruelly and unjustly with him and felt, somehow, that he was paying Him back in kind when he stabbed thus into his wife's soul. Moreover he no longer loved her, because of the unconscious injury she had brought upon his home and his name.

Total vs. Limited Omniscience

When the narration is totally omniscient, the narrator can reveal the thoughts and feelings of any of the story's characters. But when the narration is limited omniscient, the narrator can only reveal the thoughts and feelings of one character.

In James Thurber's "The Secret Life of Walter Mitty," we only know what's going on in Walter Mitty's mind. The limited omniscient narrator explains, interprets, and evaluates Mitty's actions. We know everything Mitty is thinking, but only Mitty, not those of any other character. This is because Mitty's thoughts are the only ones necessary for us to understand the central idea. This limited omniscience increases our understanding of the character and creates an intimacy with him. As a result, we share his senses and feelings more strongly. The character is the unifying element of the story. And this is nearly true of all stories where the limited omniscient narrator is used.

Though it might seem the ideal choice, and the easiest, a writer faces certain disadvantages with an omniscient point of view. Because an all-knowing authority makes the reader conscious of the author's presence, it lacks subtlety and restricts reader involvement. The omniscient view may lead to an excessively direct presentation of characters, too much telling and not enough showing.

Contributions Omniscience Makes to a Story

Omniscience creates *absolute credibility*. We are in the characters' head, reading the characters' thoughts and feelings directly; the thoughts are completely reliable. We may not like what they are thinking, but we have not doubt they are really thinking it.

In Limited Omniscience we are trapped by the character's view of the world and in total omniscience we are trapped to the views of multiple characters. But no matter how many characters' thoughts we are privy to, we are restricted to what they are thinking. We may get to know the narrator(s) deeply, but we have to remind ourselves that the actions of other characters in the story may not be as the narrator(s) perceive them. This limitation of omniscience is why it is almost always used in combination with the Dramatic Point of View, so readers get the omniscient narrator's view of the world as well as a more objective view.

Even a thoroughly omniscient point of view does not begin inside the narrator's head and never leave. The narration usually weaves in and out of the character's thoughts. When we are privy to those thoughts, the view is omniscient. When the narration steps out of the thoughts, it is Third Person Dramatic. James Thurber does this in "The Secret Life of Walter Mitty." As Mitty waits for his wife to finish at the hairdresser, he picks up a magazine in the waiting room:

> "He picked up a copy of Liberty and sank down into the chair. 'Can Germany Conquer the World Through the Air?' Walter Mitty looked at the pictures of bombing planes and of ruined streets.
>   . . . 'The cannonading has got the wind up in young Raleigh, sir,' said the sergeant. Captain Mitty looked up at him through tousled hair. 'Get him to bed,' he said wearily. 'With the others. I'll fly alone.'"

The description of Mitty picking up the magazine and reading the title of the article is in a Dramatic Point of View. But in the next paragraph the view shifts to omniscient as Mitty imagines himself as a captain heroically taking the place of one of his exhausted men.

Reading a character's mind is a powerful perspective, so even with the two points of view combined we can easily label the Mitty story as primarily omniscient.

THE DRAMATIC POINT OF VIEW

The dramatic point of view presents only the words and actions of the characters. We're never told the characters' thoughts and feelings. Consequently, we must interpret their thoughts and feelings by what they say and do (much as we do in real life). Dramatic narration is the simplest type. It is straightforward and often reads like a news story. This lends a feeling of realism and authenticity. The reader is forced to infer the meaning from the action without the author being able to comment. The dramatic point of view creates a sense of realism because it resembles reality. It requires us to interpret the motivations of the characters. It increases our involvement in the story because we have to do more work. Because the opinions we form as we read are based on what the characters say and do, the story has a realistic "feel." (Read Ernest Hemingway's "Hills Like White Elephants" or Shirley Jackson's "The Lottery" for good examples of dramatic narration.)

Ironically, the very features that give the dramatic point of view its strength also create risks for the author. Few stories are presented from a completely dramatic point of view because of this limitation. The author cannot comment on the action. This severely limits the author's ability to influence the reader's attitude. Therefore, a writer using a dramatic narrative voice must carefully construct the story so that the possibilities for misinterpretation are minimal.

In the following example from John Steinbeck's "The Chrysanthemums," the author, in the voice of a dramatic narrator, tells us what each of the characters says and does. The author's choice of words and the tone of voice created by that choice are the clues that let us know what's going on in the characters' minds and hearts. The narrator tells us that Elisa's "breast swelled passionately" and the Tinker "looked away self-consciously." And later Steinbeck says her voice "grew husky," and that she almost touches the tinker, but then "She crouched low like a fawning dog." Steinbeck does not have to tell us that the woman is sexually frustrated; his description makes it abundantly clear.

> She was kneeling on the ground looking up at him. Her breast swelled passionately.
> The man's eyes narrowed. He looked away self-consciously. "Maybe I know," he said. "Sometimes in the night in the wagon there—"

Elisa's voice grew husky. She broke in on him. "I've never lived as you do, but I know what you mean. When the night is dark why, the stars are sharp-pointed, and there's quiet. Why, you rise up and up! Every pointed star gets driven into your body. It's like that. Hot and sharp and lovely."

Kneeling there, her hand went out toward his legs in the greasy black trousers. Her hesitant fingers almost touched the cloth. Then her hand dropped to the ground. She crouched low like a fawning dog.

Contributions the Dramatic Makes to a Story

The Dramatic Point of View contributes a *sense of realism* to a story. This view is most similar to our common, everyday perspective of the world. We cannot read other people's minds, so omniscience is not possible in our real lives. We experience First Person when people speak to us, but the most common way we look at the real world is from the outside. We often make judgments about others based solely on our impressions of what they wear, what car they drive, how they talk, who they talk to, what classes they're taking, and many other superficial factors. This strictly outside perspective is the Dramatic Point of View.

This outside perspective also contributes a *sense of objectivity*. As readers, seeing characters' actions and appearances and hearing their voices in conversation does not tell us what we must think of the characters; we seem to get to decide for ourselves, just as in real life. Objective narrators make us feel they are being honest with us. But while it seems objective, it's not, because the authors are selective about telling us how the characters look, what they do, and what they say. We feel as if we are drawing conclusions, but the evidence is rigged. The author's description is subtly guiding us in how we perceive a character.

In the preceding quote from Steinbeck's "The Chrysanthemums," Elisa's sexual frustration may seem clear, but we have had to derive it from the outside description of her appearance, behavior, and conversation, and Steinbeck is very careful to choose words and phrases to guide us to her frustration.

COMBINATIONS AND CONSISTENCY IN POINT OF VIEW

Because its length doesn't match that of a novel, a short story usually has a single primary point of view. It is the one that is most prevalent and most important in helping us understand the story, its characters, and its central idea. Some stories are absolutely consistent in using one point of view. Shirley Jackson's "The Lottery," for example, is completely Dramatic and John A. Williams' "Son in the Afternoon" is completely First Person.

But most stories have bits of more than one point of view. "The Secret Life of Walter Mitty" and "Desiree's Baby" are primarily Omniscient, but sometimes step out of a character's thoughts to describe surroundings or actions. This is not a lack of consistency. It is the nature of the narrator.

Reading Exercise:

See if you can determine the central idea in James Thurber's "The Secret Life of Walter Mitty." After you've read the story, try writing a central idea statement. Then identify the point of view and see if you can determine how important Thurber's choice was in the execution of the central idea.

CHAPTER FIVE

Setting

"It was about dusk, one evening during the supreme madness of the carnival season, that I encountered my friend . . . We came at length to the foot of the descent, and stood together upon the damp ground of the catacombs of the Montresors."

[from "The Cask of Amontillado" by Edgar Allan Poe]

The setting of a story is where and when the events happen. It includes the conditions: the physical, emotional, economic, political, social, and psychological environment inhabited by the characters. The choice of a setting is rarely an arbitrary decision.

The author often uses the setting to enrich the Central idea. At the beginning of a story, we may be given the physical setting and there may be references to the time and place, but more often our awareness of the setting evolves gradually.

Good stories are more subtle about it. Rather than making an outright statement, ("It happened in January of 1937 in a small East Texas town.") the author provides details and clues, like the description of a character's clothing, the dialect the character speaks, or even the character's vehicle—a horse-drawn carriage, say, or a dune buggy—and lets us infer the time and place from those details.

SPECIFIC VS. GENERAL SETTINGS

A story's setting may be either specific or general. For example, if the story takes place in January of 1937 in a small East Texas town, it's specific. But if the time and place are never clearly specified, the setting is general. Whether a story's setting is specific or general usually depends on the central idea. The author tells us only those details that are essential to the Central Idea.

Perhaps the author wants to show the effects a particular period in history or certain geographical or social conditions has on people. By providing very specific and detailed information about the setting, the author can support a central idea related to changes in the social, moral, and religious environment of a particular part of the world. For example, in "The Bride Comes to Yellow Sky," Stephen Crane illustrates the effect of the arrival of "civilization" on the old west. Clearly, the story must take place in the old west, but more specifically, it must take place at a time when the area was becoming more civilized. In another example, Tim O'Brien's story "The Things They Carried" takes place during the Vietnam war. The particular war may not be as important, however, as what a young man must endure in any war.

Or an author may want to make a comment about the human condition or about humanity in general. In such an instance, the setting may be deliberately vague. This gives the story a universal significance. The implication is that what happens to the people in the story can happen to people at any time in any place.

Similarly, when authors do not concentrate on setting, it is usually because they are interested in the human behavior. They want us to see the characters as human beings, not as Americans in 1940 or Russians in 2010. They want us to see that people are the same no matter where or when they live. In Shirley Jackson's "The Lottery," for example, the rich details of the summer's green grass and blooming flowers adds vividness to the story, as does the presentation of small town life. But while the story is vaguely modern and vaguely north American, we cannot tell exactly when and where the story takes place. Therefore, no matter when the story is read, it will always seem familiar and relevant.

We assume the setting is always an intentional choice. Whether specific or general, the author has carefully chosen to portray the setting in that way.

THE SETTING AND THE CENTRAL IDEA

Even though the setting is general, it may be significant because the author's central idea has universal association. A good test of this is to ask if the meaning of the story would be drastically affected if the setting were changed to a specific time and place. If the answer is no, the choice of a general setting may have been intentional in order to show the universality of the theme.

More often than not, the setting supports the central idea of the story, so any changes in the setting significantly alter the story. For example, if the setting is a lonely house in the country at night during a raging storm, the characters' actions and attitudes are likely to be different than they might be if the setting were during the day in an apartment in the city in the summer.

Likewise, if the setting is the vast ocean surrounding four ship-wrecked men, the Central Idea may have to do with nature's indifference toward man's fate, as in Stephen Crane's story "The Open Boat." In another example, in "Paul's Case" by Willa Cather, the contrast between the environment Paul hates and the one he desires underscores the central conflict of the story.

Look at this setting in John Steinbeck's "The Chrysanthemums:"

The high grey-flannel fog of winter closed off the Salinas Valley from the sky and from all the rest of the world. On every side it sat like a lid on the mountains and made of the great valley a closed pot. On the broad, level land floor the gang plows bit deep and left the black earth shining like metal where the share had cut. On the foothill ranches across the Salinas River, the yellow stubble fields seemed to be bathed in pale cold sunshine, but there was no sunshine in the valley now in December. The thick willow scrub along the river flamed with sharp and positive yellow leaves.

It was a time of quiet and of waiting. The air was cold and tender. A light wind blew up from the southwest so that the farmers were mildly hopeful of a good rain before long; but fog and rain did not go together.

Steinbeck uses the image of the fog sitting *like a lid on the mountains* and making "a closed pot" of the valley to establish his meaning through symbolism and figurative imagery. We learn later in the story that this setting parallels the main character's restricted life and repressed emotional conflict. It is directly related to the central idea.

In this next passage, from Kate Chopin's "Desiree's Baby," Chopin describes L'Abri, the plantation home of the main characters:

It was a sad looking place, which for many years had not known the gentle presence of a mistress, old Monsieur Aubigny having married and buried his wife in France, and she having loved her own land too well ever to leave it. The roof came down steep and black like a cowl, reaching out beyond the wide galleries that encircled the yellow stuccoed house. Big, solemn oaks grew close to it, and their thick-leaved, far-reaching branches shadowed it like a pall.

The plantation is gloomy and foreboding, totally lacking light and happiness. (Light is generally associated with happiness; dark, with sadness.) The setting mirrors the natural temperament of Armand, Desiree's husband. It also foreshadows the tragedy that befalls Armand, Desiree, and their baby. Chopin's choice of such a setting complements the characters and the conflict. Most importantly, the story is set in the antebellum South on a plantation. It's a time of strong and clear racial attitudes, which are essential to the central idea of the story.

Reading Exercise:

See if you can determine the relationship between the Setting and the central idea in Edgar Allan Poe's "The Cask of Amontillado." After you've read the story, write a central idea statement and identify the aspects of the setting that relate to it.

CHAPTER SIX

Language

"Did you ever hear of planting hands?"

"Can't say I have ma'am."

"Well, I can only tell you what it feels like. It's when you're picking off the buds you don't want. Everything goes right down into your fingertips. You watch your fingers work. They do it themselves. You can feel how it is. They pick and pick the buds. They never make a mistake. They're with the plant. Do you see? Your fingers and the plant. You can feel that, right up your arm. They know. They never make a mistake. You can feel it. When you're like that you can't do anything wrong. Do you see that? Can you understand that?"

[from "The Chrysanthemums" by John Steinbeck]

The essence of any story is its language: its diction, images, symbolism, irony, dialog, and syntax. Joining words and sentences into a cohesive narrative is what drives the other elements. Understanding and interpreting a story fully is impossible without closely analyzing the aspects of its language. Only by reading, and rereading, can we reach a full appreciation of the story and the work that went into its creation.

Language is what makes short stories special. It is what makes them literature instead of news articles, editorials, or cookbooks. Any good writer would do well to make use of the literary techniques we will discuss in the following chapter, but writers of short stories—as well as novels, poems, and plays—depend on such techniques. For example, you have no trouble knowing the difference in a textbook chapter describing a battle of the American Civil War and Stephen Crane's novel of the Civil War *The Red Badge of Courage*. The subject is the same, but the language used to present the subject is not.

DICTION

Diction refers to the writer's choice of words. Good writers search for "just the right word." This "word searching" focuses on the connotation and denotation of words.

Denotation and Connotation

The *denotation* of a word is its exact dictionary definition. The *connotation* is the suggested or associated meaning, usually a positive or negative one. While the denotation of a word like "trash" may be "useless matter," its connotation suggests filth, slovenliness, and so on. The writer can imply a great deal about something by using a strongly connotative word. For example, when describing a character's clothing, the writer can choose any of the nouns in the list below. Like the word "clothing" itself, these words refer to the way the character is dressed, but each has a different connotation.

- Your choice of *apparel* is very interesting.
- Where did you find that *get-up*?
- His *garb* is unfamiliar to us.
- I changed into my *work gear*.
- He wore real fancy *duds*.
- Is formal *attire* required?
- His *raiment* bore the mark of a nobleman.

The formality of the word "apparel" suggests elegance, while the word "get-up" suggests a costume. "Garb" sounds like something distinctive, perhaps silly or inappropriate. "Work gear" is more industrial. "Fancy duds" might be used to describe western wear. "Attire" sounds very polite, and like "apparel," it's associated with elegance. "Raiment", on the other hand, is an archaic word commonly associated with medieval times, perhaps of royal or noble bearing. On your own, look up the various meanings of "outfit," "livery," and "regalia."

The following adjectives may be used to describe a character who is slightly built: slender, slim, lean, gaunt, scrawny, skinny, thin, delicate, attenuated, or emaciated. The choice of which word to use depends on what the writer wants you to associate with the character.

The examples below illustrate the importance of diction and how the connotations of the words chosen for naming and describing things and actions imply the writer's attitude toward the subject and create a specific image for the reader.

Paul was startled for a moment, and had the feeling of wanting to put her out; what business had she here among all these fine people and gay colors? He looked her over and decided that she was not appropriately dressed and must be a fool to sit downstairs in such togs.

In the example above, from Willa Cather's "Paul's Case," the connotative diction creates a contrast between the woman, who is wearing "togs," and the rest of the crowd, who are wearing "gay colors."

> A newly married pair had boarded this coach at San Antonio. The man's face was reddened from many days in the wind and sun, and a direct result of his new black clothes was that his brick-colored hands were constantly performing in a most conscious fashion. From time to time he looked down respectfully at his attire. He sat with a hand on each knee, like a man waiting in a barber's shop. The glances he devoted to other passengers were furtive and shy.
>
> The bride was not pretty, nor was she very young. She wore a dress of blue cashmere, with small reservations of velvet here and there, and steel buttons abounding. She continually twisted her head to regard her puff sleeves, very stiff, straight, and high. They embarrassed her. It was quite apparent that she had cooked, and that she expected to cook, dutifully. The blushes caused by the careless scrutiny of some passengers as she had entered the car were strange to see upon this plain, under-class countenance, which was drawn in placid, almost emotionless lines.

Before the narrator in Stephen Crane's "The Bride Comes to Yellow Sky" reveals the direction this story will take, he has established the nature of his characters through the diction. The man has "brick-colored" hands. The diction connotes not only redness, but also hardness and strength. He looks down at his "attire," which supports the earlier suggestion of formal clothing: it's both "new" and "black."

The bride's dress has small "reservations of velvet." That is not a usual use of the word; it connotes a very conservative dress. And her "countenance" is "under-class." Crane carefully chose that word because it tells us that the bride is not from a wealthy or even middle-class background, but calling it "lower-class" would have prompted the negativity of that term.

IMAGERY

The mental impressions evoked by words and phrases are the imagery of a story. An effective description creates an image, a sensory impression, in the reader's mind. The image is more than visual. The author can appeal to any of the senses; hearing, sight, smell, touch, and taste to vivify events, characters, settings, and the other elements.

Literal and Figurative Images

If a word or phrase can only be interpreted one way, it is said to be literal. A literal image is created by the use of such unambiguous words and phrases. A figurative image, on the other hand, relies on the associated meanings of a word or phrase. A statement like . . . "His mother entered the room" creates a simple, literal and denotative image. We have a mental picture of a woman entering the room. All we know is that the woman is the speaker's mother. The writer is not suggesting anything more.

But when the writer says "The odor of tobacco preceded his mother's cold and haughty entrance," figurative and literal meanings associated with "cold" and "haughty" come into play, as well as the implications of the smell of tobacco. These associations demand that the reader understand that the word "cold" is not meant literally. We not only know that the speaker's mother has entered the room, but we also have a feeling for the woman. It's a feeling that touches our senses and, if we correctly understand its meaning, "cold" tells us the woman is unfriendly and aloof. That is what figurative imagery contributes to the story.

"Haughty" means proud, arrogant, and snobbish, and adds to the image the perception of the woman as proud, arrogant, and snobbish. We don't need to be familiar with the associated meaning of the word because there is none. That is a literal use of imagery. The connotation of "haughty" is negative.

It benefits all of us to read a story with a good dictionary at hand. Even words we know sometimes reveal additional, helpful meanings if we look them up.

Similes and Metaphors

The most common forms of figurative imagery are the simile and the metaphor. A simile is a direct comparison introduced by the word "like" or "as." A metaphor is an implied comparison. The simile says "A is *like* B," whereas the metaphor says that "A *is* B."

The metaphor is stronger, more encompassing, than the simile. It is one thing to say someone eats like a pig, but a stronger, more generalized insult to say someone is a pig.

Steinbeck begins "The Chrysanthemums" this way: "On every side it sat like a lid on the mountains and made of the valley a closed pot." This description begins with a simile: the fog is like a lid. It closes with a metaphor: the fog "made of the great valley a closed pot." The valley, with the fog over it, does not look like a pot, it is a pot, a closed pot. Steinbeck uses the simile and the metaphor to describe the valley, but there is more here than a simple physical description. The metaphor of the closed pot represents Elisa's situation. She is trapped. She is like something in a pot with a lid on it.

When an author uses figurative rather than literal language, the image is more vivid. For example:

- Instead of a character's voice being harsh and screechy, it may sound like fingernails raking across a chalkboard.
- Instead of someone leaving quickly, she may fly from the room.
- Instead of a room being stale or musty, it may smell like an old pair of sneakers.
- Instead of a man wandering aimlessly around town, he may be a rudderless craft at the mercy of wind and currents.

Those images are also more vivid because they involve the comparison of two dissimilar things: the voice and the chalkboard-raking sound, walking and flying, air and sneaker odor, walking and floating. By comparing one thing with something extremely different from itself, an author gives that thing more meaning.

Imagery and Other Elements

The examples that follow illustrate the uses of imagery to create an immediate sense of character, setting, and tone.

Imagery and Character

"But as they approached Miss Dove's room their disorder began to vanish. They pulled their excitement in, like a proud but well-broken pony."

"The hat was summertime. It was deep and soft like summer. It caused deep soft scallops of shadow, like summer shadows under the densest trees, to fall across her face."

Imagery and Setting

"The buggy is mine. It is made of wicker, rather unraveled, and the wheels wobble like a drunkard's legs."

Imagery and Tone

"Possibly we doze; but the beginnings of dawn splash us like cold water: we're up, wide-eyed and wandering while we wait for others to waken."

"A cheery crunch, scraps of miniature thunder sound as the [pecan] shells collapse and the golden mound of sweet oily ivory meat mounts in the milk-glass bowl."

"Then Sam's horn rang in the wet gray woods and again and again; there was a boiling wave of dogs about them, with Tennie's Jim and Boon Hoggan whipping them back after each had had a taste of the blood."

Allusions

An allusion is a type of imagery that uses a reference to a mythological, religious, historical, literary, or contemporary figure, place, or event. For example, a character may be described as living in a place resembling the Augean stables, or he may be called a Hamlet of decision-makers. These involve references to mythology (the Augean stables) and literature (Shakespeare's Hamlet). A character may live in a setting so lush it is said to be a Garden of Eden (religious—Christianity) or she may aspire to take a hajj to Mecca (religious—Islam). A character playing softball may be said to have the stature of Jose Altuve (contemporary, referring to the Houston Astros second baseman. When Altuve retires and some time passes, allusions to him will be historical) and will be effective only if the reader has some knowledge and understanding of them. An author who uses allusions runs the risk that a reader may not be familiar with them. Such references limit their understanding to those readers with knowledge of the specific references. This highlights the responsibility of the reader. While you may not know the allusion immediately, you can usually tell if an allusion is being used. It is up to you to look up the reference, a task made very easy in this world of online search engines.

Repetition

Repetition emphasizes an image and underscores its importance to the central idea of the story. Sometimes an author creates an image and refers to it later. In "The Chrysanthemums," Steinbeck makes frequent references to Elisa Allen's hands. They are repeatedly described as strong, vital, or full of energy. At the end of the story, the image of Elisa crying weakly is made more effective because it stands in sharp contrast to the repeated images of her strength.

SYMBOLISM

A symbol is something that represents or suggests something else. We live with and respond to symbols, and we take them for granted. For example, if we see a building with a cross on top, we assume it is a Christian church. In the United States, if we form a circle with our thumb and forefinger and raise our hand for someone to see, we are indicating our approval that everything is "okay." If we're driving down a street and see a blinking red light, we recognize it as a signal to stop; red symbolizes danger. And if we see a gigantic pair of glasses above an office, we assume it's the office of an optometrist.

As these examples illustrate, a symbol represents or suggests something else. In each case, an object or action communicates a message. Some authors use symbols in their work for a similar reason to represent an idea. A character, an object, or an incident that embodies an idea or quality can be a symbol. Symbolism allows an author to imply things, to convey ideas without actually stating them; it is literary shorthand, which compresses several meanings into a single person, object, or event.

Universal Symbols

Some symbols are recognized quickly and universally. Because they are used so widely, an author can assume we'll understand them. Very few symbols, however, are recognized worldwide. In the Euro/American culture, a dove represents peace; a long journey signifies life; a character's immersion in water suggests baptism or initiation into a way of life; springtime often symbolizes life or rebirth; and winter suggests death. But those symbols are not recognized in all parts of the world. The star in Arthur Clarke's story by that title is a Christian symbol associated with the birth of Christ.

Contextual Symbols

Some symbols derive meaning from their context in a particular work. The furniture and clothing burned by Armand at the end of "Desiree's Baby" by Kate Chopin become symbols of his marriage to Desiree. The chrysanthemums in the story of that name represent the children

Elisa does not have and the nurturing part of herself she wants the tinker to take symbolically to the outside world on her behalf; the discarded sprouts symbolize the destruction of that dream.

Characters as Symbols

Characters may be symbolic because of what they do or even because of the name the author gives them. There is symbolism (as well as irony, which we discuss later) in the choice of Fortunato as one character's name in Poe's "The Cask of Amontillado." The character may have been fortunate, or he may have acquired a fortune before the story begins, but he soon becomes a symbol of someone very unfortunate.

Objects as Symbols

The symbolic use of objects is even more common than symbolic characters. In Crane's "The Bride Comes to Yellow Sky," the marshal does not have a gun. A gun, symbolic of manhood, is also symbolic of authority and, even more important to the central idea of this story, of the fact that the town is becoming civilized.

Similarly, in John Steinbeck's "The Chrysanthemums," the flowers in Elisa's gardens become symbols of the children she has never borne. Therefore, the tinker's disregard for the flowers takes on a larger meaning.

Actions as Symbols

Symbolic action, like characters and objects, can embody ideas. Suicide may be one of the most symbolic actions anyone can take. In Willa Cather's "Paul's Case," Paul's suicide is an action that defines the entire story. The boy is trapped; death is the only escape.

When Armand burns the furniture in Kate Chopin's "Desiree's Baby," his actions symbolize his feelings and, on a larger scale, the intensity of racism.

Symbolism, like imagery, is helpful in expressing various meanings or ideas concisely. Also, as the preceding examples demonstrate, symbols strengthen or completely carry the meaning of a story. An author chooses symbols that are more than apt; they add depth to the story and are appropriate to the central idea.

Allegory: *The Symbolic Story*

An allegory is a story in which symbolism is dominant; virtually every action, character, and place represents something an abstraction that usually promotes moral values or qualities. In an allegory, the idea conveyed is more important than the narrative itself. Allegory is somewhat rare in modern fiction, but "The White Knight" by Eric Nicol is one example; Nathaniel Hawthorne's "The Celestial Railroad," a wry modernization of *The Pilgrim's Progress*, is another. Some college history books even discuss the allegorical meaning of *The Wizard of Oz* as it comments on the political, economic, and social circumstances of early 20th century America: Dorothy symbolizes traditional American values, the munchkins ordinary citizens, the tinman industrial workers, the scarecrow agricultural workers, the lion William Jennings Bryan (a politician of the time), the yellow brick road the gold standard, the wicked witches the evil corporations, etc.

IRONY

Irony is the use of language to express a discrepancy between appearance and reality. It's useful to a writer because, like imagery and symbolism, irony compresses or implies meaning in a brief statement. There are three basic types of irony: verbal, dramatic, and situational.

Verbal Irony

Verbal irony involves an obvious discrepancy between what a speaker says and what the reader knows the character really means. But it is more than just a simple lie. In the following dialogue from Poe's "The Cask of Amontillado," verbal irony appears as Montresor and Fortunato discuss the latter's cough. Montresor, who is taking Fortunato into the catacombs to kill him, replies in a sarcastic way:

> "Come," I said, with decision, "we will go back; your health is precious. You are rich, respected, admired, beloved; you are happy, as once I was. You are a man to be missed. For me it is no matter. We will go back; you will be ill, and I cannot be responsible. Besides, there is Luchresi—"
> "Enough," he said; "the cough is a mere nothing; it will not kill me. I shall not die of a cough."
> "True true," I replied . . ."

From the context, we know that Montresor despises Fortunato and is not likely to let him turn back. We also appreciate the ironic significance of Montressor's reply that Fortunato "truly shall not die of a cough."

Dramatic Irony

When there is a discrepancy between what a character says or perceives and what the reader knows to be true, dramatic irony is at work. In Thurber's "The Secret Life of Walter Mitty," the reader knows things about Mitty that his wife does not realize. Because of Thurber's use of dramatic irony, our impression of Mitty is quite different from that of his wife.

> Something struck his shoulder. "I've been looking all over this hotel for you," said Mrs. Mitty. "Why do you have to hide in this old chair? How did you expect me to find you?"
> "Things close in," said Walter Mitty vaguely.
> "What?" Mrs. Mitty said. "Did you get the what's-its-name? The puppy biscuit? What's in that box?"
> "Overshoes," said Mitty.
> "Couldn't you have put them on in the store?"
> "I was thinking," said Walter Mitty. "Does it ever occur to you that I am sometimes thinking?"
> She looked at him. "I'm going to take your temperature when I get you home," she said.

Mrs. Mitty thinks Walter is sick, but we know what's going on because we have been inside his mind. The Omniscient point of view creates dramatic irony because the reader knows what a character is thinking while the other characters do not.

Steinbeck uses dramatic irony in "The Chrysanthemums" when Elisa responds to her husband's offer to take her to the fights:

> "Oh no," she says, "I don't want to go. I'm sure I don't.
> It will be enough if we can have wine. It will be plenty."

The reader, unlike Elisa's husband, knows that she desperately wants to experience things she has never known; however, wine with dinner is the only excitement she seems prepared to risk.

Sometimes Dramatic Irony continues for the entire story. For example, Henry never knows that his wife is unsettled and discontent in "The Chrysanthemums." Sometimes Dramatic Irony stops during the story. For example, when the tinker first pretends interest in Elisa's flowers, we know he doesn't really care about them; Elisa thinks he does. When Elisa sees the sprouts discarded later in the story, that dramatic irony concludes. Now she knows what we already knew.

Situational Irony

A more interesting and usually more important kind of irony is that which involves a discrepancy between what a character (or the reader) expects to happen and what actually does happen. The conflict and the central idea of a story may both turn on an ironic situation.

For example, it is ironic that Armand, the husband and father in "Desiree's Baby," finally discovers that he, not the loving wife he drove away, is black. It is also ironic in "The Most Dangerous Game" that General Zaroff, the world-famous big game hunter, becomes the hunted one.

Bruno Bettelheim has said, "If the artist uses irony to achieve his goal, he presents his vision as if seen in a mirror that distorts, to make us aware of what would otherwise escape us, to force us to respond to that which we would rather avoid." The writer juxtaposes contrasting ideas so that a character (or the reader) must view the world in a new and different way. In that way, the writer uses irony to convey the central idea, the writer's view.

DIALOGUE

Dialogue refers to the words spoken between two or more characters. Dialogue, which is easy to spot because it is set off by quotation marks, serves a variety of purposes:

- To inform (or misinform) the reader
- To reveal or develop a conflict
- To move the plot (story line) forward
- To build suspense
- To reveal character

Dialogue often provides indirect, less obvious clues to character, conflict, and other story elements, as in the following examples:

> "Tried to sneak up on me," he said. "Tried to sneak up on me!" His eyes grew more baleful. As Potter made a slight movement, the man thrust his revolver venomously forward. "No; don't you do it, Jack Potter. Don't you move a finger toward a gun just yet. Don't you move an eyelash. The time has come for me to settle with you, and I'm goin' to do it my own way, and loaf along with no interferin'. So if you don't want a gun bent on you, just mind what I tell you."

Potter looked at his enemy. "I ain't got a gun on me, Scratchy," he said. "Honest, I ain't." He was stiffening and steadying, but yet somewhere at the back of his mind a vision of the Pullman floated: the sea-green figured velvet, the shining brass, silver, and glass, the wood that gleamed as darkly brilliant as the surface of a pool of oil all the glory of the marriage, the environment of the new estate.

"You know I fight when it comes to fighting, Scratchy Wilson; but I ain't got a gun on me. You'll have to do all the shootin' yourself."

His enemy's face went livid. He stepped forward, and flashed his weapon to and fro before Potter's chest. "Don't you tell me you ain't got no gun on you, you whelp. Don't tell me no lie like that. There ain't a man in Texas ever seen you without no gun. Don't take me for no kid." His eyes blazed with light, and his throat worked like a pump.

In the above passage from Stephen Crane's "The Bride Comes to Yellow Sky," the characters are confronting each other, but we get the impression that they aren't deadly serious, despite the fact that one is carrying a gun.

Notice that the writer gets around the awkward repetition of 'he said' by using descriptions of the character's movements to tell us who is speaking. A new paragraph is a sign that the speaker has changed. So is the accompaniment of an action with a line of dialogue, as in this next example:

"Henry," she asked, "could we have wine at dinner?"

"Sure we could. Say! That will be fine."

She was silent for a while; then she said, "Henry, at those prize fights do the men hurt each other very much?"

"Sometimes a little, not often. Why?"

"Well, I've read how they break noses, and blood runs down their chests. I've read how the fighting gloves get heavy and soggy with blood."

He looked around at her. "What's the matter, Elisa. I didn't know you read things like that." He brought the car to a stop, then turned to the right over the Salinas River bridge.

"Do any women ever go to the fights?" she asked.

"Oh, sure, some. What's the matter, Elisa? Do you want to go? I don't think you'd like it, but I'll take you if you really want to go."

She relaxed limply in the seat. "Oh, no. I don't want to go. I'm sure I don't." Her face was turned away from him. "It will be enough if we can have wine. It will be plenty."

When Elisa's husband looks around at her, in this passage from John Steinbeck's "The Chrysanthemums," we know that the next line of dialogue is his. This is a dialogue between a husband and wife whose relationship is not very deep. The husband's statements, contrasted with the questions from his wife (which even he recognizes as unusual) reveal her mood and the nature of the relationship between them.

Sometimes the writer uses other methods to show us character, as in this next example:

> "Did you say something, Sammy?"
> "I said I quit."
> "I thought you did."
> "You didn't have to embarrass them."
> "It was they who were embarrassing us."
> I started to say something that came out "Fiddle-de-do." It's a saying of my grandmother's, and I know she would have been pleased.
> "I don't think you know what you're saying," Lengel said.
> "I know you don't," I said. "But I do."

In "A & P," Updike has Sammy quit his job in an effort to impress the girls who have just been asked to leave the store. The manager is direct and commanding in his speech, but Sammy is clearly confused because he can't admit his real reason for quitting. The "Fiddle-de-do" at the end of the example reaffirms that. Without having him say so directly, Updike shows us what kind of a person he is: a teenager whose raging hormones cause him to take an action he knows very soon he'll regret for a long time.

Dialogue is part of the story as a whole. Take note of things like the mood of the character speaking, the situation the character is in, and the character's relationship to others.

SYNTAX

Syntax refers to sentence structure, the arrangement of words within a sentence. It may be the single most important factor in the telling of a story, as in this excerpt from "Desiree's Baby":

> Desiree had not changed the thin white garment nor the slippers which she wore. Her hair was uncovered and the sun's rays brought a golden gloss from ice brown meshes. She did not take the broad, beaten road which led to the far-off plantation of Valmonde. She walked across a deserted field, where the stubble bruised her tender feet, so delicately shod, and tore her thin

gown to shreds. She disappeared among the reeds and willows that grew thick along the banks of the deep, sluggish bayou; and she did not come back again.

Each of the sentences in that passage begins with a basic subject-verb structure. This focuses the reader's attention on the action and conveys Desiree's single-mindedness and determination. It leads us to the final phrase "she did not come back again" in a way that underscores its finality and harshness.

In this next passage, from Arthur Clarke's "The Star," the author achieves a serious tone by first laying out the arguments that his colleagues will give (notice how they are equally structured) and then leads us to the solemn pronouncement "there is no God."

> I know the answers that my colleagues will give when they get back to Earth. They will say that the universe has no purpose and no plan, that since a hundred suns exploded every year in our galaxy, at this very moment some race is dying in the depths of space. Whether that race has done good or evil during its lifetime will make no difference in the end: there is no divine justice, for there is no God.

The syntax underscores what's been happening with the character. The two balanced phrases "the universe has no purpose and no plan, that since a hundred suns exploded every year in our galaxy, at this very moment some race is dying in the depths of space" lead to the next statement, that it "will make no difference in the end," which is punctuated by the final two phrases.

The Periodic Sentence

A sentence that is not grammatically complete until the very end is called a periodic sentence. The writer creates suspense or prolongs our interest with such a sentence because the main idea (and our understanding of it) appears at the end. The closing sentence of "Desiree's Baby" follows this structure:

> "But above all," she wrote, "night and day, I thank God for having so arranged our lives that our dear Armand will never know that his mother, who adores him, belongs to the race that is spread with the brand of slavery."

Only at the very end do we realize the irony of Armand's actions and the great injustice that Desiree has suffered. The ending startles us, partly as a result of the syntax of the final sentence. Arranged any other way, the ending might not have been as effective.

Reading Exercise:

See if you can determine the central idea in John Steinbeck's "The Chrysanthemums." After you've read the story, try writing a central idea statement. Then look at the metaphors and similes in the story and determine how they define the setting, or a character or conflict and how, in turn, those things support the central idea.

CHAPTER SEVEN

Tone

"When the letter reached Desiree she went with it to her husband's study, and laid it open upon the desk before which he sat. She was like a stone image: silent, white, motionless after she placed it there. In silence he ran his cold eyes over the written words. He said nothing. "Shall I go, Armand?" she asked in tones sharp with agonized suspense."

"Yes, go."

"Do you want me to go?"

"Yes. I want you to go."

[from "Desiree's Baby" by Kate Chopin]

The tone of a story reveals the author's attitude toward the story's subject. Sensitivity to a story's tone is crucial to identifying the central idea. In fact, the tone of a story often provides the only evidence to support an interpretation.

The word "tone" is usually associated with sound, as in the quality of a spoken voice. The tone of voice often reveals our feelings more than the words themselves. But how can a writer create tone without sound?

In speech, the pitch and volume of the speaker's voice, as well as facial expressions, relate the intent. For example, if we say "Be sure to return my textbook tomorrow," our tone and facial expression reveal whether:

- You're tired of loaning things to people who never return them. (Your tone is angry or hostile and you are scowling.)
- You're concerned because you need the book to study for a test. (Your tone suggests worry and anxiety and your brow is furrowed.)
- You don't want the book back, and the person borrowing it knows you don't. (Your tone is humorous or ironic and you're smiling.)

DISCOVERING AND DESCRIBING THE TONE

We cannot hear an author's voice, so tone must be expressed in other ways. There is a one-to-one correlation between tone and language, so the tone is often created through the various techniques of language we described in the previous chapter. Here is how they affect a story's tone.

Similes and Metaphors

The choice of comparative elements provides a clue to the author's attitude toward the subject. Consider these similes from Arthur Clarke's "The Star":

> I know how it must have blazed low in the east before sunrise, like a beacon in that oriental dawn.

Clarke compares the star of the magi to a beacon, which is precisely the purpose it served for the wise men. This is a **solemn** comparison.

> Our ship fell toward this gigantic bull's-eye like an arrow into its target.

The ship's path to the planet is compared to the path of an arrow toward its target. The arrow has no choice; it is directed by the archer. The implication is that the space ship, too, is being directed by something beyond its control. These similes help to set the serious tone of the story.

In the following examples from "The Bride Comes to Yellow Sky," notice how Stephen Crane's metaphors help to establish the story's tone:

> Face to face with this girl in San Antonio, and spurred by his sharp impulse, he had gone headlong over all the social hedges.

This metaphor uses the image of someone diving over a hedge. Crane calls it a "social hedge" to add some symbolism to the metaphor. The hedge separates the yards of social status. By saying the marshal went "headlong" over the hedge, he gives the marshal's action an air of **recklessness**.

> Save for the busy drummer and his companions in the saloon, Yellow Sky was dozing.

Here, Crane establishes the town as a single entity. Rather than saying that the people in the town are quiet or sleeping, he says the town is dozing. (Notice that he also avoids the cliché of calling it a "sleepy village.") The diction here is important too, since dozing implies a light nap, a sleep that is not deep. The tone is one of **calm**.

Allusions

In "The Star," Clarke makes a couple of references to the founder of the main character's religious order:

> My colleagues have asked me that, and I have given what answers I can. Perhaps you could have done better, Father Loyola, but I have found nothing in the Exercitia Spiritualia that helps me here.

> The Rubens engraving of Loyola seems to mock me as it hangs there above the spectrophoto-meter tracings. What would you, Father, have made of this knowledge that has come into my keeping, so far from the little world that was all the universe you knew? Would your faith have risen to the challenge, as mine has failed to do?

These references help to underscore the deep philosophical nature of the story's main conflict. Loyola was a writer who discussed the question of God's decisions. He argued that faith is a necessary principle in matters that we cannot understand. This reference also establishes the **serious, philosophically troublesome** tone of the story.

Repetition

In James Thurber's "The Secret Life of Walter Mitty," the words "pocketa-pocketa" are repeated throughout. In Mitty's imagination they represent an airplane's engine, then an anaesthetizer, and finally the sound of flame throwers:

> The pounding of the cylinders increased; pocketa–pocketa–pocketa–pocketa–pocketa.
> A huge, complicated machine, connected to the operating table, with many tubes and wires, began at this moment to go pocketa–pocketa–pocketa."
> The pounding of the cannon increased; there was the rat–tat–tatting of machine guns, and from somewhere came the menacing pocketa–pocketa–pocketa of the new flame-throwers.

This repetition connects Mitty's daydreams and enhances the **humorous** tone of the story.

Diction

Edgar Allan Poe's choice of words and the phrasing of his stories established a tone for the horror story genre still popular today.

> In an instant he had reached the extremity of the niche, and finding his progress arrested by the rock, stood stupidly bewildered. A moment more and I had fettered him to the granite. In its surface were two iron staples, distant from each other about two feet, horizontally. From one of these depended a short chain, from the other a padlock. Throwing the links about his waist, it was but the work of a few seconds to secure it. He was too much astounded to resist. Withdrawing the key I stepped back from the recess.

Notice that Fortunato's progress was "arrested", that he stood "stupidly belwildered", and that Montresor "throws" the links about Fortunato's waist. Those words, combined with the precision with which the narrator describes the event, create a **dispassionate** and **evil sounding** tone.

Symbolism

In "The Chrysanthemums," John Steinbeck creates a symbol out of the boxing matches. In the beginning of the story, Henry good-naturedly teases Elisa about going to the fights:

> ". . . I thought," he continued, "I thought how it's Saturday afternoon, and we might go into Salinas for dinner at a restaurant and then to a picture show to celebrate, you see."
> "Good," she repeated. "Oh, yes. That will be good."
> Henry put on his joking tone. "There's fights tonight. How'd you like to go to the fights?"
> "Oh, no." she said breathlessly. "No, I wouldn't like fights."

But later, near the story's end, when Elisa asks Henry about the fights, Steinbeck is able to show us the intensity of her emotions:

> She was silent for a while; then she said, "Henry, at those prize fights do the men hurt each other very much?"

"Sometimes a little, not often. Why?"

"Well, I've read how they break noses, and blood runs down their chests. I've read how the fighting gloves get heavy and soggy with blood."

He looked around at her. "What's the matter, Elisa. I didn't know you read things like that." He brought the car to a stop, then turned to the right over the Salinas River bridge.

"Do any women ever go to the fights?" she asked.

"Oh, sure, some. What's the matter, Elisa? Do you want to go? I don't think you'd like it, but I'll take you if you really want to go."

She relaxed limply in the seat. "Oh, no. I don't want to go. I'm sure I don't."

The fights become a symbol of Elisa's **anger** and **frustration**. The discussion between Elisa and Henry is symbolic of the way Elisa feels.

Dialogue

As the exchange between Elisa and Henry demonstrates, the importance of dialogue in establishing tone is directly related to how the dialogue is used. John Updike's "A & P" relies completely upon the narrator's words. Sammy's choice of words tells us how he feels, but at the same time, they also tell us how Updike feels about the events of the story:

"You'll feel this for the rest of your life," Lengel says, and I know that's true, too, but remembering how he made that pretty girl blush makes me so scrunchy inside I punch the No Sale tab and the machine whirs "pee-pul" and the drawer splats out. One advantage to this scene taking place in summer, I can follow this up with a clean exit, there's no fumbling around getting your coat and galoshes, I just saunter into the electric eye in my white shirt that my mother ironed the night before, and the door heaves itself open, and outside the sunshine is skating around on the asphalt.

I look around for my girls, but they're gone, of course.

Lengel is the one who tells Sammy (and the reader) in a very **serious** tone that he'll feel the repercussions of what he does for the rest of his life, but then Sammy adds that the girl blushing made him "scrunchy inside."

He also includes the fact that his mother ironed his shirt the night before and describes the cash register sound as "pee-pul" (reminiscent of Walter Mitty's "pocketa-pocketa"). The **frivolous** tone of those words contrasts with Lengel's remarks. And when Sammy calls the girls "my girls" and adds "of course" to the end of his remarks, we can tell that the entire incident is not really a tragic event in the teenager's life. The tone tells us that the author sees this as something that all teenage boys must "live and learn" about a **matter-of-fact** and **realistic** tone.

Syntax

At the end of "I'm a Fool" by Sherwood Anderson, the first person narrator says,

> I wish I had that fellow right here that had on a Windsor tie and carried a cane. I'd smash him for fair. Gosh darn his eyes. He's a big fool that's what he is.
> And if I'm not another you just go find me one and I'll quit working and be a bum and give him my job. I don't care nothing for working, and earning money, and saving it for no such boob as myself.

The first paragraph ends with the narrator calling the fellow with the Windsor tie a fool, but Anderson saves the narrator's conclusion, that he's the biggest "boob" of all, for the last (see "The Periodic Sentence" section following). Also notice how the second paragraph uses a trio of comments leading to the conclusion. This syntactical method of using threes (as in the 1-2-3 punch) is not uncommon, and Anderson uses it twice. First, the narrator says,

[1] I'll quit working and
[2] be a bum and
[3] give him my job.

Then he says he doesn't care for

[1] working, and
[2] earning money, and
[3] saving it. . .

The effect is an **aw shucks** tone of **disappointment**, much the same as that of Updike's narrator in "A & P."

The Periodic Sentence

Kate Chopin's "Desiree's Baby" concludes with a periodic sentence, saving the final revelation for the very last and leading up to it with information that underscores the story's irony:

> "But above all," she wrote, "night and day, I thank God for having so arranged our lives that our dear Armand will never know that his mother, who adores him, belongs to the race that is spread with the brand of slavery."

"The race that is spread with the brand of slavery" tells us that Armand, not Desiree, is the source of the gene that made their baby mulatto. If the reader hasn't suspected this, the element of surprise gives the story its final **melodramatic** impact.

Irony

An author may also use irony to reveal the tone of the story and establish the preferred attitude toward the characters and events. Irony can transform an ordinary or humorous incident into one of great significance or tragedy.

Such use of irony can be the sole determinant of a story's central idea. In the previous example from "Desiree's Baby," irony plays a major role in the effect the story has on the reader. In Updike's "A & P," the irony in the fact that the girls Sammy wants so badly to impress completely miss his heroic gesture (his resignation), contributes significantly to the **realistic** tone of the story.

DEFINING THE TONE

Discovering a story's tone is often as simple as answering questions like "What words describe my reaction to the story?" or "How does this story make me feel?"

The tone is usually responsible for the reader's emotional response. Therefore, in most cases, the words used to describe the emotional response to a story can also describe its tone.

The tone of each of the following passages can be described with a few words. Notice how the words suggest the overall feel of the passage.

A Comical/Humorous Tone

> When Cass Edmonds and Uncle Buck ran back to the house they heard Uncle Buddy cursing and bellowing in the kitchen, then the fox and the dogs came out of the kitchen and crossed the hall into the dogs' room and they heard them run through the dogs' room into his and Uncle Buck's room, then they saw them cross the hall again into Uncle Buddy's room into the kitchen again and this time it sounded like the whole kitchen chimney had come down and Uncle Buddy bellowing like a steamboat blowing, and this time the fox and the dogs and five or six sticks of firewood all came out of the kitchen together with Uncle Buddy in the middle of them hitting at everything in sight with another stick. It was a good race.

The above passage from William Faulkner's "Was" derives its humor from a chaotic chase sequence, much like those in slapstick comedies. The passage consists of only two sentences; that helps create the tone. The first sentence is very long and describes the wild confusion of the chase. Exaggerated imagery ("bellowing like a steamboat blowing") also contributes to the amusement. The second sentence adds to the comic tone because it's both brief and merely a comment on the action described in the first, providing a contrast also common to humor.

A Sorrowful/Sad Tone

> The dream was gone. Something had been taken from him. In a sort of panic he pushed the palms of his hands into his eyes and tried to bring up a picture of the waters lapping on Sherry Island and the moonlit veranda, and gingham on the golf-links and the dry sun and the gold color of her neck's soft down. And her mouth damp to his kisses and her eyes plaintive with melancholy and her freshness like new fine linen in the morning. Why, these things were no longer in the world! They had existed and they existed no longer.
>
> For the first time in years the tears were streaming down his face.
>
> But they were for himself now.

This second selection, from F. Scott Fitzgerald's "Winter Dreams," suggests **nostalgia**, a longing for the past. This creates the sorrowful or **sad** tone that borders on sentimentality. It appeals to our emotions and sense of nostalgia by describing a man's reaction to his lost love. The romantic images ("the moonlit veranda," "her mouth damp to his kisses") are memories of an irrecoverable past. The tone of the passage makes it obvious that the author wants us to share the grief of a man who suddenly realizes that the dreams of his youth are lost forever.

Eerie/Fearful/Terrifying

So far, I had not opened my eyes. I felt that I lay upon my back, unbound. I reached out my hand, and it fell heavily upon something damp and hard. There I suffered it to remain for many minutes, while I strove to imagine where and what I could be. I longed, yet dared not to employ my vision. I dreaded the first glance at objects around me. It was not that I feared to look upon things horrible, but that I grew aghast lest there should be nothing to see. At length, with a wild desperation at heart, I quickly unclosed my eyes. My worst thoughts, then, were confirmed. The blackness of eternal night encompassed me. I struggled for breath. The intensity of the darkness seemed to oppress and stifle me. The atmosphere was intolerably close.

The tone of this third passage from Edgar Allan Poe's "The Pit and the Pendulum" is typical of a horror story. The narrator is afraid to open his eyes for fear of what he may *not* see. Sure enough, when he finally opens his eyes, he finds a darkness so intense that he "struggled for breath." The author's use of fear of the unknown and imprisonment in total darkness creates the tone appropriate to a story of **terror** and **suspense**.

These short passages illustrate our point, but a single passage seldom reflects the tone of an entire story. Other words could have been chosen to describe any one of these passages, but the proper vocabulary is important in describing tone. A proper analysis, just like a well-written story, requires a good vocabulary.

TONE AND THE ELEMENTS OF FICTION

Another way the author creates tone is through the arrangement and manipulation of the elements of fiction. Some of these elements are dominant in the preceding examples, but all of these devices may not be of equal importance in any one story. If one element is the most significant in establishing tone, we refer to it as the dominant element.

For example, an author may use little or no figurative language and not specify the setting. Instead, the writer may rely almost exclusively on conflict and dialogue to produce the tone. (Read Ernest Hemingway's "The Killers" for a good example of this technique.) Or the point of view may be the most important factor in the tone of one story, while the personality of a central character may be most important in another.

Every author chooses the element or elements that best convey the attitude most appropriate to the central idea.

Character

The personality of a central character may help to establish the tone of a story. In the following passage John Steinbeck reveals Elisa's personality and this also helps to establish the passionate tone of the story:

> She was kneeling on the ground looking up at him. Her breast swelled passionately.
>
> The man's eyes narrowed. He looked away self-consciously. "Maybe I know," he said. "Sometimes in the night in the wagon there."
>
> Elisa's voice grew husky. She broke in on him. "I've never lived as you do, but I know what you mean. When the night is dark why, the stars are sharp-pointed, and there's quiet. Why, you rise up and up! Every pointed star gets driven into your body. It's like that. Hot and sharp and lovely."
>
> Kneeling there, her hand went out toward his legs in the greasy black trousers. Her hesitant fingers almost touched the cloth. Then her hand dropped to the ground. She crouched low like a fawning dog.

Elisa is on the verge of surrendering to her repressed sexual desires. The phrase "hot and sharp and lovely" describes not only the stars, but also her sensuous feelings and her awareness of them. Her "kneeling," her breathing "passionately," her crouching "like a fawning dog," all contribute to a sensual image. The tone of the passage helps reveal the author's attitude toward Elisa's situation: she is a sensitive person, craving love and affection and we sympathize with her restricted life because the connotations of the words used lead us to feel the tone of **repression**.

Conflict

The basis of a story's conflict can set the tone. "The Star" by Arthur Clarke is based on a philosophical and religious conflict between the new evidence the space traveler finds and his own faith in God. It is an internal conflict and, because it deals with a serious issue, the tone is **serious** as well.

Point of View

The point of view or narrative voice of a story may also be a clue to the tone. When making judgments about the accuracy and significance of information, we must consider the source. Therefore, the tone of a story may depend on whose voice we hear. Notice how the omniscient point of view, in this scene from Kate Chopin's "Desiree's Baby," establishes the tone:

> In silence he ran his cold eyes over the written words. He said nothing. "Shall I go, Armand?" she asked in tones sharp with agonized suspense. "Yes, go."
> "Do you want me to go?"
> "Yes, I want you to go."
> He thought Almighty God had dealt cruelly and unjustly with him; and felt, somehow, that he was paying Him back in kind when he stabbed thus into his wife's soul. Moreover he no longer loved her, because of the unconscious injury she had brought upon his home and his name. She turned away like one stunned by a blow, and walked slowly toward the door, "Goodbye, Armand," she moaned. He did not answer her. That was his last blow at Fate.

The revelation of each character's consciousness effectively conveys the author's **bleak, mournful** attitude toward the effects of racial fear and hatred.

Language

In Dorothy Parker's "Arrangement in Black and White," we "hear" the words of the main character, and her syntax and diction tell us much about her. We recognize the contrast between the impression she thinks she's making and what she really feels solely on the basis of her tone. Notice, in the following examples, how this works.

> ". . . I said to Burton, 'It's a good thing for you Walter Williams is colored,' I said, 'or you'd have lots of reason to be jealous .'"

The implication that Burton need not be jealous of a black man lets us in on the woman's view of blacks as inferior.

> ". . . I think you're simply marvelous, giving this perfectly marvelous party for him, and having him meet all these white people, and all. Isn't he terribly grateful?

If the guest were white would he need to be *grateful*? Again, the woman tips her hand.

> . . . he had this old colored nurse, this regular old nigger mammy, and he just simply loves her. Why, every time he goes home, he goes out in the kitchen to see her.

He loves her, but he goes to the kitchen to see her because she's not allowed to come into the living room. And notice that the woman calls the nurse a *regular old nigger mammy.*

> They're just like children, just as easy-going, and always singing and laughing and everything. Aren't they the happiest things you ever saw in your life?

Here's yet another example of how the syntax and diction set the tone of **superiority** the narrator of story. Black people, to the woman with the pink velvet poppies in her hair, aren't equal; they're "just like children."

Setting

The setting can create or reinforce the tone through the description of the conditions related to the setting (the time of day or year, the weather, and the appearance of the location). The choice of the catacombs for the physical setting of Poe's "The Cask of Amontillado" establishes the somber and frightening tone of the story, especially when contrasted with the choice of season: the carnival.

Shift in Tone

Sometimes the tone of a story is consistent throughout. Other times, however, a story begins with one tone and shifts to another. Russell Maloney's "Inflexible Logic" begins with the absurd notion that given enough time, chimpanzees on typewriters will pound out great works of literature. When the character sets a number of chimps in front of typewriters and they immediately begin producing flawless copies of great works, a **whimisical** tone is established. When another character enters the room at the end of the story and begins shooting the chimps, the tone shifts to an **appalling** and **shocking** one. Another example is in Roald Dahl's "The Way Up to Heaven." The unnecessary meanness of the husband stikes an initial tone of **callousness**. When his wife leaves their apartment building for a long journey knowing he is trapped in the elevator, the story ends with a tone of justifiable **revenge**.

Such shifts in tone are important because while the final tone may be quite different from that in the beginning, the overall effect of the story is a combination of the two working together.

Reading Exercise:

See if you can determine the central idea in Kate Chopin's "Desiree's Baby." After you've read the story, try writing a central idea statement. Then see if you can write a sentence stating the tone of the story. When you've completed, see if you can identify the relationship between the two.

CHAPTER EIGHT

The Creative Writing Process

To many, the process of creating a fictional work of literature—a short story, play, or novel—conjures up an image of an intense person writing furiously, creating great literature. The person is possessed, out of control, and at the mercy of some gut-wrenching emotion. But nothing could be further from the truth.

Most good writers are in complete control when it comes to their art. They know what they're doing. The fact that a few of them may not be able to explain their motives doesn't change the fact that their decisions are deliberate and that they are directed by a central idea or a character or setting or some other element the author is focusing on. The point is that an author is crafting the story carefully, with purpose. Perhaps it's because we still hear writers talk about their vision or inspiration that the image of the possessed artist persists.

John Steinbeck's writing is a model of conciseness. His style is direct and the syntax simple. The sentences flow so smoothly that the reader doesn't sense the author at work. But he's there, and what he has created is the result of much time and effort writing and rewriting until it's just right. In "The Chrysanthemums," Steinbeck tells the story of a woman who is unfulfilled. She is, all at once, strong and vulnerable, and these characteristics lead to her victimization by an itinerant worker, a tinker. Readers are unaware of what went into the development of the story, but records reveal that Steinbeck spent many hours shaping it.

The idea for the story appears to have germinated for a while before Steinbeck put pen to paper. It was written during the same period he was working on his novel *Tortilla Flat*. The central idea for the story was already clear, but how it ought to begin was not. The following excerpt is, as far as we know, his first attempt at writing it. The excerpt appears in the same journal as the first version of *Tortilla Flat*. (If you notice any errors in punctuation or spelling in the excerpts in this chapter, that's because you're looking at the unedited, original text. This is *exactly* the way Steinbeck wrote it.)

On a shelf over the kitchen sink, a little oblong mirror with fluted edges stood. In front of it lay four big hair pins, bent out of shape, shiny where the enamel was broken off at the U. Elisa,

73

washing the noonday dishes, paused now and then to look at the mirror. . . .

Shortly after attempting this opening, Steinbeck writes these remarks:

Purple ink again. Apparently it doesn't make a difference in the writing. I'll give it a try. It looks pretty pale to me though. But it was a bargain not to be overlooked. How it will work on my post cards fine.

Steinbeck is now rambling and goes on to express concerns about family and coming events. Then he returns to his efforts at completing the story, writing two full pages, but finally gives it up, concluding, "This is the day's work. There's no sureness of touch in me today. I don't seem to be able to get at this story."

The next page of his journal, which may have been started at a later time, consists of a letter to an hypothetical observer, whom he calls his "Little Turnip." In it, he talks about the creative writing process and provides us with some insight into the difficulties the writer encounters:

". . . this morning I want to issue a warning against certain tendencies in the writing of short stories. I had a story, Ralph, and on a day when I did not feel like writing I sat down to write it . . . Subconsciously I knew it was wrong from the beginning. But I blundered on, putting down words every one of which had an untrue ring. And so, Ralph, if you ever take up short stories as you no doubt will (everyone does) I implore you not to go on working when you have that feeling in your bones."

Following this passage, "The Chrysanthemums" begins with what became the final version—a description of the fog settling over the valley. Steinbeck has finally found an approach that satisfies him.

THE REVISION PHASE

Writing the story was just the beginning. Many portions of "The Chrysanthemums" were revised several times. At least four versions of it exist; three have appeared in print. Though some of the changes were the result of the work of Steinbeck's editors (he was notoriously weak in his use of commas), many of the changes were his.

The remainder of this chapter presents comparisons between the author's manuscript version, which appears in his journal, and *The Long Valley* version, which is the most frequently published.

Character Revisions

Many of the changes in the story affect the character of Elisa. It's quite likely that as the story developed Elisa became more real to Steinbeck, and so her character became easier to shape. Consider these two descriptions of Elisa.

The Manuscript Version	*The Final Version*
Elisa was thirty-five, but she looked older in her gardening costume, a man's black hat, pulled low down over her eyes, clodhopper shoes, and a big corduroy apron littered with pockets for snips, a little trowel and seeds. Elisa wore heavy leather gloves to protect her hands.	She was thirty-five. Her face was lean and strong and her eyes were clear as water. Her figure looked blocked and heavy in her gardening costume, a man's black hat, pulled low down over her eyes, clodhopper shoes, a figured print dress almost completely covered by a big corduroy apron with four big pockets to hold the snips, the trowel and scratcher, the seeds and the knife she worked with. She wore heavy leather gloves to protect her hands while she worked.

Notice that her age, while still mentioned, becomes less of a factor than her physical appearance. That she looks older is dropped from the description; that she looks blocked and heavy is added.

Conflict Revisions

The conflict in "The Chrysanthemums" is subtle. The initial external struggle is between Henry and Elisa (Later an external conflict develops between Elisa and the tinker). Steinbeck conveys the awkwardness between Elisa and Henry through his descriptions of their behavior.

The Manuscript Version

Henry looked down toward the tractor shed. When he looked back at her he was safe.

The Final Version

Henry looked down toward the tractor shed, and when he brought his eyes back to her, they were his own again.

The external conflict between Henry and Elisa is also evident in the dialogue. In this next example, we can see how Steinbeck reworked Henry's words to clarify the character's confusion. That Henry cannot understand Elisa's dilemma is important to the development of her internal conflict.

The Manuscript Version

"Nice? You think I look nice? What do you mean by 'nice'?"

Henry blundered on. "I mean you look strong strong and happy."

"I am strong? How strong? What do you mean 'strong'?" Henry was bewildered. "You're playing something" he said helplessly. "You look strong enough to break a calf over your knee, happy enough to eat it like a watermelon." For a second she lost her self . . . before how strong.

The Final Version

"Nice? You think I look nice? What do you mean by 'nice'?"

Henry blundered on. "I don't know. I mean you look different strong and happy."

"I am strong? Yes, strong. What do you mean 'strong'?"

He looked bewildered. "You're playing some kind of a game," he said helplessly. "It's a kind of a play. You look strong enough to break a calf over your knee, happy enough to eat it like a watermelon."

For a second she lost her rigidity . . . She grew complete again. "I am strong," she boasted. "I never knew before how strong."

Point of View Revisions

In the following example, Steinbeck shifts the position of the narrator slightly in order to add the dropping of the coin more dramatic action.

The Manuscript Version	*The Final Version*
She went into the house and brought him a fifty-cent piece.	Elisa brought him a fifty-cent piece from the house and dropped it in his hand.

In this next example, Steinbeck maintains the point of view. Elisa still looks over her shoulder, but Steinbeck alters the action. Instead of throwing back her shoulders, she throws out her chest. The result is the same, but there is a great deal of difference between the two.

The Manuscript Version	*The Final Version*
She tightened her stomach, threw back her shoulders, she turned and looked over her shoulder at her back.	She tightened her stomach and threw out her chest. She turned and looked over her shoulder at her back.

Setting Revisions

Following the tangential discussion with his little turnip, Steinbeck attempted to begin the story again. He probably thought it through and realized that a macro-vision of the setting would be more effective than the earlier version. The metaphor of the closed pot must have seemed especially apt. Here is how the second attempt began:

> The high gray flannel fog of winter closed off the Salinas valley from the sky and from the rest of the world. On all sides it sat like a lid on the mountains and made of the great valley a closed pot. On the broad level floor of the valley, the gang plows churned the dark rich and left the black earth shining like metal where the shares had cut.

But this is not the way the beginning ultimately appeared in print. The final, most frequently published version of the story begins this way:

> The high gray flannel fog of winter closed off the Salinas valley from the sky and from all the rest of the world. On every side it sat like a lid on the mountains and made of the great valley a closed pot. On the broad, level land floor the gang plows bit deep and left the black earth shining like metal where the shares had cut.

Notice these subtle changes to the description.

- the addition of the word "all" to the first sentence, requiring the word's deletion from the second
- the addition of the word "land" to the third sentence, emphasizing the earthy nature of the setting
- the change in verbs, from "churned" to "bit deep," in the third sentence

Language Revisions

Changes in the syntax, diction, and imagery, as well as the addition of symbols, have a major impact on the story. Here are just a few.

Syntax

The sequence of words is another feature that contributes to the effect. Notice how the placement of the description "lean and rangy mongrel" near the end of the sentence increases its impact.

The Manuscript Version	*The Final Version*
A lean and rangy mongrel dog walked sedately underneath the wagon behind the wheels.	Underneath the wagon, between the hind wheels, a lean and rangy mongrel dog walked sedately.

Diction

Sometimes one word can make an important difference. For example, in *The Manuscript Version* of the story, Steinbeck used the word "quietly" to describe Elisa's voice:

"Oh no," she said quietly. "I wouldn't like fights."

However, in the final version of the story the word has changed to *breathlessly*, and the word *no* is repeated:

"Oh no," she said breathlessly. "No, I wouldn't like fights."

To speak quietly is to be reticent, without feeling. But speaking breathlessly suggests a strong feeling. In the final version, Elisa nearly has her breath taken away at the thought of the fights. And twice she tells Henry no.

Syntax and diction usually work together to create the sound of a phrase or a sentence. Steinbeck had an excellent ear for the English language. In many ways, the changes he made were aimed at improving the sound; to make the story read more smoothly. In the next two samples, he adds phrases to convey Elisa's feelings and he also simplifies the action to make it more dramatic.

The Manuscript Version	*The Final Version*
She heard the gate being shut. In a few moments Henry's step sounded on the porch.	She heard the gate bang shut and set herself for Henry's arrival. His step sounded on the porch.

Imagery

Near the end of the story, Elisa and Henry talk about going to the fights. Steinbeck recognized the impact of the image of the boxing gloves soggy with blood and strengthened it by adding that they were "heavy" as well. Henry's response is modified, too. In the final version he adds, "I don't think you'll like it," which is a further indication of Henry's lack of understanding and inability to relate to Elisa.

The Manuscript Version	*The Final Version*
"Well, I've read how they break noses, and blood runs down their chests, and the fighting gloves get soggy with blood." "Do you want to go? I'll take you if you really want to go."	"Well, I've read how they break noses, and blood runs down their chests. I've read how the fighting gloves get heavy and soggy with blood." "Do you want to go? I don't think you'd like it, but I'll take you if you really want to go."

Symbolism

The symbolic sexual interplay between Elisa and the tinker is a critical part of the story. The final version strengthens this interplay by eliminating some words and making the sentences more direct.

The Manuscript Version

"Well, I can only tell you what it feels like to have them. It's when you're budding. Everything goes right down to your fingertips. You watch your fingers work. You can feel how it is. They pick and pick the buds . . . They may pick a bud off that looks biggest, but it isn't the best . . . Every pointed star gets driven into you, into your body . . . Hot and sharp and all lovely."

The Final Version

"Well, I can only tell you what it feels like. It's when you're picking off the buds you don't want. Everything goes right down to your fingertips. You watch your fingers work. They can do it themselves. You can feel how it is. They pick and pick the buds . . . They know. They never make a mistake. You can feel it . . . Every pointed star gets driven into your body . . . Hot and sharp and—lovely."

Irony

"The Chrysanthemums" makes its point through the use of irony, which is shown through Elisa's naïveté and the tinker's exploitation of her situation. In this illustration, Steinbeck added the metaphor of the fawning dog to illustrate how Elisa relates to the tinker and to underscore the ironic contrast of her strength with her weakness.

The Manuscript Version

Kneeling there her hand went out toward his legs in the (greasy dirty) dirty black trousers, almost touched the cloth. Her hand dropped to the ground. She crouched low and cleared her throat on the rising sobs. She heard his voice coming from a distance. 'It's nice, just like you say. . . .' Her lip curled back. 'How do you know? How can you tell?' she said. He felt the contempt in her tone.

The Final Version

Kneeling there, her hand went out toward his legs in the greasy black trousers. Her hesitant fingers almost touched the cloth. Then her hand dropped to the ground. She crouched low like a fawning dog. He said, "It's nice, just like you say."

Tone

Many of the earlier changes presented here had an effect on the tone of the story. Changes in wording, syntax, and diction modify the overall tone, as do the following additional changes. In these two examples, the rewording of the passages sharpens the tone of sadness and loneliness mixed with frustration.

The Manuscript Version	*The Final Version*
"My mother had it too. She could stick anything in the ground and make it grow. She said it was planters' hands."	"My mother had it. She could stick anything in the ground and make it grow. She said it was having planters' hands that knew how to do it."
"When you're like that you can't make a mistake. Do you see that! Can you understand that?" Her eyes were wet.	"When you're like that you can't do anything wrong. Do you see that? Can you understand that?"

Although many of Steinbeck's revisions might seem trivial, their impact is not. Much like sculptors who must painstakingly smooth some edges and sharpen others to make the work fit the concept, serious writers pay attention to the details of a story. They know that therein lies the difference between a good story and a great one.

CHAPTER NINE

Additional Methods of Analysis

The earlier chapters of this book focus on the analysis of short stories through a basic format involving three parts: a summary of the story, an interpretation of the central idea, and a discussion of the primary elements. While this approach serves the beginner well, alternative approaches to analysis can reveal even more. In fact, an analysis through a dominant element, an analysis with an evaluation, or a comparison/contrast analysis is often better suited to many stories.

ANALYSIS THROUGH A DOMINANT ELEMENT

In many stories one element serves as the author's primary means for conveying the central idea. When this occurs, a single element will overshadow the others. They become subservient to that single element. Analyzing such a story requires that the central idea be defined through the dominant element. A subsequent discussion of the elements then focuses on the primary element, rather than on the central idea.

John Updike's "A & P" is a good example of a story in which the element of character is central. The crux of the story depends on a change in Sammy's character. It is this change, one of the many steps toward maturation, that forms the central idea. An effective analysis of "A & P" would rely on the relationship of the other elements (setting, conflict, tone, language, and point of view) to character. Such an analysis would explore the way the setting shapes the character, the way the first person point of view provides the insight into character that is necessary for a successful central idea, the fact that the real conflict in the story is internal and, therefore, directly tied to the character, and so on.

In the following student example, the dominant element of point of view unifies the analysis. All other elements result from its development, as is often true of a first person narrative. The first person is usually the main character, and his or her perspective on the story dominates the central idea and directs the others. Notice how she uses quotes and details from the story to support statements about the character's personality.

Alice Munro's "How I Met My Husband"
by Dana Ross

"How I Met My Husband" by Alice Munro is the story of a country girl's first encounter with luxury and sophistication. The first person narrative is the dominant element of the story as Edie's perspective is essential to revealing the author's theme. Munro's story illuminates the beauty of appreciating and making the most of what one has and shows how this wisdom may come more easily to simple, hard-working people than to those of different backgrounds and values.

Edie's character is a key ingredient to the story's theme and by choosing to tell it from her point of view, Munro creates a very effective story. Edie's narrative reveals her conscientious, principled, no-nonsense approach to life. Her sincere appreciation of simple things is appealing to the reader, and her honest and sensible nature makes her a very likable character. Her simple observations, like realizing that taking a bath too often in a luxurious bathroom might make it less special, and that someone of simple background can probably imagine a life of luxury easier than someone of luxury could imagine an unadorned life, exemplify her wisdom.

Her perceptiveness of human nature can be seen time and again as she sees past what people say. "Asking people to stay, just like that, is certainly a country thing . . . but not to Mrs. Peebles, from the way she said, 'oh yes, we have plenty of room,'" is a good example of this. Her frank opinions about people could make her appear smug and self-righteous, but because of the respect the reader feels for her, these are interpreted more as honest evaluations by a person with a strong sense of values.

Comparisons of Edie's homespun attitude with some of the other characters' attitudes are made through the author's use of point of view, and lead directly to the central idea. The contrast of Edie's wholesome simplicity with Mrs. Peeble's hollow sophistication humbles the reader and makes her examine her own values. The difference between Edie's honest, hard-working ways and Loretta Bird's gossiping, lazy ones increases the reader's admiration for Edie. The most potent effects of the first person point of view come from telling the story years after it has taken place, allowing the reader to see how Edie has matured. Edie has a good head on her shoulders even as a naive girl due, at least in part, to her upbringing in a strict, farming family that makes do with the bare necessities. The traits instilled in her childhood remain through the years and she becomes an honorable, upright, and kind woman. For years she allows her husband to believe that she went to the mailbox daily to see him, when she really was waiting for a letter from another man "because I like for people to think what pleases them and makes them happy."

Edie's conflict and the way she deals with it are revealed most effectively through the first person point of view. Her first job exposes Edie to many new things, luxuries, city people, and a worldly man, all things that would excite and interest a young girl, and quite possibly lead her astray. These things, the man in particular, do affect Edie but her good sense prevails.

As Edie sees it, "If there are women all through life waiting, and women busy and not waiting, I knew which I had to be. Even though there might be things the second kind of woman has to pass up and never know about, it still is better." By accepting her place in life and knowing that a life of hard work would be one with less inner turmoil, she is able to resolve her conflict without much difficulty. The manner in which Edie handles her conflict establishes her as a heroine of ordinary circumstances, and this in conjunction with the unpretentious narrative makes the theme of the story universally appealing and easy to accept.

The traditional rural traits that Edie possesses are not necessarily shared by all people residing in the country. The story takes place at a time when city people are opting to live in the country, bringing different sets of values with them. The cultural conflicts this creates unfold vividly in the rural setting of the story, and they are made more apparent by telling the story through the eyes of a genuine country girl. The stark differences in the women of the story emphasize that where one lives is irrelevant.

The values one adopts are what leads to a healthy state of mind. The veterinarian's character lends hope that Edie's wholesome attitude is not entirely a result of her country upbringing but possible for any person with the right approach to life.

All the elements of "How I Met My Husband" rest on Edie's down-to-earth narration. Munro's use of the first person narrative gives a simple story a powerful impact. Spending time wisely and productively offers more rewards than wasting time wishing for what might never be, and basic goodness and hard work can enable one to more fully appreciate what life has to offer.

ANALYSIS THROUGH EVALUATION

Our individual likes and dislikes often cause us to judge things on the basis of bias or prejudice rather than by objective means. We may declare that something is good or bad when all we really mean is that we like or don't like it. Although you may not like a story, it may be well-written. And a story you do like may not be well-written. In other words, the quality of a story is intrinsic; it's separate from our personal feelings. Quality is determined by applying the objective criteria like those detailed in this book.

An evaluation judges the level of a story's quality. Regardless of what we evaluate, we can't conduct a logical debate until we agree on a clear set of standards. Once the standards are agreed upon, a story provides the evidence for judging whether or not the story meets the standards.

Establishing Criteria for Evaluating Short Stories

Three major criteria are commonly used to evaluate short stories. These criteria, explained in the following sections, depend on the elements discussed in the earlier chapters of this text.

The Elements Must All Work Together

A story should be judged by how effectively all of the elements work together to achieve the central idea. Each element works with every other element to accomplish the story's goal. With that premise, you can review each element, its relationship to the other elements, and its relationship to the central idea. If this relationship is weak or lacking in some way, if a piece does not fit, then the story lacks the right combination of elements to be effective.

For example, a story in which the central idea is closely related to the personality of a particular character must use the other elements to support it. We must ask: Does the setting illuminate the character's personality? Does the language reinforce the character's traits? Does the tone tell us something about the character? Is the point of view supportive of the characterization?

The elements all working together is a good but very general criterion. More specific criteria may be more useful, as illustrated below.

The Specific Elements of Fiction

Any element of fiction may be used as a criterion for evaluation. For example, one might say "The best stories have clear, easily accessible central ideas" while someone else might say "The best stories have central ideas that are challenging and more difficult to find." One might say "The best stories are those with deep internal conflicts that provide a psychological profile of the central character," while someone else might say "The best stories are those with strong social conflicts that make a commentary on society that may still be relevant today." Someone might say "The best stories are those written in first person point of view," while someone else might say "The best stories are written omnisciently." Considering the other elements of fiction, you can imagine the almost infinite number of possibilities for evaluative criteria.

The Situation Must Be Plausible

Even though we live in the real world rather than the fictional world of the story, the central idea must have "real world" significance. The story must speak to a human condition that is common to all of us, as well as to the specific characters of the story.

This is not to say that the story must be completely realistic or that it must mirror our reality. Instead, it should be true to itself. Whatever norms exist in the fictional world the author establishes must be plausible. The human (or even nonhuman) behavior, attitudes, and values should ring true.

Probability, not possibility, is the key factor. When Alice follows the white rabbit into Wonderland, we know that she has left our world and entered one with very different ways, but we quickly learn to accept them. They are plausible in the context of Lewis Carroll's story.

When Arthur C. Clarke's narrator says, in the beginning of "The Star," that "It is three thousand light years to the Vatican," we are forewarned. We cannot apply our present ideas of the universe and space travel because the story is set in the future. Nonetheless, the story provides human emotions that are authentic and plausible, and the scientific basis of the story is probable enough to make us believe.

Could the story happen the way it happened? Do the words and actions of the characters seem authentic within the limits the author has set? These are the questions of plausibility we must ask when evaluating the story.

The Story Must Stay Fresh

A good story yields new insights through repeated readings. It remains fresh and provocative long after the first reading. Frequently, it gnaws at one's mind. Rather than boring us, repeated readings should offer new ideas, even new and different interpretations. A story that yields everything on the first reading lacks this freshness.

Freshness, plausibility, and the effective relationship of all elements to the central idea are not the only standards for evaluation; other criteria may be equally valid. However, a judgment about quality is meaningless without such clearly stated criteria.

The following student essay evaluates a short story using specific criteria stated in the introductory paragraph and developed in the succeeding paragraphs.

Charlotte Perkins Gilman's "The Yellow Wallpaper" by Sara Graham-Costain

"The Yellow Wallpaper," by Charlotte Perkins Gilman, is the story of a woman losing her sanity. Bedridden by mental illness and forbidden by her husband to work or socialize, she studies the wallpaper daily. Eventually, she begins to see things moving within it and goes crazy, tearing the wallpaper to shreds. It is a haunting story and an excellent work of short fiction, because it meets these criteria: the elements work well together, the situation is plausible, and the story bears repetition. Gilman manipulates these aspects of short fiction so well that she clearly and effectively evokes her theme that the constant rejection of one's ideas and feelings can alienate a person to the point that she becomes imprisoned in her own mind.

The point of view is the dominant element, providing insight into the woman's character. Using the first person, Gilman allows the reader to see the work through the eyes of her main character. The story is written as a private journal and all of the other elements are perceived through the main character's thought. "I would not say it to a living soul, of course," she writes, "but this is dead paper and a great relief to my mind." This clearly relates to the theme, as it shows her isolation from the rest of the world, even her husband, John. Because he forbids her to think about her condition, she focuses her attention on the house.

In this way, the setting becomes an important element of the story. The peeling yellow wallpaper, with its confusing patterns, is a metaphor for her state of mind and she becomes lost in it. As her illness progresses, her perceptions about the wallpaper change. "Behind that outside pattern, the dim shapes get clearer everyday." It is at this point that she begins to see a woman caged within the wallpaper. Here again, the point of view is intertwined with the other elements. Finally, she becomes the woman within her fantasy, telling her husband, "I've got out at last, in spite of you. And I've pulled off most of the paper, so you can't put me back." She imagines that the wallpaper is a prison, in the same sense that she has become a prisoner, exemplifying the author's theme.

All of these story elements are dependent upon one another and Gilman's masterful use of language ties them together. It sets the tone for the story and helps reveal the character's state of mind. After she begins to retreat into her fantasy world, she writes in her a diary description of the wallpaper that is becoming the focus of her attention, "Nobody could climb through that pattern it strangles so; I think that is why it has so many heads. They get through and then the pattern strangles them off and makes their eyes white." This creates a disturbing tone, revealing to the reader that the main character's thinking is unsound, while at the same time creating a vivid picture of her encroaching madness.

The repeated use of the connotative word, "strangle," emphasizes the theme by reflecting her feelings of oppression. It is her husband who oppresses her and this conflict between husband and wife is another element which the author successfully integrates into the story. John is a doctor who trivializes his wife's illness and rejects any ideas that she has regarding her needs. Although she believes that "congenial work, with excitement and change," would do her good, he forbids it. The more that John rejects her, the deeper she withdraws into herself. Since she must say what she thinks and feels in some way, she writes in her journal and gets pulled deeper into the fantasy prison of the yellow wallpaper. All of the elements of the story work together in this way to emphasize the theme.

Even though the world that the woman creates within the yellow wallpaper is insane and unbelievable, the story is painfully plausible. The characters, the conflict, and even the imagery are so clearly illustrated that the reader is drawn into the story. It is clear that she believes what she sees and the descriptions of what she sees are so vivid and precise that the reader can see them as well. The conflict and theme are universal and could affect anyone. The lack of communication, the lack of understanding, the domineering male who takes control of his wife's life, these are things any reader can empathize with. It happens to many married couples. The reader, understanding her feelings of imprisonment and her need to create a fantasy world, is therefore able to accept and even feel her distorted reality. This makes the action of the story even more moving. The insanity which grows out of the conflict is believable because the conflict is believable.

The author's use of language also helps to create a plausible story. The reader becomes so involved in her thought process, gets so involved in the story because of the detail used to describe it. For example, in describing the oppressive smell of the wallpaper, she writes, ". . . the smell is here. It creeps all over the house. I find it hovering in the dining room, skulking in the parlor, hiding in the hall, lying in wait for me on the stairs." Through her use of language and her detailed description of the steady progression of the woman's illness, Gilman makes the madness so believable that it has the ring of universal truth.

Even though the story was written in 1892, it reads and feels as if it could've been written yesterday. Based on experiences from Gilman's own life (after giving birth to a daughter, she suffered a similar mental breakdown), the story gnaws at the reader. It has the immediacy of a real experience, even though it takes us into an unreal world. On first reading, one senses something strange about the house; perhaps it's haunted. The wallpaper is shredded and there's only one piece of furniture, a bed with legs that look like they've been chewed on. A foul odor permeates the bedroom.

It makes the reader think there's something wrong with the house, ". . . else why should it be let so cheaply?" This feeling of suspense, of waiting for something to happen, makes the story exciting and engaging on a dramatic level. But the story becomes more complicated. On further analysis, it is the extent of detail she uses in describing the progression of her illness, where layers of meaning can be deciphered through repeated readings.

Gilman's theme, that the constant rejection of one's ideas and feelings can alienate a person to the point that she becomes imprisoned in her own mind, unfolds beautifully due to her masterful integration of these various aspects. All of the elements work well together, the story is believable, and new insight may be gained through repeated reading. These aspects combined, serve to create a through provoking and haunting story of the highest caliber.

ANALYSIS THROUGH COMPARISON/CONTRAST

Another approach to analysis is through comparison and contrast. To compare is to identify similarities, to discuss the aspects of two or more things as they are like one another. To contrast is to identify the differences, to discuss those aspects that are unlike one another. In addition, the reasons for the similarities and differences should be addressed.

Although two stories may have the same central idea, the reader should be able to identify the causes behind the authors' choices. These choices—the arrangement and emphasis of elements in a story—are related to the central idea, but it is a mistake to assume that the elements of two stories with the same central idea would be the same. Every author is unique, and each chooses to reach the same point or achieve the same purpose through different means.

Much of the pleasure of reading comes from understanding how an author constructs the story so that the central idea is achieved. An even greater pleasure and deeper understanding is possible when we become aware of the ways in which different authors achieve the same purpose, but in different ways. Comparison/contrast focuses our attention on such similarities and differences, making us aware of the variety in literature.

In the following example, a student looks at the similarities and differences between two stories with a common central idea: how people escape from the harsh reality of their lives. The student analyzes each of the elements and discusses how the authors have used them to support their approach to the idea. The student compares the main characters; explains how the conflicts, while similar, are resolved differently; explains how the point of view in each story is the same (omniscient); and notes the differences in language and tone. The final paragraph sums up the different approaches by emphasizing their primary difference, a serious as opposed to a humorous tone.

A Comparative Analysis of Katherine Mansfield's "Miss Brill" and James Thurber's "The Secret Life of Walter Mitty" by Mark Hall

Katherine Mansfield draws a sad picture of escapism in her short story "Miss Brill." It is the story of how a single woman fills her lonely Sunday afternoons by attending band concerts in a nearby park. Miss Brill loses herself completely in her surroundings and feels much at home, as if this park is her only niche in life. This illusion is rudely shattered by a young couple sitting beside her on the bench. A few harsh words, closely followed by a few vulgar ones, burst Miss Brill's bubble.

Another form of escapism is found in James Thurber's "The Secret Life of Walter Mitty." Mr. Mitty is the henpecked husband of a seemingly overbearing, domineering woman. Mitty escapes his insufferable life by imagining himself in a variety of adventurous episodes. Mansfield's purpose seems to be to point out the futility of escapism, while Thurber's seems to be that escapism is not only necessary, but also an entertaining, beneficial pastime. The apathy and sadness Miss Brill exhibits at the end of the story suggests her inability to meet life head-on. Perhaps she will find another form of pleasurable escape, but the reader is left thinking this will probably not happen. Mitty is a very similar character, with the key difference being his elasticity. He has the ability to snap back each time the world destroys his illusions. Mitty, therefore, is a very static character, but Miss Brill's experience produces a dynamic change. Miss Brill's conflict is brought to the reader's attention when the young couple on her bench are rudely inconsiderate of her presence. She imagines herself to be a key character in her mocked-up play of life, but the young man makes her aware of her unimportance. Walter Mitty has his bubble burst every day, however, and finds it an easy thing to deal with life's little obstacles. In both stories the characters' escapes are rudely shattered, but Mitty simply throws himself into a new adventure, whereas Miss Brill has a very important part of her life permanently destroyed.

Mansfield uses the limited omniscient point of view to focus the reader's attention strictly on Miss Brill's perception of those around her. The reader becomes intimately aware of Miss Brill and feels the pain so thoughtlessly inflicted by the coarse young man. Thurber also uses the limited omniscient point of view to familiarize the reader with Walter Mitty. The shift in Mitty's thinking from reality to fantasy is deceptive, but the point of view is consistent throughout. Both authors are very effective in their use of the omniscient narrative voice.

While the physical settings are very different, the psychological settings in both stories are very similar. Both characters are unable to deal with life, and both seek escape as an adjustive reaction. This defense mechanism acts as an emotional insulator for both Miss Brill and Walter Mitty. The actual time and geographical location do not seem to have much bearing on either author's story. The total setting (emotional, psychological, physical) brings each author's theme into clearer focus.

Mansfield's language differs significantly from that used by Thurber. Eloquence and gracefulness are typical of Mansfield's style, while Thurber writes with a very tongue-in-cheek manner. Mansfield uses personification and imagery in her very literary approach, and it is highly effective because it seems to be appropriate to Miss Brill's way of thinking. Thurber's narrative is more direct and seems very appropriate to his main character. He uses a recurring phrase (pocketa-pocketa) in most of Mitty's daydreams; this helps unify the story even though Mitty's mind flashes from one fantasy to the next.

Even for the reader who approaches Mansfield's story for the first time, the tone is quickly evident as one of forced (and false) gaiety. Miss Brill seems to try to trill her way through life, totally rejecting any negative thoughts or happenings. This use of tone is the most effective part of the story. Miss Brill is obviously being set up for a harsh fall, and the reader is prepared for this because of the tone. On the other hand, Thurber's story is ironic and humorous. Mitty continually imagines himself in fantastic situations, only to be yanked from his reveries by the real world.

Because of Thurber's special brand of humor, the reader looking purely for entertainment will find "The Secret Life of Walter Mitty" to be the more enjoyable story. Thurber's story does not require the reader to ponder too deeply the merits of Mitty's lifestyle, simply because his fantasies are so blatant. Mansfield's story would be more appreciated by the reader looking for intricacy. Miss Brill is a sad and lonely character, a good candidate for psychoanalysis. Mitty, however, is a charming blunderer with whom most readers can easily identify.

—*—

The next example compares two different authors' treatment of the "battle of the sexes." Notice how the student focuses on the use of irony in both stories.

A Comparative Analysis of Roald Dahl's "The Way Up to Heaven" and James Thurber's "The Catbird Seat" by Lee Anne Aspra

Roald Dahl's "The Way Up to Heaven," a scathing portrayal of the relationship of a long-married couple, illustrates the universal themes of victory versus oppression and the triumph of good over evil. The backdrop for this central idea is the account of Mrs. Foster's struggle to catch a plane for a greatly anticipated trip to Paris, juxtaposed with her husband's not-so-subtle attempts to thwart her plans. Their departure for the airport has again been delayed by Mr. Foster who conveniently "forgets" something in the house just as they are preparing to drive off. When he returns to retrieve the missing item, Mrs. Foster hurries behind, but stops abruptly at the unmistakable sound of the elevator jamming inside. Instead of continuing into the house, she runs back to the car and races to the airport, leaving her husband trapped behind in the elevator.

James Thurber, too, has designed a very amusing tale around the theme of justice prevailing in "The Catbird Seat." In this case, the story centers around a Mr. Erwin Martin, file room manager of the esteemed firm, F & S, and the newly appointed special advisor to the president, Mrs. Ulgine Barrows. It seems that Mrs. Barrows proposes a complete revision of the existing organization of F & S, which includes ridding the firm of Mr. Martin, whose loyal, flawless tenure exceeds 22 years. What transpires is Mr. Martin's scheme to "rub out" Mrs. Barrows, whose hiring he considers a simple error in judgment by the company president. Capitalizing on his pristine reputation as a non-smoking teetotaler, he pays a visit to the home of Mrs. Barrows, intent on killing her, and winds up falling into the perfect method for doing her in. That is to say, he helps her do herself in. As in "The Way Up to Heaven," justice finds a way.

In both stories, the chief protagonists are of sterling character. Mrs. Foster has served her husband loyally and without question throughout their marriage and Mr. Foster has taken advantage of her deferential nature. He is hostile and manipulative, choosing to exploit her weaknesses, which actually amount only to having a compulsive need to be on time for every occasion. Thurber's characters have a similar dichotomy. But this time it's Mr. Martin who is a bit of a compulsive, needing to fastidiously maintain his filing system without interference. Mrs. Barrow blasts herself onto the scene like a tornado, a vulgar, bombastic assault on Mr. Martin's orderly world and he sees eliminating her as the only possible solution to his torment. The protagonists in these stories find revenge and freedom in the end, and in both cases their adversaries cut their own throats.

The conflicts are similar as well and both internal and external issues are represented. Mrs. Foster and Mr. Martin have rather modest wants. They don't ask for much out of this world, and both of them have a person in their life who systematically seeks to oppress and crush them. In addition, the conflict of righteousness against unrighteousness touches on the central theme. But the lead characters are vindicated. Perhaps not in a way one could recommend as the proper course of action, but they are freed nonetheless.

Both stories are set in New York City in what appears to be the same time period, the 1940's. Mr. and Mrs. Foster share an affluent life, living in a six-story house with four servants and a chauffeur. But it is not money and comfort that Mrs. Foster lacks; it is quite clearly love and respect. The ugliness that her husband displays knows no social bounds. In contrast, Mr. Martin leads a completely unassuming life, living alone and not bothering a soul. His domain is his office and his precious files. Both settings add richness and definition to these stories. Obviously the elevator, as the setting of Mr. Foster's demise, is an essential detail in Dahl's sketch while it is entirely appropriate for Thurber to use New York City as the main prop for his satire on the murder story.

Roald Dahl and James Thurber have used similar aspects of language to tell their stories. The most distinctive is that of irony, the unifying feature of both. Another is the use of description which in the case of "The Catbird Seat" creates a hilarious picture of Mrs. Barrows. One visualizes a large, domineering woman who yells instead of speaks and borrows all sorts of silly baseball chants and epithets such as "Don't scrape the bottom of the pickle barrel" and "Are you sitting in the catbird seat?" The narrator has a marvelous time telling of her "quacking voice" and "braying laugh," and before it's over the reader is convinced of Mr. Martin's need to remove her from the picture. Dahl gives a darkly ironic twist to his story. Mrs. Foster overcomes her oppression by leaving a trapped Mr. Foster in the elevator and dashing off to Paris for weeks. His death will naturally be seen as an accident, although Mr. Foster himself will know that his wife finally defended herself and delivered the last word. It is the same for Mrs. Barrows. She knows that the normally composed Mr. Martin visited her apartment and behaved outrageously, and that this was his way of getting back at her. He barely had to swing a punch, instead relying on her character and behavior to do the work of getting rid of her.

In the final analysis, both Dahl and Thurber write entertaining stories of revenge. The reader is riveted by suspense, sensing an astonishing finale that is richly rewarded. "The Way Up to Heaven" is not nearly as comical as "The Catbird Seat," but it is equally engaging, leaving the reader feeling superbly satisfied with the outcome. One is called to perhaps cheer a little louder for Mrs. Foster than for Mr. Martin, since she is truly being victimized by a mean little man to the point of acute mental torment; however, Mrs. Barrows is sufficiently portrayed as a detriment to Mr. Martin's sanity to warrant the reader's sympathy.

READING FOR COMPARISON/CONTRAST

The turmoil of coming of age is a popular theme, but the experience varies with the background, environment, and circumstances of the character. "A & P" by John Updike chronicles the experience of a middle-class adolescent boy to depict a universal weakness. The main character in Willa Cather's "Paul's Case" has some typical adolescent traits in common with Updike's Sammy, but there are critical differences. After you read both stories, consider these questions:

- What are the differences between the main characters in each story?
- What creates these differences?
- What is the statement in each story that defines the main character's understanding of the events that have taken place?
- What role do Mr. Lengel and the father play in the stories?
- How is the point of view different in each story and what effect does it have?

CHAPTER TEN

Sample Essays

The following examples were written by students enrolled over the years in our classes. They have kindly allowed us to include them to illustrate the various techniques we've outlined in this book. While certainly not perfect, they do represent the wide variety of writing styles and the range of skills and critical abilities students bring to the subject. As such, they stand as reasonable models of what a good student can be expected to achieve.

An Analysis of Kate Chopin's "The Story of an Hour"
by Brandi Grissom

Kate Chopin's "The Story of an Hour" is the story of Louise Mallard, a weak, repressed housewife who is liberated in learning of her husband's death in a train accident. Realizing that her husband's death will allow her to live life for herself and on her own terms, Louise finds joy in knowledge of herself and desires she had never before known. Louise's self-exaltation comes to an abrupt end when, at the end of the story, Mr. Mallard enters the house, killing the free self she had only just discovered. Chopin reveals in her story that only through assertion of the true self can one find life worth living, and that death of the true self can bring death of the physical self.

A repressed housewife who becomes a self-assured "goddess of Victory," Louise Mallard is an extraordinarily dynamic character. At the outset of the story, Louise is viewed as feeble by her friends and family. They fear the news of her husband's death will overcome Louise's weak heart and kill her. Upon learning of husband's death, Louise is consumed in a storm of grief. As the storm passes, Louise is possessed by an epiphany, altering forever her sense of self. She realizes she is no longer sheltered by repression from her true self. Passionately, Louise embraces the procession of years she is now free to live on her own terms. An awareness of self encompasses Louise. No longer must she repress her own will to placate that of her husband. No longer must she feign love for a husband of convenience. Drinking in the elixir of life and its newfound freedom, Louise discovers joy in her heart. For the first time, she is excited about life, and all of the days ahead that would truly be hers alone. In asserting her true self, Louise experiences an inner strength that infuses her with a zeal for life.

The conflict in Chopin's story is an internal one. Louise must choose between repression and self-assertion. Knowing that with the return of her husband, the freedom she has just discovered will be revoked, Louise's heart is broken, and she dies. After feeling the "monstrous joy" that accompanies the realization of the value of life experienced without repression, the sadness of returning to that state is more than Louise can bear. The inevitable death of the true self she has just discovered causes Louise's physical death. Although it is not the joy of her husband's return that kills her, as the doctor suggests, it is joy that kills Louise. She has felt the joy of self-assertion and its freedom, and the loss of that joy leads to her death.

Louise's dramatic inner transformation is revealed to the reader in Chopin's effective use of the omniscient point-of-view. Knowledge of Louise's inner thoughts and emotions is critical to the reader's understanding of Chopin's theme. While Louise's sister makes relentless importunities that Louise not be overcome by sadness, the reader is able to understand that the opposite is occurring inside of Louise. Louise is having the time of her life, unlike anything she had experienced before. In hearing Louise's thoughts and experiencing the rapture of freedom along with her, the reader understands the devastation Louise feels in knowing the brief triumph over repression would vanish as quickly as it had possessed her. Only through knowledge of Louise's thoughts and emotions is the irony of the doctor's attribution of her death to joy that kills apparent.

The setting in the story is symbolic of the new life Louise is experiencing. Louise looks out her bedroom window to see trees "all aquiver with the new spring life": a foreshadowing of the new life she will soon find in freedom from the repression she has always known. The environment outside Louise's window mirrors her own feelings. Just as Louise's "storm of grief" is passing, her cheeks still wet with tears, the air outside is delicious from the breath of rain. Just as Louise notices, for what seems to be the first time, the richness of life outside her window, she will also realize for the first time, the richness of life within herself. Chopin reveals that Louise drinks in the elixir of life from that open window. It is the window to Louise's soul.

Chopin's use of language effectively conveys the intensity of the emotions that overcome Louise. Repetition of the word "free" reveals the exaltation Louise experiences in being released from possession by her husband's will. The diction aptly portrays the significance, emotionally and physically, of Louise's transformation. Tumultuously, Louise's bosom, the seat of passion, rose and fell as the "monstrous joy" possessed her. As the elixir of life "courses" through her once weak heart, Louise's "pulses beat fast." When Louise's fancy runs "riot along those days ahead of her", the reader feels the excitement Louise feels. Through the image of Louise as a winged "goddess of Victory", her inner strength from triumph over repression becomes palpable. That strength is reaffirmed in Chopin's use of words that connote potency. Louise has a "clear and exalted perception" of herself. The years to come belong to Louise "absolutely". The "powerful will" now belongs to Louise, instead of the husband who controlled her. Self-assertion finally becomes the "strongest impulse of her being".

The tone of Chopin's story is ironic. With her husband dead, Louise was truly alive. The death of the inner-self Louise discovered in her brief moments of self-assertion was affected by her husband's life. Within an hour, Louise experienced the exaltation of absolute freedom the total devastation from loss of it. The ultimate irony occurs as the doctor pronounces Louise's death from heart disease, joy that kills. Only the reader knows that Louise's heart was diseased by repression. Joy killed Louise only in the sense that it was taken from her as quickly as she had discovered it.

An Analysis of Nathaniel Hawthorne's "Young Goodman Brown" by Carlos Salinas

Nathaniel Hawthorne's "Young Goodman Brown" is a story of a young newlywed, Goodman Brown, and a particular night he spends in the forest. Goodman Brown travels into the forest one night on an "errand" and is soon joined by an un-named companion who bears such a resemblance to Brown that, "they might have been taken for father and son." As Goodman Brown goes deeper into the forest, he finds that his companion is indeed the devil. On several occasions Goodman Brown stops and tells the devil he will not go on, but the devil persuades and tempts him to keep going. While in the forest, Goodman Brown is convinced that his wife, Faith, is ready to offer her soul over to the dark side. It is not until Goodman Brown looks to save his wife by crying out to Heaven that his nightmare is finally ended, and he wakes up alone in the forest. Hawthorne suggests that faith is tempted everyday, and the devil will stop at nothing to try to turn anyone he can to the dark side.

The central character, Goodman Brown, is a simple young man from a good family of devout Christians. The similarity in appearance between Goodman Brown and the devil is significant because of the subtle way in which the devil tempts young Brown. The familiarity gives Goodman Brown an unknowing kinship with the devil, thus weakening his faith. The devil yet again tries to familiarize himself with Goodman Brown when he tells of his friendship with Brown's father and grandfather. In a line that sounds as though it came from The Rolling Stone's song "Sympathy for the Devil," the devil says, "I helped your grandfather, the constable, when he lashed the Quaker woman so smartly through the streets of Salem. And it was I that brought your father a pitch-pine knot, kindled at my own hearth, to set fire to an Indian village, in King Phillip's war." The devil continues to tempt young Brown, even though his faith appears to be strong. Young Goodman Brown shows he is a prideful man when he defends his family name by saying, "We are people of prayer and good works to boot, and abide no such wickedness." Throughout the story Goodman Brown shows his wanting to be good and how the mind is willing, but the flesh is weak.

The central conflict in "Young Goodman Brown" is an external one. Goodman Brown is torn between his faith as a Christian, and the apparent temptations that the devil has placed before him. Young Goodman Brown appears to be a good, Christian, God fearing young man, but his faith is put to the test when he enters the forest that night. The devil again tempts young Brown when he appears to have a conversation with Goody Cloyse, the woman who taught Brown catechism in his youth. It is at this point when Goodman Brown's faith is beginning to be shaken a little. Again his faith is weakened when he notices the minister and the deacon riding on the path to gather at the witch-meeting. These are people who had major influences on Goodman Brown's life and whom he respected deeply, and to see them as witches and wizards deeply confuses young Brown.

Hawthorne uses a limited omniscient point of view in this story. In this mode the reader can sense the feelings and thoughts of Goodman Brown. It is essential that the reader be given insight into the mind of Goodman Brown, because without it they most likely would be lost. The thoughts and emotions that go through the mind of young Brown show the struggle he goes through and how his faith is slowly chipped away and finally broken. A complete omniscient point of view in this story would give too much information and be unnecessary. You need not know the devil's thoughts to know what he is up to; he wants the soul of young Goodman Brown. The young man's feelings are well documented when he, "approached the congregation, with whom he felt a loathful brotherhood, by the sympathy of all that was wicked in his heart."

The setting of this story is colonial Salem, a village just northeast of Boston. The village has historical value in that it is where the "Salem Witch Trials" took place, thus reflecting the major theme in the story. Hawthorne uses the setting of the story to his advantage, and the historical background behind the town of Salem makes the story more believable. The dark mood of Salem reflects the whole theme of witchcraft and so do the characters, all except one. The pink ribbons of Faith make her stand out as a pure, tender creature in the wicked town. Even her name, Faith, is in direct contrast with the setting of the story.

The use of language in Hawthorne's "Young Goodman Brown" is extraordinary. The story is full of symbolism, as well as irony and foreshadowing. It is ironic that Goodman Brown's wife's name is Faith. The irony is shown when young Brown is about to lose his faith, it is Faith who helps restore it. And it is Faith who gives a hint of things to come when she says, "A lone woman is troubled with such dreams and such thoughts that she's afeard of herself, sometimes. Pray, tarry with me this night, dear husband, of all nights in the year!" She is pleading with her husband to stay home (especially this night) because she has a bad feeling about what is to come. The symbolism throughout the story has to deal with good and evil. When Goodman Brown is in the forest and he looks up to the sky and he starts to feel his resolve coming back to him, but no sooner do clouds roll over the sky covering up the Heavens. The woods also have a symbolic meaning as a place of mystery and solitude. Imagery is also displayed throughout the story, for instance when Hawthorne describes the meeting in the forest: "At one extremity of an open space, hemmed in by the dark wall of the forest, arose a rock, bearing some rude, natural resemblance either to an altar or a pulpit, and surrounded by four blazing pines, their tops aflame, their stems untouched, like candles at an evening meeting. The mass of foliage, that had overgrown the summit of the rock, was all on fire, blazing high into the night, and fitfully illuminating the whole field." The imagery paints a picture of a bonfire-like atmosphere where Goodman Brown is ready to give up his soul.

The tone in this story is a fearful one. Goodman Brown is afraid of what will happen in the forest, he is afraid throughout the whole story. He is afraid he will be seen in the woods, so he hides. He is afraid of what will happen to Faith so he rushes through the forest to find her. But above all, Goodman Brown is afraid of losing his faith, and though he wakes up from his dream, he knows he lost his faith and he is unable to recover from it, and he ends up leading a very sad life because of it. Perhaps it's just a pun, but I find it very significant that had Goodman Brown never left his Faith, he would never have lost his faith.

An Analysis of Character in Guy de Maupassant's "The Necklace" by Rachel Back

"The Necklace" by Guy de Maupassant is the story of a woman of modest upbringing who dreams of being wealthy. In the story, Mathlide's pride and vanity cause her downfall. This collapse forces her to become everything she despises in order to understand the narrowness of her idea that she needs money to be happy. In understanding the symbolism of the necklace and the metamorphosis of the character's personality, Mathlide plays an essential role. Therefore, the central character is the critical element of the story. The roundness of Mathlide's personality and the dynamic change she undergoes make it possible for the reader to understand these two substantial elements.

The symbolism of the necklace would not be as profound without the awareness of Mathlide's personality. She is bewitched by the diamonds' sparkle and beauty, but does not realize that it is a mere imitation. Her ignorance regarding the quality of the jewelry proves two important things. The first is that Mathlide is not the refined, elegant person she believes herself to be. She cannot tell a genuine diamond from a fake, which proves that despite having the necessary apparel to appear regal and wealthy, she does not have the knowledge or the discriminating taste of the truly elite. The second and more important matter that the phony necklace reveals is Mathlide's "fake" persona. She is insincere, unkind, and delights herself by believing that she is better than everyone. She endures the life of a middle-class housewife unhappily and fails to realize how fortunate she is. The omniscient narrator reveals that she feels that she married beneath her. The fact is that she married a caring man who gave up his indulgences so that she could buy a dress for the ball.

Mathlide's need to feel superior contributes to her rude and petulant attitude. An example of this is when she throws the invitation to the grand ball across the room in anger because she does not have anything proper to wear. She is angry because the invitation is a reminder of the fact that she is not an actual member of the upper echelon. Also, when Mathlide has a lovely dress, she again becomes irritated because she does not have any jewelry to wear. She says, ". . . there's nothing so humiliating as looking poor in the company of rich women." She chooses to blame others for her lack of self-esteem and contentment with who she is. She is constantly reminded of her lack of social standing, and reacts with anger to cover her shame.

The glittering diamond necklace is a symbol of Mathlide's dreams. She spends so much time thinking about the things that she wants that she does not take the time to appreciate what is right before her. The author devotes two paragraphs to Mathlide's daydreams of her imaginary home, which is richly decorated, filled with servants, exquisite pieces of furniture, gleaming silver, and gourmet meals. Mathlide is a dreamer, but she's lazy. She will never achieve the status that the necklace represents because she does not feel that she should work for it. The author states, "She was one of those pretty and charming women born, as though fate had blundered, into a family of junior clerks." Mathlide believes that she was meant to be a wealthy woman, but was cheated. When Mathlide sees the diamond necklace for the first time, the reader almost feels that Mathlide is familiar with it. Mathlide immediately wants the necklace because she identifies herself with the beauty and distinction of it. At this point in the story, Mathlide considers herself worthy of the necklace, not knowing that it is a cheap imitation, just as she is.

The sharpness of the central character is significant in appreciating the metamorphosis of Mathlide's personality. After losing the necklace, the change in Mathlide's life is dramatic. She becomes the kind of woman she always believed that she loathed. She does heavy housework, haggles over prices with the grocer, and dresses like a poor woman. After ten years of this toil, the debts are paid; however, Mathlide does not return to being the snobby, fretful woman she once was. She is old and hardened, but the change is more than physical. The author subtly reveals to the reader that Mathlide has a confidence that beauty or money cannot provide. She is proud of her life, of what she has accomplished, and who she is. This strength of character is so great that Mathlide is not intimidated as she approaches a still young and beautiful Madame Forestier. No longer consumed with what people will think of her clothes or status, she has the ability to regard herself equal to others, without needing to be superior. She has discovered what has eluded her for so long, that confidence and respect do not come with money. She has learned about the two types of pride, false and merited. False pride caused her downfall and merited pride brought her up out of the ashes to a place where she could assuredly hold her head high.

These elements of "The Necklace" are revealed through Maupassant's skillful development of the central character. The symbolism of the diamond necklace would be lost without the roundness of Mathlide's disposition, and the evolution of her personality would go unnoticed without the dynamic nature of her change.

A Comparative Analysis of John Updike's "A & P" and Sherwood Anderson's "I'm a Fool"
by Dwight Paul Waites

In the story "A & P" John Updike presents the tribulations of a nineteen-year-old adolescent in conflict with his small town middle class upbringing and the desire to enhance his self-image. In this portrayal, Sammy finds himself involved in unexpected events while at work one day at the local grocery store. He becomes fixated on three teenage girls who enter the store dressed in nothing but bathing suits. Throughout their visit he mentally studies their movements as if he has never encountered anything so enticing and sublime. The trouble begins when the manager of the grocery store, who is also a Sunday school teacher with a strong impression of what is publicly decent, approaches the girls and begins to explain how inappropriate it is for them to walk around in public dressed that way. Sammy decides that the best way to make an impression on these girls is to stand up for them even at the expense of his job. He tells the manager, "I quit," and then continues to tell him off. To Sammy's dismay, the girls missed his display of valiance and he is left with nothing more than his bravado for company.

Sherwood Anderson displays the same aspect of adolescent life through his story about Henry, a young middle-class boy who ends up making the same mistake as Sammy, although Henry does not execute his self-promotion in quite the same manner. At age nineteen Henry works as a stable boy for racehorses. Once he turns twenty, he gets a more socially acceptable job with better pay. On one of his days off, he puts on his new suit and goes to the races. He eventually sits with another young man and two girls in the section with the more well-to-do people. When the opportunity arises Henry flaunts his knowledge of horses by providing information on which horse is the best on which to bet. Needing a way to relate to these obviously wealthier kids, he lies and says that he is the son of a wealthy businessman and that the horse they had bet on was his father's property. After the races he and his new love find themselves alone and discover a mutual infatuation. When the girl and her friends leave, the girl says she will write Henry. Henry realizes his impulsiveness has led him nowhere as the girl, if she writes, will discover his lies. Her letter is sure to be returned to her marked in such a way to show that he is not Mr. Mather's son.

The similarities of these two characters go beyond simply age. Both seem to come from a middle class upbringing. They seem to understand this class placement and allow their "birthright" to guide some of their actions. Although somewhat impulsive, they take risks that might carry them beyond their immediate status. They both demonstrate a yearning to feel special and noticed. The authors seem to highlight the worthlessness that sometimes accompanies adolescents as they discover things which seem to be just beyond their reach.

Both Updike and Anderson illustrate the common conflict that exists in adolescent youth. Sammy and Henry display internal conflicts between their limitations due to social class and the need to be admired. That need to be admired and the feeling that admiration will not come from the truth is more of an issue with Henry. He feels that he has to lie about his upbringing and place in life in order to be accepted. The truth is the girl likes him for himself, not for the lie about his "father being rich and all that." Sammy on the other hand does not lie. His conflict becomes an external one between him and the grocery store manager. He feels that if he comes to the girls' rescue he will win their favor, so he challenges his boss for deriding the girls. The fact is that both boys are capable of rectifying the situations they are in, but they are not yet wise enough to know this. On the positive side, both now have knowledge of the presence of this type of conflict and both can learn from their mistakes.

The first-person point-of-view is used in both these stories to focus the reader's attention strictly on the boys' perceptions of the world. In using this point of view readers are made to feel that these boys embody very real emotions, giving them a sense of realism. Readers may even identify a time in their own lives when youthful indiscretion caused unnecessary conflict. This type of narrative also allows insight into both Sammy's and Henry's perception of their experiences and what led up to them. In "I'm a Fool,: Henry remembers the situation and recounts his past experience, whereas in "A & P" Sammy narrates his experience as it happens. Henry's narration as an account of his past allows readers insight into how people gain wisdom from youthful mistakes.

While the physical settings are very different, the psychological settings in both stories are very similar. The need for social approval found in both boys stems from their middle class upbringing. The differences as they go about trying to achieve approval also relates to the setting. Sammy's rebellion can be seen as a reaction to the basic morality he faces in his hometown, a very ordinary and uneventful small town. Henry's lying can be seen as a reaction to the strict class separation present during that time of history. A horse track is used as the main setting because it is a place where there is some blurring of the division between classes.

The language techniques used by both authors are seemingly different although they achieve the same message. Updike uses dialogue to reveal the conflict within Sammy and also to display his youthfulness. The store manager, a friend of Sammy's parents, says, "you don't want to do this to your Mom and Dad." Readers are forced to see Sammy's youth and innocence. Anderson achieves the same result when Henry uses phrases such as "gee whizz" and "craps amighty." Although the authors use different techniques, both appeal to the audience's views on adolescence.

The tone achieved by these stories is based on humor at the expense of growing up. Both Updike and Anderson handily illustrate the impulsivity of youth who yearn to be accepted. Although "I'm a Fool" clearly shows the wisdom that stems from these youthful mistakes and "A & P" does not, purpose is still achieved by both. "A & P" focuses more on the entertainment aspect of life while Anderson makes more of a statement about life's lessons in "I'm a Fool." Each of these stories is written in a folksy, down-to-earth manner. The type of experience a reader is searching for dictates one's preference for one over the other. Both authors manage to achieve entertainment value while demonstrating social truths.

Zoe Colaluca
Professor Lydic
English 1302
22 April 2015

A Documented Analysis of Language in John Updike's "A & P"

John Updike's "A & P" is about an adolescent grocery store clerk named Sammy, who, while on the job, encounters three young girls in bathing suits. The story consists almost entirely of Sammy giving vivid first person descriptions of the girls' bodies, especially the one he names "Queenie." The girls stand out among the nameless, faceless ordinary shoppers who surround them, drawing attention from everyone, most of it unfavorable. When the girls finally go to check out, the manager reprimands them for their lack of clothing, and in order to impress them by standing up for them, Sammy quits his job in protest, saying to the manager "You didn't have to embarrass them" (Updike 120). Updike uses imagery and symbolism to illustrate his central idea that being rebellious in a conformist world can have unfortunate ramifications.

The main element of language Updike employs is imagery, both literal and figurative. We see literal imagery when Updike goes into great detail describing "Queenie" and the rest of her gang through the eager eyes of the narrator Sammy. For example, when Sammy's attention lands on the leader, his eyes home in on her bathing suit straps "looped loose around the cool tops of her arms" and "the suit had slipped a little on her, so all around the top of the cloth there was a shining rim" (Updike 115). The careful attention shown by his gaze and the positive connotation of "cool" and "shining" show clearly that Sammy does not give her just a passing glance. This use of literal imagery teaches us about the story in that it shows us how the girls present themselves as separate from the crowd. As Corey Evan Thompson states in "Updike's 'A & P,'" "the girls are naked and natural, strongly juxtaposed against the confinement and artificiality of the A & P." Literal imagery also tells us about our narrator because in his overtly sexual description of the girls, Sammy reveals his immaturity. He sees them as "brainless" sources of visual pleasure (Emmett 10). Aside from their pleasing appearance, however, Sammy is also drawn to the girls, especially Queenie, because they are exotic in comparison to the rest of the "sheep" who inhabit the A & P on a daily basis. According to Lawrence Dessner, Sammy "admires Queenie for her 'confident carriage'" and wants the same thing for himself, which is a crucial part of his character (qtd. in Werlock).

The second element of language Updike uses is figurative imagery. One of the most notable similes In the story is when Sammy says that all the customers "are like sheep pushing their carts down the aisle (Updike 116). Sammy's humorous jab at the A & P customers emphasizes that he is living in a conformist society and views himself as separate from it. In fact, as Adam Begley observes in his book *Updike*, "a grocery store in the middle of a typical middle-class town in the United States is a quintessential example of a conformist society" (128). When people walk into an establishment like A & P, they often exhibit many behaviors that Sammy likens to sheep, keeping to themselves while "checking [things] off their list" (Updike 116). They meander among one another while quietly going about their business in the tightly packed space. So when Queenie dares to walk "against the usual traffic" in her barely-there ensemble, the other customers "jerk, or hop, or hiccup" but almost immediately go back to their individual tasks in true sheep fashion (Updike 116). Sammy uses the larger metaphor of mindless behavior to show that he finds these behaviors both annoying and laughable, which is why he both criticizes the ordinary people and is drawn to the girls.

Important symbolism appears later in the story, for it is not until almost the end that Sammy feels something for the girls other than lust. It starts when the girls go over to the butcher and he "sizes up their joints as they are leaving;" in this moment Sammy realizes that he actually "feel[s] sorry for them" (Updike 117). The butcher's look symbolizes Sammy's own, and he is beginning to see the girls as real people with feelings and not just objects for his viewing pleasure. However, it is not until the store manager Lengel begins to lecture them on their choice in clothing that Sammy's internal change takes place. After Lengel mortifies the girls by scolding them in front of everyone, Sammy decides to quit. While some of his initial immaturity still remains because his actions are largely motivated by his wanting to be the girls' "unsuspected hero," his response comes from a good place (Updike 118). He knows in his heart that Lengel may have gone too far and that he "didn't have to embarrass them," and decides to stand up for them, and for himself, by quitting (Updike 120). When Sammy finally sheds his A & P uniform, he is also symbolically shedding the expectations of a conformist society. Underneath his uniform is revealed "a white shirt that [his] mother ironed the night before," which according to David Wheeler symbolizes "purity, freedom, and a sense of identity" (12). As Sammy exits the store the reality of "how hard the world was going to be to me hereafter" finally crashes down on him, but whatever may happen for him, he is finally separated from his absolute conformity. Sammy's action is only an initial step to a more complete maturity, however. As Austin Community College English professor David Lydic notes,

> Sammy has revealed the shirt ironed by his mom and clearly has no place to go except home, at least eventually, so he's made an important independent decision, an internal change, but hasn't changed his life. He is still attached to his family and dependent on them. He will mature more.

The A & P and its customers symbolize conformity, Sammy quitting his job is a moment of realization symbolizing a move toward maturity as he understands that there are consequences for his actions, and remaining in his ironed white shirt symbolizes his lingering connection to the ordinary, conformist world. As with us all, Sammy's journey to more complete maturity will take time.

The three elements of language employed in "A & P"—literal imagery, figurative imagery, and symbolism—work to support the central idea because they help us understand a phase in Sammy's journey to freedom. First, the literal imagery is used to document how Sammy initially feels about his surroundings—ordinary, unexciting, predictable—and about the girls—lust and a desire to "emulate Queenie's confidence" (Wheeler 13). Next, the figurative imagery emphasizes Sammy's feeling of separation and superiority towards the A & P customers. It is here that we begin to see Sammy's inclination toward non-conformity. Finally, the symbolism the end of the story helps solidify Sammy's internal change and growth in maturity, and his transition into a harsh reality of the real world, realizing that non-conformist choices can be painful. Sammy essentially personifies this central idea, and through the use of the several elements of language, we gain a sense of how the story's meaning is played out.

WORKS CITED

Begley, Adam. *Updike*, Harper, 2014.   *ebook*
    Amazon.com. updike-Adam-Begley.

Emmett, Paul J. "A Slip that Shows Updike's   *Print Article in Professional Journal*
    'A & P.'" *Journal of Contemporary
    Literature*, vol. 15, no. 2, March 1985,
    pp, 9–10.

Lydic, David. Personal Interview. 10 April 2015.   *Personal Interview*

Thompson, Corey Evans. "Updike's 'A & P.'"   *Online Article*
    The Explicator, vol. 59, 2001, no. 4.
    dx.doi.org/10.1080/00144940109597.

Updike, John. "A & P." *Analyzing Short*   *Primary Source*
    Stories, edited by Joe Lostracco and
    George Wilkerson, 8th ed., Kendall Hunt
    Publishers, 2014, pp. 114–120.

Werlock, Abby H.P. "A & P." *Facts on File*   *Database*
    Companion to the American Short Story,
    vol. 1, 2009, *Bloom's Literature,* Facts
    on File, Inc., fofweb.com/activelink2.asp?.

Wheeler, David. *"A & P"—John Updike:*   *Print Book*
    *Sammy's Rebellion and the Importance
    of Narrator.* Dog's Tail Books, 2011.

CHAPTER ELEVEN

Analyzing Other Forms of Literature

ANALYZING A NOVEL

Compared to the short story, a novel might be considered a *long* story, but there's more to it than that. The novelist doesn't simply take a short story and make it longer,* but there is some debate about the length at which a short story *becomes* a novel. More typically, it's the scope of a novel in every aspect (central idea, plot, conflict, character, setting, point of view, and language) that defines it as something more than a short story; it's broader and deeper. Rather than a single plot, there may be a number of interwoven plots; rather than a single conflict, there may be a number of conflicts; rather than a small number of characters, there may be many, and so forth with the other elements. Consequently, a short story usually can be read in one sitting, whereas the reader of a novel is likely to leave it and return to continue reading at a later time.

In more modern terms, we can think of it this way: we might be able to sum up a short story in a Tweet, but we'd need an e-mail to sum up a novel. And of course, we might pick up a novel and become so engrossed in it that we can't stop reading until we've reached the end. We might find exceptions to all of these rules, but for the most part, the elements discussed in our study of the short story appear in the novel in an expanded form.

Central Idea

While a short story does not have just one possible central idea, its brevity means it will have fewer possibilities than a novel. Short stories strive for a more focused effect, while the wider scope of novels means they are able to convey a greater number of perhaps equally important ideas. Some say a short story has a central idea, a novel has themes.

---

*There are some rare instances where that has been done, for example, *Ender's Game* by Orson Scott Card.

Plot

The plot of a novel is usually more complex than that of a short story. As a series of events, the plot in a novel generally covers a longer period of time than that covered in a short story, and there also may be subplots. The writer can track a series of events for each character in the novel and those events may have nothing in common or they may overlap. So the writer's task becomes one of telling the story in a way that won't confuse the reader.

Frederick Forsyth's *The Day of the Jackal* is a good example of the use of two plots. There is the professional killer known as the Jackal and the Police Inspector Lebel. The focus shifts back and forth from one character to another, describing what each is doing, as the Jackal plans an assassination and Inspector Lebel does his best to trap and catch him. It's not until the end of the novel that the two characters are involved in a single event, making for an exciting story as their two lives converge.

On the other hand, in Mark Twain's *The Adventures of Huckleberry Finn*, rather than two plots converging at the end, we see a series of events (subplots) and the impact they have on Huck as he grows into manhood. During that process, one of the subplots Twain introduces involves two families (the Grangerfords and the Shepherdsons). The Grangerfords take in Huck for a time, during which the feud between the families escalates into violence. Huck is a witness to it all but leaves because he cannot abide the situation, especially as it involves allegedly God-fearing people. In that series of events, Huck is a secondary character.

Conflict

Although there tends to be a single, major conflict, there may be a number of lesser conflicts as a novel makes its way to the conclusion. Some conflicts may be resolved, some not. The main character may encounter obstacles, each posing its own problems and forcing the character to choose one path or another. In the classic tales, the main character survives, and learns from, these clashes. Huck Finn does so when he struggles with the fact that he knowingly broke the law by helping Jim, the runaway slave.

> Jim said it made him all over trembly and feverish to be so close to freedom. Well, I can tell you it made me all over trembly and feverish, too, to hear him, because I begun to get it through my head that he WAS most free—and who was to blame for it? Why, ME. I couldn't get that out of my conscience, no how nor no way. It got to troubling me so I couldn't rest; I couldn't stay still in one place. It hadn't ever come home to me before, what this thing was that I was doing. But now it did; and it stayed with me, and scorched me

more and more. I tried to make out to myself that I warn't to blame, because I didn't run Jim off from his rightful owner; but it warn't no use, conscience up and says, every time, "But you knowed he was running for his freedom, and you could a paddled ashore and told somebody." That was so—I couldn't get around that noway.

The result of that conflict between breaking the law and obeying the law by turning in his friend resolves his conflict and produces a profound change in Huck, a change in his character that reflects one of the major themes of Twain's novel.

Characters

As with the other elements, a novel is likely to have more characters, each with its own story, each woven into a single narrative tapestry. The short story is likely to have a single, round, character usually dynamic but sometimes static (usually the *main* character), whereas the novel may have many characters who are, at the very least, well-developed (i.e., round), even though some probably will be static.

Setting

More than likely, a novel will have many settings, and the story is likely to take place over a longer period of time than that covered in a short story. The novelist can jump back and forth, not only from one location to another, but also from one moment in time to another. Kurt Vonnegut's classic novel *Slaughterhouse Five* is based on the notion that Billy Pilgrim, the main character, has "come unstuck in time." Rather than following his life in the traditional chronological order, the story jumps back and forth between the events of his life, and between his past and his future.

Point of View

As with a short story, a novel usually adopts a single point of view. The story is told by the main character, a minor character, or an omniscient narrator; however, novelists have the added luxury of shifting the point of view (so long as it does not confuse the reader.) In William Faulkner's *As I Lay Dying*, the point of view shifts among 15 different characters. The children and other relatives "take turns" describing the events surrounding the death of Addie Bundren, the mother of a poor family in Mississippi. Each has a different perspective on her death. (The most poignant is that of her son Vardaman, who is about 7 years old, who says "My mother is a fish.") Even Addie herself speaks.

Language

Language devices remain the same as those employed in short stories, though there are more instances of them. Dialogue can play a more important role in a novel, and symbolism is often expanded to take on greater importance. In *Animal Farm*, George Orwell uses symbolism extensively to create an allegory, a story wherein the characters and setting (animals on a farm) represent elements of the real world (humans in society). Similarly, metaphors, similes, syntax, and diction often take on greater importance and are more prominent than in a short story.

ANALYZING A PLAY

Few plays are written simply to be read; therefore, the author of a play faces a unique challenge. Whereas there is little separation between the author of a short story or a novel and the reader, the playwright must depend on others to deliver the play to an audience. A director, actors, lighting designer, costumer, hair and make-up artists, musicians, special effects designer, and others may be needed to produce the play. As a result, the play we see performed on stage may be quite different from the author's original vision. Shakespeare would be very surprised to see what some actors and directors have done with—or should we say *to*—his work.

Plot

The complexity of a play's plot falls somewhere between that of a short story and a novel. There may be subplots, but because the play is performed, viewers don't have the luxury of being able to go back and re-read an earlier scene as they can when reading a story. Thus, the plot is usually uncomplicated enough, and involves few enough characters, that a viewer can keep track of what's going on.

Conflict

As with a story or novel, there is bound to be a conflict that drives the play forward. And, as with the novel, there may be minor conflicts, both internal and external. But how do we know about the conflict taking place within an individual character? We find out through a couple of language devices unique to plays, the *soliloquy* and the *aside*. In a soliloquy, a character thinks *aloud*, revealing through speech what he or she is thinking or feeling. The most famous of these is Hamlet's "to be or not to be" speech:

> To be, or not to be: that is the question:
> Whether 'tis nobler in the mind to suffer

The slings and arrows of outrageous fortune,
Or to take arms against a sea of troubles,
And by opposing end them?

Hamlet is considering suicide: "to be" (to live) or not to be (to die). In this soliloquy, his conflicting thoughts and feelings are revealed to us.

In the second scene of *Hamlet*, King Claudius, Hamlet's Uncle, greets him, saying "my cousin Hamlet, and my son" and Hamlet turns to the audience and delivers an aside, saying to us "A little more than kin, and less than kind," to let us know that he does not share the feelings Claudius has expressed, he does not regard himself as a "son" to Claudius.

Conflicts in a play are often more obvious than in a short story or novel. Primarily using dialogue and their own gestures and movements, actors must make the conflicts—even their internal ones—clear to everyone in the performance venue, even those in the rear of the balcony.

Characters

Characterization may be the most critical aspect of a play. A good actor can make a good play better, but a bad actor can ruin the author's work. Some playwrights include a great deal of direction in their script, trying to explain how the character looks, speaks, and acts in an attempt to head off an actor's misinterpretation. For example, George Bernard Shaw included extensive descriptions of the characters in his play *Major Barbara*. Lady Brittomart is described as

> . . . a woman of fifty or thereabouts, well dressed and yet careless of her dress, well bred and quite reckless of her breeding, well mannered and yet appallingly outspoken and indifferent to the opinion of her interlocutory, amiable and yet peremptory, arbitrary, and high-tempered to the last bearable degree, and withal a very typical managing matron of the upper class, treated as a naughty child until she grew into a scolding mother, and finally settling down with plenty of practical ability and worldly experience, limited in the oddest way with domestic and class limitations, conceiving the universe exactly as if it were a large house in Wilton Crescent, though handling her corner of it very effectively on that assumption, and being quite enlightened and liberal as to the books in the library, the pictures on the walls, the music in the portfolios, and the articles in the papers.

The audience doesn't see this description, but the director and actors do and they must decide to what extent they are obliged to adhere to it and what methods they can use to convey the more abstract direction. It might be easy to create character who looks "fifty or thereabouts," but it is much more difficult to show a woman "conceiving the universe exactly as if it were a large house in Wilton Crescent." If the playwright is alive, it's possible that he or she can exert a great deal of influence on the performance. If the playwright's heirs hold the rights to the play, they might also have some influence. But if the playwright is dead and the rights have expired, it's "open season." So it is that much of Shakespeare has been adapted, revised, and sometimes modified beyond recognition.

Setting

A play is nearly always presented in a theater; therefore, the setting is restricted by the limitations of that theater. This holds true especially if the play demands a realistic setting. Hence, instead of trying to reproduce the Grand Canyon or the surface of the moon, the setting may be represented symbolically or suggested through the use of a few props. Or there may be no set at all and the producer, director, and actors may rely on the audience's imagination. The photo below shows a setting for a scene in Thornton Wilder's *Our Town*. Notice that the actors work with basic props like tables and chairs, but use ladders to suggest a second floor to the house. Is it realistic? No, but it suggests enough to allow the audience to imagine it.

Source: Photo courtesy of Timothy Mather and the Menomonie Theater Guild.

Compare the *Our Town* set to the realistic set shown below, designed for John Steinbeck's *Of Mice and Men*. George and Lenny, the main characters in the play, are spending the night in a barn. The barn walls and the hay leave nothing to the imagination. The only distinction between this and a real barn is the "fourth wall"—the front of the stage which allows the audience to see the action. It is as if one wall in a room has been removed and we can see what goes on without the actors knowing. Generally, the actors pretend there is a real wall there, but occasionally they may speak directly to the audience through this imaginary wall. This is referred to as "breaking the fourth wall."

Change of setting may also present difficulties for a play. It is simple in a novel to simply state, "many days later they were standing in the seaside fortress on Cyprus," but a play must show the fortress. In *Shakespeare's Othello*, Act I ends in Venice and Act I begins in Cyprus. The action and dialogue must indicate that time has passed and the stage crew must move around and replace pieces of the set to make the transition.

Source: Photofest

Point of View

Who tells the story in a play? The point of view of a play is uniquely different from that of a short story or novel. In one sense, we might say that the actors tell the story. After all, they are the voices of the playwright. But in most cases, the play is the recreation of the real or imagined experience of the author. Rather than being told what this or that character did or said (as might happen with a short story or novel), we "see" what they do and "hear" what they say through the near-exclusive use of the third person dramatic point of view.

Sometimes, though, the playwright will use a narrator. He or she may be a character in the play or, hypothetically, outside of it. In *The Glass Menagerie* by Tennessee Williams, Tom Wingfield, the younger brother of Laura, the play's main character, talks directly to the audience. An aspiring poet, Tom works at a shoe warehouse to support the family. He is frustrated by the numbing routine of his job and escapes from it through movies, literature, and alcohol. As the play opens, he speaks to the audience, through the first person point of view, setting the scene and establishing the tone.

> The play is memory. Being a memory play, it is dimly lit, it is sentimental, it is not realistic . . .
> I am the narrator of the play, and also a character in it.
> The other characters are my mother, Amanda, my sister, Laura, and a gentleman caller, who appears in the final scenes.
> He is the most realistic character, being an emissary from a world of reality that we were somehow set apart from.
> But since I have a poet's weakness for symbols, I am using this character also as a symbol; he is the long delayed but always expected something that we live for.

Thornton Wilder's *Our Town* opens similarly, but rather than the narrator being a character who moves in and out of the play, he is the Stage Manager. He speaks directly to the audience through first person, as Tom Wingfield does, but acts more as the audience's guide for the evening, rather than an interpreter of the meaning.

Wilder's directions specify that there should not be a curtain or scenery. When the audience arrives they see a half-lit, empty stage. When the play is scheduled to begin, the lights go down briefly as the Stage Manager steps out, then almost immediately, the lights come up and the Stage Manager speaks:

> This play is called "Our Town." The day is May 7, 1901. The time is just before dawn.

Source: Photofest

(A rooster crows.)

The sky is beginning to show some streaks of light over in the East there, behind our mount'in.

(He pauses)

Well, I'd better show you how our town lies.

Up here is Main Street.

Way back there is the railway station.

Polish Town's across the tracks.

Over there is the Congregational Church; across the street's the Presbyterian. Methodist and Unitarian are over there. Baptist is down in the holla' by the river. Catholic Church is over beyond the tracks.

Here's the Town Hall and Post Office combined; jail's in the basement.

Here's the grocery store and here's Mr. Morgan's drugstore. Most everybody in town manages to look into those two stores once a day.

Public School's over yonder. High School's still farther over. Quarter of nine mornings, noontimes, and three o'clock afternoons, the hull town can hear the yelling and screaming from those schoolyards.

This is our doctor's house, Doc Gibbs'. This is the back door.

This is Mrs. Gibbs' garden. Corn . . . peas . . . beans . . . hollyhocks . . . heliotrope . . . and a lot of burdock.

And this is Mrs. Webb's garden. Just like Mrs. Gibbs'. Only it's got a lot of sunflowers, too.

Nice town, y'know what I mean?

Language

The primary language device in any play is the dialogue, the words spoken by the actors to one another. It is generally between and within those words that the other language devices occur. And it is here that a major difference occurs between literature that is delivered directly from the writer to the reader and literature that relies on support from others.

With literature that is delivered directly from the writer, devices like symbols are stated directly, but in a play, making the audience aware of them requires more. In *The Glass Menagerie*, when Tom says to the audience "I am using this character also as a symbol; he is the long delayed but always expected something that we live for," the author is letting the audience know that the gentleman caller is a symbol. And later, Tom makes a joke by playing with the term "long distance," so that it becomes a metaphor for his father's behavior.

> There is a fifth character in the play who doesn't appear except in the larger-than-life-size photograph over the mantel.
>
> This is our father who left us a long time ago.
>
> He was a telephone man who fell in love with long distances; he gave up his job with the telephone company and skipped the light fantastic out of town.

Other language devices are often presented in the same way. At one point in *Our Town*, the Stage Manager says "The day's running down like a tired clock."

Metaphors, similes, symbols, diction, and syntax are all reflected in what the characters say and how they say it, rather than in a prose description that we read as the story unfolds.

ANALYZING A SCREENPLAY

While both plays and films are intended to be seen in order to offer the fullest experience, some plays are written to be read, whereas screenplays aren't generally published for a reading audience. But just like the author of a play, the screenwriter has to depend on others to deliver his or her work to an audience. A movie is a technical production; in addition to the director, actors, lighting designer, costumer, hair and make-up artist, musicians, special effects designer, and others may be needed to produce the play. As a result, the play we see performed on stage may be quite different from the author's original vision. In addition, some screenplays are adaptations of stage plays or novels. In those instances, the author of the original work has one more person to rely on to convert his or her work from his or her novel or short story to the script for a film. And the screenwriter must also comprehend the original writer's vision when creating the film script.

This distinction between the final script and the work's earlier iterations is important because when we analyze a screenplay, as distinct from the final product (the film), our analysis is limited to the script. But once the film is produced, the distinctions between the writing and the other aspects that go into the film (acting, direction, cinematography, etc.) become blurred. If the film fails, it may not be due to the script because a terrible film may be based on an excellent story and even have begun with a fine screenplay.

Plot

The plot of a screenplay, like that of the stage play, is likely to be more complex, but the complexity goes beyond a play's. The screenplay can move us around in time and space. It can cover decades because of the advantages of things like costumes, hair and make-up, and special effects. Whereas the play is performed in "real time" with only short pauses for costume and set changes, the filmmaker can start and stop the camera and the editor can make transitions seamless; the camera can stop shooting and the entire cast and crew can move from one place to another and the film editor can cut the scenes together smoothly.

There may be subplots, too, and with today's technology, a recorded film may work more like a piece of literature, in the sense that the viewer can go back and replay an earlier scene just as a reader can go back in the book and reread it.

Conflict

Regardless of the form, a conflict is nearly always necessary. It's what keeps us reading or watching. And there are usually internal and external conflicts in a screenplay. However, like the stage play (and unlike the novel), we learn about the internal conflict through language devices such as the *soliloquy* and the *aside*. Furthermore, in a screenplay, the author also can have a character express an internal conflict through a *voice-over*. [More on these in the "Point of View" section.]

Characters

The main distinction between the presentation of the characters in a stage play and a screenplay is that with a play the playwright is dependent upon the actors in the roles, the actors' interpretations, and the director's concept of the play. On a stage, once an actor says the line, it can't be taken back. She may say it differently for the next performance, but the audience seeing the play has seen the only "version" they are likely to see. But when a film is shot, the actors can perform a scene again and again, often experimenting in separate "takes" with different ways to say a line or different actions to incorporate into their delivery. Later, in the "cutting room," the director can choose the "take" he or she prefers and discard the rest.

Setting

When it comes to screenplays, the writer has as much latitude as the novelist. The only limit is that which is imposed by the budget. The choice of setting(s) is only limited to where a camera can go, and today, with the "magic" of special effects, the camera can go anywhere.

One of the most famous settings for a film is established at the very beginning of *Star Wars Episode IV* (originally released as simply **Star Wars**):

A long time ago in a galaxy far, far away

In addition to telling us the general setting for the film, this opening also lets us know that we should not apply the logic and restrictions of our world to that of the characters and events we are about to see. The scrolling text goes on to narrow down the situation to a civil war and explain that spies for the Rebel Alliance have stolen plans to the Galactic Empire's Death Star, an armored space station capable of annihilating an entire planet. George Lucas, who wrote the screenplay (and directed the film) had no problem with establishing this setting because he was writing a film and knew that it could be set anywhere and at any time.

Point of View

One way to regard the point of view in a screenplay is to think of it as the camera's location, primarily a third person dramatic perspective. The writer can include directions to the cinematographer to indicate his or her preference of camera angle and position, thus controlling what the audience sees and hears, unlike a stage play, where the position of the audience does not change. But once again, such decisions may not rest with the author of the screenplay. Once the script is sold, it's very likely that they will be made by the director and/or the cinematographer.

The *soliloquy* is not common in a film (especially in these days of "action movies") and the aside is very rare, as it would require the actor to speak directly to the camera, a technique most commonly used in comedy. But there are times when a character will talk to himself and we hear him through a "voice-over," the voice of a character in the film or an omniscient third-person narrator. In *Ferris Bueller's Day Off*, Ferris sometimes comments (we can recognize his voice) and frequently talks directly to us a first person point of view. For example, Ferris has feigned illness to avoid going to school. After his parents have left the house, thinking he is ill, he says,

> They bought it. Incredible! One of the worst performances of my career and they never doubted it for a second. How could I possibly be expected to handle school on a day like this? This is my ninth sick day this semester. It's getting pretty tough coming up with new illnesses. If I go for ten, I'm probably gonna have to barf up a lung, so I'd better make this one count. The key to faking out the parents is the clammy hands. It's a good non-specific symptom. I'm a big believer in it. A lot of people will tell you that a good phony fever is a dead lock, but, uh, you get a nervous mother, you could wind up in a doctor's office. That's worse than school. You fake a stomach cramp, and when you're bent over, moaning and wailing, you lick your palms. It's a little childish and stupid, but then, so is high school.

The story is about Ferris Bueller, so it's natural that he tells us the story; but it's a film, so for the most part, he and the other characters *show*, *not tell* us.

Language

Like a play, dialogue is the primary device and the other devices issue from there. The similes, metaphors, symbols, syntax, and diction are part of the language spoken by the characters and in soliloquies, asides, and voice-overs. Here are some examples of these language devices from screenplays.

METAPHOR	*Fasten your seatbelts. It's going to be a bumpy night.*	Margo Channing (Bette Davis) in *All About Eve*
SIMILE	*Mama always said life was like a box of chocolates. You never know what you're gonna get.*	Forest Gump (Tom Hanks) in *Forest Gump*
SYNTAX	*One morning I shot an elephant in my pajamas. How he got in my pajamas, I don't know.*	Capt. Geoffrey T. Spaulding (Groucho Marx) in *Animal Crackers*

VERBAL IRONY	*Gentlemen, you can't fight in here! This is the War Room!*	President Merkin Muffley (Peter Sellers) in *Dr. Strangelove*
DICTION	*Surely you can't be serious. I am serious . . . and don't call me Shirley.*	Ted Striker and Dr. Rumack (Robert Hayes and Leslie Nielson) in *Airplane*
METAPHOR	*Life is a banquet, and most poor suckers are starving to death!*	Mame Dennis (Rosalind Russell) in *Auntie Mame*
METAPHOR	*I'm the king of the world!*	Jack Dawson (Leonardo DiCaprio) in *Titanic*

ANALYZING A POEM

The primary (sometimes only) element of a poem is the language. Narrative poems tell a story, so they will have narrative elements, like a plot, a setting, a conflict, and characters, but those elements are always secondary to the language devices, like similes, metaphors, allusions, repetition, diction, symbolism, and dialogue. And of course, a poem can have rhyme and meter.

In the past (especially before the printing press), nearly all literature was poetry, partly because rhyme and meter made it easier to remember and recite and partly because that form is more pleasant to listen to. Listening to a poem or a story (which most often was also a poem) being recited was one of the few entertainments in those days. But eventually, poets recognized that their poems didn't need to have rhyme or meter. They were free to focus on the other devices. Once writing became common and the printing press allowed writing to be produced in greater quantity, writers could become more complex because they could write it down and study it. The greater sophistication led to poets *in addition to singers.*

Before going further, take a look at this classic poem by Robert Frost. (It's probably familiar since it is frequently used in English courses.)

> The Road Not Taken
> Two roads diverged in a yellow wood,
> And sorry I could not travel both
> And be one traveler, long I stood
> And looked down one as far as I could

To where it bent in the undergrowth;
Then took the other, as just as fair,
And having perhaps the better claim,
Because it was grassy and wanted wear;
Though as for that the passing there
Had worn them really about the same,
And both that morning equally lay
In leaves no step had trodden black.
Oh, I kept the first for another day!
Yet knowing how way leads on to way,
I doubted if I should ever come back.
I shall be telling this with a sigh
Somewhere ages and ages hence:
Two roads diverged in a wood, and I
I took the one less traveled by,
And that has made all the difference.

Is there a plot? Yes, sort of; the events are minimal. A traveler comes to a crossroads. He has to choose between two paths. He chooses one that doesn't look as well-traveled and reflecting on that choice he realizes it made a big difference.

Is there a conflict? Perhaps. We get the sense that the traveler experienced an internal conflict—which road should I take? A setting? Obviously, it's a "yellow wood." Characters? Just the speaker/narrator, the traveler. So there's the point of view—the "I" indicates that the traveler is telling us what happened. And there's rhyme and meter, though not of the sort a rapper might use. It's more subtle and nonintrusive.

Hence, what predominates in this poem is the language. To a literal reader, it seems clumsy. That reader might ask why Frost didn't simply relate the events, i.e., write a little story, like this:

I was out walking and came to a place where the road split in two. Of course, I could only go one way, so I looked down each road and figured they were about the same, except that one was a little grassier and didn't seem to have been used as much. So I took that one. I told myself I could always come back and take the other road, but I knew I never would and that made a really big difference.

Obviously, it's not the same. The difference is that the poem emphasizes certain things that are under the surface and that additional meaning is clearer if we understand the devices he used.

Symbolism

If we read the poem solely as paraphrased in the paragraph version above, there is no readily apparent symbolism. But because it is a poem, we become more open to the symbol projected by the words. Frost creates a symbol when he introduces the "two roads (that) diverged in a yellow wood. The use of a "crossroad" to represent choices is fairly common and Frost is counting on that familiarity to establish the symbolic nature of his poem.

Metaphors (and Similes)

Much of what we say is some kind of metaphor. For the most part, we use "figures of speech," metaphors we already know and understand. If we'd like to meet someone, we might ask a friend to "hook us up." And the more sensitive the subject, the more we "beat around the bush." For example, rather than saying a couple got divorced, we might say they simply "drifted apart" (comparing them to a pair of boats). Or rather than saying we were rejected when asking someone for a date, we might say we "struck out" or "got shot down," which metaphorically says what happened.

Metaphors and symbols are the parts of our language that keeps us in touch with our emotions. Understanding what the metaphors and symbols mean—that's the key to understanding what's *really* going on.

What an author chooses for the metaphorical comparison is a clue to the author's attitude toward the subject. Frost has chosen to compare life to a journey down a road where at one point we have to choose. "Two roads diverged in a wood," the speaker says, and he "took the one less traveled." And he extends that metaphor to explain that though we might believe we can come back "another day" if we don't like where that road took us, that's just not likely to happen.

Diction

Choosing the right word is critical for a poet. Frost says, "Two roads diverged." He could have said one road divided, one road parted ways, or any number of terms to describe the situation, but he chose "diverged," more than likely because that word specifically refers to going in different directions and that meaning is most pertinent to the meaning of the poem. Diction, choosing just the right word, becomes more important in poetry than in any other form of literature. Remember, keeping a good dictionary handy in order to look up the exact meaning of words is valuable.

Syntax

The way words are put together has tremendous impact on how we respond to them. Frost does not say "I stood for a long time." He says "long I stood." And that rearrangement of those three words shifts the emphasis to "long." Of the three things—what he did (stood), who stood there ("I"), and how long he stood there—the length of time is the most important and the syntax, "long I stood," emphasizes that.

The Periodic Sentence

Frost has saved the "punch line" for the end of the poem. He uses a periodic sentence ("And that has made all the difference.") to bring home the theme . . . "the difference" (which was the result of the choice). The whole matter of coming to a divergence in the road (a decision in life) leads to the sequence of life events that causes him to look back and realize that things might have been different if he had chosen the other road (the other life choice.) The reader does not know whether the difference was positive or negative, just that his choice had made a difference.

Irony

Many readers get the sense that the speaker in this poem is not entirely happy with the choice he made. He is, after all, telling us about it "with a sigh." He had to take one of the roads ("I could not travel both / And be one traveler"), so he took the one which was "just as fair . . . Because it was grassy and wanted wear." Now, later in his life, as he relates the experience, he realizes, "ages and ages hence" that he may regret the choice. However, a sigh can be a sound of contentment or of resignation. We don't really know what kind of sigh the narrator is taking because *he* doesn't yet know: "I shall be telling this with a sigh/Ages and ages hence." He is projecting into the future and doesn't know yet himself.

SUGGESTED READINGS

Novels

- *The Adventures of Huckleberry Finn, by Mark Twain*
- *As I Lay Dying by William Faulkner*
- *Slaughterhouse Five by Kurt Vonnegut*
- *Animal Farm by George Orwell*

Plays

- *Our Town by Thornton Wilder*
- *The Glass Menagerie by Tennessee Williams*
- *Hamlet by William Shakespeare*
- *Major Barbara by George Bernard Shaw*
- *Of Mice and Men by John Steinbeck*

Screenplays

- *Ferris Bueller's Day Off by John Hughes*
- *All About Eve by Joseph L. Mankiewicz*
- *Forest Gump Screenplay by Eric Roth, based on a novel by Winston Groom*
- *Animal Crackers by Morrie Ryskind (based on the musical play by George S. Kaufman), with additional writing credits for Harry Ruby and Bert Kalmar*
- *Dr. Strangelove (or How I stopped Worrying and Learned to Love the Bomb) by Terry Southern and Stanley Kubrick, with Peter George*
- *Airplane by Jim Abrahams, David Zucker, and Jerry Brucker (uncredited: Arthur Hailey, Hal Bartlett, and John C. Champion)*
- *Auntie Mame by Betty Comden and Adolph Green*
- *Titanic by James Cameron*

Poems

- "Where the Sidewalk Ends" by Shel Silverstein
- "If You Forget Me" by Pablo Neruda
- "Stopping by Woods on a Snowy Evening" by Robert Frost
- "Still I Rise" by Maya Angelou
- "Do Not Go Gentle Into That Good Night" by Dylan Thomas
- "Dream Deferred" by Langston Hughes
- "Anyone Lived in a Pretty How Town," by e.e. Cummings
- "I wandered lonely as a Cloud" by William Wordsworth
- "Shall I Compare Thee to a Summer's Day" by Williams Shakespeare
- "Howl" by Allen Ginsberg

STORIES
for
Further Study and Analysis

A & P
John Updike

In walks these three girls in nothing but bathing suits. I'm in the third checkout slot, with my back to the door, so I don't see them until they're over by the bread. The one that caught my eye first was the one in the plaid green two-piece. She was a chunky kid, with a good tan and a sweet broad soft-looking can with these two crescents of white just under it, where the sun never seems to hit, at the top of the backs of her legs. I stood there with hand on a box of Hi Ho crackers trying to remember if I rang it up or not. I ring it up again and the customer starts giving me hell. She's one of those cash register-watchers, a witch about fifty with rouge on her cheekbones and no eye makeup. She'd been watching cash registers for fifty years and probably never seen a mistake before.

By the time I get her feathers smoothed and her goodies into a bag—she gives me a little snort in passing, if she'd been born at the right time they would have burned her over in Salem—by the time I get her on her way the girls had circled around the bread and were coming back, without a pushcart, back my way along the counters, in the aisle between the checkouts and the Special bins. They didn't even have shoes on. There was this chunky one, with the two piece—it was bright green and the seams on the bra were still sharp and her belly was still pretty pale so I guessed she just got it (the suit)—there was this one, with one of those chubby berry-faces, the lips all bunched together under her nose, this one, and a tall one, with black hair that hadn't quite frizzed right, and one of these sunburns right across under the eyes, and a chin that was too long—you know, the kind of girl the other girls think is very "striking" and "attractive" but never quite makes it, as they very well know, which is why they like her so much—and then the third one, that wasn't quite so tall. She was the queen. She kind of led them, the other two peeking around and making their shoulders round. She didn't look around, not this queen, she just walked straight on slowly, on these long white primadonna legs. She came down a little hard on her heels, as if she didn't walk in bare feet that much, putting down her heels and then letting the weight move along to her toes as if she was testing the floor with every step, putting a little deliberate extra action into it. You never know for sure how girls' minds work (do you really think it's a mind in there or just a little buzz like a bee in a glass jar?) but you got the idea she had talked the other two into coming in here with her, and now she was showing them how to do it, walk slow and hold yourself straight.

She had on a kind of dirty-pink—beige maybe, I don't know—bathing suit with a little nubble all over it and what got me, the straps were down. They were off her shoulders looped loose around the cool tops of her arms, and I guess as a result the suit had slipped a little on her, so all around the top of the cloth there was this shining rim. If it hadn't been there you wouldn't have known there could have been anything whiter than those shoulders. With the straps pushed off, there was nothing between the top of the suit and the top of her head except just her, this clean bare plane of the top of her chest down from the shoulder bones like a dented sheet of metal tilted in the light. I mean, it was more than pretty.

She had a sort of okay hair that the sun and salt had bleached, done up in a bun that was unraveling, and a kind of prim face. Walking into the A & P with the straps down, I suppose it's the only kind of face you can have. She held her head so high her neck, coming up out of those white shoulders, looked kind of stretched, but I didn't mind. The longer her neck was, the more of her there was.

She must have felt in the corner of her eye me and over my shoulder Stoksie in the second slot watching, but she didn't tip. Not this queen. She kept her eyes moving across the racks, and stopped, and turned so slow it made my stomach rub the inside of my apron, and buzzed to the other two, who kind of huddled against her for relief, and they all three of them went up the cat-and-dog-food-breakfast-cereal-macaroni-rice-raisins-seasonings-spreads-spaghetti-soft-drinks-crackers-and-cookies aisle. From the third slot I looked straight up this aisle to the meat counter, and I watched them all the way. The fat one with the tan sort of fumbled with the cookies, but on second thought she put the package back. The sheep pushing their carts down the aisle—the girls were walking against the usual traffic (not that we have one-way signs or anything)—were pretty hilarious. You could see them, when Queenie's white shoulders dawned on them, kind of jerk, or hop, or hiccup, but their eyes snapped back to their own baskets and on they pushed. I bet you could set off dynamite in an A & P and the people would by and large keep reaching and checking oatmeal off their lists and muttering "Let me see, there was a third thing, began with A, asparagus, no, ah, yes, applesauce!" or whatever it is they do mutter. But there was no doubt, this jiggled them. A few houseslaves in pin curlers even looked around after pushing their carts past to make sure what they had seen was correct.

You know, it's one thing to have a girl in a bathing suit down on the beach, where what with the glare nobody can look at each other much anyway, and another thing in the cool of the A & P, under the fluorescent lights, against all those stacked packages, with her feet paddling along naked over our checkerboard green-and-cream rubber floor.

"Oh Daddy," Stoksie said beside me. "I feel so faint."

"Darling," I said. "Hold me tight." Stoksie's married, with two babies chalked up on his fuselage already, but as far as I can tell that's the only difference. He's twenty-two, and I was nineteen this April.

"Is it done?" he asks, the responsible married man finding his voice. I forgot to say he thinks he's going to be manager some sunny day, maybe in 1990 when it's called the Great Alexandrov and Petrooshki Tea Company or something.

What he meant was, our town is five miles from a beach, with a big summer colony out on the Point, but we're right in the middle of town, and the women generally put on a shirt or shorts or something before they get out of the car into the street. And anyway, these are usually women with six children and varicose veins mapping their legs and nobody, including them, could care less. As I say, we're right in the middle of town and if you stand at our front doors you can see two banks and the Congregational church and the newspaper store and three real-estate offices and about twenty-seven old freeloaders tearing up Central Street because the sewer broke again. It's not as if we're on the Cape, we're north of Boston and there's people in this town haven't seen the ocean for twenty years.

The girls had reached the meat counter and were asking McMahon something. He pointed, they pointed, and they shuffled out of sight behind a pyramid of Diet Delight peaches. All that was left for us to see was old McMahon patting his mouth and looking after them sizing up their joints. Poor kids, I began to feel sorry for them, they couldn't help it.

Now here comes the sad part of the story, at least my family says it's sad, but I don't think it's so sad myself. The store's pretty empty, it being Thursday afternoon, so there was nothing much to do except lean on the register and wait for the girls to show up again. The whole store was like a pinball machine and I didn't know which tunnel they'd come out of. After a while they came around out of the far aisle, around the light bulbs, records at discount of the Caribbean Six or Tony Martin Sings or some such gunk you wonder they waste the wax on, six packs of candy bars, and plastic toys done up in cellophane that fall apart when a kid looks at them anyway. Around they come, Queenie still leading the way, and holding a little gray jar in her hand. Slots Three through Seven are unmanned and I could see her wondering between Stoksie and me, but Stoksie with his usual luck draws an old party in baggy gray pants who stumbles up with four giant cans of pineapple juice (what do these bums do with all that pineapple juice? I've often asked myself) so the girls come to me. Queenie puts down the jar and I take it into my fingers icy cold. Kingfish Fancy Herring Snacks in Pure Sour Cream: 49 cents. Now her hands are empty, not a ring or a bracelet, bare as God made them, and I wonder where the money's coming from. Still with that prim look she lifts a folded dollar bill out of the hollow at the center of her nubbled pink top. The jar went heavy in my hand. Really, I thought that was so cute.

Then everybody's luck begins to run out. Lengel comes in from haggling with a truck full of cabbages on the lot and is about to scuttle into that door marked MANAGER behind which he hides all day when the girls touch his eye. Lengel's pretty dreary, teaches Sunday school and the rest, but he doesn't miss that much. He comes over and says, "Girls, this isn't the beach."

Queenie blushes, though maybe it's just a brush of sunburn I was noticing for the first time, now that she was so close. "My mother asked me to pick up a jar of herring snacks." Her voice kind of startled me, the way voices do when you see the people first, coming out so flat and dumb yet kind of tony, too, the way it ticked over "pick up" and "snacks." All of a sudden I slid right down her voice into her living room. Her father and the other men were standing around in ice-cream coats and bow ties and the women were in sandals picking up herring snacks on toothpicks off a big glass plate and they were all holding drinks the color of water with olives and sprigs of mint in them. When my parents have somebody over they get lemonade and if it's a real racy affair Schlitz in tall glasses with "They'll Do It Every Time" cartoons stenciled on.

"That's all right," Lengel said. "But this isn't the beach." His repeating this struck me as funny, as if it had just occurred to him, and he had been thinking all these years the A & P was a great big dune and he was the head lifeguard. He didn't like my smiling—as I say he doesn't miss much—but he concentrates on giving the girls that sad Sunday-school-superintendent stare.

Queenie's blush is no sunburn now, and the plump one in plaid, that I liked better from the back—a really sweet can—pipes up, "We weren't doing any shopping. We just came in for one thing."

"That makes no difference," Lengel tells her, and I could see from the way his eyes went that he hadn't noticed she was wearing a two-piece before. "We want you decently dressed when you come in here."

"We are decent," Queenie says suddenly, her lower lip pushing, getting sore now that she remembers her place, a place from which the crowd that runs the A & P must look pretty crummy. Fancy Herring Snacks flashed in her very blue eyes.

"Girls, I don't want to argue with you. After this come in here with your shoulders covered. It's our policy." He turns his back. That's policy for you. Policy is what the kingpins want. What the others want is juvenile delinquency.

All this while, the customers had been showing up with their carts but, you know, sheep, seeing a scene, they had all bunched up on Stoksie, who shook open a paper bag as gently as peeling a peach, not wanting to miss a word. I could feel in the silence everybody getting nervous, most of all Lengel, who asks me, "Sammy, have you rung up their purchase?"

I thought and said "No" but it wasn't about that I was thinking. I go through the punches, 4, 9, GROC, TOT—it's more complicated than you think, and after you do it often enough it begins to make a little song, that you hear words to, in my case "Hello (bing) there, you (gung) hap-py pee-pul (splat)!"—the splat being the drawer flying out. I uncrease the bill, tenderly as you may imagine, it just having come from between the two smoothest scoops of vanilla I had ever known there were, and pass a half and a penny into her narrow pink palm, and nestle the herrings in a bag and twist the neck and hand it over, all the time thinking.

The girls, and who'd blame them, are in a hurry to get out, so I say "I quit" to Lengel quick enough for them to hear, hoping they'll stop and watch me, their unsuspected hero. They keep right on going, into the electric eye; the door flies open and they flicker across the lot to their car. Queenie and Plaid and Big Tall Goony-Goony (not that as raw material she was so bad), leaving me with Lengel and a kink in his eyebrow.

"Did you say something, Sammy?"

"I said I quit."

"I thought you did."

"You didn't have to embarrass them."

"It was they who were embarrassing us."

I started to say something that came out "Fiddle-de-do." It's a saying of my grandmother's, and I know she would have been pleased.

"I don't think you know what you're saying," Lengel said.

"I know you don't," I said. "But I do." I pull the bow at the back of my apron and start shrugging it off my shoulders. A couple of customers that had been heading for my slot begin to knock against each other, like scared pigs in a chute.

Lengel sighs and begins to look very patient and old and gray. He's been a friend of my parents for years. "Sammy, you don't want to do this to your Mom and Dad," he tells me. It's true. I don't. But it seems to me that once you begin a gesture it's fatal not to go through with it. I fold the apron, "Sammy" stitched in red on the pocket, and put it on the counter, and drop the bow tie on top of it. The bow tie is theirs, if you've ever wondered. "You'll feel this for the rest of your life," Lengel says, and I know that's true, too, but remembering how he made that pretty girl blush makes me so scrunchy inside I punch the No Sale tab and the machine whirs "pee-pul" and the drawer splats out. One advantage to this scene taking place in summer, I can follow this up with a clean exit, there's no fumbling around getting your coat and galoshes, I just saunter into the electric eye in my white shirt that my mother ironed the night before, and the door heaves itself open, and outside the sunshine is skating around on the asphalt.

I look around for my girls, but they're gone, of course. There wasn't anybody but some young married screaming with her children about some candy they didn't get by the door of a powder-blue Falcon station wagon. Looking back in the big windows, over the bags of peat moss and aluminum lawn furniture stacked on the pavement, I could see Lengel in my place in the slot, checking the sheep through. His face was dark gray and his back stiff, as if he's just had an injection of iron, and my stomach kind of fell as I felt how hard the world was going to be to me hereafter.

A JURY OF HER PEERS
Susan Glaspell

When Martha Hale opened the storm-door and got a cut of the north wind, she ran back for her big woolen scarf. As she hurriedly wound that round her head her eye made a scandalized sweep of her kitchen. It was no ordinary thing that called her away—it was probably further from ordinary than anything that had ever happened in Dickson County. But what her eye took in was that her kitchen was in no shape for leaving: her bread all ready for mixing, half the flour sifted and half unsifted.

She hated to see things half done; but she had been at that when the team from town stopped to get Mr. Hale, and then the sheriff came running in to say his wife wished Mrs. Hale would come too—adding, with a grin, that he guessed she was getting scared and wanted another woman along. So she had dropped everything right where it was.

"Martha!" now came her husband's impatient voice. "Don't keep folks waiting out here in the cold."

She again opened the storm—door, and this time joined the three men and the one woman waiting for her in the big two-seated buggy.

After she had the robes tucked around her she took another look at the woman who sat beside her on the back seat. She had met Mrs. Peters the year before at the county fair, and the thing she remembered about her was that she didn't seem like a sheriff's wife. She was small and thin and didn't have a strong voice. Mrs. Gorman, sheriff's wife before Gorman went out and Peters came in, had a voice that somehow seemed to be backing up the law with every word. But if Mrs. Peters didn't look like a sheriff's wife, Peters made it up in looking like a sheriff. He was to a dot the kind

137

of man who could get himself elected sheriff—a heavy man with a big voice, who was particularly genial with the law-abiding, as if to make it plain that he knew the difference between criminals and non-criminals. And right there it came into Mrs. Hale's mind, with a stab, that this man who was so pleasant and lively with all of them was going to the Wrights' now as a sheriff.

"The country's not very pleasant this time of year," Mrs. Peters at last ventured, as if she felt they ought to be talking as well as the men.

Mrs. Hale scarcely finished her reply, for they had gone up a little hill and could see the Wright place now, and seeing it did not make her feel like talking. It looked very lonesome this cold March morning. It had always been a lonesome-looking place. It was down in a hollow, and the poplar trees around it were lonesome-looking trees. The men were looking at it and talking about what had happened. The county attorney was bending to one side of the buggy, and kept looking steadily at the place as they drew up to it.

"I'm glad you came with me: Mrs. Peters said nervously, as the two women were about to follow the men in through the kitchen door.

Even after she had her foot on the door-step, her hand on the knob, Martha Hale had a moment of feeling she could not cross that threshold. And the reason it seemed she couldn't cross it now was simply because she hadn't crossed it before. Time and time again it had been in her mind, "I ought to go over and see Minnie Foster"—she still thought of her as Minnie Foster, though for twenty years she had been Mrs. Wright. And then there was always something to do and Minnie Foster would go from her mind. But *now* she could come.

The men went over to the stove. The women stood close together by the door. Young Henderson, the county attorney, turned around and said, "Come up to the fire, ladies."

Mrs. Peters took a step forward, than stopped. "I'm not—cold," she said. And so the two women stood by the door, at first not even so much as looking around the kitchen.

The men talked for a minute about what a good thing it was the sheriff had sent his deputy out that morning to make a fire for them, and then Sheriff Peters stepped back from the stove, unbuttoned his outer coat, and leaned his hands on the kitchen table in a way that seemed to mark the beginning of official business. "Now, Mr. Hale," he said in a sort of semi-official voice, "before we move things about, you tell Mr. Henderson just what it was you saw when you came here yesterday morning."

The county attorney was looking around the kitchen.

"By the way," he said, "has anything been moved?" He turned to the sheriff. "Are things just as you left them yesterday?"

Peters looked from cupboard to sink; from that to a small worn rocker a little to one side of the kitchen table.

"It's just the same."

"Somebody should have been left here yesterday," said the county attorney.

"Oh—yesterday," returned the sheriff, with a little gesture as if yesterday having been more than he could bear to think of. "When I had to send Frank to Morris Center for that man who went crazy—let me tell you, I had my hands full *yesterday*. I knew you could get back from Omaha by today, George, and as long as I went over everything here myself—"

"Well, Mr. Hale," said the county attorney, in a way of letting what was past and gone go, "tell just what happened when you came here yesterday morning."

Mrs. Hale, still leaning against the door, had that sinking feeling of the mother whose child is about to speak a piece. Lewis often wandered along and got things mixed up in a story. She hoped he would tell this straight and plain, and not say unnecessary things that would just make things harder for Minnie Foster. He didn't begin at once, and she noticed that he looked queer—as if standing in that kitchen and having to tell what he had seen there yesterday morning made him almost sick.

"Yes, Mr. Hale?" the county attorney reminded.

"Harry and I had started to town with a load of potatoes," Mrs. Hale's husband began.

Harry was Mrs. Hale's oldest boy. He wasn't with them now, for the very good reason that those potatoes never got to town yesterday and he was taking them this morning, so he hadn't been home when the sheriff stopped to say he wanted Mr. Hale to come over to the Wright place and tell the county attorney his story there, where he could point it all out. With all Mrs. Hale's other emotions came the fear that maybe Harry wasn't dressed warm enough—they hadn't any of them realized how that north wind did bite.

"We come along this road," Hale was going on, with a motion of his hand to the road over which they had just come, "and as we got in sight of the house I says to Harry, 'I'm goin' to see if I can't get John Wright to take a telephone.' You see," he explained to Henderson, "unless I can get somebody to go in with me they won't come out this branch road except for a price I can't pay. I'd spoke to Wright about it once before; but he put me off, saying folks talked too much anyway, and all he asked was peace and quiet—guess you know about how much he talked himself. But I thought maybe if I went to the house and talked about it before his wife, and said all the women-folks liked the telephones, and that in this lonesome stretch of road it would be a good thing—well, I said to Harry that that was what I was going to say—though I said at the same time that I didn't know as what his wife wanted made much difference to John—"

Now, there he was!—saying things he didn't need to say. Mrs. Hale tried to catch her husband's eye, but fortunately the county attorney interrupted with:

"Let's talk about that a little later, Mr. Hale. I do want to talk about that, but I'm anxious now to get along to just what happened when you got here."

When he began this time, it was very deliberately and carefully:

"I didn't see or hear anything. I knocked at the door. And still it was all quiet inside. I knew they must be up—it was past eight o'clock. So I knocked again, louder, and I thought I heard somebody say 'Come in.' I wasn't sure—I'm not sure yet. But I opened the door—this door," jerking a hand toward the door by which the two women stood, "and there, in that rocker"—pointing to it—"sat Mrs. Wright."

Everyone in the kitchen looked at the rocker. It came into Mrs. Hale's mind that that rocker didn't look in the least like Minnie Foster—the Minnie Foster of twenty years before. It was a dingy red, with wooden rungs up the back, and the middle rung was gone, and the chair sagged to one side.

"How did she—look?" the country attorney was inquiring.

"Well," said Hale, "she looked—queer."

"How do you mean—queer?"

As he asked it he took out a note-book and pencil. Mrs. Hale did not like the sight of that pencil. She kept her eye fixed on her husband, as if to keep him from saying unnecessary things that would go into that note-book and make trouble.

Hale did speak guardedly, as if the pencil had affected him too.

"Well, as if she didn't know what she was going to do next. And kind of done up."

"How did she seem to feel about your coming?"

"Why, I don't think she minded—one way or other. She didn't pay much attention. I said, 'Ho' do, Mrs. Wright? It's cold, ain't it?' And she said, 'Is it?'—and went on pleatin' at her apron.

"Well, I was surprised. She didn't ask me to come up to the stove, or to sit down, but just set there, not even lookin' at me. And so I said: 'I want to see John.'

"And then she—laughed. I guess you would call it a laugh.

"I thought of Harry and the team outside, so I said, a little sharp, 'Can I see John?' 'No, says she—kind of dull like. 'Ain't he home?' says I. Then she looked at me. 'Yes: says she, 'he's home.' 'Then why can't I see him?' I asked her, out of patience with her now. 'Cause he's dead,' says she, just as quiet and dull—and fell to pleatin' her apron. 'Dead?' says I, like you do when you can't take in what you've heard.

"She just nodded her head, not getting a bit excited, but rockin' back and forth. "'Why—where is he?' says I, not knowing *what* to say.

"She just pointed upstairs—like this"—pointing to the room above.

"I got up, with the idea of going up there myself. By this time I didn't know what to do. I walked from there to here; then I says: 'Why, what did he die of?'

"'He died of a rope around his neck: says she; and just went on pleatin' at her apron."

Hale stopped speaking, and stood staring at the rocker, as if he were still seeing the woman who had sat there the morning before. Nobody spoke; it was as if everyone were seeing the woman who had sat there the morning before.

"And what did you do then?" the county attorney at last broke the silence.

"I went out and called Harry. I thought I might need help. I got Harry in, and we went upstairs." His voice fell almost to a whisper. "There he was—lying over the—"

"I think I'd rather have you go into that upstairs," the county attorney interrupted, "where you can point it all out. Just go on now with the rest of the story." "Well, my first thought was to get that rope off. It looked—"

He stopped, his face twitching.

"But Harry, he went up to him, and he said, 'No, he's dead all right, and we'd better not touch anything.' So we went downstairs.

"She was still sitting that same way. 'Has anybody been notified?' I asked.

'No,' says she, unconcerned.

"'Who did this, Mrs. Wright?' said Harry. He said it business-like, and she stopped pleatin' at her apron. I don't know,' she says. 'You don't *know?*' says Harry. 'Weren't you sleepin' in the bed with him?' 'Yes,' says she, 'but I was on the inside.' 'Somebody slipped a rope round his neck and strangled him, and you didn't wake up?' says Harry. I didn't wake up: she said after him.

"We may have looked as if we didn't see how that could be, for after a minute she said, 'I sleep sound.'

"Harry was going to ask her more questions, but I said maybe that weren't our business; maybe we ought to let her tell her story first to the coroner or the sheriff. So Harry went fast as he could over to High Road—the Rivers' place, where there's a telephone."

"And what did she do when she knew you had gone for the coroner?" The attorney got his pencil in his hand all ready for writing.

"She moved from that chair to this one over here"—Hale pointed to a small chair in the corner—"and just sat there with her hands held together and looking down. I got a feeling that I ought to make some conversation, so I said I had come in to see if John wanted to put in a telephone; and at that she started to laugh, and then she stopped and looked at me—scared."

At the sound of a moving pencil the man who was telling the story looked up. "I dunno—maybe it wasn't scared," he hastened; "I wouldn't like to say it was. Soon Harry got back, and then Dr. Lloyd came, and you, Mr. Peters, and so I guess that's all I know that you don't."

He said that last with relief, and moved a little, as if relaxing. Everyone moved a little. The county attorney walked toward the stair door.

"I guess we'll go upstairs first—then out to the barn and around there."

He paused and looked around the kitchen.

"You're convinced there was nothing important here?" he asked the sheriff. "Nothing that would—point to any motive?"

The sheriff too looked all around, as if to re-convince himself.

"Nothing here but kitchen things," he said, with a little laugh for the insignificance of kitchen things.

The county attorney was looking at the cupboard—a peculiar, ungainly structure, half closet and half cupboard, the upper part of it being built in the wall, and the lower part just the old-fashioned kitchen cupboard. As if its queerness attracted him, he got a chair and opened the upper part and looked in. After a moment he drew his hand away sticky.

"Here's a nice mess," he said resentfully.

The two women had drawn nearer, and now the sheriff's wife spoke.

"Oh—her fruit," she said, looking to Mrs. Hale for sympathetic understanding. She turned back to the county attorney and explained: "She worried about that when it turned so cold last night. She said the fire would go out and her jars might burst."

Mrs. Peters' husband broke into a laugh.

"Well, can you beat the women! Held for murder, and worrying about her preserves!"

The young attorney set his lips.

"I guess before we're through with her she may have something more serious than preserves to worry about."

"Oh, well," said Mrs. Hale's husband, with good-natured superiority, "women are used to worrying over trifles."

The two women moved a little closer together. Neither of them spoke. The county attorney seemed suddenly to remember his manners—and think of his future.

"And yet," said he, with the gallantry of a young politician, "for all their worries, what would we do without the ladies?"

The women did not speak, did not unbend. He went to the sink and began washing his hands. He turned to wipe them on the roller towel—whirled it for a cleaner place.

"Dirty towels! Not much of a housekeeper, would you say, la-dies?"

He kicked his foot against some dirty pans under the sink.

"There's a great deal of work to be done on a farm," said Mrs. Hale stiffly.

"To be sure. And yet"—with a little bow to her—"I know there are some Dickson County farm-houses that do not have such roller towels." He gave it a pull to expose its full length again.

"Those towels get dirty awful quick. Men's hands aren't al-ways as clean as they might be."

"Ah, loyal to your sex, I see," he laughed. He stopped and gave her a keen look. "But you and Mrs. Wright were neighbors. I sup-pose you were friends, too."

Martha Hale shook her head.

"I've seen little enough of her of late years. I've not been in this house—it's more than a year."

"And why was that? You didn't like her?"

"I liked her well enough," she replied with spirit. "Farm-ers' wives have their hands full, Mr. Henderson. And then"—She looked around the kitchen.

"Yes?" he encouraged.

"It never seemed a very cheerful place," said she, more to her-self than to him.

"No," he agreed; "I don't think anyone would call it cheerful. I shouldn't say she had the homemaking instinct."

"Well, I don't know as Wright had, either," she muttered.

"You mean they didn't get on very well?" he was quick to ask.

"No; I don't mean anything," she answered, with decision. As she turned a little away from him, she added: "But I don't think a place would be any the cheerfuler for John Wright's bein' in it."

"I'd like to talk to you about that a little later, Mrs. Hale," he said. "I'm anxious to get the lay of things upstairs now."

He moved toward the stair door, followed by the two men.

"I suppose anything Mrs. Peters does'll be all right?" the sher-iff inquired. "She was to take in some clothes for her, you know—and a few little things. We left in such a hurry yesterday."

The county attorney looked at the two women whom they were leaving alone there among the kitchen things.

"Yes—Mrs. Peters," he said, his glance resting on the woman who was not Mrs. Peters, the big farmer woman who stood behind the sheriff's wife. "Of course Mrs. Peters is one of us," he said, in a manner of entrusting responsibility. "And keep your eye out, Mrs. Peters, for anything that might be of use. No telling; you women might come upon a clue to the motive—and that's the thing we need."

Mr. Hale rubbed his face after the fashion of a show man getting ready for a pleasantry.

"But would the women know a clue if they did come upon it?" he said; and, having delivered himself of this, he followed the others through the stair door.

The women stood motionless and silent, listening to the footsteps, first upon the stairs, then in the room above them.

Then, as if releasing herself from something strange, Mrs. Hale began to arrange the dirty pans under the sink, which the county attorney's disdainful push of the foot had deranged.

"I'd hate to have men comin' into my kitchen," she said testily—"snoopin' round and criticizin'."

"Of course it's no more than their duty," said the sheriff's wife, in her manner of timid acquiescence.

"Duty's all right," replied Mrs. Hale bluffly; "but I guess that deputy sheriff that come out to make the fire might have got a little of this on." She gave the roller towel a pull. "Wish I'd thought of that sooner! Seems mean to talk about her for not having things slicked up, when she had to come away in such a hurry."

She looked around the kitchen. Certainly it was not "slicked up." Her eye was held by a bucket of sugar on a low shelf. The cover was off the wooden bucket, and beside it was a paper bag-half full.

Mrs. Hale moved toward it.

"She was putting this in there," she said to herself—slowly.

She thought of the flour in her kitchen at home—half sifted, half not sifted. She had been interrupted and had left things half done. What had interrupted Minnie Foster? Why had that work been left half done? She made a move as if to finish it, unfinished things always bothered her—and then she glanced around and saw that Mrs. Peters was watching her—and she didn't want Mrs. Peters to get that feeling she had got of work begun and then—for some reason—not finished.

"It's a shame about her fruit," she said, and walked toward the cupboard that the county attorney had opened, and got on the chair, murmuring: "I wonder if it's all gone."

It was a sorry enough looking sight, but "Here's one that's all right," she said at last. She held it toward the light. "This is cherries, too." She looked again. "I declare I believe that's the only one."

With a sigh, she got down from the chair, went to the sink and wiped off the bottle.

"She'll feel awful bad, after all her hard work in the hot weather. I remember the afternoon I put up my cherries last summer."

She set the bottle on the table, and, with another sigh, started to sit down in the rocker. But she did not sit down. Something kept her from sitting down in that chair. She straightened—stepped back, and, half turned away, stood looking at it, seeing the woman who sat there "pleatin' at her apron."

The thin voice of the sheriff's wife broke in upon her: "I must be getting those things from the front room closet." She opened the door into the other room, started in, stepped back. "You coming with me, Mrs. Hale?" she asked nervously. "You—you could help me get them."

They were soon back—the stark coldness of that shut-up room was not a thing to linger in.

"My!" said Mrs. Peters, dropping the things on the table and hurrying to the stove.

Mrs. Hale stood examining the clothes the woman who was being detained in town had said she wanted.

"Wright was close!" she exclaimed, holding up a shabby black skirt that bore the marks of much making over. I think maybe that's why she kept so much to herself. I s'pose she felt she couldn't do her part; and then, you don't enjoy things when you feel shabby. She used to wear pretty clothes and be lively—when she was Minnie Foster, one of the town girls, singing in the choir. But that—oh, that was twenty years ago."

With a carefulness in which there was something tender, she folded the shabby clothes and piled them at one corner of the table. She looked at Mrs. Peters, and there was something in the other woman's look that irritated her.

"She don't care," she said to herself. "Much difference it makes to her whether Minnie Foster had pretty clothes when she was a girl."

Then she looked again, and she wasn't so sure; in fact, she hadn't at any time been perfectly sure about Mrs. Peters. She had that shrinking manner, and yet her eyes looked as if they could see a long way into things.

"This all you was to take in?" asked Mrs. Hale.

"No," said the sheriff's wife; "she said she wanted an apron. Funny thing to want," she ventured in her nervous little way, "for there's not much to get you dirty in jail, goodness knows. But I suppose just to make her feel more natural. If you're used to wearing an apron—. She said they were in the bottom drawer of this cupboard. Yes—here they are. And then her little shawl that always hung on the stair door."

Suddenly Mrs. Hale took a quick step toward the other woman.

"Mrs. Peters!"

"Yes, Mrs. Hale?"

"Do you think she—did it?"

A frightened look blurred the other things in Mrs. Peters' eyes.

"Oh, I don't know," she said, in a voice that seemed to shrink away from the subject.

"Well, I don't think she did," affirmed Mrs. Hale stoutly. "Asking for an apron, and her little shawl. Worryin' about her fruit."

"Mr. Peters says—" Footsteps were heard in the room above; she stopped, looked up, then went on in a lowered voice: "Mr. Peters says—it looks bad for her. Mr. Henderson is awful sarcastic in a speech, and he's going to make fun of her saying she didn't wake up."

For a moment Mrs. Hale had no answer. Then, "Well, I guess John Wright didn't wake up—when they was slippin' that rope under his neck," she muttered.

"No, it's *strange*," breathed Mrs. Peters. "They think it was such a—funny way to kill a man."

She began to laugh; at sound of the laugh, abruptly stopped.

"That's just what Mr. Hale said," said Mrs. Hale, in a resolutely natural voice.

"There was a gun in the house. He says that's what he can't understand."

"Mr. Henderson said, coming out, that what was needed for the case was a motive. Something to show anger—or sudden feeling."

"Well, I don't see any signs of anger around here," said Mrs. Hale. "I don't—"

She stopped. It was as if her mind tripped on something. Her eye was caught by a dish-towel in the middle of the kitchen table. Slowly she moved toward the table. One half of it was wiped clean, the other half messy. Her eyes made a slow, almost unwilling turn to the bucket of sugar and the half empty bag beside it. Things begun—and not finished.

After a moment she stepped back, and said, in that manner of releasing herself:

"Wonder how they're finding things upstairs? I hope she had it a little more red up there. You know,"—she paused, and feeling gathered,—"it seems kind of *sneaking;* locking her up in town and coming out here to get her own house to turn against her!"

"But, Mrs. Hale," said the sheriff's wife, "the law is the law."

'I s'pose 'tis," answered Mrs. Hale shortly.

She turned to the stove, saying something about that fire not being much to brag of. She worked with it a minute, and when she straightened up she said aggressively:

"The law is the law—and a bad stove is a bad stove. How'd you like to cook on this?"—pointing with the poker to the broken lining. She opened the oven door and started to express her opinion of the oven; but she was swept into her own thoughts, thinking of what it would mean, year after year, to have that stove to wrestle with. The thought of Minnie Foster trying to bake in that oven—and the thought of her never going over to see Minnie Foster—.

She was startled by hearing Mrs. Peters say: "A person gets discouraged—and loses heart."

The sheriff's wife had looked from the stove to the sink—to the pail of water which had been carried in from outside. The two women stood there silent, above them the footsteps of the men who were looking for evidence against the woman who had worked in that kitchen. That look of seeing into things, of seeing through a thing to something else, was in the eyes of the sheriff's wife now. When Mrs. Hale next spoke to her, it was gently:

"Better loosen up your things, Mrs. Peters. We'll not feel them when we go out."

Mrs. Peters went to the back of the room to hang up the fur tippet she was wearing. A moment later she exclaimed, "Why, she was piecing a quilt," and held up a large sewing basket piled high with quilt pieces.

Mrs. Hale spread some of the blocks on the table.

"It's log-cabin pattern," she said, putting several of them together. "Pretty, isn't it?"

They were so engaged with the quilt that they did not hear the footsteps on the stairs. Just as the stair door opened Mrs. Hale was saying:

"Do you suppose she was going to quilt it or just knot it?"

The sheriff threw up his hands.

"They wonder whether she was going to quilt it or just knot it!"

There was a laugh for the ways of women, a warming of hands over the stove, and then the county attorney said briskly:

"Well, let's go right out to the barn and get that cleared up."

"I don't see as there's anything so strange," Mrs. Hale said resentfully, after the outside door had closed on the three men—"our taking up our time with little things while we're waiting for them to get the evidence. I don't see as it's anything to laugh about."

"Of course they've got awful important things on their minds," said the sheriff's wife apologetically.

They returned to an inspection of the blocks for the quilt. Mrs. Hale was looking at the fine, even sewing, and preoccupied with thoughts of the woman who had done that sewing, when she heard the sheriff's wife say, in a queer tone:

"Why, look at this one."

She turned to take the block held out to her.

"The sewing," said Mrs. Peters, in a troubled way. "All the rest of them have been so nice and even—but—this one. Why, it looks as if she didn't know what she was about!"

Their eyes met—something flashed to life, passed between them; then, as if with an effort, they seemed to pull away from each other. A moment Mrs. Hale sat there, her hands folded over that sewing which was so unlike all the rest of the sewing. Then she had pulled a knot and drawn the threads.

"Oh, what are you doing, Mrs. Hale?" asked the sheriffs wife, startled.

"Just pulling out a stitch or two that's not sewed very good,"
said Mrs. Hale mildly.

"I don't think we ought to touch things," Mrs. Peters said, a
little helplessly.

"I'd just finish up this end," answered Mrs. Hale, still in that
mild, matter-of-fact fashion.

She threaded a needle and started to replace bad sewing with
good. For a little while she sewed in silence. Then, in that thin,
timid voice, she heard:

"Mrs. Hale!"

"Yes, Mrs. Peters?"

"What do you suppose she was so—nervous about?"

"Oh, *I* don't know," said Mrs. Hale, as if dismissing a thing
not important enough to spend much time on. "I don't know as she
was-nervous. I sew awful queer sometimes when I'm just tired."

She cut a thread, and out of the corner of her eye looked up at
Mrs. Peters. The small, lean face of the sheriff's wife seemed to
have tightened up. Her eyes had that look of peering into something. But the next moment she moved, and said in her thin, indeci-
sive way:

"Well, I must get those clothes wrapped. They may be through
sooner than we think. I wonder where I could find a piece of
paper—and string."

"In that cupboard, maybe," suggested Mrs. Hale, after a glance
around.

One piece of the crazy sewing remained unripped. Mrs. Peters'
back turned, Martha Hale now scrutinized that piece, compared it
with the dainty, accurate sewing of the other blocks. The difference
was startling. Holding this block made her feel queer, as if the distracted thoughts of the woman who had perhaps turned to it to try
and quiet herself were communicating themselves to her.

Mrs. Peters' voice roused her.

"Here's a bird-cage," she said. "Did she have a bird, Mrs. Hale?"

"Why, I don't know whether she did or not." She turned to
look at the cage Mrs. Peters was holding up. "I've not been here
in so long." She sighed. "There was a man round last year selling
canaries cheap—but I don't know as she took one. Maybe she did.
She used to sing real pretty herself."

Mrs. Peters looked around the kitchen.

"Seems kind of funny to think of a bird here." She half laughed—an attempt to put up a barrier. "But she must have had one—or why would she have a cage? I wonder what happened to it."

"I suppose maybe the cat got it," suggested Mrs. Hale, resuming her sewing.

"No; she didn't have a cat. She's got that feeling some people have about cats—being afraid of them. When they brought her to our house yesterday, my cat got in the room, and she was real upset and asked me to take it out."

"My sister Bessie was like that," laughed Mrs. Hale.

The sheriff's wife did not reply. The silence made Mrs. Hale turn round. Mrs. Peters was examining the bird-cage.

"Look at this door," she said slowly. "It's broke. One hinge has been pulled apart."

Mrs. Hale came nearer.

"Looks as if someone must have been—rough with it."

Again their eyes met—startled, questioning, apprehensive. For a moment neither spoke nor stirred. Then Mrs. Hale, turning away, said brusquely: "If they're going to find any evidence, I wish they'd be about it. I don't like this place."

"But I'm awful glad you came with me, Mrs. Hale." Mrs. Peters put the bird cage on the table and sat down. "It would be lonesome for me—sitting here alone."

"Yes, it would, wouldn't it?" agreed Mrs. Hale, a certain determined naturalness in her voice. She picked up the sewing, but now it dropped in her lap, and she murmured in a different voice: "But I tell you what I *do* wish, Mrs. Peters. I wish I had come over sometimes when she was here. I wish—I had."

"But of course you were awful busy, Mrs. Hale. Your house—and your children."

"I could've come," retorted Mrs. Hale shortly. "I stayed away because it weren't cheerful—and that's why I ought to have come. I"—she looked around "I've never liked this place. Maybe because it's down in a hollow and you don't see the road. I don't know what it is, but it's a lonesome place, and always was. I wish I had come over to see Minnie Foster sometimes. I can see now—" She did not put it into words.

"Well, you mustn't reproach yourself." counseled Mrs. Peters. "Somehow, we just don't see how it is with other folks till—something comes up."

"Not having children makes less work," mused Mrs. Hale, after a silence, "but it makes a quiet house—and Wright out to work all day—and no company when he did come in. Did you know John Wright, Mrs. Peters?"

"Not to know him. I've seen him in town. They say he was a good man."

"Yes—good," conceded John Wright's neighbor grimly. "He didn't drink, and kept his word as well as most, I guess, and paid his debts. But he was a hard man, Mrs. Peters. Just to pass the time of day with him—." She stopped, shivered a little. "Like a raw wind that gets to the bone." Her eye fell upon the cage on the table before her, and she added, almost bitterly: "I should think she would've wanted a bird!"

Suddenly she leaned forward, looking intently at the cage. "But what do you s'pose went wrong with it?"

"I don't know," returned Mrs. Peters; "unless it got sick and died."

But after she said it she reached over and swung the broken door. Both women watched it as if somehow held by it.

"You didn't know—her?" Mrs. Hale asked, a gentler note in her voice.

"Not till they brought her yesterday," said the sheriff's wife.

"She—come to think of it, she was kind of like a bird herself. Real sweet and pretty, but kind of timid and—fluttery. How—she—did—change."

That held her for a long time. Finally, as if struck with a happy thought and relieved to get back to everyday things, she exclaimed:

"Tell you what, Mrs. Peters, why don't you take the quilt in with you? It might take up her mind."

"Why, I think that's a real nice idea, Mrs. Hale," agreed the sheriff's wife, as if she too were glad to come into the atmosphere of a simple kindness. "There couldn't possibly be any objection to that, could there? Now, just what will I take? I wonder if her patches are in here—and her things."

They turned to the sewing basket.

"Here's some red," said Mrs. Hale, bringing out a roll of cloth. Underneath that was a box. "Here, maybe her scissors are in here—and her things." She held it up. "What a pretty box! I'll warrant that was something she had a long time ago when she was a girl."

She held it in her hand a moment; then, with a little sigh, opened it.

Instantly her hand went to her nose.

"Why—!"

Mrs. Peters drew nearer—then turned away.

"There's something wrapped up in this piece of silk," faltered Mrs. Hale. "This isn't her scissors," said Mrs. Peters in a shrinking voice.

Her hand not steady, Mrs. Hale raised the piece of silk. "Oh, Mrs. Peters!" she cried. "It's—"

Mrs. Peters bent closer.

"It's the bird," she whispered.

"But, Mrs. Peters!" cried Mrs. Hale. *"Look* at it! Its neck—look at its neck! It's all—other side *to.* "

She held the box away from her.

The sheriff's wife again bent closer.

"Somebody wrung its neck," said she, in a voice that was slow and deep.

And then again the eyes of the two women met—this time clung together in a look of dawning comprehension, of growing horror. Mrs. Peters looked from the dead bird to the broken door of the cage. Again their eyes met. And just then there was a sound at the outside door.

Mrs. Hale slipped the box under the quilt pieces in the basket, and sank into the chair before it. Mrs. Peters stood holding to the table. The county attorney and the sheriff came in from outside.

"Well, ladies," said the county attorney, as one turning from serious things to little pleasantries, "have you decided whether she was going to quilt it or knot it?"

"We think," began the sheriff's wife in a flurried voice, "that she was going to—knot it."

He was too preoccupied to notice the change that came in her voice on that last.

"Well that's very interesting, I'm sure," he said tolerantly. He caught sight of the bird-cage. "Has the bird flown?"

"We think the cat got it," said Mrs. Hale in a voice curiously even.

He was walking up and down, as if thinking something out.

"Is there a cat?" he asked absently.

Mrs. Hale shot a look up at the sheriff's wife.

"Well not *now*," said Mrs. Peters. "They're superstitious, you know; they leave."

She sank into her chair.

The county attorney did not heed her. "No sign at all of anyone having come in from the outside," he said to Peters, in the manner of continuing an interrupted conversation. "Their own rope. Now let's go upstairs again and go over it, piece by piece. It would have to have been someone who knew just the—"

The stair door closed behind them and their voices were lost. The two women sat motionless, not looking at each other, but as if peering into something and at the same time holding back. When they spoke now it was as if they were afraid of what they were saying, but as if they could not help saying it.

"She liked the bird," said Martha Hale, low and slowly. "She was going to bury it in that pretty box."

"When I was a girl" said Mrs. Peters, under her breath, "my kitten—there was a boy took a hatchet, and before my eyes—before I could get there—" She covered her face an instant. "If they hadn't held me back I would have"—she caught herself, looked upstairs where footsteps were heard, and finished weakly—"hurt him."

Then they sat without speaking or moving.

"I wonder how it would seem," Mrs. Hale at last began, as if feeling her way over strange ground—"never to have had any children around?" Her eyes made a slow sweep of the kitchen, as if seeing what that kitchen had meant through all the years. "No, Wright wouldn't like the bird," she said after that—"a thing that sang.

"She used to sing. He killed that too." Her voice tightened.

Mrs. Peters moved uneasily.

"Of course we don't know who killed the bird."

"I knew John Wright," was Mrs. Hale's answer.

"It was an awful thing was done in this house that night, Mrs. Hale," said the sheriff's wife. "Killing a man while he slept—slipping a thing round his neck that choked the life out of him."

Mrs. Hale's hand went out to the bird-cage.

"His neck. Choked the life out of him."

"We don't *know* who killed him," whispered Mrs. Peters wildly. "We don't *know.*"

Mrs. Hale had not moved. "If there had been years and years of—nothing, then a bird to sing to you, it would be awful—still—after the bird was still."

It was as if something within her not herself had spoken, and it found in Mrs. Peters something she did not know as herself.

"I know what stillness is," she said, in a queer, monotonous voice. "When we homesteaded in Dakota, and my first baby died—after he was two years old—and me with no other then—"

Mrs. Hale stirred.

"How soon do you suppose they'll be through looking for evidence?"

"I know what stillness is," repeated Mrs. Peters, in just that same way. Then she too pulled back. "The law has got to punish crime, Mrs. Hale," she said in her tight little way.

"I wish you'd seen Minnie Foster," was the answer, "when she wore a white dress with blue ribbons, and stood up there in the choir and sang."

The picture of that girl, the fact that she had lived neighbor to that girl for twenty years, and had let her die for lack of life, was suddenly more than she could bear.

"Oh, I *wish* I'd come over here once in a while!" she cried. "That was a crime! That was a crime! Who's going to punish that?"

"We mustn't take on," said Mrs. Peters, with a frightened look toward the stairs.

"I might 'a' *known* she needed help! I tell you, it's *queer,* Mrs. Peters. We live close together, and we live far apart. We all go through the same things—it's all just a different kind of the same thing. If it weren't—why do you and I *understand?* Why do we *know—what* we know this minute?"

She dashed her hand across her eyes. Then, seeing the jar of fruit on the table, she reached for it and choked out:

"If I was you I wouldn't *tell* her her fruit was gone! Tell her it *ain't.* Tell her it's all right—all of it. Here—take this in to prove it to her! She—she may never know whether it was broke or not."

She turned away.

Mrs. Peters reached out for the bottle of fruit as if she were glad to take it—as if touching a familiar thing, having something to do, could keep her from something else. She got up, looked about for something to wrap the fruit in, took a petticoat from the pile of clothes she had brought from the front room, and nervously started winding that round the bottle.

"My!" she began, in a high, false voice, "it's a good thing the men couldn't hear us! Getting all stirred up over a little thing like a—dead canary." She hurried over that. "As if that could have anything to do with—with—My, wouldn't they *laugh?*"

Footsteps were heard on the stairs.

"Maybe they would," muttered Mrs. Hale—"maybe they wouldn't."

"No, Peters," said the county attorney incisively; "it's all perfectly clear, except the reason for doing it. But you know juries when it comes to women. If there was some definite thing—something to show. Something to make a story about. A thing that would connect up with this clumsy way of doing it."

In a covert way Mrs. Hale looked at Mrs. Peters. Mrs. Peters was looking at her. Quickly they looked away from each other. The outer door opened and Mr. Hale came in.

"I've got the team round now," he said. "Pretty cold out there."

"I'm going to stay here awhile by myself," the county attorney suddenly announced. "You can send Frank out for me, can't you?" he asked the sheriff. "I want to go over everything. I'm not satisfied we can't do better."

Again, for one brief moment, the two women's eyes found one another.

The sheriff came up to the table.

"Did you want to see what Mrs. Peters was going to take in?"

The county attorney picked up the apron. He laughed.

"Oh, I guess they're not very dangerous things the ladies have picked out." Mrs. Hale's hand was on the sewing basket in which the box was concealed. She felt that she ought to take her hand off the basket. She did not seem able to. He picked up one of the quilt blocks which she had piled on to cover the box. Her eyes felt like fire. She had a feeling that if he took up the basket she would snatch it from him.

But he did not take it up. With another little laugh, he turned away, saying:

"No; Mrs. Peters doesn't need supervising. For that matter, a sheriff's wife is married to the law. Ever think of it that way, Mrs. Peters?"

Mrs. Peters was standing beside the table. Mrs. Hale shot a look up at her; but she could not see her face. Mrs. Peters had turned away. When she spoke, her voice was muffled.

"Not—just that way," she said.

"Married to the law!" chuckled Mrs. Peters' husband. He moved toward the door into the front room, and said to the county attorney: "I just want you to come in here a minute, George. We ought to take a look at these windows."

"Oh—windows," said the county attorney scoffingly.

"We'll be right out, Mr. Hale," said the sheriff to the farmer, who was still waiting by the door.

Hale went to look after the horses. The sheriff followed the county attorney into the other room. Again—for one moment—the two women were alone in that kitchen.

Martha Hale sprang up, her hands tight together, looking at that other woman, with whom it rested. At first she could not see her eyes, for the sheriff's wife had not turned back, since she turned away at that suggestion of being married to the law. *But* now Mrs. Hale made her turn back. Her eyes made her turn back. Slowly, unwillingly, Mrs. Peters turned her head until her eyes met the eyes of the other woman. There was a moment when they held each other in a steady, burning look in which there was no evasion nor flinching. Then Martha Hale's eyes pointed the way to the basket in which was hidden the thing that would make certain the conviction of the other woman—that woman who was not there and yet who had been there with them all through the hour.

For a moment Mrs. Peters did not move. And then she did it. With a rush forward, she threw back the quilt pieces, got the box, tried to put it in her handbag. It was too big. Desperately she opened it, started to take the bird out. *But* there she broke—she could not touch the bird. She stood helpless, foolish.

There was the sound of a knob turning in the inner door. Martha Hale snatched the box from the sheriff's wife, and got it in the pocket of her big coat just as the sheriff and the county attorney came back into the kitchen.

"Well, Henry," said the county attorney facetiously, "at least we found out that she was not going to quilt it. She was going to—what is it you call it, ladies?"

Mrs. Hale's hand was against the pocket of her coat.

"We call it—knot it, Mr. Henderson."

ARRANGEMENT IN BLACK AND WHITE

Dorothy Parker

The woman with the pink velvet poppies twined round the assisted gold of her hair traversed the crowded room at an interesting gait combining a skip with a sidle, and clutched the lean arm of her host.

"Now I got you!" she said. "Now you can't get away!"

"Why, hello," said her host. "Well. How are you?"

"Oh, I'm finely," she said. "Just simply finely. Listen. I want you to do me the most terrible favor. Will you? Will you please? Pretty please?"

"What is it?" said her host.

"Listen," she said. "I want to meet Walter Williams. Honestly, I'm just simply crazy about that man. Oh, when he sings! When he sings those spirituals! Well, I said to Burton, 'It's a good thing for you Walter Williams is colored,' I said, 'or you'd have lots of reason to be jealous.' I'd really love to meet him. I'd like to tell him I've heard him sing. Will you be an angel and introduce me to him?"

"Why, certainly," said her host. "I thought you'd met him. The party's for him. Where is he, anyway?"

"He's over there by the bookcase," she said. "Let's wait till those people get through talking to him. Well, I think you're simply marvelous, giving this perfectly marvelous party for him, and having him meet all these white people, and all. Isn't he terribly grateful?"

"I hope not," said her host.

"I think it's really terribly nice," she said. "I do. I don't see why on earth it isn't perfectly all right to meet colored people. I haven't any feeling at all about it not one single bit. Burton oh, he's just the other way. Well, you know, he comes from Virginia, and you know how they are."

"Did he come tonight?" said her host.

"No, he couldn't," she said. "I'm a regular grass widow tonight. I told him when I left, 'There's no telling what I'll do,' I said. He was just so tired out, he couldn't move. Isn't it a shame?"

"Ah," said her host.

"Wait till I tell him I met Walter Williams!" she said. "He'll just about die. Oh, we have more arguments about colored people. I talk to him like I don't know what, I get so excited. 'Oh, don't be so silly,' I say. But I must say for Burton, he's a heap broader-minded than lots of these Southerners. He's really awfully fond of colored people. Well, he says himself, he wouldn't have white servants. And you know, he had this old colored nurse, this regular old nigger mammy, and he just simply loves her. Why, every time he goes home, he goes out in the kitchen to see her. He does, really, to this day. All he says is, he says he hasn't got a word to say against colored people as long as they keep their place. He's always doing things for them, giving them clothes and I don't know what all. The only thing he says, he says he wouldn't sit down at the table with one for a million dollars. 'Oh,' I say to him, 'you make me sick, talking like that.' I'm just terrible to him. Aren't I terrible?"

"Oh, no, no, no," said her host. "No, no."

"I am," she said. "I know I am. Poor Burton! Now, me, I don't feel that way at all. I haven't the slightest feeling about colored people. Why, I'm just crazy about some of them. They're just like children, just as easy-going, and always singing and laughing and everything. Aren't they the happiest things you ever saw in your life? Honestly, it makes me laugh just to hear them. Oh, I like them. I really do. Well, now, listen, I have this colored laundress, I've had her for years, and I'm devoted to her. She's really a character. And I want to tell you, I think of her as my friend. That's the way I think of her. As I say to Burton, 'Well, for Heaven's sakes, we're all human beings!' Aren't we?"

"Yes," said her host. "Yes, indeed."

"Now this Walter Williams," she said. "I think a man like that's a real artist. I do. I think he deserves an awful lot of credit. Goodness, I'm so crazy about music or anything, I don't care what color he is. I honestly think if a person's an artist, nobody ought to have any feeling at all about meeting them. That's absolutely what I say to Burton. Don't you think I'm right?"

"Yes," said her host, "Oh, yes."

"That's the way I feel," she said. "I just can't understand people being narrow-minded. Why, I absolutely think it's a privilege to meet a man like Walter Williams. Yes, I do. I haven't any feeling at all. Well, my goodness, the good Lord made him, just the same as He did any of us. Didn't He?"

"Surely," said her host. "Yes, indeed."

"That's what I say," she said. "Oh, I get so furious when people are narrow-minded about colored people. It's just all I can do not to say something. Of course, I do admit when you get a bad colored man, they're simply terrible. But as I say to Burton, there are some bad white people, too, in this world. Aren't there?"

"I guess there are," said her host.

"Why, I'd really be glad to have a man like Walter Williams come to my house and sing for us, some time," she said. "Of course, I couldn't ask him on account of Burton, but I wouldn't have any feeling about it at all. Oh, can't he sing! Isn't it marvelous, the way they all have music in them? It just seems to be right in them.

"Come on, let's us go on over and talk to him. Listen, what shall I do when I'm introduced? Ought I to shake hands? Or what?"

"Why, do whatever you want," said her host.

"I guess maybe I'd better," she said. "I wouldn't for the world have him think I had any feeling. I think I'd better shake hands, just the way I would with anybody else.

"That's just exactly what I'll do."

They reached the tall young Negro, standing by the bookcase. The host performed introductions; the Negro bowed.

"How do you do?" he said.

The woman with the pink velvet poppies extended her hand at the length of her arm and held it so for all the world to see, until the Negro took it, shook it, and gave it back to her.

"Oh, how do you do, Mr. Williams," she said. "Well how do you do. I've just been saying, I've enjoyed your singing so awfully much. I've been to your concerts, and we have you on the phonograph and everything. Oh, I just enjoy it!"

She spoke with great distinctness, moving her lips meticulously, as if in parlance with the deaf.

"I'm so glad," he said.

"I'm just simply crazy about that 'Water Boy' thing you sing," she said. "Honestly, I can't get it out of my head. I have my husband nearly crazy, the way I go around humming it all the time. Oh, he looks just as black as the ace of . . . Well. Tell me, where on earth do you ever get all those songs of yours? How do you ever get hold of them?"

"Why," he said, "there are so many different . . ."

"I should think you'd love singing them," she said. "It must be more fun. All those darling old spirituals oh, I just love them! Well, what are you doing, now? Are you still keeping up your singing? Why don't you have another concert, some time?"

"I'm having one the sixteenth of this month," he said.

"Well, I'll be there," she said. "I'll be there, if I possibly can. You can count on me. Goodness, here comes a whole raft of people to talk to you. You're just a regular guest of honor! Oh, who's that girl in white? I've seen her some place."

"That's Katherine Burke," said her host.

"Good Heavens." she said, "Is that Katherine Burke? Why, she looks entirely different off the stage. I thought she was much better-looking. I had no idea she was so terribly dark. Why, she looks almost like . . . Oh, I think she's a wonderful actress! Don't you think she's a wonderful actress, Mr. Williams? Oh, I think she's marvelous. Don't you?"

"Yes, I do," he said.

"Oh, I do, too," she said. "Just wonderful. Well, goodness, we must give someone else a chance to talk to the guest of honor. Now, don't forget, Mr. Williams, I'm going to be at that concert if I possibly can. I'll be there applauding like everything. And if I can't come, I'm going to tell everybody I know to go, anyway. Don't you forget!"

"I won't," he said. "Thank you so much."

"Oh, my dear," she said. "I nearly died! Honestly, I give you my word, I nearly passed away. Did you hear that terrible break I made? I was just going to say Katherine Burke looked almost like a nigger. I just caught myself in time. Oh, do you think he noticed?"

"I don't believe so," said her host.

"Well, thank goodness," she said, "because I wouldn't have embarrassed him for anything. Why, he's awfully nice. Just as nice as he can be. Nice manners, and everything. You know, so many colored people, you give them an inch, and they walk all over you. But he doesn't try any of that. Well, he's got more sense, I suppose. He's really nice. Don't you think so?"

"Yes," said her host.

"I liked him," she said. "I haven't any feeling at all because he's a colored man. I felt just as natural as I would with anybody. Talked to him just as naturally, and everything. But honestly, I could hardly keep a straight face. I kept thinking of Burton. Oh, wait till I tell Burton I called him 'Mister'!"

ASTRONOMER'S WIFE
Kay Boyle

There is an evil moment on awakening when all things seem to pause. But for women, they only falter and may be set in action by a single move: a lifted hand and the pendulum will swing, or the voice raised and through every room the pulse takes up its beating. The astronomer's wife felt the interval gaping and at once filled it to the brim. She fetched up her gentle voice and sent it warily down the stairs for coffee, swung her feet out upon the oval mat, and hailed the morning with her bare arms' quivering flesh drawn taut in rhythmic exercise: left, left, left my wife and fourteen children, right, right, right in the middle of the dusty road.

The day would proceed from this, beat by beat, without reflection, like every other day. The astronomer was still asleep, or feigning it, and she, once out of bed, had come into her own possession. Although scarcely ever out of sight of the impenetrable silence of his brow, she would be absent from him all the day in being clean, busy, kind. He was a man of other things, a dreamer. At times he lay still for hours, at others he sat upon the roof behind his telescope, or wandered down the pathway to the road and out across the mountains. This day, like any other, would go on from the removal of the spot left there from dinner on the astronomer's vest to the severe thrashing of the mayonnaise for lunch. That man might be each time the new arching wave, and woman the undertow that sucked him back, were things she had been told by his silence were so.

In spite of the earliness of the hour, the girl had heard her mistress's voice and was coming up the stairs. At the threshold of the bedroom she paused, and said: "Madame, the plumber is here."

The astronomer's wife put on her white and scarlet smock very quickly and buttoned it at the neck. Then she stepped carefully around the motionless spread of water in the hall.

"Tell him to come right up," she said. She laid her hands on the banisters and stood looking down the wooden stairway. "Ah, I am Mrs. Ames," she said softly as she saw him mounting. "I am Mrs. Ames," she said softly, softly down the flight of stairs. "I am Mrs. Ames," spoken soft as a willow weeping. "The professor is still sleeping. Just step this way."

The plumber himself looked up and saw Mrs. Ames with her voice hushed, speaking to him. She was a youngish woman, but this she had forgotten. The mystery and silence of her husband's mind lay like a chiding finger on her lips. Her eyes were gray, for the light had been extinguished in them. The strange dim halo of her yellow hair was still uncombed and sideways on her head.

For all of his heavy boots, the plumber quieted the sound of his feet, and together they went down the hall, picking their way around the still lake of water that spread as far as the landing and lay docile there. The plumber was a tough, hardy man; but he took off his hat when he spoke to her and looked her fully, almost insolently in the eye.

"Does it come from the wash-basin," he said, "or from the other . . . ?"

"Oh, from the other," said Mrs. Ames without hesitation.

In this place the villas were scattered out few and primitive, and although beauty lay without there was no reflection of her face within. Here all was awkward and unfit; a sense of wrestling with uncouth forces gave everything an austere countenance. Even the plumber, dealing as does a woman with matters under hand, was grave and stately. The mountains round about seemed to have cast them into the shadow of great dignity.

Mrs. Ames began speaking of their arrival that summer in the little villa, mourning each event as it followed on the other.

"Then, just before going to bed last night," she said, "I noticed something was unusual."

The plumber cast down a folded square of sack-cloth on the brimming floor and laid his leather apron on it. Then he stepped boldly onto the heart of the island it shaped and looked long into the overflowing bowl.

"The water should be stopped from the meter in the garden," he said at last.

"Oh, I did that," said Mrs. Ames, "the very first thing last night. I turned it off at once, in my nightgown, as soon as I saw what was happening. But all this had already run in."

The plumber looked for a moment at her red kid slippers. She was standing just at the edge of the clear, pure-seeming tide.

"It's no doubt the soil lines," he said severely. "It may be that something has stopped them, but my opinion is that the water seals aren't working. That's the trouble often enough in such cases. If you had a valve you wouldn't be caught like this."

Mrs. Ames did not know how to meet this rebuke. She stood, swaying a little, looking into the plumber's blue relentless eye.

"I'm sorry—I'm sorry that my husband," she said, "is still resting and cannot go into this with you. I'm sure it must be very interesting. . . ."

"You'll probably have to have the traps sealed," said the plumber grimly, and at the sound of this Mrs. Ames' hand flew in dismay to the side of her face. The plumber made no move, but the set of his mouth as he looked at her seemed to soften. "Anyway, I'll have a look from the garden end," he said.

"Oh, do," said the astronomer's wife in relief. Here was a man who spoke of action and object as simply as women did! But however hushed her voice had been, it carried clearly to Professor Ames who lay, dreaming and solitary, upon his bed. He heard their footsteps come down the hall, pause, and skip across the pool of overflow.

"Katherine!" said the astronomer in a ringing tone. "There's a problem worthy of your mettle!"

Mrs. Ames did not turn her head, but led the plumber swiftly down the stairs. When the sun in the garden struck her face, he saw there was a wave of color in it, but this may have been anything but shame.

"You see how it is," said the plumber, as if leading her mind away. "The drains run from these houses right down the hill, big enough for a man to stand upright in them, and clean as a whistle, too." There they stood in the garden with the vegetation flowering in disorder all about. The plumber looked at the astronomer's wife. "They come out at the torrent on the other side of the forest beyond there," he said.

But the words the astronomer had spoken still sounded in her in despair. The mind of man, she knew, made steep and sprightly flights, pursued illusion, took foothold in the nameless things that cannot pass between the thumb and finger. But whenever the astronomer gave voice to the thoughts that soared within him, she returned in gratitude to the long expanses of his silence. Desert-like they stretched behind and before the articulation of his scorn.

Life, life is an open sea, she sought to explain it in sorrow, and to survive women cling to the floating debris on the tide. But the plumber had suddenly fallen upon his knees in the grass and had crooked his fingers through the ring of the drains' trap-door. When she looked down she saw that he was looking up into her face, and she saw too that his hair was as light as gold.

"Perhaps Mr. Ames," he said rather bitterly, "would like to come down with me and have a look around?"

"Down?" said Mrs. Ames in wonder.

"Into the drains," said the plumber brutally. "They're a study for a man who likes to know what's what."

"Oh, Mr. Ames," said Mrs. Ames in confusion. "He's still— still in bed, you see."

The plumber lifted his strong, weathered face and looked curiously at her. Surely it seemed to him strange for a man to linger in bed, with the sun pouring yellow as wine all over the place. The astronomer's wife saw his lean cheeks, his high, rugged bones, and the deep seams in his brow. His flesh was as firm and clean as wood, stained richly tan with the climate's rigor. His fingers were blunt, but comprehensible to her, gripped in the ring and holding the iron door wide. The backs of his hands were bound round and round with ripe blue veins of blood.

"At any rate," said the astronomer's wife, and the thought of it moved her lips to smile a little, "Mr. Ames would never go down there alive. He likes going up," she said. And she, in her turn, pointed, but impudently, towards the heavens. "On the roof. Or on the mountains. He's been up on the top of them many times."

"It's a matter of habit," said the plumber, and suddenly he went down the trap. Mrs. Ames saw a bright little piece of his hair still shining, like a star, long after the rest of him had gone. Out of the depths, his voice, hollow and dark with foreboding, returned to her. "I think something has stopped the elbow," was what he said.

This was speech that touched her flesh and bone and made her wonder. When her husband spoke of height, having no sense of it, she could not picture it nor hear. Depth or magic passed her by unless a name were given. But madness in a daily shape, as elbow stopped, she saw clearly and well. She sat down on the grasses, bewildered that it should be a man who had spoken to her so.

She saw the weeds springing up, and she did not move to tear them up from life. She sat powerless, her sense veiled, with no action taking shape beneath her hands. In this way some men sat for hours on end, she knew, tracking a single thought back to its origin. The mind of man could balance and divide, weed out, destroy. She sat on the full, burdened grasses, seeking to think, and dimly waiting for the plumber to return.

Whereas her husband had always gone up, as the dead go, she knew now that there were others who went down, like the corporeal being of the dead. That men were then divided into two bodies now seemed clear to Mrs. Ames. This knowledge stunned her with its simplicity and took the uneasy motion from her limbs. She could not stir, but sat facing the mountains' rocky flanks, and harking in silence to lucidity. Her husband was the mind, this other man the meat, of all mankind.

After a little, the plumber emerged from the earth: first the light top of his head, then the burnt brow, and then the blue eyes fringed with whitest lash. He braced his thick hands flat on the pavings of the garden-path and swung himself completely from the pit.

"It's the soil lines," he said pleasantly. "The gases," he said as he looked down upon her lifted face, "are backing up the drains."

"What in the world are we going to do?" said the astronomer's wife softly. There was a young and strange delight in putting questions to which true answers would be given. Everything the astronomer had ever said to her was a continuous query to which there could be no response.

"Ah, come, now," said the plumber, looking down and smiling. "There's a remedy for every ill, you know. Sometimes it may be that," he said as if speaking to a child, "or sometimes the other thing. But there's always a help for everything amiss."

Things come out of herbs and make you young again, he might have been saying to her; or the first good rain will quench any drought; or time of itself will put a broken bone together.

"I'm going to follow the ground pipe out right to the torrent," the plumber was saying. "The trouble's between here and there and I'll find it on the way. There's nothing at all that can't be done over for the caring," he was saying, and his eyes were fastened on her face in insolence, or gentleness, or love.

The astronomer's wife stood up, fixed a pin in her hair, and turned around towards the kitchen. Even while she was calling the servant's name, the plumber began speaking again.

"I once had a cow that lost her cud," the plumber was saying. The girl came out on the kitchen-step and Mrs. Ames stood smiling at her in the sun.

"The trouble is very serious, very serious," she said across the garden. "When Mr. Ames gets up, please tell him I've gone down."

She pointed briefly to the open door in the pathway, and the plumber hoisted his kit on his arm and put out his hand to help her down.

"But I made her another in no time," he was saying, "out of flowers and things and what not."

"Oh," said the astronomer's wife in wonder as she stepped into the heart of the earth. She took his arm, knowing that what he said was true.

CARLYLE TRIES POLYGAMY
William Melvin Kelley

For a while anyway an Africamerican man named Carlyle Bedlow lived in one large, sunny room in a brownstone on lower Edgecombe Avenue in Harlem, U.S.A. Like many men he had a polygamous nature, which did not make his promiscuous. And neither had he married. But over the years he usually seemed to have two or three steady lady friends.

Often they overlapped, and sometimes they repeated. First he would have one woman, for example Glora Glamus. Then he would meet another one, like Senegale Miller. Then he would shuttle back and forth between the two. On the way he might meet a third. Then he would shuttle around among the three, traveling from the Bronx to Manhattan to Brooklyn. Then the first woman would get tired of his intermittency and break it off. Then he would meet another woman shuttling back and forth between the second two. Occasionally he would disappear to his room in Harlem, where he lived alone and never let anyone visit except his brother and his widowed mother, who rarely came because she did not like climbing the three flights of steps to his room.

Carlyle Bedlow kept his room neat and clean. Since he never entertained any women there, he had a firm narrow bed, which he made up into a couch each morning. His clothes he kept in a large closet and three black footlockers. A high-grade Navajo rug (handmade by the Etcitty sisters) covered the polished-wood floor. In the corner near the window sat an EzeeGuy chair, where by sunlight or lamp he would relax and read science-fiction novels, a pile of which he stacked beside the chair.

Sometimes he would look up from his reading and think about the two more or less steady lady friends he had kept for the past ten years. Actually Glora had occupied a place in his heart for about thirty years. In the beginning he loved her madly but could not win her because she loved Carlyle's mentor in the hustling life, the society baker and contract killer C. C. (Cooley) Johnson. Eventually, when she realized that Cooley Johnson would never love anybody, she and Carlyle began a relationship that produced a daughter, Carlotta, now twelve years old. Carlyle and Glora had broken it off fifty times, but had made up fifty-one times. Besides, they both adored Carlotta. So did Carlyle's mother, though she did not like professional barmaid Glora, considering her barky and brassy and boastful.

The second lady friend in Carlyle's life had a child for him as well, an eight-year-old daughter named Mali. He had met Mali's mama, Senegale Miller, at a jump-up given by the Rastafarian bredda who supplied high-quality society clientele, affluent former Woodstockians who had returned to the lap of luxury but secretly still smoked the blessed herb and did not want the world to know it.

Senegale Miller possessed luxuriant glistening black dread locks reaching to the small of her back which had never known scissors or comb. Raised in the cockpit country of Arawaka and descended from Maroons (who fought their way out of slavery in the seventeen-thirties), she had not worn shoes until coming to America. She stood six feet tall in her smooth cocoa-buttered chocolate-colored skin and had the grace of a seal in water. Carlyle's mother did not like Senegale either, mostly because she could not understand her thick accent, but, as she did with Carlotta, she showered Mali with gifts.

Carlotta and Mali got along very well, better than most big and little sisters. Sometimes Carlyle borrowed his brother's RoadStar sedan and without telling their mothers took the two girls anywhere they wanted to go, the beach or zoo or circus or rodeo or amusement park. He walked behind them, an unobtrusive shepherd, enjoying the sight of them whispering, cavorting, holding hands.

Recently their mothers had become jealous of each other. They had known of each other for the past three years, when Senegale had tracked him down to Glora's house in the Bronx, demanding money for Mali's school uniforms. Before that, he had kept them separated in different parts of the city, Senegale in Brooklyn and Glora in the Bronx. Once they learned about each other, they did not stop talking and asking about each other.

In the Bronx, Glora might inquire, "When you getting your monkey woman to cut off that bush of hair and get a regular look, baby?"

In Brooklyn, Senegale would comment, "Is only a foolfool woulda make him babymudda to work into said wicked atmosphere, man no see it."

In the Bronx, Glora might wonder, "Why you don't go to court for custody of that cute little Mali, then report that bitch to immigration?"

In Brooklyn, Senegale would ponder, "Why you must keep on with the old woman when you kyan find rest and fulfillment in I-arm of this daughter of King Solomon?"

At times the verbal struggle they waged in his ears became so intense that Carlyle would retreat to his sunny Harlem room and rest in his EzeeGuy until his ears repaired themselves. He would not see either woman for a week. His brother, who knew something of his dilemma, told him that the blessed Koran gave a man permission to maintain four women, which did not help. Carlyle could barely manage two.

"Then you must cut one loose, my brother. Keep the relationship with your offspring, but call it off with one of the mothers." His brother had decided to wait till the Provider sent him a woman, abstaining from sex for several years, though Carlyle suspected he had a woman stashed somewhere. "You must choose!"

But Carlyle loved both women, Glora for her mocha beauty and her fast mouth, Senegal for her chocolate beauty and her independent spirit, and could not choose between them. Reclining in his EzeeGuy, he would puff a spliff and try to envision life without one or the other of them. He had always loved Glora; Senegale had stomped into his life with her goofy believe in the divinity of Ethiopia just when he started to get sour, making him aware of some motivating force in the world besides money. Until Senegale came along he had not known how much he loved Glora, because falling in love with Senegale reminded him that he had love inside himself to give. So suddenly he also found himself in love with Glora again.

*   *   *

Carlyle could not decide between them. But something had to change. Then one day he encountered Brother Ben selling juice and astrology books at the corner of 125th Street and Frederick Douglass, and the brother launched into his tired polygamy rap, which goes: Vietnam + Homosexuality + Prison + Heroin + AIDS + Crack had so reduced the male Africamerican population as to make polygamy the only way for Africamerican culture to sustain itself. Each man had to accept his responsibility. Each woman had to realize that only by accepting the other woman in her man's life could she get a man to call her own. Then of course once a man had gathered his women together he might organize them to make dried-flower arrangements or some such product—

"But Brother Ben," Carlyle interrupted. "You have a nuclear family under your own roof, a wife you've loved for years and two beautiful daughters like mine. And besides, no other woman would have you!"

Brother Ben blinked but continued his rap undeterred as Carlyle ambled away. But Brother Ben had made one usable point: perhaps Carlyle should bring together his two warring lady friends for a sitdown. Given them the opportunity to say bad things to each other face to face without making Carlyle's brain the battleground. Perhaps they could work out what he could not. At least they might blow off some bad gas.

Carlyle arranged to have both meet him on a Tuesday evening at one of Harlem's few surviving gems, the Golden Grouse Bar & Restaurant. He liked breakfast better than dinner at the Grouse but did not expect anybody to eat very much. However, red-clad Glora tipped in first and quick ordered an immense fried-chicken dinner with scalloped potatoes and tossed salad and peach cobbler and the Grouse's special punch. Before the food had arrived, Senegale appeared in olive drab, her dreadlocks wrapped (out and back like a praying mantis) in the Nationalists colors. She carried various tubs of her own I-tall delicacies because she did not trust the cook at the Grouse to keep the bacon grease out of the peanut oil.

The two women sat silently glaring across the table at each other and consumed all that the waitress and Senegal had carried to the table, near the end of the thirty-minute meal Senegale sampling the peach cobbler and Glora quenching her thirst with the home-made ginger beer. Together they covered their belches and tittered.

Then they both put fire under his sorry brown butt! "Thought the sight of this simple country cow pie would do what? But make I tell all the world that I-woman never fear no old higgler till yet, no see it! Sure don't see what jive hustle he think he pulling with this tired B.S. but this sister came a long way to tell e'vrybody that this just won't hardly go down! Because I-love that I-woman keeping for said man spring from the most high mountain of New Zion! Besides this brother have deluded himself into thinking that because I love him that mean I need him when he be too dim to see I got my own house on Barnes Avenue in the Bronx all bought and paid for with mops and tips, and also got by far the best of his never-do-nothing buttocks in his daughter Carlotta. Which I-sister kyan strenuously affirm and illustrate as him give I-woman noth-ing of value but sweet likkle Mali, and she quite valu-able." They glowered at him.

So now what, bumbasukka?

"I just wanted to see if we all couldn't maybe find a way to get along," Carlyle said simple. "I can't help myself but I love you both. And I been mainly true to you two for the past ten years." He heard and despised the quite desperation in his voice. "I mean, the kids don't seem to defend each other."

The women agreed. Dem two pickney hitch up like sea and sand, no see it. Looking so cute and fly in they little matching out-fits, hooking it up on the phone when this fool think he sneaking them out on the sly to take them someplace like my child don't come tell her mama ev'ry ting that be goin' on, turkey! All the while dem aburn up phone wire, no see it, talkin' bout my sister dis and my sister dat, Carlotta why and Carlotta what for. And many times Carlotta have said, "Mama, why can't Mali spend the night?" Well they could certainly agree to arrange that. Senegal expressed her gratitude that Mali would spend time on safer Bronx streets than those in the part of Brooklyn in which she presently resided where posses marauded in broad daylight and as soon as she found suitable accommodations, perhaps with members of her extended family in New Jersey, she would willingly offer similar hospitality to Carlotta. Strangely enough, Glora's aforementioned two-family semi-detached featured a smaller second-floor space, which she had recently listed with Sister Edward's Realty, seeking tenants, five hundred dollars a month for two-bedrooms-kitchen living-room-bath, use of washer-dryer, easy walking distance to the I.R.T.—but Senegale knew the way because she had already visited there at least once. They shook on it, bracelets and bangles jangling.

On the first of the following month, two jaunty I-dren driving a yellow van, puffing spliffs and blasting St. Donald Drummond and the Skatalites on their trunk-size cassette player, delivered Senegal and Mali Miller, along with two mahogany beds, a sofa and an overstuffed chair, a dish cabinet, a kitchen table and chairs, large cartons of clothes, books, utensils, dishes and pots, a cast-iron Dutchie, tools, raffia, leather hides for belts and sandals, and one calico puss cat named Kiki, to chez Glora Glamus, Bronx, N.Y. Soon the house filled with incessant female activity. Carlotta and Mali and their girlfriends (neighborhood pre-teens quickly forming a crew) seemed to make no distinction upstairs and downstairs, roaming freely throughout every room under the roof, as likely to sleep in one as in the other of their two bedrooms, eating wherever hunger and opportunity struck them, though both avoided Glora's rhubarb pie as well as Senegale's steamed okra. And the two women began to take the step-aerobics class and do weights at the local NUBODi exercise salon on White Plains Road, working off their stress and excess energy with the rest of the sisters. Around the corner on Paulding Avenue, Carlyle's mother loved living near to both of her two darlings, though she still barely tolerated their mothers.

After completing his hustling chores, Carlyle Bedlow spends more time in his one large room in the brownstone on lower Edgecombe Avenue, Harlem, U.S.A. Since he no longer travels to Brooklyn except on business to the Promenade or Park Slope, and can visit his two daughters at one address, he gets to see them both more often than in the days before polygamy, a definite improvement in his life. But now that his two lady friends live within whispering distance of each other Carlyle finds his sexual style stunted. Whenever he hopes to bed down with one woman, he knows the other woman knows his exact whereabouts and keeps expecting one or the other of the kids to burst through the door. Occasionally he gets over. But more often than not cool winds sweep his loins. The women load him with lists of things to do and buy. He completes his errands for them, then returns to the solitude and quiet of his room. His brother visits, assuring him that Carlyle has done the honest, manly thing, brought out everything into the open, creating a healthier environment for his children, that with each woman knowing where she fits into the Grand Scheme, they will all live happily ever after. For a while anyway.

DÉSIRÉE'S BABY
Kate Chopin

An author intentionally creates characters and a conflict, chooses a particular point of view and setting, and carefully selects the story's language in order to control the reader's attitude and give a story its specific tone.

The following example, a story about a couple living in the 1800's, makes a clear statement about the bigotry of that time and, perhaps, our own. The discussion of the plot in Chapter Three explains how this story uses the flashback technique to set up the circumstances that are critical to the surprise ending. A slow, careful reading of the first six paragraphs yields clues to that ending. Each item is important and has an impact on the development of the central idea.

Because the story is set in Louisiana, the French influence is evident. Words like "corbielle" and "cochon de lait" and expressions like "mais si" not only locate the story, but also help establish the tone. ("Corbielle" are wedding presents; "cochon de lait" translates literally as "suckling pig," but is used affectionately here; "mais si" literally means "but, yes" but is better translated as "of course.") Chopin's diction, though more than one hundred years old, helps to establish the social class of the characters. As you read, look at how the language establishes a close relationship between the setting and the tone. Polite expressions contrast significantly with the harsh nature of the content of the remarks and that also contributes to the tone. One element may be emphasized more than the others. That emphasis affects the tone, as does the change in the tone, from the beginning to the end of the story. Notice how it reflects the change in character.

As the day was pleasant, Madame Valmondé drove over to L'Abri to see Désirée and the baby.

It made her laugh to think of Désirée with a baby. Why, it seemed but yesterday that Désirée was little more than a baby herself; when Monsieur in riding through the gateway of Valmondé had found her lying asleep in the shadow of the big stone pillar.

The little one awoke in his arms and began to cry for "Dada."

That was as much as she could do or say. Some people thought she might have strayed there of her own accord, for she was of the toddling age. The prevailing belief was that she had been purposely left by a party of Texans, whose canvas-covered wagon, late in the day, had crossed the ferry that Coton Maïs kept, just below the plantation. In time Madame Valmondé abandoned every speculation but the one that Désirée had been sent to her by a beneficent Providence to be the child of her affection, seeing that she was without child of the flesh. For the girl grew to be beautiful and gentle, affectionate and sincere,—the idol of Valmondé.

It was no wonder, when she stood one day against the stone pillar in whose shadow she had lain asleep, eighteen years before, that Armand Aubigny riding by and seeing her there, had fallen in love with her. That was the way all the Aubignys fell in love, as if struck by a pistol shot. The wonder was that he had not loved her before; for he had known her since his father brought him home from Paris, a boy of eight, after his mother died there. The passion that awoke in him that day, when he saw her at the gate, swept along like an avalanche, or like a prairie fire, or like anything that drives headlong over all obstacles.

Monsieur Valmondé grew practical and wanted things well considered; that is, the girl's obscure origin. Armand looked into her eyes and did not care. He was reminded that she was nameless. What did it matter about a name when he could give her one of the oldest and proudest in Louisiana? He ordered the corbeille from Paris, and contained himself with what patience he could until it arrived; then they were married.

Madame Valmondé had not seen Désirée and the baby for four weeks. When she reached L'Abri she shuddered at the first sight of it, as she always did. It was a sad looking place, which for many years had not known the gentle presence of a mistress, old Monsieur Aubigny having married and buried his wife in France, and she having loved her own land too well ever to leave it. The roof came down steep and black like a cowl, reaching out beyond the wide galleries that encircled the yellow stuccoed house. Big, solemn oaks grew close to it, and their thick-leaved, far-reaching branches shadowed it like a pall. Young Aubigny's rule was a strict one, too, and under it his negroes had forgotten how to be gay, as they had been during the old master's easy-going and indulgent lifetime.

The young mother was recovering slowly, and lay full length, in her soft white muslins and laces, upon a couch. The baby was beside her, upon her arm, where he had fallen asleep, at her breast. The yellow nurse woman sat beside a window fanning herself.

Madame Valmondé bent her portly figure over Désirée and kissed her, holding her an instant tenderly in her arms. Then she turned to the child.

"This is not the baby!" she exclaimed, in startled tones. French was the language spoken at Valmondé in those days.

"I knew you would be astonished," laughed Désirée, "at the way he has grown. The little cochon de lait! Look at his legs, mamma, and his hands and fingernails—real fingernails. Zandrine had to cut them this morning. Isn't it true, Zandrine?"

The woman bowed her turbaned head majestically, "Mais si, Madame."

"And the way he cries," went on Désirée, "is deafening. Armand heard him the other day as far away as La Blanche's cabin."

Madame Valmondé had never removed her eyes from the child. She lifted it and walked with it over to the window that was lightest. She scanned the baby narrowly, then looked as searchingly at Zandrine, whose face was turned to gaze across the fields.

"Yes, the child has grown, has changed," said Madame Valmondé, slowly, as she replaced it beside its mother. "What does Armand say?"

Désirée's face became suffused with a glow that was happiness itself.

"Oh, Armand is the proudest father in the parish, I believe, chiefly because it is a boy, to bear his name; though he says not,— that he would have loved a girl as well. But I know it isn't true. I know he says that to please me. And mamma," she added, drawing Madame Valmondé's head down to her and speaking in a whisper, "he hasn't punished one of them—not one of them—since baby is born. Even Négrillon, who pretended to have burnt his leg that he might rest from work—he only laughed, and said Négrillon was a great scamp. Oh, mamma, I'm so happy; it frightens me."

What Désirée said was true. Marriage, and later the birth of his son had softened Armand Aubigny's imperious and exacting nature greatly. This was what made the gentle Désirée so happy, for she loved him desperately. When he frowned she trembled, but loved him. When he smiled, she asked no greater blessing of God.

But Armand's dark, handsome face had not often been disfigured by frowns since the day he fell in love with her.

When the baby was about three months old, Désirée awoke one day to the conviction that there was something in the air menacing her peace. It was at first too subtle to grasp. It had only been a disquieting suggestion; an air of mystery among the blacks; unexpected visits from far-off neighbors who could hardly account for their coming. Then a strange, an awful change in her husband's manner, which she dared not ask him to explain. When he spoke to her, it was with averted eyes, from which the old love-light seemed to have gone out. He absented himself from home; and when there, avoided her presence and that of her child, without excuse. And the very spirit of Satan seemed suddenly to take hold of him in his dealings with the slaves. Désirée was miserable enough to die.

She sat in her room, one hot afternoon, in her peignoir, listlessly drawing through her fingers the strands of her long, silky brown hair that hung about her shoulders. The baby, half naked, lay asleep upon her own great mahogany bed, that was like a sumptuous throne, with its satin-lined half-canopy. One of La Blanche's little quadroon boys—half naked too—stood fanning the child slowly with a fan of peacock feathers. Désirée's eyes had been fixed absently and sadly upon the baby, while she was striving to penetrate the threatening mist that she felt closing about her. She looked from her child to the boy who stood beside him, and back again; over and over. "Ah!" It was a cry that she could not help; which she was not conscious of having uttered. The blood turned like ice in her veins, and a clammy moisture gathered upon her face.

She tried to speak to the little quadroon boy; but no sound would come, at first. When he heard his name uttered, he looked up, and his mistress was pointing to the door. He laid aside the great, soft fan, and obediently stole away, over the polished floor, on his bare tiptoes.

She stayed motionless, with gaze riveted upon her child, and her face the picture of fright.

Presently her husband entered the room, and without noticing her, went to a table and began to search among some papers which covered it.

"Armand," she called to him, in a voice which must have stabbed him, if he was human. But he did not notice. "Armand," she said again. Then she rose and tottered towards him. "Armand," she panted once more, clutching his arm, "look at our child. What does it mean? Tell me."

He coldly but gently loosened her fingers from about his arm and thrust the hand away from him. "Tell me what it means!" she cried despairingly.

"It means," he answered lightly, "that the child is not white; it means that you are not white."

A quick conception of all that this accusation meant for her nerved her with unwonted courage to deny it. "It is a lie; it is not true, I am white! Look at my hair, it is brown; and my eyes are gray, Armand, you know they are gray. And my skin is fair," seizing his wrist. "Look at my hand; whiter than yours, Armand," she laughed hysterically.

"As white as La Blanche's," he returned cruelly; and went away leaving her alone with their child.

When she could hold a pen in her hand, she sent a despairing letter to Madame Valmondé.

"My mother, they tell me I am not white. Armand has told me I am not white. For God's sake tell them it is not true. You must know it is not true. I shall die. I must die. I cannot be so unhappy, and live."

The answer that came was as brief:

"My own Désirée: Come home to Valmondé; back to your mother who loves you. Come with your child."

When the letter reached Désirée she went with it to her husband's study, and laid it open upon the desk before which he sat. She was like a stone image: silent, white, motionless after she placed it there.

In silence he ran his cold eyes over the written words. He said nothing.

"Shall I go, Armand?" she asked in tones sharp with agonized suspense.

"Yes, go."

"Do you want me to go?"

"Yes. I want you to go."

He thought Almighty God had dealt cruelly and unjustly with him; and felt, somehow, that he was paying Him back in kind when he stabbed thus into his wife's soul. Moreover he no longer loved her, because of the unconscious injury she had brought upon his home and his name.

She turned away like one stunned by a blow, and walked slowly towards the door, hoping he would call her back.

"Good-by, Armand," she moaned.

He did not answer her. That was his last blow at fate.

Désirée went in search of her child. Zandrine was pacing the sombre gallery with it. She took the little one from the nurse's arms with no word of explanation, and descending the steps, walked away, under the live-oak branches.

It was an October afternoon; the sun was just sinking. Out in the still fields the negroes were picking cotton.

Désirée had not changed the thin white garment nor the slippers which she wore. Her hair was uncovered and the sun's rays brought a golden gleam from its brown meshes. She did not take the broad, beaten road which led to the far-off plantation of Valmondé. She walked across a deserted field, where the stubble bruised her tender feet, so delicately shod, and tore her thin gown to shreds. She disappeared among the reeds and willows that grew thick along the banks of the deep, sluggish bayou; and she did not come back again.

Some weeks later there was a curious scene enacted at L'Abri. In the centre of the smoothly swept back yard was a great bonfire. Armand Aubigny sat in the wide hallway that commanded a view of the spectacle; and it was he who dealt out to a half dozen negroes the material which kept this fire ablaze.

A graceful cradle of willow, with all its dainty furnishings, was laid upon the pyre, which had already been fed with the richness of a priceless layette. Then there were silk gowns, and velvet and satin ones added to these; laces, too, and embroideries; bonnets and gloves; for the corbeille had been of rare quality.

The last thing to go was a tiny bundle of letters; innocent little scribblings that Désirée had sent to him during the days of their espousal. There was the remnant of one back in the drawer from which he took them. But it was not Désirée's; it was part of an old letter from his mother to his father. He read it. She was thanking God for the blessing of her husband's love:—

"But, above all," she wrote, "night and day, I thank the good God for having so arranged our lives that our dear Armand will never know that his mother, who adores him, belongs to the race that is cursed with the brand of slavery."

HAIRCUT
Ring Lardner

I got another barber that comes over from Carterville and helps me out Saturdays, but the rest of the time I can get along all right alone. You can see for yourself that this ain't no New York City and besides that, the most of the boys works all day and don't have no leisure to drop in here and get themselves prettied up.

You're a newcomer, ain't you? I thought I hadn't seen you round before. I hope you like it good enough to stay. As I say, we ain't no New York City or Chicago, but we have pretty good times. Not as good, though, since Jim Kendall got killed. When he was alive, him and Hod Meyers used to keep this town in an uproar. I bet they was more laughin' done here than any town its size in America.

Jim was comical, and Hod was pretty near a match for him. Since Jim's gone, Hod tries to hold his end up just the same as ever, but it's tough goin' when you ain't got nobody to kind of work with.

They used to be plenty fun in here Saturdays. This place is jampacked Saturdays, from four o'clock on. Jim and Hod would show up right after their supper round six o'clock. Jim would set himself down in that big chair, nearest the blue spittoon. Whoever had been settin' in that chair, why they'd get up when Jim come in and give it to him.

You'd of thought it was a reserved seat like they have sometimes in a theaytre. Hod would generally always stand or walk up and down or some Saturdays, of course, he'd be settin' in this chair part of the time, gettin' a haircut.

Well, Jim would set there a w'ile without opening his mouth only to spit, and then finally he'd say to me, "Whitey,"—my right name, that is, my right first name, is Dick, but everybody round here calls me Whitey—Jim would say, "Whitey, your nose looks like a rosebud tonight. You must of been drinkin' some of your aw de cologne."

So I'd say, "No, Jim, but you look like you'd been drinkin' something of that kind or somethin' worse."

Jim would have to laugh at that, but then he'd speak up and say, "No, I ain't had nothin' to drink, but that ain't sayin' I wouldn't like somethin'. I wouldn't even mind if it was wood alcohol."

Then Hod Meyers would say, "Neither would your wife." That would set everybody to laughin' because Jim and his wife wasn't on very good terms. She'd of divorced him only they wasn't no chance to get alimony and she didn't have no way to take care of herself and the kids. She couldn't never understand Jim. He was kind of rough, but a good fella at heart.

Him and Hod had all kinds of sport with Milt Sheppard. I don't suppose you've seen Milt. Well, he's got an Adam's apple that looks more like a mush-melon. So I'd be shavin' Milt and when I'd start to shave down here on his neck, Hod would holler, "Hey, Whitey, wait a minute! Before you cut into it, let's make up a pool and see who can guess closest to the number of seeds."

And Jim would say, "If Milt hadn't of been so hoggish, he'd of ordered a half a cantaloupe instead of a whole one and it might not of stuck in his throat."

All the boys would roar at this and Milt himself would force a smile, though the joke was on him. Jim certainly was a card!

There's his shavin' mug, setting on the shelf, right next to Charley Vail's. "Charles M. Vail." That's the druggist. He comes in regular for his shave, three times a week. And Jim's is the cup next to Charley's. "James H. Kendall." Jim won't need no shavin' mug no more, but I'll leave it there just the same for old time's sake. Jim certainly was a character!

Years ago, Jim used to travel for a canned goods concern over in Carterville. They sold canned goods. Jim had the whole northern half of the State and was on the road five days out of every week. He'd drop in here Saturdays and tell his experiences for that week. It was rich.

I guess he paid more attention to playin' jokes than makin' sales. Finally the concern let him out and he come right home here and told everybody he'd been fired instead of sayin' he'd resigned like most fellas would of.

It was a Saturday and the shop was full and Jim got up out of that chair and says, "Gentlemen, I got an important announcement to make. I been fired from my job."

Well, they asked him if he was in earnest and he said he was and nobody could think of nothin' to say till Jim finally broke the ice himself. He says, "I been sellin' canned goods and now I'm canned goods myself."

You see, the concern he'd been workin' for was a factory that made canned goods. Over in Carterville. And now Jim said he was canned himself. He was certainly a card!

Jim had a great trick that he used to play w'ile he was travelin'. For instance, he'd be ridin' on a train and they'd come to some little town like, well, like, well, like, we'll say, like Benton. Jim would look out the train window and read the signs of the stores.

For instance, they'd be a sign, "Henry Smith, Dry Goods." Well, Jim would write down the name and the name of the town and when he got to wherever he was goin' he'd mail back a postal card to Henry Smith at Benton and not sign no name to it, but he'd write on the card, well somethin' like "Ask your wife about that book agent that spent the afternoon last week," or "Ask your Missus who kept her from gettin' lonesome the last time you was in Carterville." And he'd sign the card, "A Friend."

Of course, he never knew what really come of none of these jokes, but he could picture what probably happened and that was enough.

Jim didn't work very steady after he lost his position with the Carterville people. What he did earn, coin' odd jobs round town why he spent pretty near all of it on gin, and his family might of starved if the stores hadn't of carried them along. Jim's wife tried her hand at dressmakin', but they ain't nobody goin' to get rich makin' dresses in this town.

As I say, she'd of divorced Jim, only she seen that she couldn't support herself and the kids and she was always hopin' that some day Jim would cut out his habits and give her more than two or three dollars a week.

They was a time when she would go to whoever he was workin' for and ask them to give her his wages, but after she done this
once or twice, he beat her to it by borrowin' most of his pay in advance. He told it all round town, how he had outfoxed his Missus.
He certainly was a caution!

But he wasn't satisfied with just outwittin' her. He was sore the
way she had acted, tryin' to grab off his pay. And he made up his
mind he'd get even. Well, he waited till Evans's Circus was adver-
tised to come to town. Then he told his wife and two kiddies that
he was goin' to take them to the circus. The day of the circus, he
told them he would get the tickets and meet them outside the entrance to the tent.

Well, he didn't have no intentions of bein' there or buyin' tickets or nothin'. He got full of gin and laid round Wright's poolroom
all day. His wife and the kids waited and waited and of course he
didn't show up. His wife didn't have a dime with her, or nowhere
else, I guess. So she finally had to tell the kids it was all off and
they cried like they wasn't never goin' to stop.

Well, it seems, w'ile they was cryin', Doc Stair come along
and he asked what was the matter, but Mrs. Kendall was stubborn
and wouldn't tell him, but the kids told him and he insisted on ta-
kin' them and their mother in the show. Jim found this out afterwards and it was one reason why he had it in for Doc Stair.

Doc Stair come here about a year and a half ago. He's a mighty
handsome young fella and his clothes always look like he has them
made to order. He goes to Detroit two or three times a year and
w'ile he's there must have a tailor take his measure and then make
him a suit to order. They cost pretty near twice as much, but they
fit a whole lot better than if you just bought them in a store.

For a w'ile everybody was wonderin' why a young doctor like
Doc Stair should come to a town like this where we already got old
Doc Gamble and Doc Foote that's both been here for years and all
the practice in town was always divided between the two of them.

Then they was a story got round that Doc Stair's gal had
thronged him over, a gal up in the Northern Peninsula somewhere,
and the reason he come here was to hide himself away and forget
it. He said himself that he thought they wasn't nothin' like general
practice in a place like ours to fit a man to be a good all round doctor. And that's why he'd came.

Anyways, it wasn't long before he was makin' enough to live on, though they tell me that he never dunned nobody for what they owed him, and the folks here certainly has got the owin' habit, even in my business. If I had all that was comin' to me for just shaves alone, I could go to Carterville and put up at the Mercer for a week and see a different picture every night. For instance, they's old George Purdy—but I guess I shouldn't ought to be gossipin'.

Well, last year, our coroner died, died of the flu. Ken Beatty, that was his name. He was the coroner. So they had to choose another man to be coroner in his place and they picked Doc Stair. He laughed at first and said he didn't want it, but they made him take it. It ain't no job that anybody would fight for and what a man makes out of it in a year would just about buy seeds for their garden. Doc's the kind, though, that can't say no to nothin' if you keep at him long enough.

But I was goin' to tell you about a poor boy we got here in town—Paul Dickson. He fell out of a tree when he was about ten years old. Lit on his head and it done somethin' to him and he ain't never been right. No harm in him, but just silly. Jim Kendall used to call him cuckoo; that's a name Jim had for anybody that was off their head, only he called people's head their bean. That was another of his gags, callin' head bean and callin' crazy people cuckoo. Only poor Paul ain't crazy, but just silly.

You can imagine that Jim used to have all kinds of fun with Paul. He'd send him to the White Front Garage for a left-handed monkey wrench. Of course they ain't no such thing as a left-handed monkey wrench.

And once we had a kind of a fair here and they was a baseball game between the fats and the leans and before the game started Jim called Paul over and sent him way down to Schrader's hardware store to get a key for the pitcher's box.

They wasn't nothin' in the way of gags that Jim couldn't think up, when he put his mind to it.

Poor Paul was always kind of suspicious of people, maybe on account of how Jim had kept foolin' him. Paul wouldn't have much to do with anybody only his own mother and Doc Stair and a girl here in town named Julie Gregg. That is, she ain't a girl no more, but pretty near thirty or over.

When Doc first come to town, Paul seemed to feel like here was a real friend and he hung round Doc's office most of the w'ile;

the only time he wasn't there was when he'd go home to eat or sleep or when he seen Julie Gregg coin' her shoppin'.

When he looked out Doc's window and seen her, he'd run downstairs and join her and tag along with her to the different stores. The poor boy was crazy about Julie and she always treated him mighty nice and made him feel like he was welcome, though of course it wasn't nothin' but pity on her side.

Doc done all he could to improve Paul's mind and he told me once that he really thought the boy was getting better, that they was times when he was as bright and sensible as anybody else.

But I was goin' to tell you about Julie Gregg. Old man Gregg was in the lumber business, but got to drinkin' and lost the most of his money and when he died, he didn't leave nothin' but the house and just enough insurance for the girl to skimp along on.

Her mother was a kind of a half invalid and didn't hardly ever leave the house. Julie wanted to sell the place and move somewhere else after the old man died, but the mother said she was born here and would die here. It was tough on Julie as the young people round this town—well, she's too good for them.

She'd been away to school and Chicago and New York and different places and they ain't no subject she can't talk on, where you take the rest of the young folks here and you mention anything to them outside of Gloria Swanson or Tommy Meighan and they think you're delirious. Did you see Gloria in Wages of Virtue? You missed somethin'!

Well, Doc Stair hadn't been here more than a week when he came in one day to get shaved and I recognized who he was, as he had been pointed out to me, so I told him about my old lady. She's been ailin' for a couple years and either Doc Gamble or Doc Foote, neither one, seemed to be helpin' her. So he said he would come out and see her, but if she was able to get out herself, it would be better to bring her to his office where he could make a completer examination.

So I took her to his office and w'ile I was waitin' for her in the reception room, in come Julie Gregg. When somebody comes in Doc Stair's office, they's a bell that rings in his inside office so he can tell they's somebody to see him.

So he left my old lady inside and come out to the front office and that's the first time him and Julie met and I guess it was what they call love at first sight. But it wasn't fifty-fifty. This young fella was the slickest lookin' fella she'd ever seen in this town and she went wild over him. To him she was just a young lady that wanted to see the doctor.

She'd came on about the same business I had. Her mother had been doctorin' for years with Doc Gamble and Doc Foote and without no results. So she'd heard they was a new doc in town and decided to give him a try. He promised to call and see her mother that same day.

I said a minute ago that it was love at first sight on her part. I'm not only judgin' by how she acted afterwards but how she looked at him that first day in his office. I ain't no mind reader, but it was wrote all over her face that she was gone.

Now Jim Kendall, besides bein' a jokesmith and a pretty good drinker, well Jim was quite a lady-killer. I guess he run pretty wild durin' the time he was on the road for them Carterville people, and besides that, he'd had a couple little affairs of the heart right here in town. As I say, his wife would have divorced him, only she couldn't.

But Jim was like the majority of men, and women, too, I guess. He wanted what he couldn't get. He wanted Julie Gregg and worked his head off tryin' to land her. Only he'd of said bean instead of head.

Well, Jim's habits and his jokes didn't appeal to Julie and of course he was a married man, so he didn't have no more chance than, well, than a rabbit. That's an expression of Jim's himself. When somebody didn't have no chance to get elected or some-thin', Jim would always say they didn't have no more chance than a rabbit.

He didn't make no bones about how he felt. Right in here, more than once, in front of the whole crowd, he said he was stuck on Julie and anybody that could get her for him was welcome to his house and his wife and kids included. But she wouldn't have nothin' to do with him; wouldn't even speak to him on the street. He finally seen he wasn't gettin' nowheres with his usual line so he decided to try the rough stuff. He went right up to her house one evenin' and when she opened the door he forced his way in and grabbed her. But she broke loose and before he could stop her, she run in the next room and locked the door and phoned to Joe

Barnes. Joe's the marshal. Jim could hear who she was phonin' to and he beat it before Joe got there.

Joe was an old friend of Julie's pa. Joe went to Jim the next day and told him what would happen if he ever done it again.

I don't know how the news of this little affair leaked out. Chances is that Joe Barnes told his wife and she told somebody else's wife and they told their husband. Anyways, it did leak out and Hod Meyers had the nerve to kid Jim about it, right here in this shop. Jim didn't deny nothin' and kind of laughed it off and said for us all to wait; that lots of people had tried to make a monkey out of him, but he always got even.

Meanw'ile everybody in town was wise to Julie's bein' wild mad over the Doc. I don't suppose she had any idea how her face changed when him and her was together; of course she couldn't of, or she'd of kept away from him. And she didn't know that we was all noticin' how many times she made excuses to go up to his office or pass it on the other side of the street and look up in his window to see if he was there. I felt sorry for her and so did most other people.

Hod Meyers kept rubbin' it into Jim about how the Doc had cut him out. Jim didn't pay no attention to the kiddie' and you could see he was plannin' one of his jokes.

One trick Jim had was the knack of changin' his voice. He could make you think he was a girl talkie' and he could mimic any man's voice. To show you how good he was along this line, I'll tell you the joke he played on me once.

You know, in most towns of any size, when a man is dead and needs a shave, why the barber that shaves him soaks him five dollars for the job; that is, he don't soak him, but whoever ordered the shave. I just charge three dollars because personally I don't mind much shavin' a dead person. They lay a whole lot stiller than live customers. The only thing is that you don't feel like talkie' to them and you get kind of lonesome.

Well, about the coldest day we ever had here, two years ago last winter, the phone rung at the house w'ile I was home to dinner and I answered the phone and it was a woman's voice and she said she was Mrs. John Scott and her husband was dead and would I come out and shave him.

Old John had always been a good customer of mine. But they live seven miles out in the country, on the Streeter road. Still I didn't see how I could say no.

So I said I would be there, but would have to come in a jitney and it might cost three or four dollars besides the price of the shave. So she, or the voice, it said that was all right, so I got Frank Abbott to drive me out to the place and when I got there, who should open the door but old John himself! He wasn't no more dead than, well, than a rabbit.

It didn't take no private detective to figure out who had played me this little joke. Nobody could of thought it up but Jim Kendall. He certainly was a card!

I tell you this incident just to show you how he could disguise his voice and make you believe it was somebody else talkie'. I'd of swore it was Mrs. Scott had called me. Anyways, some woman.

Well, Jim waited till he had Doc Stair's voice down pat; then he went after revenge.

He called Julie up on a night when he knew Doc was over in Carterville. She never questioned but what it was Doc's voice. Jim said he must see her that night; he couldn't wait no longer to tell her somethin'. She was all excited and told him to come to the house. But he said he was expectin' an important long distance call and wouldn't she please forget her manners for once and come to his office. He said they couldn't nothin' hurt her and nobody would see her and he just must talk to her a little w'ile. Well, poor Julie fell for it.

Doc always keeps a night light in his office, so it looked to Julie like they was somebody there.

Meanw'ile Jim Kendall had went to Wright's poolroom, where they was a whole gang amusin' themselves. The most of them had drank plenty of gin, and they was a rough bunch even when sober. They was always strong for Jim's jokes and when he told them to come with him and see some fun they give up their card games and pool games and followed along.

Doc's office is on the second floor. Right outside his door they's a flight of stairs leadin' to the floor above. Jim and his gang hid in the dark behind these stairs.

Well, Julie come up to Doc's door and rung the bell and they was nothin' coin'. She rung it again and she rung it seven or eight times. Then she tried the door and found it locked. Then Jim made some kind of a noise and she heard it and waited a minute, and then she says, "Is that you, Ralph?" Ralph is Doc's first name.

They was no answer and it must of came to her all of a sudden that she'd been bunked. She pretty near fell downstairs and the whole gang after her. They chased her all the way home, hollerin', "Is that you, Ralph?" and "Oh, Ralphie, dear, is that you?" Jim says he couldn't holler it himself, as he was laughin' too hard.

Poor Julie! She didn't show up here on Main Street for a long, long time afterward.

And of course Jim and his gang told everybody in town, everybody but Doc Stair. They was scared to tell him, and he might of never knowed only for Paul Dickson. The poor cuckoo, as Jim called him, he was here in the shop one night when Jim was still gloatin' yet over what he'd done to Julie. And Paul took in as much of it as he could understand and he run to Doc with the story.

It's a cinch Doc went up in the air and swore he'd make Jim suffer. But it was a kind of a delicate thing, because if it got out that he had beat Jim up, Julie was bound to hear of it and then she'd know that Doc knew and of course knowin' that he knew would make it worse for her than ever. He was goin' to do somethin', but it took a lot of figurin'.

Well, it was a couple days later when Jim was here in the shop again, and so was the cuckoo. Jim was goin' duck-shootin' the next day and had come in lookin' for Hod Meyers to go with him. I happened to know that Hod had went over to Carterville and wouldn't be home till the end of the week. So Jim said he hated to go alone and he guessed he would call it off. Then poor Paul spoke up and said if Jim would take him he would go along. Jim thought a w'ile and then he said, well, he guessed a half-wit was better than nothin'.

I suppose he was plottin' to get Paul out in the boat and play some joke on him, like pushin' him in the water. Anyways, he said Paul could go. He asked him had he ever shot a duck and Paul said no, he'd never even had a gun in his hands. So Jim said he could set in the boat and watch him and if he behaved himself, he might lend him his gun for a couple of shots. They made a date to meet in the mornin' and that's the last I seen of Jim alive.

Next mornin', I hadn't been open more than ten minutes when Doc Stair come in. He looked kind of nervous. He asked me had I seen Paul Dickson. I said no, but I knew where he was, out duck-shootin' with Jim Kendall. So Doc says that's what he had heard, and he couldn't understand it because Paul had told him he wouldn't never have no more to do with Jim as long as he lived.

He said Paul had told him about the joke Jim had played on Julie. He said Paul had asked him what he thought of the joke and the Doc told him that anybody that would do a thing like that ought not to be let live. I said it had been a kind of a raw thing, but Jim just couldn't resist no kind of a joke, no matter how raw. I said I thought he was all right at heart, but just bubblin' over with mischief. Doc turned and walked out.

At noon he got a phone call from old John Scott. The lake where Jim and Paul had went shootin' is on John's place. Paul had came runnin' up to the house a few minutes before and said they'd been an accident. Jim had shot a few ducks and then give the gun to Paul and told him to try his luck. Paul hadn't never handled a gun and he was nervous. He was shakin' so hard that he couldn't control the gun. He let fire and Jim sunk back in the boat, dead.

Doc Stair, bein' the coroner, jumped in Frank Abbott's flivver and rushed out to Scott's farm. Paul and old John was down on the shore of the lake. Paul had rowed the boat to shore, but they'd left the body in it, waiting for Doc to come.

Doc examined the body and said they might as well fetch it back to town. They was no use leavin' it there or callin' a jury, as it was a plain case of accidental shootin'.

Personally I wouldn't never leave a person shoot a gun in the same boat I was in unless I was sure they knew somethin' about guns. Jim was a sucker to leave a new beginner have his gun, let alone a half-wit. It probably served Jim right, what he got. But still we miss him round here. He certainly was a card! Comb it wet or dry?

HARRISON BERGERON
Kurt Vonnegut

THE YEAR WAS 2081, and everybody was finally equal. They weren't only equal before God and the law. They were equal every which way. Nobody was smarter than anybody else. Nobody was better looking than anybody else. Nobody was stronger or quicker than anybody else. All this equality was due to the 211th, 212th, and 213th Amendments to the Constitution, and to the unceasing vigilance of agents of the United States Handicapper General.

Some things about living still weren't quite right, though. April, for instance, still drove people crazy by not being springtime. And it was in that clammy month that the H-G men took George and Hazel Bergeron's fourteen-year-old son, Harrison, away.

It was tragic, all right, but George and Hazel couldn't think about it very hard. Hazel had a perfectly average intelligence, which meant she couldn't think about anything except in short bursts. And George, while his intelligence was way above normal, had a little mental handicap radio in his ear. He was required by law to wear it at all times. It was tuned to a government transmitter. Every twenty seconds or so, the transmitter would send out some sharp noise to keep people like George from taking unfair advantage of their brains.

George and Hazel were watching television. There were tears on Hazel's cheeks, but she'd forgotten for the moment what they were about.

On the television screen were ballerinas.

A buzzer sounded in George's head. His thoughts fled in panic, like bandits from a burglar alarm.

"That was a real pretty dance, that dance they just did," said Hazel.

"Huh?" said George.

"That dance—it was nice," said Hazel.

"Yup," said George. He tried to think a little about the ballerinas. They weren't really very good—no better than anybody else would have been, anyway. They were burdened with sashweights and bags of birdshot, and their faces were masked, so that no one, seeing a free and graceful gesture or a pretty face, would feel like something the cat drug in. George was toying with the vague notion that maybe dancers shouldn't be handicapped. But he didn't get very far with it before another noise in his ear radio scattered his thoughts.

George winced. So did two out of the eight ballerinas.

Hazel saw him wince. Having no mental handicap herself she had to ask George what the latest sound had been.

"Sounded like somebody hitting a milk bottle with a ball peen hammer," said George.

"I'd think it would be real interesting, hearing all the different sounds," said Hazel, a little envious. "All the things they think up."

"Um," said George.

"Only, if I was Handicapper General, you know what I would do?" said Hazel. Hazel, as a matter of fact, bore a strong resemblance to the Handicapper General, a woman named Diana Moon Glampers. "If I was Diana Moon Glampers," said Hazel, "I'd have chimes on Sunday—just chimes. Kind of in honor of religion."

"I could think, if it was just chimes," said George.

"Well—maybe make 'em real loud," said Hazel. "I think I'd make a good Handicapper General."

"Good as anybody else," said George.

"Who knows better'n I do what normal is?" said Hazel.

"Right," said George. He began to think glimmeringly about his abnormal son who was now in jail, about Harrison, but a twenty-one-gun salute in his head stopped that.

"Boy!" said Hazel, "that was a doozy, wasn't it?"

It was such a doozy that George was white and trembling and tears stood on the rims of his red eyes. Two of the eight ballerinas had collapsed to the studio floor, were holding their temples.

"All of a sudden you look so tired," said Hazel. "Why don't you stretch out on the sofa, so's you can rest your handicap bag on the pillows, honeybunch." She was referring to the forty-seven pounds of birdshot in canvas bag, which was padlocked around George's neck. "Go on and rest the bag for a little while," she said. "I don't care if you're not equal to me for a while."

George weighed the bag with his hands. "I don't mind it," he said. "I don't notice it any more. It's just a part of me."

"You been so tired lately—kind of wore out," said Hazel. "If there was just some way we could make a little hole in the bottom of the bag, and just take out a few of them lead balls. Just a few."

"Two years in prison and two thousand dollars fine for every ball I took out," said George. "I don't call that a bargain."

"If you could just take a few out when you came home from work," said Hazel. "I mean—you don't compete with anybody around here. You just set around."

"If I tried to get away with it," said George, "then other people'd get away with it and pretty soon we'd be right back to the dark ages again, with everybody competing against everybody else. You wouldn't like that, would you?"

"I'd hate it," said Hazel.

"There you are," said George. "The minute people start cheating on laws, what do you think happens to society?"

If Hazel hadn't been able to come up with an answer to this question, George couldn't have supplied one. A siren was going off in his head.

"Reckon it'd fall all apart," said Hazel.

"What would?" said George blankly.

"Society," said Hazel uncertainly. "Wasn't that what you just said?"

"Who knows?" said George.

The television program was suddenly interrupted for a news bulletin. It wasn't clear at first as to what the bulletin was about, since the announcer, like all announcers, had a serious speech impediment. For about half a minute, and in a state of high excitement, the announcer tried to say, "Ladies and gentlemen—"

He finally gave up, handed the bulletin to a ballerina to read.

"That's all right—" Hazel said of the announcer, "he tried. That's the big thing. He tried to do the best he could with what God gave him. He should get a nice raise for trying so hard."

"Ladies and gentlemen" said the ballerina, reading the bulletin. She must have been extraordinarily beautiful, because the mask she wore was hideous. And it was easy to see that she was the strongest and most graceful of all the dancers, for her handicap bags were as big as those worn by two-hundred-pound men.

And she had to apologize at once for her voice, which was a very unfair voice for a woman to use. Her voice was a warm, luminous, timeless melody. "Excuse me—" she said, and she began again, making her voice absolutely uncompetitive.

"Harrison Bergeron, age fourteen," she said in a grackle squawk, "has just escaped from jail, where he was held on suspicion of plotting to overthrow the government. He is a genius and an athlete, is under-handicapped, and should be regarded as extremely dangerous."

A police photograph of Harrison Bergeron was flashed on the screen—upside down, then sideways, upside down again, then right side up. The picture showed the full length of Harrison against a background calibrated in feet and inches. He was exactly seven feet tall.

The rest of Harrison's appearance was Halloween and hardware. Nobody had ever worn heavier handicaps. He had outgrown hindrances faster than the H-G men could think them up. Instead of a little ear radio for a mental handicap, he wore a tremendous pair of earphones, and spectacles with thick wavy lenses. The spectacles were intended to make him not only half blind, but to give him whanging headaches besides.

Scrap metal was hung all over him. Ordinarily, there was a certain symmetry, a military neatness to the handicaps issued to strong people, but Harrison looked like a walking junkyard. In the race of life, Harrison carried three hundred pounds.

And to offset his good looks, the H-G men required that he wear at all times a red rubber ball for a nose, keep his eyebrows shaved off, and cover his even white teeth with black caps at snaggletooth random.

"If you see this boy," said the ballerina, "do not—I repeat, do not—try to reason with him."

There was the shriek of a door being torn from its hinges.

Screams and barking cries of consternation came from the television set. The photograph of Harrison Bergeron on the screen jumped again and again, as though dancing to the tune of an earthquake.

George Bergeron correctly identified the earthquake, and well he might have—for many was the time his own home had danced to the same crashing tune. "My God—" said George, "that must be Harrison!"

The realization was blasted from his mind instantly by the sound of an automobile collision in his head.

When George could open his eyes again, the photograph of Harrison was gone. A living, breathing Harrison filled the screen.

Clanking, clownish, and huge, Harrison stood in the center of the studio. The knob of the uprooted studio door was still in his hand. Ballerinas, technicians, musicians, and announcers cowered on their knees before him, expecting to die.

"I am the Emperor!" cried Harrison. "Do you hear? I am the Emperor! Everybody must do what I say at once!" He stamped his foot and the studio shook.

"Even as I stand here—" he bellowed, "crippled, hobbled, sickened—I am a greater ruler than any man who ever lived! Now watch me become what I *can* become!"

Harrison tore the straps of his handicap harness like wet tissue paper, tore straps guaranteed to support five thousand pounds.

Harrison's scrap-iron handicaps crashed to the floor.

Harrison thrust his thumbs under the bar of the padlock that secured his head harness. The bar snapped like celery. Harrison smashed his headphones and spectacles against the wall.

He flung away his rubber-ball nose, revealed a man that would have awed Thor, the god of thunder.

"I shall now select my Empress!" he said, looking down on the cowering people. "Let the first woman who dares rise to her feet claim her mate and her throne!"

A moment passed, and then a ballerina arose, swaying like a willow.

Harrison plucked the mental handicap from her ear, snapped off her physical handicaps with marvelous delicacy. Last of all, he removed her mask.

She was blindingly beautiful.

"Now" said Harrison, taking her hand, "shall we show the people the meaning of the word dance? Music!" he commanded.

The musicians scrambled back into their chairs, and Harrison stripped them of their handicaps, too. "Play your best," he told them, "and I'll make you barons and dukes and earls."

The music began. It was normal at first—cheap, silly, false. But Harrison snatched two musicians from their chairs, waved them like batons as he sang the music as he wanted it played. He slammed them back into their chairs.

The music began again and was much improved.

Harrison and his Empress merely listened to the music for a while—listened gravely, as though synchronizing their heartbeats with it.

They shifted their weights to their toes.

Harrison placed his big hands on the girl's tiny waist, letting her sense the weightlessness that would soon be hers.

And then, in an explosion of joy and grace, into the air they sprang!

Not only were the laws of the land abandoned, but the law of gravity and the laws of motion as well.

They reeled, whirled, swiveled, flounced, capered, gamboled, and spun.

They leaped like deer on the moon.

The studio ceiling was thirty feet high, but each leap brought the dancers nearer to it. It became their obvious intention to kiss the ceiling.

They kissed it.

And then, neutralizing gravity with love and pure will, they remained suspended in air inches below the ceiling, and they kissed each other for a long, long time.

It was then that Diana Moon Glampers, the Handicapper General, came into the studio with a double-barreled ten-gauge shotgun. She fired twice, and the Emperor and the Empress were dead before they hit the floor.

Diana Moon Glampers loaded the gun again. She aimed it at the musicians and told them they had ten seconds to get their handicaps back on.

It was then that the Bergerons' television tube burned out.

Hazel turned to comment about the blackout to George.

But George had gone out into the kitchen for a can of beer.

George came back in with the beer, paused while a handicap signal shook him up. And then he sat down again. "You been crying?" he said to Hazel.

"Yup," she said.

"What about?" he said.

"I forget," she said. "Something real sad on television." "What was it?" he said.

"It's all kind of mixed up in my mind," said Hazel.

"Forget sad things," said George.

"I always do," said Hazel.

"That's my girl," said George. He winced. There was the sound of a riveting gun in his head.

"Gee—I could tell that one was a doozy," said Hazel.

"You can say that again," said George.

"Gee—" said Hazel, "I could tell that one was a doozy."

INFLEXIBLE LOGIC
Russell Maloney

When the six chimpanzees came into his life, Mr. Bainbridge was thirty-eight years old. He was a bachelor and lived comfortably in a remote part of Connecticut, in a large old house with a carriage drive, a conservatory, a tennis court, and a well-selected library. His income was derived from impeccably situated real estate in New York City, and he spent it soberly, in a manner which could give offence to nobody. Once a year, late in April, his tennis court was resurfaced, and after that anybody in the neighborhood was welcome to use it; his monthly statement from Brentano's seldom ran below seventy-five dollars; every third year, in November, he turned in his old Cadillac coupé for a new one; he ordered his cigars, which were mild and rather moderately priced, in shipments of one thousand from a tobacconist in Havana; because of the international situation he had cancelled arrangements to travel abroad, and after due thought had decided to spend his traveling allowance on wines, which seemed likely to get scarcer and more expensive if the war lasted. On the whole, Mr. Bainbridge's life was deliberately, and not too unsuccessfully, modeled after that of an English country gentleman of the late eighteenth century, a gentleman interested in the arts and in the expansion of science, and so sure of himself that he didn't care if some people thought him eccentric.

Mr. Bainbridge had many friends in New York, and he spent several days of the month in the city, staying at his club and looking around. Sometimes he called up a girl and took her out to a theatre and a night club. Sometimes he and a couple of classmates got a little tight and went to a prizefight. Mr. Bainbridge also looked in now and then at some of the conservative art galleries, and liked occasionally to go to a concert. And he liked cocktail parties, too, because of the fine footling conversation and the extraordinary number of pretty girls who had nothing else to do with the rest of their evening. It was at a New York cocktail party, however, that Mr. Bainbridge kept his preliminary appointment with doom. At one of the parties given by Hobie Packard, the stockbroker, he learned about the theory of the six chimpanzees.

It was almost six-forty. The people who had intended to have one drink and go had already gone, and the people who intended to stay were fortifying themselves with slightly dried canapés and talking animatedly. A group of stage and radio people had coagulated in one corner, near Packard's Capehart, and were wrangling about various methods of cheating the Collector of Internal Revenue. In another corner was a group of stockbrokers, talking about the greatest stockbroker of them all, Gauguin. Little Marcia Lupton was sitting with a young man, saying earnestly, "Do you really want to know what my greatest ambition is? I want to be myself," and Mr. Bainbridge smiled gently, thinking of the time Marcia had said that to him. Then he heard the voice of Bernard Weiss, the critic, saying, "Of course he wrote one good novel. It's not surprising. After all, we know that if six chimpanzees were set to work pounding six typewriters at random, they would, in a million years, write all the books in the British Museum."

Mr. Bainbridge drifted over to Weiss and was introduced to Weiss's companion, a Mr. Noble. "What's this about a million chimpanzees, Weiss?" he asked.

"Six chimpanzees," Mr. Weiss said. "It's an old cliché of the mathematicians. I thought everybody was told about it in school."

Law of averages, you know, or maybe it's permutation and combination. The six chimps, just pounding away at the typewriter keys, would be bound to copy out all the books ever written by man. There are only so many possible combinations of letters and numerals, and they'd produce all of them—see? Of course they'd also turn out a mountain of gibberish, but they'd work the books in, too. All the books in the British Museum."

Mr. Bainbridge was delighted; this was the sort of talk he liked to hear when he came to New York. "Well, but look here," he said, just to keep up his part in the foolish conversation, "what if one of the chimpanzees finally did duplicate a book, right down to the last period, but left that off? Would that count?"

"I suppose not. Probably the chimpanzee would get around to doing the book again, and put the period in."

"What nonsense!" Mr. Noble cried.

"It may be nonsense, but Sir James Jeans believes it," Mr. Weiss said, huffily. "Jeans or Lancelot Hogben. I know I ran across it quite recently."

Mr. Bainbridge was impressed. He read quite a bit of popular science, and both Jeans and Hogben were in his library. "Is that so?" he murmured, no longer feeling frivolous. "Wonder if it has ever actually been tried? I mean has anybody ever put six chimpanzees in a room with six typewriters and a lot of paper?"

Mr. Weiss glanced at Mr. Bainbridge's empty cocktail glass and said drily, "Probably not."

Nine weeks later, on a winter evening, Mr. Bainbridge was sitting in his study with his friend James Mallard, an assistant professor of mathematics at New Haven. He was plainly nervous as he poured himself a drink and said, "Mallard, I've asked you to come here—Brandy? Cigar?—for a particular reason. You remember that I wrote you some time ago, asking your opinion of . . . of a certain mathematical hypothesis or supposition."

"Yes," Professor Mallard said, briskly. "I remember perfectly. About the six chimpanzees and the British Museum. And I told you it was a perfectly sound popularization of a principle known to every schoolboy who had studied the science of probabilities."

"Precisely," Mr. Bainbridge said. "Well, Mallard, I made up my mind . . . It was not difficult for me, because I have, in spite of that fellow in the White House, been able to give something every year to the Museum of Natural History, and they were naturally glad to oblige me. . . . And after all, the only contribution a layman can make to the progress of science is to assist with the drudgery of experiment. . . . In short, I—"

"I suppose you're trying to tell me that you have procured six chimpanzees and set them to work at typewriters in order to see whether they will eventually write all the books in the British Museum. Is that it?"

"Yes, that's it," Mr. Bainbridge said. "What a mind you have, Mallard. Six fine young males, in perfect condition. I had a—I suppose you'd call it a dormitory—built out in back of the stable. The typewriters are in the conservatory. It's light and airy in there, and I moved most of the plants out. Mr. North, the man who owns the circus, very obligingly let me engage one of his best animal men. Really, it was no trouble at all."

Professor Mallard smiled indulgently. "After all, such a thing is not unheard of," he said. "I seem to remember that a man at some university put his graduate students to work flipping coins, to see if heads and tails came up an equal number of times. Of course they did."

Mr. Bainbridge looked at his friend very queerly. "Then you believe that any such principle of the science of probabilities will stand up under an actual test?"

"Certainly."

"You had better see for yourself." Mr. Bainbridge led Professor Mallard downstairs, along a corridor, through a disused music room, and into a large conservatory. The middle of the floor had been cleared of plants and was occupied by a row of six typewriter tables, each one supporting a hooded machine. At the left of each typewriter was a neat stack of yellow copy paper. Empty wastebaskets were under each table. The chairs were the unpadded, spring-backed kind favored by experienced stenographers. A large bunch of ripe bananas was hanging in one corner, and in another stood a Great Bear water-cooler and a rack of Lily cups. Six piles of typescript, each about a foot high, were ranged along the wall on an improvised shelf. Mr. Bainbridge picked up one of the piles, which he could just conveniently lift, and set it on a table before Professor Mallard. "The output to date of Chimpanzee A, known as Bill," he said simply.

"Oliver Twist," by Charles Dickens, Professor Mallard read out. He read the first and second pages of the manuscript, then feverishly leafed through to the end. "You mean to tell me," he said, "that this chimpanzee has written—"

"Word for word and comma for comma," said Mr. Bainbridge. "Young, my butler, and I took turns comparing it with the edition I own. Having finished 'Oliver Twist,' Bill is, as you see, starting the sociological works of Vilfredo Pareto, in Italian. At the rate he has been going, it should keep him busy for the rest of the month."

"And all the chimpanzees"—Professor Mallard was pale, and enunciated with difficulty—"they aren't all—"

"Oh, yes, all writing books which I have every reason to believe are in the British Museum. The prose of John Donne, some Anatole France, Conan Doyle, Galen, the collected plays of Somerset Maugham, Marcel Proust, the memoirs of the late Marie of Rumania, and a monograph by a Dr. Wiley on the marsh grasses of Maine and Massachusetts. I can sum it up for you, Mallard, by telling you that since I started this experiment, four weeks and some days ago, none of the chimpanzees has spoiled a single sheet of paper."

Professor Mallard straightened up, passed his handkerchief across his brow, and took a deep breath. "I apologize for my weakness," he said. "It was simply the sudden shock. No, looking at the thing scientifically—and I hope I am at least as capable of that as the next man—there is nothing marvellous about the situation. These chimpanzees, or a succession of similar teams of chimpanzees, would in a million years write all the books in the British Museum. I told you some time ago that I believed that statement. Why should my belief be altered by the fact that they produced some of the books at the very outset? After all, I should not be very much surprised if I tossed a coin a hundred times and it came up heads every time. I know that if I kept at it long enough, the ratio would reduce itself to an exact fifty per cent. Rest assured, these chimpanzees will begin to compose gibberish quite soon. It is bound to happen. Science tells us so. Meanwhile, I advise you to keep this experiment secret. Uninformed people might create a sensation if they knew."

"I will, indeed," Mr. Bainbridge said. "And I'm very grateful for your rational analysis. It reassures me. And now, before you go, you must hear the new Schnabel records that arrived today."

During the succeeding three months, Professor Mallard got into the habit of telephoning Mr. Bainbridge every Friday afternoon at five-thirty, immediately after leaving his seminar room. The Professor would say, "Well?," and Mr. Bainbridge would reply, "They're still at it, Mallard. Haven't spoiled a sheet of paper yet." If Mr. Bainbridge had to go out on Friday afternoon, he would leave a written message with his butler, who would read it to Professor

Mallard: "Mr. Bainbridge says we now have Trevelyan's 'Life of Macaulay,' the Confessions of St. Augustine, 'Vanity Fair,' part of Irving's 'Life of George Washington,' the Book of the Dead, and some speeches delivered in Parliament in opposition to the Corn Laws, sir." Professor Mallard would reply, with a hint of a snarl in his voice, "Tell him to remember what I predicted," and hang up with a clash.

The eleventh Friday that Professor Mallard telephoned, Mr. Bainbridge said, "No change. I have had to store the bulk of the manuscript in the cellar. I would have burned it, except that it probably has some scientific value."

"How dare you talk of scientific value?" The voice from New Haven roared faintly in the receiver. "Scientific value! You—you—chimpanzee!" There were further inarticulate sputterings, and Mr. Bainbridge hung up with a disturbed expression. "I am afraid Mallard is overtaxing himself," he murmured.

Next day, however, he was pleasantly surprised. He was leafing through a manuscript that had been completed the previous day by Chimpanzee D, Corky. It was the complete diary of Samuel Pepys, and Mr. Bainbridge was chuckling over the naughty passages, which were omitted in his own edition, when Professor Mallard was shown into the room. "I have come to apologize for my outrageous conduct on the telephone yesterday," the Professor said.

"Please don't think of it any more. I know you have many things on your mind," Mr. Bainbridge said. "Would you like a drink?"

"A large whiskey, straight, please," Professor Mallard said. "I got rather cold driving down. No change, I presume?"

"No, none. Chimpanzee F, Dinty, is just finishing John Florio's translation of Montaigne's essays, but there is no other news of interest."

Professor Mallard squared his shoulders and tossed off his drink in one astonishing gulp. "I should like to see them at work," he said. "Would I disturb them, do you think?"

"Not at all. As a matter of fact, I usually look in on them around this time of day. Dinty may have finished his Montaigne by now, and it is always interesting to see them start a new work. I would have thought that they would continue on the same sheet of paper, but they don't, you know. Always a fresh sheet, and the title in capitals."

Professor Mallard, without apology, poured another drink and slugged it down. "Lead on," he said.

It was dusk in the conservatory, and the chimpanzees were typing by the light of student lamps clamped to their desks. The keeper lounged in a corner, eating a banana and reading Billboard. "You might as well take an hour or so off," Mr. Bainbridge said. The man left.

Professor Mallard, who had not taken off his overcoat, stood with his hands in his pockets, looking at the busy chimpanzees. "I wonder if you know, Bainbridge, that the science of probabilities takes everything into account," he said, in a queer, tight voice. "It is certainly almost beyond the bounds of credibility that these chimpanzees should write books without a single error, but that abnormality may be corrected by—these!" He took his hands from his pockets, and each one held a .38 revolver. "Stand back out of harm's way!" he shouted.

"Mallard! Stop it!" the revolvers barked, first the right hand, then the left, then the right. Two chimpanzees fell, and a third reeled into a corner. Mr. Bainbridge seized his friend's arm and wrested one of the weapons from him.

"Now I am armed, too, Mallard, and I advise you to stop!" he cried. Professor Mallard's answer was to draw a bead on Chimpanzee E and shoot him dead. Mr. Bainbridge made a rush, and Professor Mallard fired at him. Mr. Bainbridge, in his quick death agony, tightened his finger on the trigger of his revolver. It went off, and Professor Mallard went down. On his hands and knees he fired at the two chimpanzees which were still unhurt, and then collapsed.

There was nobody to hear his last words. "The human equation . . . always the enemy of science . . ." he panted. "This time . . . vice versa . . . I, a mere mortal . . . savior of science . . . deserve a Nobel . . ."

When the old butler came running into the conservatory to investigate the noises, his eyes were met by a truly appalling sight. The student lamps were shattered, but a newly risen moon shone in through the conservatory windows on the corpses of the two gentlemen, each clutching a smoking revolver. Five of the chimpanzees were dead. The sixth was Chimpanzee F. His right arm disabled, obviously bleeding to death, he was slumped before his typewriter. Painfully, with his left hand, he took from the machine the completed last page of Florio's Montaigne. Groping for a fresh sheet, he inserted it, and typed with one finger, UNCLE TOM'S CABIN, by Harriet Beecher Stowe. Chapte . . ." Then he, too, was dead.

OFFLOADING FOR MRS. SCHWARTZ

George Saunders

Elizabeth always thought the fake stream running through our complex was tacky. Whenever I'd sit brooding beside it after one of our fights she'd hoot down on me from the balcony. Then I'd come in and we'd make up. Oh would we. I think of it. I think of it and think of it. Finally in despair I call GuiltMasters. GuiltMasters are Jean and Bob Fleen, a brother/sister psychiatric practice. In their late-night TV ads they wear cowls and capes and stand on either side of a sobbing neurotic woman in sweater and slacks. By the end of the bit she's romping through a field of daisies. I get Jean Fleen. I tell her I've done a bad thing I can't live with. She says I've called the right place. She says there's nothing so shameful it can't be addressed by GuiltMasters. I take a deep breath and spill my guts. There's a silence from Jean's end. Then she asks can I hold. Upbeat Muzak comes on. Several minutes later Bob comes on and asks can they call me back. I wait by the phone. One hour, two hours, all night. Nothing. The sun comes up. Brad from Complex Grounds turns on the bubbler and the whitewater begins to flow. I don't shower. I don't shave. I put on the same pants I had on before. It's too much. Three years since her death and still I'm a wreck. I think of fleeing the city. I think of working on a shrimper, or setting myself on fire downtown. Instead I go to work.

In spite of my problems, personal interactive holography marches on. All morning I hopefully dust. Nobody comes in. At noon I work out a little tension by running amok in one of my modules. I choose Bowling With the Pros. A holographic smoothie in a blazer greets me and affably asks if I'm as tired as he is of perennially overhooking the ball when what I really need is to consistently throw strikes. I tell him fuck off. In a more sophisticated module he'd ask why the hostility, but my equipment is outdated and instead he looks confused and tries to shake my hand. What crappy verisimilitude. No wonder I'm in the red. No wonder my rent's overdue. He asks isn't bowling a lovely recreation? I tell him I'm in mourning. He says the hours spent in a bowling alley with friends certainly make for some fantastic memories years down the line. I tell him my life's in the crapper. He grins and says let's bowl, let's go in and bowl, let's go in and bowl a few frames—with the Pros! I take him by the throat. Of course he Dysfunctions. Of course I'm automatically unbooted. I doff my headset and dismount the treadmill. Once again it's just me and my failing shop. Once again the air reeks of microwaved popcorn. Once again I am only who I am.

Wonderful, I think, you've fouled your own four-hundred-dollar module. And I have. So I trash it. I write it off to grief management. I go to lunch. I opt for an autodispensed FreightFurter. Of course I overmicrowave and the paper cowcatcher melds with the bun and the little engineer's face runs down his overalls. It's even more inedible than unusual. I chuck it. I can't afford another. I chuck it and go wait for my regulars.

At two Mr. Bomphil comes in looking guilty and as always requests Violated Prom Queen, then puts on high heels and selects Treadmill Three. Treadmill Three is behind a beam, so he's free to get as worked up as he likes, which is very. I try not to hear him moan. I try not to hear him call each football-team member by name.

He's followed by Theo Kiley, an appliance salesmen who lays down a ream of Frigidaire specs and asks for Legendary American Killers Stalk You. I strap on his headset. I insert his module. For twenty minutes he hems and haws with Clyde Barrow. Finally he slips up and succumbs to a burst of machine-gun fire, then treats himself to a Sprite. "Whew," he says. "Next time I'll know to avoid the topic of his mom." I remind him he's got an outstanding bill. He says thanks. He says his bill and his ability to match wits with great criminals are the only outstanding things he's got. We laugh. We laugh some more. He shakes his head and leaves. I curse him under my breath, then close up early and return to my lonely home.

Next day Mrs. Gaither from Corporate comes to town. Midway through my Significant Accomplishments Assessment, armless Mr. Feltriggi comes to the door and as usual rings the bell with his face. I let him in and he unloads his totebag of cookbooks for sale. Today it's "Crazy Cajun Carnival" and "Going Bananas with Bananas: A Caribbean Primer." But I know what he really wants. With my eyes I tell him wait. Finally Gaither finishes raking my sub-par Disbursement Ledger over the coals and goes across the mall to O My God for some vintage religious statuary. I slip the headset on Feltriggi and run Youth Roams Kansas Hometown, 1932. It's all homemade bread and dirt roads and affable dogcatchers. What a sweet grin appears. How he greets each hometowner with his ghost limbs and beams at the chirping of the holographic birds. He kneels awhile in Mrs. Lawler's larder, sniffing spices that remind him of his mother elbow-deep in flour. He drifts out to the shaded yard and discusses Fascism with the iceman near some swaying wheat. His posture changes for the better. He laughs aloud. He's young again and the thresher has yet to claim his arms.

Gaither comes back with a St. Sebastian cookie jar. I nudge Feltriggi and tell him that's all for today. He takes off the headset and offers me a cookbook in payment. I tell him forget it. I tell him that's what friends are for. It's seventy bucks a session and he knows it. He rams his head into my chest as a sign of affection.

"That type of a presence surely acts to deflate revenues," Gaither says primly as Feltriggi goes out.

"No lie," I say. "That's why I nearly beat him up every time he comes in here."

"I'm not sure that's appropriate," she says.

"Me neither," I say. "That's why I usually don't really do it."

"I see," she says. "Let's talk briefly about personal tragedy. No one's immune. But at what point must mourning cease? In your case, apparently never."

I think: You never saw Elizabeth lanky and tan and laughing in Napa.

"I like your cookie jar," I say.

"Very well," she says, "Seal your own doom."

She says she's shocked at the dryness of my treadmill bearings and asks if I've ever heard of oil. She sighs and gives me her number at the Quality Inn in case I think of anything that might argue against Franchise Agreement Cancellation. Then out she goes, sadly shaking her head.

It's only my livelihood. It's only every cent Elizabeth left me. I load up my mobil pack. I select my happiest modules. Then I go off to my real job, my penance, my albatross.

Rockettown's our ghetto. It's called Rockettown because long ago they put up a building there in which to build rockets. But none were built and the building's now nothing, which is what it's always been, except for a fenced-off dank corner that was once used to store dilapidated fireplugs and is now a filthy daycare for the children of parents who could care less. All around Rockettown little houses went up when it was thought the building would soon be full of people making rockets and hauling down impressive wages. They're bad little houses, put up quick, and now all the people who were young and had hoped to build rockets are old and doddering and walk by the empty building mumbling why why why.

In the early days of my grief Father Luther told me to lose myself in service by contacting ElderAid, Inc. I got Mrs. Ken Schwartz. Mrs. Ken Schwartz lives in Rockettown. She lives in Rockettown remembering Mr. Ken Schwartz and cursing him for staying so late at Menlo's TenPin on nights when she forgets he's been dead eighteen years. Mrs. Ken Schwartz likes me and my happy modules. Especially she likes Viennese Waltz. Boy does she. She's bedridden and lonely and sometimes in her excitement bruises her arms on her headboard when the orchestra starts to play. Tonight she says she's feeling weak. She says she used to be a different person and wishes she could go back to the days when she was loved. She mourns Fat Patrice and their jovial games of Old Maid. She mourns the front-yard oak the city felled without asking her. Mostly she mourns Mr. Ken Schwartz.

I pull out all the stops. I set Color on high contrast. I tape sensors to her lips and earlobes. I activate the Royalty Subroutine. Soon the prince is lavishing her with praise. Soon they're sneaking off from the ball for some tender words and a kiss or two on a stone bench beside the Danube. Soon I'm daubing her eyes with tissue while she weeps at the beauty of the fishermen bowing from their little boats as they realize it's the prince himself trying to retrieve her corsage from the river. I make tea. I read my magazine.

Finally I stroke her forehead while humming Strauss and slowly fading the volume.

"You," she says, smiling sweetly when she's all the way back. "You're too good to me."

"No one could be too good to you," I say.

"Oh you," she says. "You're a saint."

No, I think, I'm a man without a life, due to you. Then I feel ashamed and purposely bash my shin against the bedframe while tucking her in. I get her some juice. I check her backdoor lock. All around the room are dirty plates I've failed to get to the sink and old photos of Mr. Ken Schwartz assessing the condition of massive steamboilers while laughing confidently.

Out on the street it's cold and a wino's standing in a dumpster calling a stray cat Uncle Chuck. I hustle directly to my Omni, fearing for my gear. I drive through frightening quarters of the city, nervously toggling my defrost lever, thinking of Mrs. Ken Schwartz. The last few months she's gone badly downhill. She's unable to feed herself or autonomously use the bathroom. Talk about losing yourself in service to a greater extent than planned. I'm over there night and day and still it's not enough. She needs a live-in but they don't come cheap, and my shop hasn't turned a profit in months. What to do? I think and think. I think so much I lose track of where I am and blunder by The Spot. You fool, I think, you ass, how much additional pain would you like? Here a drunk named Tom Clifton brought his Coupe De Ville onto the sidewalk as Elizabeth shopped for fruit on the evening of a day when we'd fought like hell. On the evening of a day when I'd called her an awful name. What name? I can't say the word. I even think it and my gut burns. I'm a saint.

The fight started when I accused her of flirting with our neighbor Len Kobb by bending low on purpose. I was angry and implied that she couldn't keep her boobs in her top to save her life. If I could see her one last time I'd say: thanks very much for dying at the worst possible moment and leaving me holding the bag of guilt. I'd say: if you had to die, couldn't you have done it when we were getting along? I madly flee The Spot. There are boat lights in the harbor and a man in a tux inexplicably jogging through the park. There's a moon bobbing up between condemned buildings.

There's the fact that tomorrow I'm Lay Authority Guest at the Lyndon Baines Johnson School for Precocious Youth. I'm slated to allow interested kids to experience the module entitled Hop-Hop the Bunny Masters Fractions. Frankly I fear I'll be sneered at. How interested could a mob of gifted kids be in a rabbit and a lisping caterpillar subdividing acorns ad nauseam? But I've promised the principal, Mrs. Briff. And I'm not in a position to decline any revenue source. So at an hour of the night when other men my age are rising from their beds to comfort screaming newborns I return to the mall for my Hop-Hop module. I use my pass key. Something's strange. Modules are strewn everywhere. The cashbox sits on the fax machine. One of my treadmills lies on its side.

"How is all of this fancy equipment used?" someone asks from behind me, pressing a sharp knife to my throat, "More specifically, which of it is worth the most? And remember sir, you're answering for your life."

He sounds old but feels strong. I tell him it's hard to explain. I offer to demonstrate.

He says do so, but slowly. I fit him with a headset. I gently guide him to a treadmill, then run Sexy Nurses Scrub You Down. Immediately his lips get moist. Immediately he pops a mild bone and loosens his grip on the knife and I'm able to coldcock him with the FedEx tape gun. He drops drooling to my nice carpet. A man his age should be a doting grandfather, not a crook threatening me with death. I feel violated. Such a man was Tom Clifton, past his prime and bitter. How does someone come to this?

I strap him down and set my console for Scan.

It seems his lousy name is Hank. I hear his portly father calling it out across a cranberry bog. I know the smell of his first baseball cap. Through his eyes I see the secret place under the porch where he hid whenever his fat kissing aunt came. Later I develop a love for swing. It seems he was a Marine at Iwo who on his way to bootcamp saw the aging Ty Cobb at a depot. I sense his panic on the troop transport, then quickly doff my headset as he hits the beach and the bullets start to fly.

To my horror, I see that his eyelids are fluttering and his face is contorting. My God, I think, this is no Scan, this is a damn Offload. I check the console, and sure enough, via one incorrect switch setting, I've just irrevocably transferred a good third of his memories to my hard drive.

When he comes to, he hops off the table looking years younger, suddenly happy-go-lucky, asks where he is, and trots blithely out the door, free now of bootcamp, free of Iwo, free of all memory of youthful slaughter, free in fact of any memory at all of the first twenty years of his life. I'm heartsick. What have I done? On the other hand, it stopped him from getting up and trying to kill me. On the other hand, it appears he left here a happier man, perhaps less inclined to felony.

I grab my Hop-Hop module. On the cover is Hop-Hop, enthusiastically giving the thumbs-up to an idealized blond boy lifting an enormous 4 into a numerator. As if being robbed weren't enough, first thing tomorrow morning a roomful of genius kids is going to eat me alive.

Then, crossing the deserted Food Court, I get a brainstorm. I hustle back to the shop and edit out Hank's trysts with starving women in Depression-era hobo camps and his one homo fling with his cousin Julian. I edit the profanity out of Iwo. I edit out the midnight wanks, the petty thefts, the unkind words, all but the most inoffensive of the bodies of his buddies on the pale sand beach.

Next morning I herd kid after kid behind my white curtain and let them experience Hank's life. They love it. They leave jabbering knowledgeably about the Pacific Theater and the ultimate wisdom of using the Bomb. They leave humming "American Patrol." They leave praising Phil Rizzuto's fielding and cursing the Brown Shirts. They pat old Mr. Panchuko, the geriatric janitor, on the back and ask him what caliber machine gun he operated at the Bulge. He stands scratching his gut, stunned, trying to remember. The little Klotchkow twins jitterbug. Andy Pitlin, all of three feet tall, hankers aloud for a Camel.

Mrs. Briff is more than impressed. She asks what else do I have. I ask what else does she want. She says for starters how about the remainder of the century. I tell her I'll see what I can do.

The kids come out of it with a firsthand War Years experience and I come out of it with a check for five hundred dollars, enough to hire a temporary live-in for Mrs. Ken Schwartz. Which I gladly do. A lovely Eurasian named Wei, a student of astrophysics who, as I'm leaving them alone for the first time, is brushing out Mrs. Ken Schwartz's hair and humming "Let Me Call You Sweetheart."

"Will you stay forever?" I ask her.

"With all due respect," she replies, "I will stay as long as you can pay me."

Two weeks later, Briff's on my tail for more modules and Wei's on my tail for her pay. I tell Mrs. Ken Schwartz all, during one of her fifteen-minute windows of lucidity. When lucid she's shrewd and bright. She understands her predicament. She understands the limitations of my gear. She understands that I can't borrow her memories, only take them away forever.

She says she can live without the sixties.

I haul my stuff over to her place and take what I need. I edit out her mastectomy, Ken Schwartz's midlife crisis and resulting trip to Florida, and her constant drinking in his absence. I stick to her walking past a protest and counseling a skinny girl on acid to stay in school. It's not great but I've got a deadline. I call it America in Tumult–The Older Generation Looks On In Dismay.

I have it couriered over to Briff, dreading her response. But to my amazement she sends a cash bonus. She reports astounding increases in grandparental bonding. She reports kids identifying a Mercury Cougar with no prompting and disgustedly calling each other Nixon whenever a trust is betrayed.

Thereafter I retain Wei on a weekly basis by whittling away at Mrs. Schwartz's memories. I submit Pearl Harbor–Week Prior to Infamy. I submit The Day the Music Died–Buddy Holly Remembered, which unfortunately is merely Mrs. Schwartz hearing the news on a pink radio, then disinterestedly going back to cleaning her oven. Finally Briff calls, hacked off. She says she wants some real meat. She asks how about the entire twenties, a personal favorite of hers. She's talking flappers. She's talking possible insights on Prohibition. I stonewall. I tell her give me a few days to exhaustively check my massive archive. I call Mrs. Ken Schwartz. She says during the twenties she was a lowly phone operator in Pekin, Illinois. She sounds disoriented, and wearily asks where her breasts are. Clearly this has gone far enough.

I call Briff and tell her no more modules. She ups her offer to three thousand a decade. She's running for school board and says my modules are the primary arrow in her quiver. But what am I supposed to do? Turn Mrs. Schwartz into a well-cared-for blank slate? Start kidnapping and offloading strangers? I say a little prayer:

God, I've botched this life but good. I've failed you in all major ways. You gave me true love and I blew it. I'm nothing. But what have you got against Mrs. Ken Schwartz? Forgive me. Help me figure this out.

And then in a flash I figure it out.

I lock the shop. On the spine of a blank module I write 1951-1992–Baby Boomers Come Into Their Own. At three thousand a decade that's twelve grand. I address an envelope to Briff and enclose an invoice. I write out some instructions and rig myself up.

Memories shmemories, I think, I'll get some new ones. These old ones give me no peace.

Then I let it rip. It all goes whizzing by: Anthony Newburg smacking me. Mom on the dock. An Agnew Halloween mask at a frat house. Bev Malloy struggling with my belt. The many seasons. The many flags, dogs, paths, the many stars in skies of many hues.

My sweet Elizabeth.

Holding hands we gape at an elk in Estes Park. On our knees in a bed of tulips I kiss her cheek. The cold clear water of Nacogdoches. The birthday banner she made of scarves in our little place on Ellington. The awful look on her face as I called her what I called her. Her hair, trailing fine and light behind her as she stormed out to buy fruit.

The grave, the grave, my sad attempt to become a franchisee.

Then I'm a paunchy guy in a room, with a note pinned to his sleeve: "You were alone in the world," it says, "and did a kindness for someone in need. Good for you. Now post this module, and follow this map to the home of Mrs. Ken Schwartz. Care for her with some big money that will come in the mail. Find someone to love. Your heart has never been broken. You've never done anything unforgivable or hurt anyone beyond reparation. Everyone you've ever loved you've treated like gold."

PAUL'S CASE
Willa Cather

A skillful author combines methods of presentation, selecting those most appropriate to the demands of the plot, the role of a particular character, and the central idea of the story.

Since the central idea of a story may be the portrayal of a certain kind of person, characterization is extremely important to analysis and understanding. "Paul's Case" tells of such a person, a boy who is seeking satisfaction in a society that denies it to him. His character is revealed to us in a variety of ways through the words of his father and his teachers and through his own thoughts which reveal a side of the boy unknown to anyone else. Understanding this character is crucial to the central idea of the story.

Cather chose the title of the story intentionally; it's not "Paul's Story;" it's "Paul's Case." Consider what that might imply. Paul is obviously unhappy, but why? Pay close attention to what others in the story think of Paul. Do they see him as "normal" or "average" for his age? Look closely at his attitudes and behavior to identify what is different about him from most other boys his age and why the author made him that way. How does that difference tie in with the central idea? For instance, the theatre represents something special to Paul; that's a clue to Paul's unhappiness. And what is the "dark corner" he speaks of?

It was Paul's afternoon to appear before the faculty of the Pittsburgh High School to account for his various misdemeanors. He had been suspended a week ago, and his father had called at the Principal's office and confessed his perplexity about his son.

Paul entered the faculty room suave and smiling. His clothes were a trifle outgrown, and the tan velvet on the collar of his open overcoat was frayed and worn; but for all that there was something of a dandy about him, and he wore an opal pin in his neatly knoted black four-in-hand, and a red carnation in his buttonhole. This latter adornment the faculty somehow felt was not properly significant of the contrite spirit befitting a boy under the ban of suspension.

Paul was tall for his age and very thin, with high, cramped shoulders and a narrow chest. His eyes were remarkable for a certain hysterical brilliancy, and he continually used them in a conscious, theatrical sort of way, peculiarly offensive in a boy. The pupils were abnormally large, as though he were addicted to belladonna, but there was a glassy glitter about them which that drug does not produce.

When questioned by the Principal as to why he was there, Paul stated, politely enough, that he wanted to come back to school. This was a lie, but Paul was quite accustomed to lying; found it, indeed, indispensable for overcoming friction. His teachers were asked to state their respective charges against him, which they did with such a rancor and aggrievedness as evinced that this was not a usual case. Disorder and impertinence were among the offences named, yet each of his instructors felt that it was scarcely possible to put into words the real cause of the trouble, which lay in a sort of hysterically defiant manner of the boy's; in the contempt which they all knew he felt for them, and which he seemingly made not the effort to conceal.

Once, when he had been making a synopsis of a paragraph at the blackboard, his English teacher had stepped to his side and attempted to guide his hand. Paul had started back with a shudder and thrust his hands violently behind him. The astonished woman could scarcely have been more hurt and embarrassed had he struck at her. The insult was so involuntary and definitely personal as to be unforgettable. In one way and another, he had made all his teachers, men and women alike, conscious of the same feeling of physical aversion. In one case he habitually sat with his hand shading his eyes; in another had made a running commentary on the lecture, with humorous intent.

His teachers felt this afternoon that his whole attitude was symbolized by his shrug and his flippantly red carnation flower, and they fell upon him without mercy, his English teacher leading the pack. He stood through it smiling, his pale lips parted over his white teeth. (His lips were continually twitching, and he had a habit of raising his eyebrows that was contemptuous and irritating to the last degree.) Older boys than Paul had broken down and shed tears under that ordeal, but his set smile did not once desert him, and his only sign of discomfort was the nervous trembling of the fingers that toyed with the buttons of his overcoat, and an occasional jerking of the other hand which held his hat. Paul was always smiling, always glancing about him, seeming to feel that people might be watching him and trying to detect something. This conscious expression, since it was as far as possible from boyish mirthfulness, was usually attributed to insolence or smartness.

As the inquisition proceeded, one of his instructors repeated an impertinent remark of the boy's, and the Principal asked him whether he thought that a courteous speech to make to a woman. Paul shrugged his shoulders slightly and his eyebrows twitched.

"I don't know," he replied. "I didn't mean to be polite or impolite, either. I guess it's a sort of way I have, of saying things regardless."

The Principal asked him whether he didn't think that a way it would be well to get rid of. Paul grinned and said he guessed so. When he was told that he could go, he bowed gracefully and went out. His bow was like a repetition of the scandalous red carnation.

His teachers were in despair, and his drawing-master voiced the feeling of them all when he declared there was something about the boy which none of them understood. He added: "I don't really believe that smile of his comes altogether from insolence; there's something sort of haunted about it. The boy is not strong for one thing. There is something wrong about the fellow."

The drawing-master had come to realize that, in looking at Paul, one saw only his white teeth and the forced animation of his eyes. One warm afternoon the boy had gone to sleep at his drawing-board, and his master had noted with amazement what a white, blue-veined face it was; drawn and wrinkled like an old man's about the eyes, the lips twitching even in his sleep.

His teachers left the building dissatisfied and unhappy; humiliated to have felt so vindictive toward a mere boy, to have uttered this feeling in cutting terms, and to have set each other on, as it were, in the gruesome game of intemperate reproach. One of them remembered having seen a miserable street cat set at bay by a ring of tormentors.

As for Paul, he ran down the hill whistling the "Soldiers' Chorus" from *Faust*, looking behind him now and then to see whether some of his teachers were not there to witness his light-heartedness. As it was now late in the afternoon and Paul was on duty that evening as usher at Carnegie Hall, he decided that he would go home to supper.

When he reached the concert hall, the doors were not yet open. It was chilly outside, and he decided to go up into the picture gallery always deserted at this hour where there were some of Raffelli's gay studies of Paris streets and an airy blue Venetian scene or two that always exhilarated him. He was delighted to find no one in the gallery but the old guard, who sat in the corner, a newspaper on his knee, a black patch over one eye and the other closed. Paul possessed himself of the place and walked confidently up and down, whistling under his breath. After a while he sat down before a blue Rico and lost himself. When he bethought him to look at his watch, it was after seven o'clock, and he rose with a start and ran downstairs, making a face at Augustus Caesar, peering out from the cast room, and an evil gesture at the Venus of Milo as he passed her on the stairway. When Paul reached the ushers' dressing room, half a dozen boys were there already, and he began excitingly to tumble into his uniform. It was one of the few that at all approached fitting, and Paul thought it very becoming though he knew the tight, straight coat accentuated his narrow chest, about which he was exceedingly sensitive. He was always excited while he dressed, twanging all over to the tuning of the strings and the preliminary flourishes of the horns in the music room; but tonight he seemed quite beside himself, and he teased and plagued the boys until, telling him that he was crazy, they put him down on the floor and sat on him.

Somewhat calmed by his suppression, Paul dashed out to the front of the house to seat the early comers. He was a model usher. Gracious and smiling he ran up and down the aisles. Nothing was too much trouble for him; he carried messages and brought programs as though it were his greatest pleasure in life, and all the people in his section thought him a charming boy, feeling that he remembered and admired them. As the house filled, he grew more and more vivacious and animated, and the color came to his cheeks and lips. It was very much as though this were a great reception and Paul were the host. Just as the musicians came out to take their places, his English teacher arrived with checks for the seats which a prominent manufacturer had taken for the season. She betrayed some embarrassment when she handed Paul the tickets, and a hauteur which subsequently made her feel very fool-ish. Paul was startled for a moment, and had the feeling of want-ing to put her out; what business had she here among all these fine people and gay colors? He looked her over and decided that she was not appropriately dressed and must be a fool to sit downstairs in such togs. The tickets had probably been sent her out of kind-ness, he reflected, as he put down a seat for her, and she had about as much right to sit there as he had.

When the symphony began, Paul sank into one of the rear seats with a long sigh of relief, and lost himself as he had done before the Rico. It was not that symphonies, as such, meant any-thing in particular to Paul, but the first sight of the instruments seemed to free some hilarious spirit within him; something that struggled there like the genie in the bottle found by the Arab fish-erman. He felt a sudden zest of life; the lights danced before his eyes and the concert hall blazed into unimaginable splendor. When the soprano soloist came on, Paul forgot even the nastiness of his teacher's being there, and gave himself up to the peculiar intox-ication such personages always had for him. The soloist chanced to be a German woman, by no means in her first youth, and the mother of many children; but she wore a satin gown and a tiara, and she had that indefinable air of achievement, that world-shine upon her, which always blinded Paul to any possible defects. After a concert was over, Paul was often irritable and wretched until he got to sleep and tonight he was even more than usually restless. He had the feeling of not being able to let down; of its being impossi-ble to give up his delicious excitement which was the only thing that could be called living at all. During the last number he with-drew and, after hastily changing his clothes in the dressing room, slipped out to the side door where the singer's carriage stood. Here he began pacing rapidly up and down the walk, waiting to see her come out. Over yonder the Schenley, in its vacant stretch, loomed big and square through the fine rain, the windows of its twelve sto-ries glowing like those of a lighted cardboard house under a Christ-mas tree. All the actors and singers of any importance stayed there when they were in Pittsburgh, and a number of the big manufactur-ers of the place lived there in the winter. Paul had often hung about the hotel, watching the people go in and out, longing to enter and leave schoolmasters and dull care behind him forever.

At last the singer came out, accompanied by the conductor, who helped her into her carriage and closed the door with a cordial auf wiedersehen which set Paul to wondering whether she were not an old sweetheart of his. Paul followed the carriage over to the hotel, walking so rapidly as not to be far from the entrance when the singer alighted and disappeared behind the swinging glass doors which were opened by a Negro in a tall hat and a long coat. In the moment that the door was ajar, it seemed to Paul that he, too, entered. He seemed to feel himself go after her up the steps, into the warm, lighted building, into an exotic, a tropical world of shiny, glistening surfaces and basking ease. He reflected upon the mysterious dishes that were brought into the dining room, the green bottles in buckets of ice, as he had seen them in the supper-party pictures of the Sunday supplement. A quick gust of wind brought the rain down with sudden vehemence, and Paul was startled to find that he was still outside in the slush of the gravel driveway; that his boots were letting in the water and his scanty overcoat was clinging wet about him; that the lights in front of the concert hall were out, and that the rain was driving in sheets between him and the orange glow of the windows above him. There it was, what he wanted tangibly before him, like the fairy world of a Christmas pantomime; as the rain beat in his face. Paul wondered whether he were destined always to shiver in the black night outside, looking up at it.

He turned and walked reluctantly toward the car tracks. The end had to come sometime; his father in his night clothes at the top of the stairs, explanations that did not explain, hastily improvised fictions that were forever tripping him up, his upstairs room and its horrible yellow wallpaper, the creaking bureau with the greasy plush collar-box, and over his painted wooden bed the pictures of George Washington and John Calvin, and the framed motto, 'Feed my Lambs,' which had been worked in red worsted by his mother, whom Paul could not remember. Half an hour later, Paul alighted from the Negley Avenue car and went slowly down one of the side streets off the main thoroughfare. It was a highly respectable street, where all the houses were exactly alike, and where business men of moderate means begot and reared large families of children, all of whom went to Sabbath School and learned the shorter catechism, and were interested in arithmetic; all of whom were as exactly alike as their homes, and of a piece of the monotony in which they lived. Paul never went up Cordelia Street without a shudder of loathing. His home was next to the house of the Cumberland minister. He approached it tonight with the nerveless sense of defeat, the hopeless feeling of sinking back forever into ugliness and commonness that he had always had when he came home. The moment he turned into Cordelia Street he felt the waters close above his head. After each of these orgies of living, he experienced all the physical depression which follows a debauch; the loathing of respectable beds, of common food, of a house permeated by kitchen odors; a shuddering repulsion for the flavorless, colorless mass of everyday existence; a morbid desire for cool things and soft lights and fresh flowers.

The nearer he approached the house, the more absolutely unequal Paul felt to the sight of it all; his ugly sleeping chamber; the old bathroom with the grimy zinc tub, the cracked mirror, the dripping spigots; his father, at the top of the stairs, his hairy legs sticking out from his nightshirt, his feet thrust into carpet slippers. He was so much later than usual that there would certainly be enquiries and reproaches. Paul stopped short before the door. He felt that he could not be accosted by his father tonight; that he could not toss again on that miserable bed. He would not go in. He would tell his father that he had no carfare, and it was raining so hard he had gone home with one of the boys and stayed out all night.

Meanwhile, he was wet and cold. He went around to the back of the house and tried one of the basement windows, found it open, and raised it cautiously, and scrambled down the cellar wall to the floor. There he stood, holding his breath, terrified by the noise he had made; but the floor above him was silent, and there was no creak on the stairs. He found a soap-box, and carried it over to the soft ring of light that streamed from the furnace door, and sat down. He was horribly afraid of rats, so he did not try to sleep, but sat looking distrustfully at the dark, still terrified lest he might have awakened his father.

In such reactions, after one of the experiences which made days and nights out of the dreary blanks of the calendar, when his senses were deadened, Paul's head was always singularly clear. Suppose his father had heard him getting in at the window and had come down and shot him for a burglar? Then, again, suppose his father had come down, pistol in hand, and he had cried out in time to save himself, and his father had been horrified to think how nearly he had killed him? Then, again, suppose a day should come when his father would remember that night, and wish there had been no warning cry to stay his hand? With this last supposition Paul entertained himself until daybreak.

The following Sunday was fine; the sodden November chill was broken by the last flash of autumnal summer. In the morning Paul had to go to church and Sabbath School, as always. On seasonable Sunday afternoons the burghers of Cordelia Street usually sat out on their front stoops, and talked to their neighbors on the next stoop, or called to those across the street in neighborly fashion. The men sat placidly on gay cushions placed upon the steps that led down to the sidewalk, while the women, in their Sunday waists, sat in rockers on the cramped porches, pretending to be greatly at their ease. The children played in the streets; there were so many of them that the place resembled the recreation grounds of a kindergarten. The men on the steps, all in their shirt-sleeves, their vests unbuttoned, sat with their legs well apart, their stomachs comfortably protruding, and talked of the prices of things, or told anecdotes of the sagacity of their various chiefs and overlords. They occasionally looked over the multitude of squabbling children, listened affectionately to their high-pitched, nasal voices, smiling to see their own proclivities reproduced in their offspring, and interspersed their legends of the iron kings with remarks about their sons' progress at school, their grades in arithmetic, and the amounts they had saved in their toy banks. On this last Sunday of November, Paul sat all afternoon on the lowest step of his stoop, staring into the street, while his sisters, in their rockers, were talking to the minister's daughters next door about how many shirtwaists they had made in the last week, and how many waffles someone had eaten at the last church supper. When the weather was warm, and his father was in a particularly jovial frame of mind, the girls made lemonade, which was always brought out in a red-glass pitcher, ornamented with forget-me-nots in blue enamel. This the girls thought very fine, and the neighbors joked about the suspicious color of the pitcher.

Today, Paul's father, on the top step, was talking to a young man who shifted a restless baby from knee to knee. He happened to be the young man who was daily held up to Paul as a model, and after whom it was his father's dearest hope that he would pattern. This young man was a ruddy complexion, with a compressed, red mouth, and faded, nearsighted eyes, over which he wore thick spectacles, with gold bows that curved about his ears. He was clerk to one of the magnates of a great steel corporation, and was looked upon in Cordelia Street as a young man with a future. There was a story that, some five years ago he was now barely twenty-six he had been a trifle dissipated, but in order to curb his appetites and save the loss of time and strength that a sowing of wild oats might have entailed, he had taken his chief's advice, oft reiterated to his employees, and at twenty-one had married the first woman whom he could persuade to share his fortunes. She happened to be an angular schoolmistress, much older than he, who also wore thick glasses, and who had now borne him four children, all nearsighted like herself. The young man was relating how his chief, now cruising in the Mediterranean, kept in touch with all the details of the business, arranging his office hours on his yacht just as though he were at home, and knocking off work enough to keep two stenographers busy. His father told, in turn, the plan his corporation was considering, of putting in an electric railway plant at Cairo. Paul snapped his teeth; he had an awful apprehension that they might spoil it all before he got there. Yet he rather liked to hear these legends of the iron kings, that were told and retold on Sundays and holidays; these stories of palaces in Venice, yachts on the Mediterranean, and high play at Monte Carlo appealed to his fancy, and he was interested in the triumphs of cash-boys who had become famous, though he had no mind for the cash-boy stage.

After supper was over, and he had helped to dry the dishes, Paul nervously asked his father whether he could go to George's to get some help in his geometry, and still more nervously asked for carfare. This latter request he had to repeat, as his father, on principle, did not like to hear requests for money, whether much or little. He asked Paul whether he could not go to some boy who lived nearer, and told him that he ought not to leave his school work until Sunday; but he gave him the dime. He was not a poor man, but he had a worthy ambition to come up in the world. His only reason for allowing Paul to usher was that he thought a boy ought to be earning a little.

Paul bounded upstairs, scrubbed the greasy odor of the dish-water from his hands with the ill-smelling soap he hated, and then shook over his fingers a few drops of violet water from the bottle he kept hidden in his drawer. He left the house with his geometry conspicuously under his arm, and the moment he got out of Cordelia Street and boarded a downtown car, he shook off the lethargy of two deadening days, and began to live again. The leading juvenile of the permanent stock company which played at one of the downtown theatres was an acquaintance of Paul's, and the boy had been invited to drop in at the Sunday night rehearsals whenever he could. For more than a year Paul had spent every available moment loitering about Charley Edward's dressing room. He had won a place among Edward's following not only because the young actor, who could not afford to employ a dresser, often found him useful, but because he recognized in Paul something akin to what churchmen term vocation. It was at the theater and at Carnegie Hall that Paul really lived; the rest was but a sleep and a forgetting. This was Paul's fairy tale, and it had for him all the allurement of a secret love. The moment he inhaled the gassy, painty, dusty odor behind the scenes, he breathed like a prisoner set free, and felt within him the possibility of doing or saving splendid, brilliant things. The moment the cracked orchestra beat out the overture from Martha, or jerked at the serenade from Rigoletto, all stupid and ugly things slid from him, and his senses were deliciously, yet delicately fired.

Perhaps it was because, in Paul's world, the natural nearly always wore the guise of ugliness, that a certain element of artificiality seemed to him necessary in beauty. Perhaps it was because his experience of life elsewhere was so full of Sabbath School picnics, petty economies, wholesome advice as to how to succeed in life, and the unescapable odors of cooking, that he found this existence so alluring, these smartly clad men and women so attractive, that he was so moved by these starry apple orchards that bloomed perennially under the limelight. It would be difficult to put it strongly enough how convincingly the stage entrance of the theater was for Paul the actual portal of romance. Certainly none of the company ever suspected it, least of all Charley Edwards. It was very like the old stories that used to float about London of fabulously rich Jews, who had subterranean halls, with palms, and fountains, and soft lamps, and richly appareled women who never saw the disenchanting light of London day. So, in the midst of that smoke-palled city, enamored of figures and grimy oil, Paul had his secret temple, his wishing-carpet, his bit of blue-and-white Mediterranean shore bathed in perpetual sunshine. Several of Paul's teachers had a theory that his imagination had been perverted by garish fiction; but the truth was he scarcely ever read at all. The books at home were not such as would either tempt or corrupt a youthful mind, and as for reading the novels that some of his friends urged upon him well, he got what he wanted much more quickly from music; any sort of music, from an orchestra to a barrel-organ. He needed only the spark, the indescribable thrill that made his imagination master of his senses, and he could make plots and pictures enough of his own. It was equally true that he was not stage-struck not, at any rate, in the usual acceptation of the expression. He had no desire to become an actor, any more than he had to become a musician. He felt no necessity to do any of these things; what he wanted was to see, to be in the atmosphere, float on the wave of it, to be carried out, blue league after league, away from everything.

After a night behind the scenes, Paul found the schoolroom more than ever repulsive; the bare floors and naked walls; the prosy men who never wore frock coats, or violets in their buttonholes; the women with their dull gowns, shrill voices, and pitiful seriousness about pretensions that govern the dative. He could not bear to have the other pupils think, for a moment, that he took these people seriously; he must convey to them that he considered it all trivial, and was there only by way of a joke, anyway. He had autographed pictures of all the members of the stock company which he showed his classmates, telling them the most incredible stories of his familiarity with these people, of his acquaintance with the soloists who came to Carnegie Hall, his suppers with them and the flowers he sent them. When these stories lost their effect, and his audience grew listless, he would bid all the boys goodbye, announcing that he was going to travel for a while; going to Naples, to California, to Egypt. Then, next Monday, he would slip back, conscious and nervously smiling; his sister was ill, and he would have to defer his voyage until spring.

Matters went steadily worse with Paul at school. In the itch to let his instructors know how heartily he despised them, and how thoroughly he was appreciated elsewhere, he mentioned once or twice that he had no time to fool with theorems; adding with a twitch of the eyebrows and a touch of that nervous bravado which so perplexed them that he was helping the people down at the stock company; they were old friends of his.

The upshot of the matter was that the Principal went to Paul's father, and Paul was taken out of school and put to work. The manager at Carnegie Hall was told to get another usher in his stead; the doorkeeper at the theater was warned not to admit him to the house; and Charley Edwards remorsefully promised the boy's father not to see him again.

The members of the stock company were vastly amused when some of Paul's stories reached them especially the women. They were hard-working women, most of them supporting indolent husbands or brothers, and they laughed rather bitterly at having stirred the boy to such fervid and florid inventions. They agreed with the faculty and with his father, that Paul's was a bad case.

The east-bound train was plowing through a January snow-storm; the dull dawn was beginning to show grey when the engine whistled a mile out of Newark. Paul started up from the seat where he had lain curled in uneasy slumber, rubbed the breath-misted window glass with his hand, and peered out. The snow was whirling in curling eddies above the white bottom lands, and the drifts lay already deep in the fields and along the fences, while here and there the tall dead grass and dried weed stalks protruded black above it. Lights shone from the scattered houses, and a gang of laborers who stood beside the track waved their lanterns. Paul had slept very little, and he felt grimy and uncomfortable. He had made the all-night journey in a day coach because he was afraid if he took a Pullman he might be seen by some Pittsburgh business man who had noticed him in Denny and Carson's office. When the whistle woke him, he clutched quickly at his breast pocket, glancing about him with an uncertain smile. But the little, clay-bespattered Italians were still sleeping, the slatternly women across the aisle were in open-mouthed oblivion, and even the crumby, crying babies were for the time stilled. Paul settled back to struggle with his impatience as best he could. When he arrived at the Jersey City station, he hurried through his breakfast, manifestly ill at ease and keeping a sharp eye about him. After he reached the Twenty-Third Street station, he consulted a cabman, and had himself driven to a men's furnishing establishment which was just opening for the day. He spent upward of two hours there, buying, buying with endless reconsidering and great care. His new street suit he put on in the fitting-room; the frock coat and dress clothes he had bundled into the cab with his new shirts. Then he drove to a hatter's and a shoe house. His next errand was at Tiffany's, where he selected silver-mounted brushes and a scarf pin. He would not wait to have his silver marked, he said. Lastly, he stopped at a trunk shop on Broadway, and had his purchases packed into various traveling bags.

It was a little after one o'clock when he drove up to the Waldorf, and, after settling with the cabman, went into the office. He registered from Washington; said his mother and father had been abroad, and that he had come down to await the arrival of their steamer. He told his story plausibly and had no trouble, since he offered to pay for them in advance, in engaging his rooms; a sleeping room, sitting room, and bath.

Not once, but a hundred times Paul had planned his entry into New York. He had gone over every detail of it with Charley Edwards, and in his scrapbook at home there were pages of description about New York hotels, cut from the Sunday papers.

When he was shown to his sitting-room on the eighth floor, he saw at a glance that everything was as it should be; there was but one detail in his mental picture that the place did not realize, so he rang for the bellboy and sent him down for flowers. He moved about nervously until the boy returned, putting away his new linen and fingering it delightedly as he did so. When the flowers came, he put them hastily into water, and then tumbled into a hot bath. Presently he came out of his white bathroom, resplendent in his new silk underwear, and playing with the tassels of his red robe.

The snow was whirling so fiercely outside his windows that he could scarcely see across the street, but within, the air was deliciously soft and fragrant. He put the violets and jonquils on the taboret beside the couch, and threw himself down with a long sigh, covering himself with a Roman blanket. He was thoroughly tired; he had been in such haste, he had stood up to such a strain, covered so much ground in the last twenty-four hours, that he wanted to think how it had all come about. Lulled by the sound of the wind, the warm air, and the cool fragrance of the flowers, he sank into deep, drowsy retrospection. It had been wonderfully simple; when they had shut him out of the theater and concert hall, when they had taken away his bone, the whole thing was virtually determined. The rest was a mere matter of opportunity. The only thing that at all surprised him as his own courage for he realized well enough that he had always been tormented by fear, a sort of apprehensive dread which, of late years, as the meshes of the lies he had told closed about him, had been pulling the muscles of his body tighter and tighter. Until now, he could not remember a time when he had not been dreading something. Even when he was a little boy, it was always there behind him, or before, or on either side. There had always been the shadowed corner, the dark place into which he dared not look, but from which something seemed always to be watching him and Paul had done things that were not pretty to watch, he knew.

But now he had a curious sense of relief, as though he had at last thrown down the gauntlet to the thing in the corner.

Yet it was but a day since he had been sulking in the traces; but yesterday afternoon that he had been sent to the bank with Denny and Carson's deposit, as usual but this time he was instructed to leave the book to be balanced. There was above two thousand dollars in checks, and nearly a thousand in the bank notes which he had taken from the book and quietly transferred to his pocket. At the bank he had made out a new deposit slip. His nerves had been steady enough to permit of his returning to the office, where he had finished his work and asked for full day's holiday tomorrow, Saturday, giving a perfectly reasonable pretext. The bank book, he knew, would not be returned before Monday or Tuesday, and his father would be out of town for the next week. From the time he slipped the bank notes into his pocket until he boarded the night train for New York, he had not known a moment's hesitation.

How astonishingly easy it had all been; here he was, the thing done; and this time there would be no awakening, no figure at the top of the stairs. He watched the snowflakes whirling by his window until he fell asleep. When he awoke, it was four o'clock in the afternoon. He bounded up with a start; one of his precious days gone already! He spent nearly an hour in dressing, watching every stage of his toilet carefully in the mirror. Everything was quite perfect; he was exactly the kind of boy he had always wanted to be.

When he went downstairs, Paul took a carriage and drove up Fifth Avenue toward the Park. The snow had somewhat abated; carriages and tradesmen's wagons were hurrying soundlessly to and fro in the winter twilight; boys in woolen mufflers were shoveling off the doorsteps; the Avenue stages made fine spots of color against the white street. Here and there on the corners whole flower gardens blooming behind glass windows, against which the snowflakes stuck and melted; violets, roses, carnations, lilies-of-the-valley somehow vastly more lovely and alluring that they blossomed thus unnaturally in the snow. The Park itself was a wonderful stage, a winterpiece. When he returned, the pause of the twilight had ceased, and the tune of the streets had changed. The snow was falling faster, lights streamed from the hotels that reared their many stories fearlessly up into the storm, defying the raging Atlantic winds. A long, black stream of carriages poured down the Avenue, intersected here and there by other streams, tending horizontally. There were a score of cabs about the entrance of his hotel, and his driver had to wait. Boys in livery were running in and out of the awning stretched across the sidewalk, up and down the red velvet carpet laid from the door to the street. Above, about, within it all, was the rumble and roar, the hurry and toss of thousands of human beings as hot for pleasure as himself, and on every side of him towered the glaring affirmation of the omnipotence of wealth.

The boy set his teeth and drew his shoulders together in a spasm of realization; the plot of all dramas, the text of all romances, the nerve-stuff of all sensations was whirling about him like the snowflakes. He burnt like a fagot in a tempest. When Paul came down to dinner, the music of the orchestra floated up the elevator shaft to greet him. As he stepped into the thronged corridors, he sank back into one of the chairs against the wall to get his breath. The lights, the chatter, the perfumes, the bewildering medley of color he had, for a moment, the feeling of not being able to stand it. But only for a moment; these were his own people, he told himself. He went slowly about the corridors, through the writing rooms, smoking rooms, reception rooms, as through he were exploring the chambers of an enchanted palace, built and peopled for him alone.

When he reached the dining room he sat down at a table near a window. The flowers, the white linen, the many-colored wine glasses, the gay toilettes of the women, the low popping of corks, the undulating repetitions of the Blue Danube from the orchestra, all flooded Paul's dream with bewildering radiance. When the roseate tinge of his champagne was added that cold, precious, bubbling stuff that creamed and foamed in his glass Paul wondered that there were honest men in the world at all. This was what all the world was fighting for, he reflected; this was what all the struggle was about. He doubted the reality of his past. Had he ever known a place called Cordelia Street, a place where fagged-looking business men boarded the early car? Mere rivets in a machine they seemed to Paul sickening men, with combings of children's hair always hanging to their coats, and the smell of cooking in their clothes. Cordelia Street Ah, that belonged to another time and country! Had he not always been thus, had he not sat here night after night, from as far back as he could remember, looking pensively over just such shimmering textures, and slowly turning the stem of a glass like this one between his thumb and middle finger? He rather thought he had.

He was not in the least abashed or lonely. He had no special desire to meet or to know any of these people; all he demanded was the right to look on and conjecture, to watch the pageant. The mere stage properties were all he contended for. Nor was he lonely later in the evening, in his loge at the Opera. He was entirely rid of his nervous misgivings, of his forced aggressiveness, of the imperative desire to show himself different from his surroundings. He felt now that his surroundings explained him. Nobody questioned the purple; he had only to wear it passively. He had only to glance down at his dress coat to reassure himself that here it would be impossible for anyone to humiliate him.

He found it hard to leave his beautiful sitting room to go to bed that night, and sat long watching the raging storm from his turret window. When he went to sleep, it was with the lights turned on in his bedroom; partly because of his old timidity, and partly so that, if he should wake in the night, there would be no wretched moment of doubt, no horrible suspicion of yellow wallpaper, or of Washington and Calvin above his bed.

On Sunday morning the city was practically snowbound. Paul breakfasted late, and in the afternoon he fell in with a wild San Francisco boy, a Freshman at Yale, who said he had run down for

a little flyer over Sunday. The young man offered to show Paul the
night side of town, and the two boys went off together after dinner, not returning to the hotel until seven o'clock the next morning. They had started out in the confiding warmth of a champagne
friendship, but their parting in the elevator was singularly cool.
The freshman pulled himself together to make his train, and Paul
went to bed. He awoke at two o'clock in the afternoon, very thirsty
and dizzy, and rang for ice water, coffee, and the Pittsburgh papers. On the part of the hotel management, Paul excited no suspicion. There was this to be said for him, that he wore his spoils
with dignity and in no way made himself conspicuous. His chief
greediness lay in his ears and eyes, and his excesses were not offensive ones. His dearest pleasures were the grey winter twilights
in his sitting room; his quiet enjoyment of his flowers, his clothes,
his wide divan, his cigarette, and his sense of power. He could not
remember a time when he had felt so at peace with himself. The
mere release from the necessity of petty lying, lying every day and
every day, restored his self respect. He had never lied for pleasure,
even at school; but to make himself noticed and admired, to assert
his difference from other Cordelia Street boys; and he felt a good
deal more manly, more honest, even, now that he had no need for
boastful pretensions, now that he could, as his actor friends used to
say, dress the part. It was characteristic that remorse did not occur
to him. His golden days went by without a shadow, and he made
each as perfect as he could.

On the eighth day of his arrival in New York, he found the
whole affair exploited in the Pittsburgh papers, exploited with a
wealth of detail which indicated that local news of a sensational
nature was at a low ebb. The firm of Denny and Carson announced
that it had no intention of prosecuting. The Cumberland minister
had been interviewed, and expressed his hope of yet reclaiming
the motherless lad, and Paul's Sabbath School teacher declared
that she would spare no effort to that end. The rumor had reached
Pittsburgh that the boy had been seen in a New York hotel, and
his father had gone East to find him and bring him home. Paul had
just come in to dress for dinner; he sank into the chair, weak in
the knees, and clasped his head in his hands. It was to be worse
than jail, even; the tepid waters of Cordelia Street were to close
over him finally and forever. The grey monotony stretched before

him in hopeless, unrelieved years—Sabbath School, Young People's Meeting, the yellow-papered room, the damp dish towels—it all rushed back upon him with sickening vividness. He had the old feeling that the orchestra had suddenly stopped, the sinking sensation that the play was over. The sweat broke out on his face, and he sprang to his feet, looked about him with his white, conscious smile, and winked at himself in the mirror. With something of the childish belief in miracles with which he had so often gone to class, all his lessons unlearned, Paul dressed and dashed whistling down the corridor to the elevator. He had no sooner entered the dining room and caught the measure of the music than his remembrance was lightened by his old elastic power of claiming the moment, mounting with it, and finding it all-sufficient. The glare and glitter about him, the mere scenic accessories had again, and for the last time, their old potency. He would show himself that he was game, he would finish the thing splendidly. He doubted, more than ever, the existence of Cordelia Street, and for the first time he drank his wine recklessly. Was he not, after all, one of these fortunate beings? Was he not still himself, and in his own place? He drummed a nervous accompaniment to the music and looked about him, telling himself over and over that it had paid. He reflected drowsily, to the swell of the violin and the chill sweetness of his wine, that he might have done it more wisely. He might have caught an outbound steamer and been well out of their clutches before now. But the other side of the world had seemed too far away and too uncertain then; he could not have waited for it; his need had been too sharp. If he had to choose over again, he would do the same thing tomorrow. He looked affectionately about the dining room, now gilded with a soft mist. Ah, it had paid indeed!

Paul was awakened next morning by a painful throbbing in his head and feet. He had thrown himself across the bed without undressing, and had slept with his shoes on. His limbs and hands were lead-heavy, and his tongue and throat were parched. There came upon him one of those fateful attacks of clear-headedness that never occurred except when he was physically exhausted and his nerves hung loose. He lay still and closed his eyes and let the tide of realities wash over him. His father was in New York; stopping at some joint or other, he told himself. The memory of successive summers on the front stoop fell upon him like a weight of black water. He had not a hundred dollars left; and he knew now, more than ever, that money was everything, the wall that stood between all he loathed and all he wanted. The thing was winding itself up; he had thought of that on his first glorious day in New York, and had even provided a way to snap the thread. It lay on his dressing table now; he had got it out last night when he came blindly up from dinner but the shiny metal hurt his eyes, and he disliked the look of it, anyway. He rose and moved about with a painful effort, succumbing now and again to attacks of nausea. It was the old depression exaggerated; all the world had become Cordelia Street. Yet somehow he was not afraid of anything, was absolutely calm; perhaps because he had looked into the dark corner at last, and knew. It was bad enough, what he saw there; but somehow not so bad as his long fear of it had been. He saw everything clearly now. He had a feeling that he had made the best of it, that he had lived the sort of life he was meant to live, and for half an hour he sat staring at the revolver. But he told himself that was not the way, so he went downstairs and took a cab to the ferry.

When Paul arrived at Newark, he got off the train and took another cab, directing the driver to follow the Pennsylvania tracks out of town. The snow lay heavy on the roadways and had drifted deep in the open fields. Only here and there the dead grass or dried weed stalks projected, singularly black, above it. Once well into the country, Paul dismissed the carriage and walked, floundering along the tracks, his mind a medley of irrelevant things. He seemed to hold in his brain an actual picture of everything he had seen that morning. He remembered every feature of both his drivers, the toothless old woman from whom he had bought the red flowers in his coat, the agent from whom he had got his ticket, and all of his fellow-passengers on the ferry. His mind, unable to cope with vital matters near at hand, worked feverishly and deftly at sorting and grouping these images. They made for him a part of the ugliness of the world, of the ache in his head, and the bitter burning on his tongue. He stooped and put a handful of snow into his mouth as he walked, but that, too, seemed hot. When he reached a little hillside, where the tracks ran through a cut some twenty feet below him, he stopped and sat down.

The carnations in his coat were drooping with cold, he noticed; their red glory over. It occurred to him that all the flowers he had seen in the show windows that first night must have gone the same way, long before this. It was only one splendid breath they had, in spite of their brave mockery at the winter outside the glass. It was a losing game in the end, it seemed, this revolt against the homilies by which the world is run. Paul took one of the blossoms carefully from his coat and scooped a little hole in the snow, where he covered it up. Then he dozed awhile, from his weak condition, seeming insensible to the cold.

The sound of an approaching train woke him and he started to his feet, remembering only his resolution, and afraid lest he should be too late. He stood watching the approaching locomotive, his teeth chattering, his lips drawn away from them in a frightened smile; once or twice he glanced nervously sidewise, as though he were being watched. When the right moment came, he jumped. As he fell, the folly of his haste occurred to him with merciless clearness, the vastness of what he had left undone. There flashed through his brain, clearer than ever before, the blue Adriatic water, the yellow of Algerian sands.

He felt something strike his chest his body being thrown swiftly through the air, on and on, immeasurably far and fast, while his limbs gently relaxed. Then, because the picture-making mechanism was crushed, the disturbing visions flashed into black, and Paul dropped back into the immense design of things.

SOLDIER'S HOME
Ernest Hemingway

Krebs went to the war from a Methodist college in Kansas. There is a picture which shows him among his fraternity brothers, all of them wearing exactly the same height and style collar. He enlisted in the Marines in 1917 and did not return to the United States until the second division returned from the Rhine in the summer of 1919.

There is a picture which shows him on the Rhine with two German girls and another corporal. Krebs and the corporal look too big for their uniforms. The German girls are not beautiful. The Rhine does not show in the picture.

By the time Krebs returned to his home town in Oklahoma the greeting of heroes was over. He came back much too late. The men from the town who had been drafted had all been welcomed elaborately on their return. There had been a great deal of hysteria. Now the reaction had set in. People seemed to think it was rather ridiculous for Krebs to be getting back so late, years after the war was over.

At first Krebs, who had been at Belleau Wood, Soissons, the Champagne, St. Mihiel, and in the Argonne did not want to talk about the war at all. Later he felt the need to talk but no one wanted to hear about it. His town had heard too many atrocity stories to be thrilled by actualities. Krebs found that to be listened to at all he had to lie, and after he had done this twice he, too, had a reaction against the war and against talking about it. A distaste for everything that had happened to him in the war set in because of the lies he had told. All of the times that had been able to make him feel cool and clear inside himself when he thought of them; the times so long back when he had done the one thing, the only thing for a man to do, easily and naturally, when he might have done something else, now lost their cool, valuable quality and then were lost themselves.

His lies were quite unimportant lies and consisted in attributing to himself things other men had seen, done, or heard of, and stating as facts certain apocryphal incidents familiar to all soldiers. Even his lies were not sensational at the pool room. His acquaintances, who had heard detailed accounts of German women found chained to machine guns in the Argonne forest and who could not comprehend, or were barred by their patriotism from interest in, any German machine gunners who were not chained, were not thrilled by his stories.

Krebs acquired the nausea in regard to experience that is the result of untruth or exaggeration, and when he occasionally met another man who had really been a soldier and they talked a few minutes in the dressing room at a dance he fell into the easy pose of the old soldier among other soldiers; that he had been badly, sickeningly frightened all the time. In this way he lost everything.

During this time, it was late summer, he was sleeping late in bed, getting up to walk down town to the library to get a book, eating lunch at home, reading on the front porch until he became bored, and then walking down through the town to spend the hottest hours of the day in the cool dark of the pool room. He loved to play pool.

In the evening he practiced on his clarinet, strolled down town, read, and went to bed. He was still a hero to his two young sisters. His mother would have given him breakfast in bed if he had wanted it. She often came in when he was in bed and asked him to tell her about the war, but her attention always wandered. His father was noncommittal.

Before Krebs went away to the war he had never been allowed to drive the family motor car. His father was in the real estate business and always wanted the car to be at his command when he required it to take clients out into the country to show them a piece of farm property. The car always stood outside the First National Bank building where his father had an office on the second floor. Now, after the war, it was still the same car.

Nothing was changed in the town except that the young girls had grown up. But they lived in such a complicated world of already defined alliances and shifting feuds that Krebs did not feel the energy or the courage to break into it. He liked to look at them, though. There were so many good-looking young girls. Most of them had their hair cut short. When he went away only little girls wore their hair like that or girls that were fast. They all wore sweaters and shirt waists with round Dutch collars. It was a pattern. He liked to look at them from the front porch as they walked on the other side of the street. He liked to watch them walking under the shade of the trees. He liked the round Dutch collars above their sweaters. He liked their silk stockings and flat shoes. He liked their bobbed hair and the way they walked.

When he was in town their appeal to him was not very strong. He did not like them when he saw them in the Greek's ice cream parlor. He did not want them themselves really. They were too complicated. There was something else. Vaguely he wanted a girl but he did not want to have to work to get her. He would have liked to have a girl but he did not want to have to spend a long time getting her. He did not want to get into the intrigue and the politics. He did not want to have to do any courting. He did not want to tell any more lies. It wasn't worth it.

He did not want any consequences. He did not want any consequences ever again. He wanted to live along without consequences. Besides he did not really need a girl. The army had taught him that. It was all right to pose as though you had to have a girl. Nearly everybody did that. But it wasn't true. You did not need a girl. That was the funny thing. First a fellow boasted how girls mean nothing to him, that he never thought about them, that they could not touch him. Then a fellow boasted that he could not get along without girls, that he had to have them all the time, that he could not go to sleep without them.

That was all a lie. It was all a lie both ways. You did not need a girl unless you thought about them. He learned that in the army. Then sooner or later you always got one. When you were really ripe for a girl you always got one. You did not have to think about it. Sooner or later it would come. He had learned that in the army.

Now he would have liked a girl if she had come to him and not wanted to talk. But here at home it was all too complicated. He knew he could never get through it all again. It was not worth the trouble. That was the thing about French girls and German girls.

There was not all this talking. You couldn't talk much and you did not need to talk. It was simple and you were friends. He thought about France and then he began to think about Germany. On the whole he had liked Germany better. He did not want to leave Germany. He did not want to come home. Still, he had come home. He sat on the front porch.

He liked the girls that were walking along the other side of the street. He liked the look of them much better than the French girls or the German girls. But the world they were in was not the world he was in. He would like to have one of them. But it was not worth it. They were such a nice pattern. He liked the pattern. It was exciting. But he would not go through all the talking. He did not want them badly enough. He liked to look at them all, though. It was not worth it. Not now when things were getting good again.

He sat there on the porch reading a book on the war. It was a history and he was reading about all the engagements he had been in. It was the most interesting reading he had ever done. He wished there were more maps. He looked forward with a good feeling to reading all the really good histories when they would come out with good detail maps. Now he was really learning about the war. He had been a good soldier. That made a difference.

One morning after he had been home about a month his mother came into his bedroom and sat on the bed. She smoothed her apron.

"I had a talk with your father last night, Harold," she said, "and he is willing for you to take the car out in the evenings."

"Yeah?" said Krebs, who was not fully awake. "Take the car out? Yeah?"

"Yes. Your father has felt for some time that you should be able to take the car out in the evenings whenever you wished but we only talked it over last night."

"I'll bet you made him," Krebs said.

"No. It was your father's suggestion that we talk the matter over."

"Yeah, I'll bet you made him," Krebs sat up in bed.

"Will you come down to breakfast, Harold?" his mother said.

"As soon as I get my clothes on," Krebs said.

His mother went out of the room and he could hear her frying something downstairs while he washed, shaved, and dressed to go

down into the dining-room for breakfast. While he was eating
breakfast his sister brought in the mail.

"Well, Hare," she said. "You old sleepyhead. What do you ever
get up for?" Krebs looked at her. He liked her. She was his best
sister. "Have you got the paper?" he asked.

She handed him *The Kansas City Star* and he shucked off its
brown wrapper and opened it to the sporting page. He folded the
Star open and propped it against the water pitcher with his cereal
dish to steady it, so he could read while he ate.

"Harold," his mother stood in the kitchen doorway, "Harold,
please don't muss up the paper, You father can't read his *Star* if
it's been mussed."

"I won't muss it," Krebs said.

His sister sat down at the table and watched him while he read.

"We're playing indoor over at school this afternoon," she said.
"I'm going to pitch."

"Good," said Krebs. "How's the old wing?"

"I can pitch better than lots of the boys. I tell them all you
taught me. The other girls aren't much good."

"Yeah?" said Krebs.

"I tell them all you're my beau. Aren't you my beau, Hare?"

"You bet."

"Couldn't your brother really be your beau just because he's
your brother?"

"I don't know."

"Sure you know. Couldn't you be my beau, Hare, if I was old
enough and if you wanted to?"

"Sure. You're my girl now."

"Am I really your girl?"

"Sure."

"Do you love me?"

"Uh, huh."

"Will you love me always?"

"Sure."

"Will you come over and watch me play indoor?"

"Maybe."

"Aw, Hare, you don't love me. If you loved me, you'd want to
come over and watch me play indoor."

Krebs's mother came into the dining-room from the kitchen. She carried a plate with two fried eggs and some crisp bacon on it and a plate of buckwheat cakes.

"You run along, Helen," she said. "I want to talk to Harold."

She put the eggs and bacon down in front of him and brought in a jug of maple syrup for the buckwheat cakes. Then she sat down across the table from Krebs.

"I wish you'd put down the paper a minute, Harold." she said.

Krebs took down the paper and folded it.

"Have you decided what you are going to do yet, Harold?" his mother said, taking off her glasses.

"No," said Krebs.

"Don't you think it's about time?" His mother did not say this in a mean way. She seemed worried.

"I hadn't thought about it," Krebs said.

"God has some work for everyone to do," his mother said. "There can be no idle hands in His Kingdom."

"I'm not in His Kingdom," said Krebs.

"We are all of us in His Kingdom."

Krebs felt embarrassed and resentful as always.

"I've worried about you so much, Harold," his mother went on. "I know the temptations you must have been exposed to. I know how weak men are. I know what your own dear grandfather, my own father, told us about the Civil War and I have prayed for you. I pray for you all day long, Harold."

Krebs looked at the bacon fat hardening on his plate.

"Your father is worried, too," his mother went on. "He thinks you have lost your ambition, that you haven't got a definite aim in life. Charley Simmons, who is just your age, has a good job and is going to be married. The boys are all settling down; they're all determined to get somewhere; you can see that boys like Charley Simmons are on their way to being really a credit to the community."

Krebs said nothing.

"Don't look that way, Harold," his mother said. "You know we love you and I want to tell you for your own good how matters stand. Your father does not want to hamper your freedom. He thinks you should be allowed to drive the car. If you want to take some of the nice girls out riding with you, we are only too pleased.

We want you to enjoy yourself. But you are going to have to settle down to work, Harold. Your father doesn't care what you start in at. All work is honorable as he says. But you've got to make a start at something. He asked me to speak to you this morning and then you can stop in and see him at his office."

"Is that all?" Krebs said.

"Yes. Don't you love your mother, dear boy?"

"No," Krebs said.

His mother looked at him across the table. Her eyes were shiny. She started crying.

"I don't love anybody," Krebs said.

It wasn't any good. He couldn't tell her, he couldn't make her see it. It was silly to have said it. He had only hurt her. He went over and took hold of her arm. She was crying with her head in her hands.

"I didn't mean it," he said. "I was just angry at something. I didn't mean I didn't love you."

His mother went on crying. Krebs put his arm on her shoulder.

"Can't you believe me, mother?"

His mother shook her head.

"Please, please, mother. Please believe me."

"All right," the mother said chokily. She looked up at him. "I believe you, Harold."

Krebs kissed her hair. She put her face up to him.

"I'm your mother," she said. "I held you next to my heart when you were a tiny baby."

Krebs felt sick and vaguely nauseated.

"I know, Mummy," he said. "I'll try and be a good boy for you."

"Would you kneel and pray with me, Harold?" his mother asked.

They knelt down beside the dining-room table and Krebs's mother prayed.

"Now, you pray, Harold," she said.

"I can't," Krebs said.

"Try, Harold."

"I can't."

"Do you want me to pray for you?"

"Yes."

So his mother prayed for him and then they stood up and Krebs kissed his mother and went out of the house. He had tried so to keep his life from being complicated. Still, none of it had touched him. He had felt sorry for his mother and she had made him lie. He would go to Kansas City and get a job and she would feel all right about it. There would be one more scene maybe before he got away. He would not go down to his father's office. He would miss that one. He wanted his life to go smoothly. It had just gotten going that way. Well, that was all over now, anyway. He would go over to the schoolyard and watch Helen play indoor baseball.

SON IN THE AFTERNOON
John A. Williams

It was hot. I tend to be a bitch when it's hot. I goosed the little Ford over Sepulveda Boulevard toward Santa Monica until I got stuck in the traffic that pours from L.A. into the surrounding towns. I'd had a very lousy day at the studio. I was, still am, a writer and this studio had hired me to check scripts and films with Negroes in them to make sure the Negro moviegoer wouldn't be offended. The signs were already clear; one day the whole of American industry would be racing pellmell to get a Negro, showcase a spade. I was kind of a pioneer. I'm a negro writer, you see. The day had been tough because of a couple of verbs slink and walk. One of those Hollywood hippies had done a script calling for a Negro waiter to slink away from the table where a dinner party was glaring at him. I said the waiter should walk, not slink, because later on he becomes a hero. The Hollywood hippie, who understood it all because he had some colored friends, said that it was essential to the plot that the waiter slink. I said you don't slink one minute and become a hero the next; there has to be some consistency. The Negro actor I was standing up for said nothing either way. He had played Uncle Tom roles so long that he had become Uncle Tom. But the director agreed with me.

Anyway . . . hear me out now. I was on my way to Santa Monica to pick up my mother, Nora. It was a long haul for such a hot day. I had planned a quiet evening: a nice shower, fresh clothes, and then I would have dinner at the Watkins and talk with some of the musicians on the scene for a quick taste before they cut to their gigs. After, I was going to the Pigalle down on Figueroa and catch Earl Grant at the organ, and still later, if nothing exciting happened, I'd pick up Scottie and make it to the Lighthouse on the Beach or

246

to the Strollers and listen to some of the white boys play. I liked the long drive, especially while listening to Sleepy Stein's show on the radio. Later, much later of course, it would be home, back to Watts. So you see, this picking up Nora was a little inconvenient. My mother was a maid for the Couchmans. Ronald Couchman was an architect, a good one I understood from Nora who has a fine sense for this sort of thing; you don't work in some hundred-odd houses during your life without getting some idea of the way a house should be laid out. Couchman's wife, Kay, was a playgirl who drove a white Jaguar from one party to another. My mother didn't like her too much; she didn't seem to care much for her son, Ronald, junior. There's something wrong with a parent who can't really love her own child, Nora thought. The Couchmans lived in a real fine residential section, of course. A number of actors lived nearby, character actors, not really big stars.

Somehow it is very funny. I mean that the maids and butlers knew everything about these people, and these people knew nothing at all about the help. Through Nora and her friends I knew who was laying whose wife; who had money and who really had money; I knew about the wild parties hours before the police, and who smoked marijuana, when, and where they got it.

To get to Couchman's driveway I had to go three blocks up one side of a palm-planted center strip and back down the other. The driveway bent gently, then swept back out of sight of the main road. The house, sheltered by slim palms, looked like a transplanted New England Colonial. I parked and walked to the kitchen door, skirting the growling Great Dane who was tied to a tree. That was the route to the kitchen door.

I don't like kitchen doors. Entering people's houses by them, I mean. I'd done this thing most of my life when I called at places where Nora worked to pick up the patched or worn sheets or the half-eaten roasts, the battered, tarnished silver, the fringe benefits of a housemaid. As a teen-ager I'd told Nora I was through with that crap; I was not going through anyone's kitchen door. She only laughed and said I'd learn. One day soon after, I called for her and without knocking walked right through the front door of this house and right on through the living room. I was almost out of the room when I saw feet behind the couch. I leaned over and there was Mr. Jorgensen and his wife making out like crazy. I guess they

thought Nora had gone and it must have hit them sort of suddenly
and they went at it like the hell-bomb was due to drop any minute.
I've been that way too, mostly in the spring. Of course, when
Mr. Jorgensen looked over his shoulder and saw me, you know what
happened. I was thrown out and Nora right behind me. It was the
middle of winter, the old man was sick and the coal bill three months
overdue. Nora was right about those kitchen doors. I learned.

My mother saw me before I could ring the bell. She opened the
door. "Hello," she said. She was breathing hard, like she'd been
running or something. "Come in and sit down. I don't know where
that Kay is. Little Ronald is sick and she's probably out gettin'
drunk again." She left me then and trotted back through the house,
I guess to be with Ronnie. I hated the combination of her white ny-
lon uniform, her dark brown face and the wide streaks of gray in
her hair. Nora had married this guy from Texas a few years after
the old man had died. He was all right. He made out okay. Nora
didn't have to work, but she just couldn't be still; she always had to
be doing something. I suggested she quit work, but I had as much
luck as her husband. I used to tease her about liking to be around
those white folks. It would have been good for her to take an extended trip around the country visiting my brothers and sisters.
Once she got to Philadelphia, she could go right out in the cemetery and sit awhile with the old man.

I walked through the Couchman home. I liked the library. I
thought if I knew Couchman I'd like him. The room made me feel
like that. I left it and went into the big living room. You could tell
that Couchman had let his wife do that. Everything in it was fast,
dart-like, with no sense of ease. But on the walls were several of
Couchman's conceptions of buildings and homes. I guess he was
a disciple of Wright. My mother walked rapidly through the room
without looking at me and said, "Just be patient, Wendell. She
should be here real soon."

"Yeah," I said, "with a snootful." I had turned back to the
drawings when Ronnie scampered into the room, his face twisted
with rage.

"Nora!" he tried to roar, perhaps the way he'd seen the parents of some of his friends roar at their maids. I'm sure Kay didn't
shout at Nora, and I don't think Couchman would. But then no one
shouts at Nora. "Nora, you come right back here this minute!" the

little bastard shouted and stamped and pointed to a spot on the floor where Nora was supposed to come to roost. I have a nasty temper. Sometimes it lies dormant for ages and at other times, like when the weather is hot and nothing seems to be going right, it's bubbling and ready to explode. "Don't talk to my mother like that, you little . . . !" I said sharply, breaking off just before I cursed. I wanted him to be large enough for me to strike. "How'd you like me to talk to your mother like that?"

The nine-year-old looked up at me in surprise and confusion. He hadn't expected me to say anything. I was just another piece of furniture. Tears rose in his eyes and spilled out onto his pale cheeks. He put his hands behind him, twisted them. He moved backwards, away from me. He looked at my mother with a "Nora, come help me" look. And sure enough, there was Nora, speeding back across the room, gathering the kid in her arms, tucking his robe together. I was too angry to feel hatred for myself.

Ronnie was the Couchman's only kid. Nora loved him. I suppose that was the trouble. Couchman was gone ten, twelve hours a day. Kay didn't stay around the house any longer than she had to. So Ronnie had only my mother. I think kids should have someone to love, and Nora wasn't a bad sort. But somehow when the six of us, her own children, were growing up we never had her. She was gone, out scuffling to get those crumbs to put into our mouths and shoes for our feet and praying for something to happen so that all the space in between would be taken care of. Nora's affection for us took the form of rushing out into the morning's five o'clock blackness to wake some silly bitch and get her coffee; took form in her trudging five miles home every night instead of taking the streetcar to save money to buy tablets for us, to use at school, we said. But the truth was that all of us liked to draw and we went through a writing tablet in a couple of hours every day. Can you imagine? There's not a goddamn artist among us. We never had the physical affection, the pat on the head, the quick, smiling kiss, the "gimmee a hug" routine.

All of this Ronnie was getting.

Now he buried his little blond head in Nora's breast and sobbed. "There, there now," Nora said, "Don't you cry, Ronnie. Ol' Wendell is just jealous, and he hasn't much sense either. He didn't mean nuthin'."

I left the room. Nora had hit it of course, hit it and passed on. I looked back. It didn't look so incongruous, the white and black together. I mean. Ronnie was still sobbing. His head bobbed gently on Nora's shoulder. The only time I ever got that close to her was when she trapped me with a bear hug so she could whale the daylights out of me after I put a snowball through Mrs. Grant's window. I walked outside and lit a cigarette. When Ronnie was in the hospital the month before, Nora got me to run her way over to Hollywood every night to see him. I didn't like that worth a damn. All right, I'll admit it: it did upset me. All that affection I didn't get nor my brothers and sisters going to that little white boy who, without a doubt, when away from her called her the names he'd learned from adults. Can you imagine a nine-year-old kid calling Nora a "girl," "our girl?" I spat at the Great Dane. He snarled and then I bounced a rock off his fanny. "Lay down, you bastard," I muttered. It was a good thing he was tied up.

I heard the low cough of the Jaguar slapping against the road. The car was throttled down, and with a muted roar it swung into the driveway. The woman aimed it for me. I was evil enough not to move. I was tired of playing with these people. At the last moment, grinning, she swung the wheel over and braked. She bounded out of the car like a tennis player vaulting over a net.

"Hi," she said tugging at her shorts.

"Hello."

"You're Nora's boy?"

"I'm Nora's son." Hell, I was as old as she was; besides, I can't stand "boy."

"Nora tells us you're working in Hollywood. Like it?"

"It's all right."

"You must be pretty talented."

We stood looking at each other while the dog whined for her attention. Kay had a nice body and it was well tanned. She was high, boy, was she high. Looking at her, I could feel myself going into my sexy bastard routine; sometimes I can swing it great. Maybe it had to do with the business inside. Kay took off her sunglasses and took a good look at me. "Do you have a cigarette?"

I gave her one and lit it. "Nice tan," I said. Most white people I know think it's a great big deal if a Negro compliments them on their tans. It's a large laugh. You have all this volleyball about

color and come summer you can't hold the white folks back from
the beaches, anyplace where they can get some sun. And of course
the blacker they get, the more pleased they are. Crazy. If there is
ever a Negro revolt, it will come during the summer and Negroes
will descend upon the beaches around the nation and paralyze the
country. You can't conceal cattle prods and bombs and pistols and
police dogs when you're showing your birthday suit to the sun.

"You like it?" she asked. She was pleased. She placed her arm
next to mine.

"Almost the same color," she said.

"Ronnie isn't feeling well," I said.

"Oh, the poor kid. I'm so glad we have Nora. She's such a
charm. I'll run right in and look at him. Do have a drink in the bar.
Fix me one too, will you?" Kay skipped inside and I went to the bar
and poured out two strong drinks. I made hers stronger than mine.
She was back soon. "Nora was trying to put him to sleep and she
made me stay out." She giggled. She quickly tossed off her drink.
"Another, please?" While I was fixing her drink she was saying
how amazing it was for Nora to have such a talented son. What she
was really saying was that it was amazing for a servant to have a
son who was not also a servant. "Anything can happen in a democ-
racy," I said. "Servants' sons drink with madames and so on."

"Oh, Nora isn't a servant," Kay said. "She's part of the family."

Yeah, I thought. Where and how many times had I heard that
before?

In the ensuing silence, she started to admire her tan again.
"You think it's pretty good, do you? You don't know how hard I
worked to get it." I moved close to her and held her arm. I placed
my other arm around her. She pretended not to see or feel it. but
she wasn't trying to get away either. In fact she was pressing closer
and the register in my brain that tells me at the precise moment
when I'm in, went off. Kay was very high. I put both arms around
her and she put both hers around me. When I kissed her, she
responded completely.

"Mom!"

"Ronnie, come back to bed," I heard Nora shout from the other
room. We could hear Ronnie running over the rug in the outer
room. Kay tried to get away from me, push me to one side, because
we could tell that Ronnie knew where to look for his Mom: he was

running right for the bar, where we were. "Oh, please," she said, "don't let him see us."

I wouldn't let her push me away.

"Stop!" she hissed. "He'll see us!" We stopped struggling just for an instant, and we listened to the echoes of the word see. She gritted her teeth and renewed her efforts to get away.

Me? I had the scene laid right out. The kid breaks into the room, see, and sees his mother in this real wriggly clinch with this colored guy who's just shouted at him, see, and no matter how his mother explains it away, the kid has the image of the colored guy and his mother for the rest of his life, see?

That's the way it happened. The kid's mother hissed under her breath, "You're crazy" and she looked at me as though she were seeing me or something about me for the very first time. I'd released her as soon as Ronnie, romping into the bar, saw us and came to a full, open-mouthed halt. Kay went to him. He looked first at me, then at his mother. Kay turned to me, but she couldn't speak.

Outside in the living room my mother called, "Wendell, where are you? We can go now."

I started to move past Kay and Ronnie. I felt many things, but I made myself think mostly, There you little bastard, there.

My mother thrust her face inside the door and said, "Good-bye, Mrs. Couchman. See you tomorrow. 'Bye, Ronnie."

"Yes," Kay said, sort of stunned. "Tomorrow." She was reaching for Ronnie's hand as we left, but the kid was slapping her hand away. I hurried quickly after Nora, hating the long drive back to Watts.

TEN MILES WEST OF VENUS
Judy Troy

After Marvelle Lyle's husband, Morgan, committed suicide—his body being found on an April evening in the willows that grew along Black Creek—Marvelle stopped going to church. Franklin Sanders, her minister at Venus United Methodist, drove out to her house on a Sunday afternoon in the middle of May to see if he could coax her back. Her house was ten miles west of Venus—seven miles on the highway and three on a two-lane road that cut through the open Kansas wheat fields and then wound back through the forest preserve. The woods at this time of year were sprinkled with white blooming pear trees.

Franklin had his radio tuned to Gussie Dell's weekly "Neighbor Talk" program. Gussie was a member of his congregation, and Franklin wanted to see what embarrassing thing she would choose to say today. The week before, she had told a story about her grandson, Norman, drawing a picture of Jesus wearing high heels. "I have respect for Norman's creativity," she had said, "I don't care if Norman puts Jesus in a garter belt."

Today, though, she was on the subject of her sister, whom Franklin had visited in the hospital just the day before. "My sister has cancer," Gussie said. "She may die or she may not. My guess is she won't. I just wanted to say that publicly."

Franklin pulled into Marvelle's driveway and turned off the radio too soon to hear whatever Gussie was going to say next; he imagined it was something unfavorable about her sister's husband, who, for years now, had been sitting outside in his chicken shed, watching television. "One of these days I'm going to dynamite him out of there," Gussie liked to say. She was generally down on

marriage, which Franklin couldn't argue with—his own marriage
being unhappy, and that fact not a secret among his parishioners.

Franklin parked his new Ford Taurus between Marvelle's old
pickup and the ancient Jeep Morgan had driven. Hanging from
the Jeep's rearview mirror were Morgan's military dog tags. He'd
been in the Vietnam War, though Franklin had never known any
details about it. Morgan Lyle had never been forthcoming about
himself, and the few times Franklin had seen him at church
Morgan had spent the length of the sermon and most of the service
smoking outside. "You have to accept him as he is," Marvelle had
once told Franklin. "Otherwise, well, all I'm saying is he doesn't
mean anything by what he says and does."

Also in the driveway—just a big gravel clearing, really, between
the house and the garage where Morgan had had his motorcycle
repair shop—was the dusty van their son, Curtis, drove. He was
thirty-one and still living at home. Franklin, who was sixty-three,
could remember Curtis as the blond-headed child who had once, in
Sunday School, climbed out of a window in order to avoid reciting
the Lord's Prayer. Now the grownup Curtis, in faded pants and no
shirt, his thinning hair pulled back into a ponytail, opened the door
before Franklin had a chance to knock. "Well, come on in, I guess,"
Curtis said. Behind him, Marvelle appeared in the kitchen doorway.

The house was built haphazardly into a hill, and was so shaded
with oak and sweetgum trees that the inside—in spring and summer, anyway—was dark during the day. The only light in the room
was a small lamp on a desk in the corner, shining down on irides-
cent feathers and other fly-tying materials. Curtis sat down at the
desk and picked up a hook.

"I'll make coffee," Marvelle told Franklin, and he followed her
into the kitchen, which was substantially brighter. An overhead
light was on, and the walls were painted white. "I thought Sunday
afternoons were when you visited the sick," Marvelle said.

"It was, but I do that on Saturdays now. I find other reasons
to get out of the house on Sundays." Franklin sat at the kitchen
table and watched her make coffee. She was a tall, muscular
woman, and she'd lost weight since Morgan's death. Her jeans
looked baggy on her; her red hair was longer than it used to be, and
uncombed. "You could stand to eat more," Franklin told her.

"You men complain when we're fat and then worry when we're thin."

"When did I ever say you were fat?" Franklin said.

Marvelle turned toward him with the coffeepot in her hand. "You're right. You never did."

Franklin looked down at the table. This afternoon, with his mind on Morgan, and not on himself or his marriage, he'd managed to push aside the memory of an afternoon years ago, when he and Marvelle had found themselves kissing in the church kitchen. "Found themselves" was just how it had seemed to him. It was, like this day, a Sunday afternoon in spring; Marvelle and his wife and two other parishioners had been planting flowers along the front walk. Marvelle had come into the kitchen for coffee just when he had. He wasn't so gray-haired then or so bottom-heavy, and they walked toward each other and kissed passionately, as if they had planned it for months.

"You've always been an attractive woman," he said quietly.

"Don't look so guilty. It was a long time ago." Marvelle sat down across from him as the coffee brewed. "The amazing thing is that it only happened once."

"No," Franklin said, "it's that I allowed it to happen at all."

"Where was God that day? Just not paying attention?" Marvelle asked.

"That was me not paying attention to God," Franklin told her.

Curtis had turned on the radio in the living room, and Franklin could faintly hear a woman singing. Louder was the sound of the coffee brewing. The kitchen table was next to a window that overlooked a sloping wooded hill and a deep ravine. These woods, too, Franklin noticed, had their share of flowering pear trees. "It looks like snow has fallen in a few select places," he said.

"Doesn't it? I saw two deer walking down there this morning. For a moment, I almost forgot about everything else."

Franklin looked at her face, which was suddenly both bright and sad.

"That's interesting," he said carefully, "because that's what church services do for me."

"Sure they do. Otherwise, you'd lose your place," Marvelle said.

"You don't realize something," Franklin told her. "I'd rather not be the one conducting them. I feel that more and more as I get older. I'd like to sit with the congregation and just partake."

"Would you? Well, I wouldn't. I wouldn't want to do either one." She got up and poured coffee into two mugs and handed one to Franklin. "How do you expect me to feel?" she asked him, standing next to the window. "Do you see God taking a hand in my life? There are people in that congregation who didn't want to see Morgan buried in their cemetery."

"You're talking about two or three people out of a hundred and twenty."

"I bet you felt that way yourself," Marvelle told him.

"You know me better than to think that," Franklin said.

Marvelle sat down and put her coffee on the table in front of her. "All right, I do. Just don't make me apologize."

"When could anybody make you do anything you didn't want to do?" Franklin said to her.

Franklin left late in the afternoon, saying goodbye to Curtis after admiring Curtis's fly-tying abilities. Marvelle accompanied him to his car walking barefoot over the gravel. "You'll be walking over coals next," Franklin said, joking.

"Are you trying to sneak God back into the conversation?" Marvelle asked him. She had her hand on his car door as he got in, and she closed the door after him.

"I'm talking about the toughness of your feet," Franklin said through the open window. "I don't expect that much from God. Maybe I used to. But the older I get, the easier I am on him. God's getting older, too, I figure."

"Then put on your seat belt," Marvelle said. She stepped back into a patch of sunlight, so the last thing he saw as he drove away was the sun on her untidy hair and on her pale face and neck.

The woods he passed were gloomier now, with the sun almost level with the tops of the tallest oaks; it was a relief to him to drive out of the trees and into the green wheat fields. The radio was broadcasting a Billy Graham sermon, which Franklin found he couldn't concentrate on. He was wondering about Gussie's sister and if she'd live, and for how long, and what her husband might be thinking, out in that chicken shed. When Franklin was at the hospital the day before, Gussie's sister hadn't mentioned her husband. She'd wanted to know exactly how Franklin's wife had redecorated their bedroom.

"Blue curtains and a flowered bedspread," he had told her, and that was all he could remember—nothing about the new chair or the wallpaper or the lamps, all of which he took note of when he went home afterward.

He was also thinking, less intentionally, about Marvelle, who was entering his thoughts as erratically as the crows flying down into the fields he was passing. She was eight or nine years older than when he'd kissed her, but those years had somehow changed into days. When Franklin tried to keep his attention on her grief, it wandered off to her hair, her dark eyes—to every godless place it could. It wasn't until he heard Billy Graham recite, "He maketh me to lie down in green pastures: He leadeth me beside the still waters," that Franklin's mind focused back on Morgan lying in the willows. From that point on he paid attention to the words, falling apart a little when he heard, "Surely goodness and mercy shall follow me all the days of my life," because he didn't know anything more moving, except maybe love, which he didn't feel entitled to; he never had.

THE CHRYSANTHEMUMS
John Steinbeck

As our reading experience expands, we become more conscious of each writer's "style," his or her own particular and unique use of language. While not every author's style is easily identified, with extensive reading you can learn to recognize the work of many of them.

As you read "The Chrysanthemums," try to recall the examples provided from the textbook. Steinbeck has an extraordinary command of the language and uses it to full advantage. Symbolism, syntax, dialogue, and the artful choice of words lead carefully to the ironic ending.

Pay careful attention to Steinbeck's adjectives, similes, metaphors, and descriptions. The words used to describe the setting and the characters are carefully selected to reinforce the themes of frustration and isolation, as does the dialogue, which contrasts with the author's descriptions of the characters.

Look for universal symbols; Steinbeck uses several of them; see if you can determine their function. Steinbeck also creates original symbols. See if you can identify them. And even the title has symbolic significance (beyond the simple fact that the main character is growing chrysanthemums).

The high grey-flannel fog of winter closed off the Salinas Valley from the sky and from all the rest of the world. On every side it sat like a lid on the mountains and made of the great valley a closed pot. On the broad, level land floor the gang plows bit deep and left the black earth shining like metal where the shares had cut. On the foot-hill ranches across the Salinas River, the yellow stubble fields seemed to be bathed in pale cold sunshine, but there was no sunshine in the valley now in December. The thick willow scrub along the river flamed with sharp and positive yellow leaves.

It was a time of quiet and of waiting. The air was cold and tender. A light wind blew up from the southwest so that the farmers were mildly hopeful of a good rain before long; but fog and rain do not go together.

Across the river, on Henry Allen's foot-hill ranch there was little work to be done, for the hay was cut and stored and the orchards were ploughed up to receive the rain deeply when it should come. The cattle on the higher slopes were becoming shaggy and rough-coated.

Elisa Allen, working in her flower garden, looked down across the yard and saw Henry, her husband, talking to two men in business suits. The three of them stood by the tractor-shed, each man with one foot on the side of the little Fordson. They smoked cigarettes and studied the machine as they talked.

Elisa watched them for a moment and then went back to her work. She was thirty-five. Her face was lean and strong and her eyes were as clear as water. Her figure looked blocked and heavy in her gardening costume, a man's black hat pulled low down over her eyes, clod-hopper shoes, a figured print dress almost completely covered by a big corduroy apron with four big pockets to hold the snips, the trowel and scratcher, the seeds and the knife she worked with. She wore heavy leather gloves to protect her hands while she worked.

She was cutting down the old year's chrysanthemum stalks with a pair of short and powerful scissors. She looked down toward the men by the tractor-shed now and then. Her face was eager and mature and handsome; even her work with the scissors was over-eager, over-powerful. The chrysanthemum stems seemed too small and easy for her energy.

She brushed a cloud of hair out of her eyes with the back of her glove, and left a smudge of earth on her cheek in doing it. Behind her stood the neat white farmhouse with red geraniums close-banked around it as high as the windows. It was a hard-swept-looking little house, with hard-polished windows, and a clean mud-mat on the front steps.

Elisa cast another glance toward the tractor-shed. The strangers were getting into their Ford coupé. She took off a glove and put her strong fingers down into the forest of new green chrysanthemum sprouts that were growing around the old roots. She spread the leaves and looked down among the close-growing stems. No aphids were there, no sow bugs or snails or cutworms. Her terrier fingers destroyed such pests before they could get started.

Elisa started at the sound of her husband's voice. He had come near quietly, and he leaned over the wire fence that protected her flower garden from cattle and dogs and chickens.

"At it again," he said. "You've got a strong new crop coming."

Elisa straightened her back and pulled on the gardening glove again. "Yes. They'll be strong this coming year." In her tone and on her face there was a little smugness.

"You've got a gift with things," Henry observed. "Some of those yellow chrysanthemums you had this year were ten inches across. I wish you'd work out in the orchard and raise some apples that big."

Her eyes sharpened. "Maybe I could do it, too. I've a gift with things, all right. My mother had it. She could stick anything in the ground and make it grow. She said it was having planters' hands that knew how to do it."

"Well, it sure works with flowers," he said.

"Henry, who were those men you were talking to?"

"Why, sure, that's what I came to tell you. They were from the Western Meat Company. I sold those thirty head of three-year-old steers. Got nearly my own price, too."

"Good," she said. "Good for you."

"And I thought," he continued, "I thought how it's Saturday afternoon, and we might go into Salinas for dinner at a restaurant, and then to a picture show—to celebrate, you see."

"Good," she repeated. "Oh, yes. That will be good."

Henry put on his joking tone. "There's fights tonight. How'd you like to go to the fights?"

"Oh, no," she said breathlessly. "No, I wouldn't like fights."

"Just fooling, Elisa. We'll go to a movie. Let's see. It's two now. I'm going to take Scotty and bring down those steers from the hill. It'll take us maybe two hours. We'll go in town about five and have dinner at the Cominos Hotel. Like that?"

"Of course I'll like it. It's good to eat away from home."

"All right then. I'll go get up a couple of horses."

She said: "I'll have plenty of time to transplant some of these sets, I guess."

She heard her husband calling Scotty down by the barn. And a little later she saw the two men ride up the pale yellow hillside in search of the steers.

There was a little square sandy bed kept for rooting the chrysanthemums. With her trowel she turned the soil over and over, and smoothed it and patted it firm. Then she dug ten parallel trenches to receive the sets. Back at the chrysanthemum bed she pulled out the little crisp shoots, trimmed off the leaves of each one with her scissors and laid it on a small orderly pile.

A squeak of wheels and plod of hoofs came from the road. Elisa looked up. The country road ran along the dense bank of willows and cottonwoods that bordered the river, and up this road came a curious vehicle, curiously drawn. It was an old spring-wagon, with a round canvas top on it like the cover of a prairie schooner. It was drawn by an old bay horse and a little gray-and-white burro. A big stubble-bearded man sat between the cover flaps and drove the crawling team. Underneath the wagon, between the hind wheels, a lean and rangy mongrel dog walked sedately. Words were painted on the canvas, in clumsy, crooked letters. "Pots, pans, knives, sisors, lawn mores, Fixed." Two rows of articles, and the triumphantly definitive "Fixed" below. The black paint had run down in little sharp points beneath each letter.

Elisa, squatting on the ground, watched to see the crazy, loose-jointed wagon pass by. But it didn't pass. It turned into the farm road in front of her house, crooked old wheels skirling and squeaking. The rangy dog darted from between the wheels and ran ahead. Instantly the two ranch shepherds flew out at him. Then all three stopped, and with stiff and quivering tails, with taut straight legs, with ambassadorial dignity, they slowly circled, sniffing daintily. The caravan pulled up to Elisa's wire fence and stopped.

Now the newcomer dog, feeling out-numbered, lowered his tail and retired under the wagon with raised hackles and bared teeth.

The man on the wagon seat called out: "That's a bad dog in a fight when he gets started."

Elisa laughed. "I see he is. How soon does he generally get started?"

The man caught up her laughter and echoed it heartily. "Sometimes not for weeks and weeks," he said. He climbed stiffly down, over the wheel. The horse and the donkey drooped like unwatered flowers.

Elisa saw that he was a very big man. Although his hair and beard were graying, he did not look old. His worn black suit was wrinkled and spotted with grease. The laughter had disappeared from his face and eyes the moment his laughing voice ceased. His eyes were dark, and they were full of the brooding that gets in the eyes of teamsters and of sailors. The calloused hands he rested on the wire fence were cracked, and every crack was a black line. He took off his battered hat.

"I'm off my general road, ma'am," he said. "Does this dirt road cut over across the river to the Los Angeles highway?"

Elisa stood up and shoved the thick scissors in her apron pocket. "Well, yes, it does, but it winds around and then fords the river. I don't think your team could pull through the sand."

He replied with some asperity: "It might surprise you what them beasts can pull through."

"When they get started?" she asked.

He smiled for a second. "Yes. When they get started."

"Well," said Elisa, "I think you'll save time if you go back to the Salinas road and pick up the highway there."

He drew a big finger down the chicken wire and made it sing. "I ain't in any hurry, ma'am. I go from Seattle to San Diego and back every year. Takes all my time. About six months each way. I aim to follow nice weather."

Elisa took off her gloves and stuffed them in the apron pocket with the scissors. She touched the under edge of her man's hat, searching for fugitive hairs. "That sounds like a nice kind of way to live." she said.

He leaned confidentially over the fence. "Maybe you noticed the writing on my wagon. I mend pots and sharpen knives and scissors. You got any of them things to do?"

"Oh, no," she said quickly. "Nothing like that."

Her eyes hardened with resistance.

"Scissors is the worst thing," he explained. "Most people just ruin scissors trying to sharpen 'em, but I know how. I got a special tool. It's a little bobbit kind of thing, and patented. But it sure does the trick."

"No. My scissors are all sharp."

"All right, then. Take a pot," he continued earnestly, "a bent pot, or a pot with a hole. I can make it like new so you don't have to buy no new ones. That's a saving for you."

"No," she said shortly. "I tell you I have nothing like that for you to do."

His face fell to an exaggerated sadness. His voice took on a whining undertone. "I ain't had a thing to do today. Maybe I won't have no supper tonight. You see I'm off my regular road. I know folks on the highway clear from Seattle to San Diego. They save their things for me to sharpen up because they know I do it so good and save them money."

"I'm sorry," Elisa said irritably. "I haven't anything for you to do."

His eyes left her face and fell to searching the ground. They roamed about until they came to the chrysanthemum bed where she had been working. "What's them plants, ma'am?"

The irritation and resistance melted from Elisa's face. "Oh, those are chrysanthemums, giant whites and yellows. I raise them every year, bigger than anybody around here."

"Kind of a long-stemmed flower? Looks like a quick puff of colored smoke?" he asked.

"That's it. What a nice way to describe them."

"They smell kind of nasty till you get used to them," he said.

"It's a good bitter smell," she retorted, "not nasty at all."

He changed his tone quickly. "I like the smell myself."

"I had ten-inch blooms this year," she said.

The man leaned farther over the fence. "Look. I know a lady down the road a piece, has got the nicest garden you ever seen. Got nearly every kind of flower but no chrysanthemums. Last time I was mending a copper-bottom washtub for her (that's a hard job but I do it good), she said to me: 'If you ever run acrost some nice chrysanthemums I wish you'd try to get me a few seeds.' That's what she told me."

Elisa's eyes grew alert and eager. "She couldn't have known much about chrysanthemums. You can raise them from seed, but it's much easier to root the little sprouts you see here."

"Oh," he said. "I s'pose I can't take none to her, then."

"Why yes you can," Elisa cried. "I can put some in damp sand, and you can carry them right along with you. They'll take root in the pot if you keep them damp. And then she can transplant them."

"She'd sure like to have some, ma'am. You say they're nice ones?"

"Beautiful," she said. "Oh, beautiful." Her eyes shone. She tore off the battered hat and shook out her dark pretty hair. "I'll put them in a flowerpot, and you can take them right with you. Come into the yard."

While the man came through the picket gate Elisa ran excitedly along the geranium-bordered path to the back of the house. And she returned carrying a big red flowerpot. The gloves were forgotten now. She kneeled on the ground by the starting bed and dug up the sandy soil with her fingers and scooped it into the bright new flowerpot. Then she picked up the little pile of shoots she had prepared. With her strong fingers she pressed them into the sand and tamped around them with her knuckles. The man stood over her. "I'll tell you what to do," she said. "You remember so you can tell the lady."

"Yes, I'll try to remember."

"Well, look. These will take root in about a month. Then she must set them out, about a foot apart in good rich earth like this, see?" She lifted a handful of dark soil for him to look at. "They'll grow fast and tall. Now remember this: In July tell her to cut them down, about eight inches from the ground."

"Before they bloom?" he asked.

"Yes, before they bloom." Her face was tight with eagerness. "They'll grow right up again. About the last of September the buds will start."

She stopped and seemed perplexed. "It's the budding that takes the most care," she said hesitantly. "I don't know how to tell you." She looked deep into his eyes, searchingly. Her mouth opened a little, and she seemed to be listening. "I'll try to tell you," she said. "Did you ever hear of planting hands?"

"Can't say I have, ma'am."

"Well, I can only tell you what it feels like. It's when you're picking off the buds you don't want. Everything goes right down into your fingertips. You watch your fingers work. They do it themselves. You can feel how it is. They pick and pick the buds. They never make a mistake. They're with the plant. Do you see? Your fingers and the plant. You can feel that, right up your arm. They know. They never make a mistake. You can feel it. When you're like that you can't do anything wrong. Do you see that? Can you understand that?"

She was kneeling on the ground looking up at him. Her breast swelled passionately.

The man's eyes narrowed. He looked away self-consciously.

"Maybe I know," he said. "Sometimes in the night in the wagon there—"

Elisa's voice grew husky. She broke in on him: "I've never lived as you do, but I know what you mean. When the night is dark—why, the stars are sharp-pointed, and there's quiet. Why, you rise up and up! Every pointed star gets driven into your body. It's like that. Hot and sharp and—lovely."

Kneeling there, her hand went out toward his legs in the greasy black trousers. Her hesitant fingers almost touched the cloth. Then her hand dropped to the ground. She crouched low like a fawning dog.

He said: "It's nice, just like you say. Only when you don't have no dinner, it ain't."

She stood up then, very straight, and her face was ashamed. She held the flowerpot out to him and placed it gently in his arms. "Here. Put it in your wagon, on the seat, where you can watch it. Maybe I can find something for you to do."

At the back of the house she dug in the can pile and found two old and battered aluminum saucepans. She carried them back and gave them to him. "Here, maybe you can fix these."

His manner changed. He became professional. "Good as new I can fix them." At the back of his wagon he set a little anvil, and out of an oily tool-box dug a small machine hammer. Elisa came through the gate to watch him while he pounded out the dents in the kettles. His mouth grew sure and knowing. At a difficult part of the work he sucked his underlip.

"You sleep right in the wagon?" Elisa asked.

"Right in the wagon, ma'am. Rain or shine I'm dry as a cow in there."

"It must be nice," she said. "It must be very nice. I wish women could do such things."

"It ain't the right kind of a life for a woman."

Her upper lip raised a little, showing her teeth. "How do you know? How can you tell?" she said.

"I don't know, ma'am," he protested. "Of course I don't know. Now here's your kettles, done. You don't have to buy no new ones."

"How much?"

"Oh, fifty cents'll do. I keep my prices down and my work good. That's why I have all them satisfied customers up and down the highway."

Elisa brought him a fifty-cent piece from the house and dropped it in his hand. "You might be surprised to have a rival some time. I can sharpen scissors, too. And I can beat the dents out of little pots. I could show you what a woman might do."

He put his hammer back in the oily box and shoved the little anvil out of sight. "It would be a lonely life for a woman, ma'am, and a scary life, too, with animals creeping under the wagon all night." He climbed over the single-tree, steadying himself with a hand on the burro's white rump. He settled himself in the seat, picked up the lines. "Thank you kindly, ma'am," he said. "I'll do like you told me; I'll go back and catch the Salinas road."

"Mind," she called, "if you're long in getting there, keep the sand damp."

"Sand, ma'am . . . Sand? Oh, sure. You mean around the chrysanthemums. Sure I will." He clucked his tongue. The beasts leaned luxuriously into their collars. The mongrel dog took his place between the back wheels. The wagon turned and crawled out the entrance road and back the way it had come, along the river.

Elisa stood in front of her wire fence watching the slow progress of the caravan. Her shoulders were straight, her head thrown back, her eyes half-closed, so that the scene came vaguely into them. Her lips moved silently, forming the words "Good-bye— good-bye." Then she whispered: "That's a bright direction. There's a glowing there." The sound of her whisper startled her. She shook herself free and looked about to see whether anyone had been listening. Only the dogs had heard. They lifted their heads toward her from their sleeping in the dust, and then stretched out their chins and settled asleep again. Elisa turned and ran hurriedly into the house.

In the kitchen she reached behind the stove and felt the water tank. It was full of hot water from the noonday cooking. In the bathroom she tore off her soiled clothes and flung them into the corner. And then she scrubbed herself with a little block of pumice, legs and thighs, loins and chest and arms, until her skin was scratched and red. When she had dried herself she stood in front of a mirror in her bedroom and looked at her body. She tightened her stomach and threw out her chest. She turned and looked over her shoulder at her back.

After a while she began to dress, slowly. She put on her newest underclothing and her nicest stockings and the dress which was the symbol of her prettiness. She worked carefully on her hair, penciled her eyebrows and rouged her lips.

Before she was finished she heard the little thunder of hoofs and the shouts of Henry and his helper as they drove the red steers into the corral. She heard the gate bang shut and set herself for Henry's arrival.

His step sounded on the porch. He entered the house calling: "Elisa, where are you?"

"In my room, dressing. I'm not ready. There's hot water for your bath. Hurry up. It's getting late."

When she heard him splashing in the tub, Elisa laid his dark suit on the bed, and shirt and socks and tie beside it. She stood his polished shoes on the floor beside the bed. Then she went to the porch and sat primly and stiffly down. She looked toward the river road where the willow-line was still yellow with frosted leaves so that under the high grey fog they seemed a thin band of sunshine. This was the only color in the grey afternoon. She sat unmoving for a long time. Her eyes blinked rarely.

Henry came banging out of the door, shoving his tie inside his vest as he came. Elisa stiffened and her face grew tight. Henry stopped short and looked at her. "Why—why, Elisa. You look so nice!"

"Nice? You think I look nice? What do you mean by 'nice'?"

Henry blundered on. "I don't know. I mean you look different, strong and happy."

"I am strong? Yes, strong. What do you mean 'strong'?"

He looked bewildered. "You're playing some kind of a game," he said helplessly. "It's a kind of a play. You look strong enough to break a calf over your knee, happy enough to eat it like a water-melon."

For a second she lost her rigidity. "Henry! Don't talk like that. You didn't know what you said." She grew complete again. "I'm strong," she boasted. "I never knew before how strong."

Henry looked down toward the tractor-shed, and when he brought his eyes back to her, they were his own again. "I'll get out the car. You can put on your coat while I'm starting."

Elisa went into the house. She heard him drive to the gate and idle down his motor, and then she took a long time to put on her hat. She pulled it here and pressed it there. When Henry turned the motor off she slipped into her coat and went out.

The little roadster bounced along on the dirt road by the river, raising the birds and driving the rabbits into the brush. Two cranes flapped heavily over the willow-line and dropped into the river bed.

Far ahead on the road Elisa saw a dark speck. She knew.

She tried not to look as they passed it, but her eyes would not obey. She whispered to herself sadly: "He might have thrown them off the road. That wouldn't have been much trouble, not very much. But he kept the pot," she explained. "He had to keep the pot. That's why he couldn't get them off the road."

The roadster turned a bend and she saw the caravan ahead. She swung full around toward her husband so she could not see the little covered wagon and the mismatched team as the car passed them.

In a moment it was over. The thing was done. She did not look back.

She said loudly, to be heard over the motor: "It will be good, tonight, a good dinner."

"Now you've changed again," Henry complained. He took one hand from the wheel and patted her knee. "I ought to take you in to dinner oftener. It would be good for both of us. We get so heavy out on the ranch."

"Henry," she asked, "could we have wine at dinner?"

"Sure we could. Say! That will be fine."

She was silent for a while; then she said: "Henry, at those prizefights, do the men hurt each other very much?"

"Sometimes a little, not often. Why?"

"Well, I've read how they break noses, and blood runs down their chests. I've read how the fighting gloves get heavy and soggy with blood."

He looked around at her. "What's the matter, Elisa? I didn't know you read things like that." He brought the car to a stop, then turned to the right over the Salinas River bridge.

"Do any women ever go to the fights?" she asked.

"Oh, sure, some. What's the matter, Elisa? Do you want to go? I don't think you'd like it, but I'll take you if you really want to go."

She relaxed limply in the seat. "Oh, no. No. I don't want to go. I'm sure I don't." Her face was turned away from him. "It will be enough if we can have wine. It will be plenty." She turned up her coat collar so he could not see that she was crying weakly—like an old woman.

THE FURIES
Paul Theroux

"I now belong to an incredibly exclusive club," Ray Testa said in his speech at his wedding reception. He savored the moment, then winked and added, "There are not many men who can say that they're older than their father-in-law."

He was fifty-eight, his new wife, Shelby, thirty-one, his father-in-law fifty-six and seemingly at ease with the idea of this balding man marrying his daughter. "She's an old soul," he said.

Ray Testa was a dentist, and for seven years Shelby had been his hygienist. "I'm thinking of leaving," Shelby said one day. Ray urged her to stay and finally pleaded, "You can't leave. I love you." She didn't smile. She swallowed air and said that she had feelings for him, too. Then, "What about Angie?"

He confessed everything to his wife.

Angie took it badly, as he'd guessed she might, but unexpectedly she said, "Why didn't you leave me years ago, when I might have met someone who really cared for me?"

He hadn't imagined that she'd object in this peevish way, for such a coldly practical reason—because his timing was inconvenient for her. He'd thought she was going to tell him how much she'd miss him, how miserable she'd be without him, not that she might have been better off with someone else.

As she stared at him, her eyes went black and depthless, and she seemed to swell physically, as though with malevolence. Ray expected a shout, but her voice was the confident whisper of a killer to his helpless victim. "I know I should say I wish you well, but I wish you ill, with all my heart. I've made it easy for you. I hope you suffer now with that woman who's taken you from me. These women who carry on with married men are demons."

270

She sounded like her mother, Gilda—Ermenegilda—sour, mustached, habitually in black, pedantically superstitious, Sicilian, always threatening the evil eye. He told himself that Angie was bitter, cruel with grief, demented by the breakup. She didn't mean what she was saying.

They had no children; they divided their assets in half, the proceeds of his more than thirty years of dentistry. Angie got the house, the dog, a lump sum; Ray the vacation home on the South Shore—he'd commute to his office from there, Shelby by his side. Shelby wasn't greedy. She said she'd never been happier. Ray did not repeat to her the vindictive curse that Angie had uttered. He had what he wanted now, a new life with a woman he loved.

People said that a second wife was often a younger version of the first one, but Shelby was in every way the opposite of Angie. She was a treasure, unconventionally beautiful, not the fleshy new graduate she'd been when he first hired her but tall and sharp-featured, with the lean, feline good health of the jogger she now was. Her mouth was almost severe—she hardly parted her lips when she spoke, and spoke always in a low, certain voice that got his attention, as in, "What about Angie?"

With the unwavering judgment of someone untested, someone innocent and upright, Shelby was alert to the obvious. Her eyes were gray, blinkless, catlike. Ray had desired her from the first, but thought that the feeling would diminish as he got to know her better. Time had passed, and his desire to possess her had become a set of physical symptoms: hunger, a swollen tongue, a drone in his head, a tingling in his hands.

Now she was his. He could not believe his luck, how she had come into his life, to lead him confidently into a future he'd once hated to contemplate. He sometimes eavesdropped on her when she was working on a patient in her focussed way and he was almost tearful with gratitude that she was his wife.

They had never argued, and so their first argument, a few months after their marriage, came as a shock to Ray. It concerned his high-school reunion—the fortieth. Ray wanted to take Shelby. She protested that she'd feel out of place. Everyone knew that a high-school reunion was hell for a spouse. She said, "I think you'll regret it."

But Ray was a big smiling boy with a boast, and Shelby eventually agreed, even to their staying the night at the hotel in his home town, where the reunion was being held.

Medford had changed. It was denser and, divided now by the Interstate, much busier, but still full of memories, as he told Shelby on their tour through the place—the brick façades that had once been the entrances to single-screen movie theatres, the armory that bulked like a granite citadel, the stairs that had led down to Joe's basement poolroom, the Italian cobbler, the Chinese laundry, the post office with the old murals of ship-building in its lobby. Now Medford had a new hotel, with a ballroom large enough to accommodate the high-school reunion.

"One night, non-smoking, king-size bed," the hotel clerk said, tapping the check-in card with her pen, but she kept glancing at Shelby, uneasily, almost with pity, as though suspecting that she had been abducted.

They drew stares later, too, as they searched the table for their name tags.

"I don't really need one. It's your night," Shelby said.

But, as she said it, Ray peeled the paper backing from a label marked "Shelby Testa" and stuck it to her beaded jacket.

A woman in a black shawl approached them as Ray was patting the label flat. The woman flourished a large yellow envelope and drew a black-and-white photograph from it, saying, "Miss Balsam's class. Third grade. Do you recognize yourself?"

"That's me, third row," Ray said. "And that's you in the front with your hands in your lap. Maura Dedrick, you were so cute!"

"Aren't I still cute?" the woman said.

She was small and thin and deeply lined, with weary eyes. No makeup, a trace of hair on her cheeks, fretful lips, her open mouth like a grommet in canvas.

"Of course you are," Ray said.

She smiled sadly, as though he had satirized her with his quick answer. Then she turned, because two other women had come to greet her.

"You remember Roberta and Annie," Maura said.

Ray said, "You married Larry," to Roberta.

"He left me," Roberta said.

"I'm divorced, too," Annie said.

Ray was aware that while they were talking to him they were eying Shelby. Annie was bigger than he remembered, not just plump and full-faced but taller—it was probably her shoes—

and she was carrying a handbag the size of a valise. Roberta was heavily made up, wearing ropes of green beads, Gypsy-like. Ray had known them as girls. They were almost old women now—older than him, he felt, for their look of abandonment, tinged with anger. When they became aware of his gaze, they recoiled in a way that made him feel intrusive. They were fifty-eight years old—everyone in the room was that age, though when he surveyed the growing crowd he could see that some had aged better than others.

"May I introduce my wife?" Ray said. "This is Shelby."

The women smiled, they clucked, but Ray saw that Maura had narrowed her eyes, and Annie had leaned closer, and Roberta seemed to snicker. Putting a protective arm around Shelby, he felt the sudden pulsing of an odd circuitry in her shoulders.

Maura said to Shelby, "Angie was so mad when I went to the junior prom with Ray. Angie was my best friend—still is."

Roberta hovered over Shelby and spoke in a deaf person's shout, "He took me to Canobie Lake. He got fresh!"

"Remember what you wrote in my yearbook?" Annie said. "'You're the ultimate in feminine pulchritude.'"

"I guess I had a way with words," Ray said.

"You had a way with your hands," Roberta said, shouting again.

Maura said to Shelby, "I've known Ray Testa since I was seven years old."

Everything that he'd forgotten was still real and immediate to them—the prom, the lake, the yearbook, Miss Balsam's third-grade class. He had lived his life without looking back, and he'd been happy. Had their disappointment made them dwell on the past, as a kind of consolation?

He said, "Shel and I need a drink."

Maura said, "I'll get it."

"Don't bother."

But she insisted, and after she slipped away they spoke with Annie and Roberta. While they chatted about the changes in Medford, he remembered the rowboat at Canobie Lake, the fumbled kiss, the way he had gripped Roberta as she snatched at his hands. And Annie—the summer night on her porch, her arms folded over her breasts, and "Don't, please." And when Maura returned with the drinks he recalled the back seat of his father's car at the drive-in, the half pint of Four Roses, and her "Cut it out." Horrible.

Maura handed over two glasses of white wine. Ray sipped his, while Shelby just held hers in both hands as if for balance.

"Drink up," Maura said.

Shelby put her glass to her lips, and Ray did the same. The warm wine had the dusty taste of chalk, and a tang he couldn't name, perhaps a metal—zinc, maybe, with the smack of cat piss. He found it hard to swallow, but to please Maura he swigged again, and he knew he was right in thinking it was foul, because Shelby did no more than wet her lips with it. Seeing Shelby struggle, Maura looked on with what he took to be satisfaction.

He remembered these women's flesh, and he sorrowed for what they had become, parodies of the girls he'd known. They had badly neglected their teeth. He had never been more keenly aware of the age difference between him and Shelby.

In the ballroom, where a small band was playing, some couples had begun to dance. As he steered Shelby onto the floor, he could feel her body go heavy, resisting the music.

"How you doing?" he heard. It was Malcolm DeYoung, gray-haired now. "Hey, who's this fine lady?"

"Shelby, I want you to meet my old friend Malcolm."

Malcolm said, "What about some food? There's a buffet over there."

They stood in the buffet line, and afterward they sat together at a table. Ray said, "I used to know everyone. But the only people I've recognized so far, apart from you, are those three"—Maura, Roberta, and Annie were at a nearby table. "The funny thing is, they were all my girlfriends, at different times."

Malcolm said, "You got a target on your back, man," and he winked at Shelby.

"I really wanted to introduce Shel to my old friends."

"Oh, and give the executive the right to rain down death from on high."

*   *   *

Malcolm put his fork down. He stood up and said, "I don't drink these days. But let me tell you something. In a little while these people are going to get toasted. I don't want to be here then. I don't think you want to, neither."

Then he left them. Ray didn't speak again, nor did Shelby say anything more. She put her knife and fork on the uneaten food in her plate, and her napkin on top, like a kind of burial. Ray squeezed her hand and said, "Ready?"

She said, "I was ready an hour ago."

They left quickly, not making eye contact, and in the hotel lobby Ray said, "Shall we go upstairs?"

"What did you do after the prom?"

"We watched the submarine races up at the Mystic Lakes."

"Show me."

He drove her through the town to the familiar turnoff, and down to the edge of the lake, where he parked, the house lights on the far shore glistening, giving life to the black water. He held Shelby's hand and kissed her, as he had in the first weeks of their love affair. He fumbled with her dress, loving its complications, delighting in the thought of her body under those silky layers slipping through his fingers, and she seemed as eager as he was.

"Here?" he asked. "Now?"

"Why not?" She shrugged the straps from her shoulders and held her breasts, and as she presented them to him their whiteness was illuminated by the headlights of a car, swinging up to park beside them.

"Cops," Ray said.

Shelby gasped and covered herself, clawing at her dress, while Ray rolled down his window. A bright overhead light came on inside the other car, which seemed full of passengers.

"You pig." It was Maura Dedrick, her face silhouetted at her window, someone beside her—Annie, maybe; someone else in the rear seat.

Ray was in such a hurry to get away that he started the car without raising the window, so he could hear Maura still calling out abuse, as he drove off, her shouts mingling with Shelby's choked sobs.

*   *   *

Back at the hotel (the reunion was still in progress—fewer people, louder music), Shelby lay in bed, shivering, repeating, "That was awful." Ray tried to soothe her, and in doing so felt useful, but when he moved to hug her she said, "Not now."

In a dark hour of the night, the phone rang like an alarm. Ray grabbed for it, and the voice had claws, the accusations of a woman wanting to hurt him. "Wrong number," he mumbled, and hung up, but was unable to get to sleep again.

In the morning, Shelby slid out of bed before he could touch her. She said, "Show me whatever you're going to show me, then let's go home."

He drove her to his old neighborhood and then slowly down the street where he had lived as a boy. The trees were gone, the wood-frame houses faded and small. Shelby sat, inattentive, distracted. At one point, he urged her to get out of the car, and he walked her to the side of a garage, where he'd carved a heart on a cinder block with a spike, the petroglyph still visible after all these years. It was here, in the garage between two houses, that he'd kissed a girl—what was her name?—one Halloween night, crushing her against the wall, tasting the candy in her mouth and running his hands over her body.

"Hello, stranger."

A great fat woman with wild hair stood, almost filling the space between the garage and the nearby house. She laughed, and put her hands on her hips. She wore bruised sneakers and no socks, and when she opened her mouth Ray could see gaps in her teeth, most of her molars missing. She raised one hand, clapping a cigarette to her lips, then blew smoke at him.

"I've been waiting for you."

"Is it—" He squinted to remember the name. "Louise?"

"Who else?" she said, then, "Who's that—your daughter?" and laughed again.

Shelby said, "I'll meet you in the car."

"She's scared," Louise said, hooting.

Ray was frightened, too, but didn't want to show it. The woman was hideous, and her sudden appearance and weird confidence made him want to run. But he sidled away slowly, saying, "Wait here. I'll be back."

"That's what you told me that night. I've been waiting ever since!"

Had he said that? Probably. As a boy, he'd told any lie for the chance to touch someone. She had scared him then; she scared him now. He had the sense that she wanted to hit him, and when she took another puff of her cigarette and tossed the butt aside he feared that she was coming for him.

"Please," he said, and put his hands up to protect his face and ran clumsily to his car.

Louise did not follow him. She watched from the passageway, potbellied, her feet apart, and as he started the car she shook another cigarette from her pack.

"I haven't seen her for years," Ray said. Shelby did not reply; she was mute, her arms folded, facing forward. "Imagine, she still lives there."

"Waiting for you."

"That's crazy."

*   *   *

But when they got home there was a further shock. As Ray parked, he noticed a white slip of paper thumbtacked to the front door. The idea that someone had come up the long driveway and through his gate to leave this note disturbed him. And he was more disturbed when he read it: "Ray, you must of gone out.

Sorry I missed you—Ellie."

"Who's Ellie?" Shelby said.

He was thinking "must of," and he knew it had to be Ellie, his college girlfriend. She'd become pregnant at just about the time they were breaking up. She'd told her parents, who'd arranged for her to have an abortion in another state—it was illegal in Massachusetts then. When it was over, her parents had written to his parents denouncing him, saying that he'd ruined their daughter's life. He had not seen her since. That was who Ellie was—Ellie Bryant.

But he said, "I don't know anyone by that name." It was the first lie he'd told Shelby in all the time he'd known her. "Maybe an old patient," he added.

For days, every evening when he returned home from the office with Shelby he expected Ellie to be waiting for him. Friday came. He knew something was wrong when he saw that the front gate, which was always latched, was ajar—a small thing, but for a frightened house owner, alert to details, it had significance. Then he heard the creak of the porch swing at the side of the house.

Shelby said, "There's someone here."

"I'll check—don't worry," he said, and braced himself for Ellie.

She was on the porch swing, facing away; he saw her back, her cold purple hands—it was November—on the chains that held the seat, the kerchief tightened around her head. She turned and the swing squeaked again.

"You!" The snarled word made her face ugly.

He had no idea who the woman was, and, before he could speak, Shelby came up behind him and said, "What are you doing here?"

"Visiting my old friend Ray Testa," the woman said.

"Are you Ellie?"

The woman frowned at the name. She said, "No. Ask him who I am. Go on, Ray, tell her."

But he didn't know. He started to gabble in fear.

"Think," she said. "You used to visit me and my husband in New Hampshire. He was a photographer. You pretended you were interested in his pictures. You were very chatty. And then, when he was away, you came back. You couldn't keep your hands off me. Always sneaking around, sniff-sniff." To Shelby, she said, "This man drove two hundred miles just to touch me."

And the effort did seem preposterous now, because the woman was gray, with papery skin, and sad eyes, and reddened gums showing in her downturned mouth.

He said, "Joyce."

"See? He knows who I am."

"What do you want?"

"Just to pay a friendly visit."

"Please go."

The woman said, "Isn't it funny? You drove all that way to see me—took half a day to get to my house—and all the probing, to make sure Richard was away. And now you can't wait to get rid of me."

With that, she stamped on the porch floorboards and hoisted herself out of the swing. She stood, leaning sideways, and she came at him with that crooked posture and a slight limp, as if she were about to fall down.

"This is how he'll treat you one day, sweetheart," she said to Shelby.

Ray let Joyce pass, then followed her to the driveway, and kept watching her—where was her car? how had she got there?—but she seemed to vanish before she reached the road.

Shelby was on the sofa in tears, her face in her hands. She recoiled when he reached for her.

"You know them," Shelby said. "All of them."

She refused to allow him to console her. She was disgusted, she said. She didn't eat that night. She slept in the spare room thereafter. He regretted their sleeping apart, until one night, soon after Joyce's visit, when he woke in his bed and became aware not of breathing but of a swelling shadow in the room.

He said, "Shelby?"

The soft laugh he heard was not Shelby's.

"You probably think you had a hard time," the woman said, becoming more substantial, emerging from the darkness as she spoke. "In those days, an abortion was a criminal offense. A doctor could lose his license for performing one. And it was painful and bloody and humiliating. It had another effect—I was never able to bear another child. My husband left me when he realized we'd never have children. I became a teacher, because I loved kids. I recently retired. I live on a pension. You destroyed my life."

Just when he thought she was going to hit him, she disappeared. In the morning, Shelby said she'd heard voices. "Who was it?"

"Talking in my sleep. I must have been dreaming."

Certain that he was lying, Shelby said that she could not bear to hear another word from him. She added, in her unanswerable, unwavering voice, "You keep saying how old and feeble they all are, and how repugnant. But don't you realize who they look like?"

He gaped at her, futilely.

"They all look like you. I sometimes think they are you. Each person in our past is an aspect of us. You need to know that."

Ray called his ex-wife, but got her answering machine. "Angie," he pleaded into it, "I don't know how you're doing it, but please stop. I'll agree to anything if you stop them showing up."

"I'm gonna talk to her. How's my breath?"

*   *   *

For several weeks, no women from his past intruded, and Ray believed that Angie had got the message. He even called again and left a thank-you on the answering machine.

Shelby demanded that they see a marriage counsellor. Ray agreed, but on the condition that the counsellor be in Boston, far from their home, so that their anonymity was assured.

"I want it to be a woman," Shelby said, and found a Dr. Patricia Devlin, whose office was near Mass General Hospital.

"Please take a seat," Dr. Devlin said on their first visit. "Make yourselves comfortable."

She read their insurance forms, running her finger down the answers to the questions on the back of the page. She was heavy, jowly, almost regal, wearing a white smock, her hair cut short, tapping her thick finger on the paper as she read. Her chair emitted complaining squeaks when she shifted in it, as if provoked by her restless thoughts.

"I'm afraid I can't take you on," she said, sighing, removing her glasses, and facing Ray, who smiled back helplessly. "Did you do this deliberately, to make me feel even worse?"

Ray said, "The appointment was Shelby's idea."

Looking hard at Ray, the doctor said, "I thought I'd seen the last of you, and heard the last of your excuses. Maybe it's unprofessional of me to say this—but it's outrageous that you should come here out of the blue, after the way you treated me." She gripped the armrests of her chair as though restraining herself. Sitting this way, her head tilted back, she looked like an emperor. "Now I must ask you to leave."

Shelby was silent in the elevator, because of the other passengers, but in the street she said, "Tell me who she is—and don't lie to me."

"We were at B.U. together," he said. "Pre-med."

"You're stalling," Shelby said.

He was. But he had been thrown by "Dr. Devlin." Her name had been Patricia Dorian—Armenian, a chemistry major. She'd been beautiful, with a sultry Central Asian cast to her face, full lips, and thick black hair. He'd taken her to a fraternity party, where they'd got drunk, and she'd said, "I feel sick. I have to lie down," and she'd fallen asleep in his room, in his bed, only to wake in the morning half-naked but fully alert, saying, "Did you touch me?

What did you do to me? Tell me!"

He'd said, truthfully, that he could not remember, but he was half-naked, too. And that was the beginning of a back-and-forth of recrimination that had ended with Patricia changing her major to psychology, so that she would not have to face Ray in the chem lab again.

"I knew her long ago," Ray said.

"Don't tell me any more," Shelby said. She turned her gray eyes on him and said, "*She* looks like you, too."

*   *   *

Shelby became humorless and doubting. She was like a much older woman, cautious in her movements, as though she feared she might trip; quieter and more reflective, almost rueful when Ray passed the bedroom and saw her lying alone—*her* bedroom. He slept in the spare room now.

He wanted to tell her that most people have flawed pasts, have acted selfishly at some point in their lives, and then moved on. New experiences take the place of old ones, new memories, better memories; and all the old selves become interred in a forgetfulness that is itself merciful. This was the process of aging, each new decade burying the previous one; that long-ago self was a stranger.

But all that these women had was the past. They dragged him back into it, into their ritual of unfulfillment, with these endless visitations—old women, old loves, old objects of desire with faces like bruised fruit.

Instead of saying this to Shelby, he called her father, who did not seem fazed by his story. He hardly reacted, and when Ray pressed him for an opinion the man said, "I can't help you."

Ray said, "She's like a stranger."

"That's my Shelby," the man said, and hung up.

Shelby still worked with him. Her father's abruptness, his grim amusement, had rattled Ray, and so he said to her, "You are everything to me now. Those women are all gone and forgotten."

This was in the office. There was a knock, the receptionist saying, "We have a new patient."

Ray went cold when he saw her tilted back in the chair, awaiting his examination. She did not even have to say, "Remember me?" He remembered her. He remembered his mistake. She was Sharon, from the cleaning company. He had been surprised, years earlier, that someone so young—no more than eighteen or so—was doing this menial job. Why wasn't she in school? he'd asked her. "I hate school," she said. "I want to make some money." She'd seemed to linger in her work, and one evening when they were alone Ray had pulled her to him while she was mopping, and kissed her, hoping for more. But she'd pushed him away, and wiped her mouth with the back of her hand, and never come back. Shelby had become his hygienist later that year, so she knew nothing of Sharon. And he'd never seen Sharon again, or thought of her—it had been only a foolish, impulsive, hopeful kiss!—until now.

She stared at him with implacable eyes; her very lack of expression seemed accusatory. He did not recall her being so plain, so fierce. She had been young, attractive, in a T-shirt and shorts, with a long-handled mop in her hands. Now she lay canted back in the chair, as Shelby hooked on her earpieces and adjusted the protective goggles. Sharon's mouth was prominent, her cold eyes blurred by the plastic. She seemed weirdly masked, with an upside-down face, from where Ray stood, slightly behind her. Her mouth began to move, the bite of the teeth reversed.

"You got yourself a hot assistant now," Sharon said. "Bet you kiss her, too, when no one's looking."

"This is my wife," Ray said. "Now open wide and let me have a look."

"I can't do this," Shelby said. She gathered the loops of the suction device and tossed them into the sink.

"Shel," he said. Then, seeing that it was hopeless, that Shelby had closed the door behind her, he attended to Sharon, his fingers in her mouth, gagging her. He wanted to pull out her tongue.

When he had finished the cleaning, he said, "You've never been here as a patient before. I haven't seen you in years. You don't need any serious work. Why did you come?"

"Just a spur-of-the-moment thing," Sharon said. "Hey, you probably think that kissing me and touching me like that was something I'd forget."

He sighed. He was going to shout, but he forced himself to speak calmly. "I'm done. I've knocked some barnacles off your teeth.

Don't come back. If you do, I will refuse to see you."

Now the goggles were off and Sharon was upright, blinking like a squirrel. She licked a smear of toothpaste from her lips and said, "I won't come back. I don't need to. I've done what I had to do."

"What was that?"

"Make you remember."

But he had not forgotten—he remembered her as a girl, alone in the corridor by his office, holding the sudden promise of pleasure. The shock to him on her return was that she had aged, that she was rawboned and resentful and no longer attractive.

Before going home to Shelby that day, he looked at himself in the bathroom mirror and hated his face. He hated what time had done to it; he hated what time had done to these women. He hated the sight of his hands. He had flirted with and pawed these old women. *They all look like you. I sometimes think they are you.*

*   *   *

Shelby treated him as though he were dangerous. She seemed afraid to be with him, afraid of who might show up unbidden, which hag from the past come to confront Ray, to remind him of what he'd done and who he was, an old beast they all haunted because they could not forgive him. She seemed to regard him as the monster that, in his worst moments, he believed himself to be, the embodiment of everything he'd done. And now, thanks to these offended women, she knew every one of his reckless transgressions.

Soon she stopped coming to work, and the two of them lived separately in the house, taking turns in the kitchen, eating their meals apart, more like hostile roommates than like a married couple—a reënactment of his last months with Angie.

He called Angie again, but this time there was no answering machine. The number had been disconnected. Then he found out why. A patient said casually, just as he'd finished putting on a crown, "Sorry about Angie."

Misunderstanding, he began to explain, and then realized that the patient was telling him that Angie had died.

It had happened two weeks before. He found the details online on the Medford *Transcript* Web site. *Collapsed and died after a short illness.* Instead of going home, he drove the seventy-five miles to the cemetery and knelt at her grave. A metal marker with her name, courtesy of the funeral home, had been inserted into the ruglike cover of new sod. He told himself that he was sorrowful, but he did not feel it: he was relieved; he felt lighter; he blamed Angie for the swarm of old lovers. This feeling scared him in the dampness of the cemetery, where he suspected that he was being watched. It was then, looking around, that he saw that Angie was buried next to her mother, a reunion of sorts.

He told Shelby that Angie had died. "It's a turning point!" They could start all over again.

"You actually seem glad that Angie's dead," Shelby said. "Poor Angie."

After Angie's death, the visitations ceased. But, demoralized, humiliated, Shelby left him. She did not divorce him at once. She demanded a house, and he provided it. She asked for severance pay from her job, and got it. They spoke through lawyers, until it was final, and he was alone.

*   *   *

Ray is not surprised, one night, when he is woken by a clatter, the sound of someone hurrying in darkness. It is a familiar sound. He awaits the visitation, hoping that it will make him less lonely. Perhaps it is Angie who has come to mock him. He wants to beg for her forgiveness. No, it is not Angie's voice. It is Shelby's, and it is triumphant. But the body, the hag's face, is his own. ♦

Paul Theroux is a novelist and a travel writer. "Deep South: Four Seasons on Back Roads" is his latest book.

http://www.newyorker.com/magazine/2013/02/25/the-furies-2

THE GIRLS IN THEIR SUMMER DRESSES

Irwin Shaw

Fifth Avenue was shining in the sun when they left the Brevoort. The sun was warm, even though it was February, and everything looked like Sunday morning—the buses and the well-dressed people walking slowly in couples and the quiet buildings with the windows closed.

Michael held Frances' arm tightly as they walked toward Washington Square in the sunlight. They walked lightly, almost smiling, because they had slept late and had a good breakfast and it was Sunday. Michael unbuttoned his coat and let it flap around him in the mild wind.

"Look out," Frances said as they crossed Eighth Street. "You'll break your neck." Michael laughed and Frances laughed with him.

"She's not so pretty," Frances said. "Anyway, not pretty enough to take a chance of breaking your neck."

Michael laughed again. "How did you know I was looking at her?"

Frances cocked her head to one side and smiled at her husband under the brim of her hat. "Mike, darling," she said.

"O.K.," he said. "Excuse me."

Frances patted his arm lightly and pulled him along a little faster toward Washington Square. "Let's not see anybody all day," she said. "Let's just hang around with each other. You and me. We're always up to our neck in people, drinking their Scotch or drinking our Scotch; we only see each other in bed. I want to go out with my husband all day long. I want him to talk only to me and listen only to me."

285

"What's to stop us?" Michael asked.

"The Stevensons. They want us to drop by around one o'clock and they'll drive us into the country."

"The cunning Stevensons," Mike said. "Transparent. They can whistle. They can go driving in the country by themselves."

"Is it a date?"

"It's a date."

Frances leaned over and kissed him on the tip of the ear.

"Darling," Michael said, "this is Fifth Avenue."

"Let me arrange a program," Frances said. "A planned Sunday in New York for a young couple with money to throw away."

"Go easy."

"First let's go to the Metropolitan Museum of Art," Frances suggested, because Michael had said during the week he wanted to go. "I haven't been there in three years and there're at least ten pictures I want to see again. Then we can take the bus down to Radio City and watch them skate. And later we'll go down to Cavanagh's and get a steak as big as a blacksmith's apron, with a bottle of wine, and after that there's a French picture at the Filmarte that everybody says—say, are you listening to me?"

"Sure," he said. He took his eyes off the hatless girl with the dark hair, cut dancer-style like a helmet, who was walking past him.

"That's the program for the day," Frances said flatly. "Or maybe you'd just rather walk up and down Fifth Avenue."

"No," Michael said. "Not at all."

"You always look at other women," Frances said. "Everywhere. Every damned place we go."

"No, darling," Michael said, "I look at everything. God gave me eyes and I look at women and men in subway excavations and moving pictures and the little flowers of the field. I casually inspect the universe."

"You ought to see the look in your eye," Frances said, "as you casually inspect the universe on Fifth Avenue."

"I'm a happily married man." Michael pressed her elbow tenderly. "Example for the whole twentieth century—Mr. and Mrs. Mike Loomis. Hey, let's have a drink," he said, stopping.

"We just had breakfast."

"Now listen, darling," Mike said, choosing his words with care, "it's a nice day and we both felt good and there's no reason why we have to break it up. Let's have a nice Sunday."

"All right. I don't know why I started this. Let's drop it. Let's have a good time."

They joined hands consciously and walked without talking among the baby carriages and the old Italian men in their Sunday clothes and the young women with Scotties in Washington Square Park.

"At least once a year everyone should go to the Metropolitan Museum of Art," Frances said after a while, her tone a good imitation of the tone she had used at breakfast and at the beginning of their walk. "And it's nice on Sunday. There're a lot of people looking at the pictures and you get the feeling maybe Art isn't on the decline in New York City, after all—"

"I want to tell you something," Michael said very seriously. "I have not touched another woman. Not once. In all the five years."

"All right," Frances said.

"You believe that, don't you?"

"All right."

They walked between the crowded benches, under the scrubby city-park trees.

"I try not to notice it," Frances said, "but I feel rotten inside, in my stomach, when we pass a woman and you look at her and I see that look in your eye and that's the way you looked at me the first time. In Alice Maxwell's house. Standing there in the living room, next to the radio, with a green hat on and all those people."

"I remember the hat," Michael said.

"The same look," Frances said. "And it makes me feel bad. It makes me feel terrible."

"Sh-h-h, please, darling, sh-h-h."

"I think I would like a drink now," Frances said.

They walked over to a bar on Eighth Street, not saying anything, Michael automatically helping her over curbstones and guiding her past automobiles. They sat near a window in the bar and the sun streamed in and there was a small, cheerful fire in the fireplace. A little Japanese waiter came over and put down some pretzels and smiled happily at them.

"What do you order after breakfast?" Michael asked.

"Brandy, I suppose," Frances said.

"Courvoisier," Michael told the waiter, "Two Courvoisiers."

The waiter came with the glasses and they sat drinking the brandy in the sunlight. Michael finished half his and drank a little water.

"I look at women," he said. "Correct. I don't say it's wrong or right. I look at them. If I pass them on the street and I don't look at them, I'm fooling you, I'm fooling myself."

"You look at them as though you want them," Frances said, playing with her brandy glass. "Every one of them."

"In a way," Michael said, speaking softly and not to his wife, "in a way that's true. I don't do anything about it, but it's true."

"I know it. That's why I feel bad."

"Another brandy," Michael called. "Waiter, two more brandies."

He sighed and closed his eyes and rubbed them gently with his fingertips. "I love the way women look. One of the things I like best about New York is the battalions of women. When I first came to New York from Ohio that was the first thing I noticed, the million wonderful women, all over the city. I walked around with my heart in my throat."

"A kid," Frances said. "That's a kid's feeling."

"Guess again," Michael said. "Guess again. I'm older now. I'm a man getting near middle age, putting on a little fat, and I still love to walk along Fifth Avenue at three o'clock on the east side of the street between Fiftieth and the Fifty-seventh Streets. They're all out then, shopping, in their furs and their crazy hats, everything all concentrated from all over the world into seven blocks—the best furs, the best clothes, the handsomest women, out to spend money and feeling good about it."

The Japanese waiter put the two drinks down, smiling with great happiness.

"Everything is all right?" he asked.

"Everything is wonderful," Michael said.

"If it's just a couple of fur coats," Frances said, "and forty-five dollar hats."

"It's not the fur coats. Or the hats. That's just the scenery for that particular kind of women. Understand," he said, "you don't have to listen to this."

"I want to listen."

"I like the girls in the offices. Neat, with their eyeglasses, smart, chipper, knowing what everything is about. I like the girls on Forty-fourth Street at lunchtime, the actresses, all dressed up on nothing a week. I like the salesgirls in the stores, paying attention to you first because you're a man, leaving lady customers waiting. I got all this stuff accumulated in me because I've been thinking about it for ten years and now you've asked for it and here it is."

"Go ahead," Frances said.

"When I think of New York City, I think of all the girls on parade in the city. I don't know whether it's something special with me or whether every man in the city walks around with the same feeling inside him, but I feel as though I'm at a picnic in this city. I like to sit near the women in the theatres, the famous beauties who've taken six hours to get ready and look at it. And the young girls at the football games, with the red cheeks, and when the warm weather comes, the girls in their summer dresses." He finished his drink. "That's the story."

Frances finished her drink and swallowed two or three times extra. "You say you love me?"

"I love you."

"I'm pretty, too," Frances said. "As pretty as any of them."

"You're beautiful," Michael said.

"I'm good for you," Frances said, pleading. "I've made a good wife, a good housekeeper, a good friend. I'd do any damn thing for you."

"I know," Michael said. He put his hand out and grasped hers.

"You'd like to be free to—" Frances said.

"Sh-h-h."

"Tell the truth." She took her hand away from under his.

Michael flicked the edge of his glass with his finger. "O.K.," he said gently. "Sometimes I feel I would like to be free."

"Well," Frances said, "any time you say."

"Don't be foolish." Michael swung his chair around to her side of the table and patted her thigh.

She began to cry silently into her handkerchief, bent over just enough so that nobody else in the bar would notice. "Someday," she said, crying, "you're going to make a move."

Michael didn't say anything. He sat watching the bartender slowly peel a lemon.

"Aren't you?" Frances asked harshly. "Come on, tell me. Talk. Aren't you?"

"Maybe," Michael said. He moved his chair back again. "How the hell do I know?"

"You know," Frances persisted. "Don't you know?"

"Yes," Michael said after a while, "I know."

Frances stopped crying then. Two or three snuffles into the handkerchief and she put it away and her face didn't tell anything to anybody. "At least do me one favor," she said.

"Sure."

"Stop talking about how pretty this woman is or that one. Nice eyes, nice breasts, a pretty figure, good voice." She mimicked his voice. "Keep it to yourself. I'm not interested."

Michael waved to the waiter. "I'll keep it to myself," he said.

Frances flicked the corners of her eyes. "Another brandy," she told the waiter.

"Two," Michael said.

"Yes, Ma'am, yes, sir," said the waiter, backing away.

Frances regarded Michael coolly across the table. "Do you want me to call the Stevensons?" she asked. "It'll be nice in the country."

"Sure," Michael said. "Call them."

She got up from the table and walked across the room toward the telephone. Michael watched her walk, thinking what a pretty girl, what nice legs.

THE LOTTERY (1948)
Shirley Jackson

The morning of June 27th was clear and sunny, with the fresh warmth of a full-summer day; the flowers were blossoming profusely and the grass was richly green. The people of the village began to gather in the square, between the post office and the bank, around ten o'clock; in some towns there were so many people that the lottery took two days and had to be started on June 26th, but in this village, where there were only about three hundred people, the whole lottery took less than two hours, so it could begin at ten o'clock in the morning and still be through in time to allow the villagers to get home for noon dinner.

The children assembled first, of course. School was recently over for the summer, and the feeling of liberty sat uneasily on most of them; they tended to gather together quietly for a while before they broke into boisterous play, and their talk was still of the classroom and the teacher, of books and reprimands. Bobby Martin had already stuffed his pockets full of stones, and the other boys soon followed his example, selecting the smoothest and roundest stones; Bobby and Harry Jones and Dickie Delacroix—the villagers pronounced this name "Dellacroy"—eventually made a great pile of stones in one corner of the square and guarded it against the raids of the other boys. The girls stood aside, talking among themselves, looking over their shoulders at the boys, and the very small children rolled in the dust or clung to the hands of their older brothers or sisters.

Soon the men began to gather, surveying their own children, speaking of planting and rain, tractors and taxes. They stood together, away from the pile of stones in the corner, and their jokes were quiet and they smiled rather than laughed. The women, wearing faded house dresses and sweaters, came shortly after their menfolk. They greeted one another and exchanged bits of gossip as they went to join their husbands. Soon the women, standing by their husbands, began to call to their children, and the children came reluctantly, having to be called four or five times. Bobby Martin ducked under his mother's grasping hand and ran, laughing, back to the pile of stones. His father spoke up sharply, and Bobby came quickly and took his place between his father and his oldest brother.

The lottery was conducted–as were the square dances, the teen club, the Halloween program–by Mr. Summers, who had time and energy to devote to civic activities. He was a round-faced, jovial man and he ran the coal business, and people were sorry for him because he had no children and his wife was a scold. When he arrived in the square, carrying the black wooden box, there was a murmur of conversation among the villagers, and he waved and called, "Little late today, folks." The postmaster, Mr. Graves, followed him, carrying a three-legged stool, and the stool was put in the center of the square and Mr. Summers set the black box down on it. The villagers kept their distance, leaving a space between themselves and the stool, and when Mr. Summers said, "Some of you fellows want to give me a hand?" there was a hesitation before two men, Mr. Martin and his oldest son, Baxter came forward to hold the box steady on the stool while Mr. Summers stirred up the papers inside it.

The original paraphernalia for the lottery had been lost long ago, and the black box now resting on the stool had been put into use even before Old Man Warner, the oldest man in town, was born. Mr. Summers spoke frequently to the villagers about making a new box, but no one liked to upset even as much tradition as was represented by the black box. There was a story that the present box had been made with some pieces of the box that had preceded it, the one that had been constructed when the first people settled down to make a village here. Every year, after the lottery, Mr. Summers began talking again about a new box, but every year the subject was allowed to fade off without anything being done. The black box grew shabbier each year: by now it was no longer completely black but splintered badly along one side to show the original wood color, and in some places faded or stained.

Mr. Martin and his oldest son, Baxter, held the black box securely on the stool until Mr. Summers had stirred the papers thoroughly with his hand. Because so much of the ritual had been forgotten or discarded, Mr. Summers had been successful in having slips of paper substituted for the chips of wood that had been used for generations. Chips of wood, Mr. Summers had argued, had been all very well when the village was tiny, but now that the population was more than three hundred and likely to keep on growing, it was necessary to use something that would fit more easily into the black box. The night before the lottery, Mr. Summers and Mr. Graves made up the slips of paper and put them in the box, and it was then taken to the safe of Mr. Summers' coal company and locked up until Mr. Summers was ready to take it to the square next morning. The rest of the year, the box was put way, sometimes one place, sometimes another; it had spent one year in Mr. Graves's barn and another year underfoot in the post office, and sometimes it was set on a shelf in the Martin grocery and left there.

There was a great deal of fussing to be done before Mr.Summers declared the lottery open. There were the lists to make up–of heads of families, heads of households in each family, members of each household in each family. There was the proper swearing-in of Mr. Summers by the postmaster, as the official of the lottery; at one time, some people remembered, there had been a recital of some sort, performed by the official of the lottery, a perfunctory tuneless chant that had been rattled off duly each year; some people believed that the official of the lottery used to stand just so when he said or sang it, others believed that he was supposed to walk among the people, but years and years ago this part of the ritual had been allowed to lapse. There had been, also, a ritual salute, which the official of the lottery had had to use in addressing each person who came up to draw from the box, but this also had changed with time, until now it was felt necessary only for the official to speak to each person approaching. Mr. Summers was very good at all this; in his clean white shirt and blue jeans, with one hand resting carelessly on the black box, he seemed very proper and important as he talked interminably to Mr. Graves and the Martins.

Just as Mr. Summers finally left off talking and turned to the assembled villagers, Mrs. Hutchinson came hurriedly along the path to the square, her sweater thrown over her shoulders, and slid into place in the back of the crowd. "Clean forgot what day it was," she said to Mrs. Delacroix, who stood next to her, and they both laughed softly. "Thought my old man was out back stacking wood," Mrs. Hutchinson went on. "and then I looked out the window and the kids was gone, and then I remembered it was the twenty-seventh and came a-running." She dried her hands on her apron, and Mrs. Delacroix said, "You're in time, though. They're still talking away up there."

Mrs. Hutchinson craned her neck to see through the crowd and found her husband and children standing near the front. She tapped Mrs. Delacroix on the arm as a farewell and began to make her way through the crowd. The people separated good-humoredly to let her through: two or three people said, in voices just loud enough to be heard across the crowd, "Here comes your, Missus, Hutchinson," and "Bill, she made it after all." Mrs. Hutchinson reached her husband, and Mr. Summers, who had been waiting, said cheerfully. "Thought we were going to have to get on without you, Tessie." Mrs. Hutchinson said. grinning, "Wouldn't have me leave m'dishes in the sink, now, would you. Joe?" and soft laughter ran through the crowd as the people stirred back into position after Mrs. Hutchinson's arrival.

"Well, now." Mr. Summers said soberly, "guess we better get started, get this over with, so's we can go back to work. Anybody ain't here?"

"Dunbar." several people said. "Dunbar. Dunbar."

Mr. Summers consulted his list. "Clyde Dunbar." he said. "That's right. He's broke his leg, hasn't he? Who's drawing for him?"

"Me. I guess," a woman said, and Mr. Summers turned to look at her. "Wife draws for her husband." Mr. Summers said. "Don't you have a grown boy to do it for you, Janey?" Although Mr. Summers and everyone else in the village knew the answer perfectly well, it was the business of the official of the lottery to ask such questions formally. Mr. Summers waited with an expression of polite interest while Mrs. Dunbar answered.

"Horace's not but sixteen vet." Mrs. Dunbar said regretfully. "Guess I gotta fill in for the old man this year."

"Right." Sr. Summers said. He made a note on the list he was holding. Then he asked, "Watson boy drawing this year?"

A tall boy in the crowd raised his hand. "Here," he said. "I'm drawing for my mother and me." He blinked his eyes nervously and ducked his head as several voices in the crowd said things like "Good fellow, Jack." and "Glad to see your mother's got a man to do it."

"Well," Mr. Summers said, "guess that's everyone. Old Man Warner make it?" "Here," a voice said, and Mr. Summers nodded.

A sudden hush fell on the crowd as Mr. Summers cleared his throat and looked at the list. "All ready?" he called. "Now, I'll read the names—heads of families first—and the men come up and take a paper out of the box. Keep the paper folded in your hand without looking at it until everyone has had a turn. Everything clear?"

The people had done it so many times that they only half listened to the directions: most of them were quiet, wetting their lips, not looking around. Then Mr. Summers raised one hand high and said, "Adams." A man disengaged himself from the crowd and came forward. "Hi. Steve." Mr. Summers said, and Mr. Adams said. "Hi. Joe." They grinned at one another humorlessly and nervously. Then Mr. Adams reached into the black box and took out a folded paper. He held it firmly by one corner as he turned and went hastily back to his place in the crowd, where he stood a little apart from his family, not looking down at his hand.

"Allen." Mr. Summers said. "Anderson. . . . Bentham." "Seems like there's no time at all between lotteries any more," Mrs. Delacroix said to Mrs. Graves in the back row. "Seems like we got through with the last one only last week."

"Time sure goes fast—Mrs. Graves said.

"Clark. . . . Delacroix."

"There goes my old man." Mrs. Delacroix said. She held her breath while her husband went forward.

"Dunbar," Mr. Summers said, and Mrs. Dunbar went steadily to the box while one of the women said. "Go on. Janey," and another said, "There she goes."

"We're next." Mrs. Graves said. She watched while Mr. Graves came around from the side of the box, greeted Mr. Summers gravely and selected a slip of paper from the box. By now, all through the crowd there were men holding the small folded papers in their large hand. turning them over and over nervously Mrs. Dunbar and her two sons stood together, Mrs. Dunbar holding the slip of paper.

"Harburt. . . . Hutchinson." "Get up there, Bill," Mrs. Hutchinson said. and the people near her laughed.

"Jones."

"They do say," Mr. Adams said to Old Man Warner, who stood next to him, "that over in the north village they're talking of giving up the lottery." Old Man Warner snorted. "Pack of crazy fools," he said. "Listening to the young folks, nothing's good enough for them. Next thing you know, they'll be wanting to go back to living in caves, nobody works any more, live that way for a while. Used to be a saying about 'Lottery in June, corn be heavy soon.' First thing you know, we'd all be eating stewed chickweed and acorns. There's always been a lottery," he added petulantly. "Bad enough to see young Joe Summers up there joking with everybody."

"Some places have already quit lotteries." Mrs. Adams said.

"Nothing but trouble in that," Old Man Warner said stoutly. "Pack of young fools."

"Martin." And Bobby Martin watched his father go forward. "Overdyke. . . . Percy."

"I wish they'd hurry," Mrs. Dunbar said to her older son. "I wish they'd hurry."

"They're almost through," her son said.

"You get ready to run tell Dad," Mrs. Dunbar said.

Mr. Summers called his own name and then stepped forward precisely and selected a slip from the box. Then he called, "Warner." "Seventy-seventh year I been in the lottery," Old Man Warner said as he went through the crowd. "Seventy-seventh time."

"Watson" The tall boy came awkwardly through the crowd. Someone said, "Don't be nervous, Jack," and Mr. Summers said, "Take your time, son."

"Zanini."

*   *   *

After that, there was a long pause, a breathless pause, until Mr. Summers. holding his slip of paper in the air, said, "All right, fellows." For a minute, no one moved, and then all the slips of paper were opened. Suddenly, all the women began to speak at once, saving. "Who is it?" "Who's got it?" "Is it the Dunbars?" "Is it the Watsons?" Then the voices began to say, "It's Hutchinson. It's Bill," "Bill Hutchinson's got it."

"Go tell your father," Mrs. Dunbar said to her older son.

People began to look around to see the Hutchinsons. Bill Hutchinson was standing quiet, staring down at the paper in his hand. Suddenly. Tessie Hutchinson shouted to Mr. Summers. "You didn't give him time enough to take any paper he wanted. I saw you. It wasn't fair!"

"Be a good sport, Tessie." Mrs. Delacroix called, and Mrs. Graves said, "All of us took the same chance."

"Shut up, Tessie," Bill Hutchinson said. "Well, everyone," Mr. Summers said, "that was done pretty fast, and now we've got to be hurrying a little more to get done in time." He consulted his next list. "Bill," he said, "you draw for the Hutchinson family. You got any other households in the Hutchinsons?"

"There's Don and Eva," Mrs. Hutchinson yelled. "Make them take their chance!"

"Daughters draw with their husbands' families, Tessie," Mr. Summers said gently. "You know that as well as anyone else."

"It wasn't fair," Tessie said.

"I guess not, Joe." Bill Hutchinson said regretfully. "My daughter draws with her husband's family; that's only fair. And I've got no other family except the kids."

"Then, as far as drawing for families is concerned, it's you," Mr. Summers said in explanation, "and as far as drawing for households is concerned, that's you, too. Right?"

"Right," Bill Hutchinson said.

"How many kids, Bill?" Mr. Summers asked formally. "Three," Bill Hutchinson said. "There's Bill, Jr., and Nancy, and little Dave. And Tessie and me."

"All right, then," Mr. Summers said. "Harry, you got their tickets back?"

Mr. Graves nodded and held up the slips of paper. "Put them in the box, then," Mr. Summers directed. "Take Bill's and put it in."

"I think we ought to start over," Mrs. Hutchinson said, as quietly as she could. "I tell you it wasn't fair. You didn't give him time enough to choose. Everybody saw that."

Mr. Graves had selected the five slips and put them in the box, and he dropped all the papers but those onto the ground where the breeze caught them and lifted them off.

"Listen, everybody," Mrs. Hutchinson was saying to the people around her.

"Ready, Bill?" Mr. Summers asked, and Bill Hutchinson, with one quick glance around at his wife and children, nodded.

"Remember," Mr. Summers said. "Take the slips and keep them folded until each person has taken one. Harry, you help little Dave." Mr. Graves took the hand of the little boy, who came willingly with him up to the box. "Take a paper out of the box, Davy." Mr. Summers said. Davy put his hand into the box and laughed. "Take just one paper." Mr. Summers said. "Harry, you hold it for him." Mr. Graves took the child's hand and removed the folded paper from the tight fist and held it while little Dave stood next to him and looked up at him wonderingly.

"Nancy next," Mr. Summers said. Nancy was twelve, and her school friends breathed heavily as she went forward switching her skirt, and took a slip daintily from the box "Bill, Jr.," Mr. Summers said, and Billy, his face red and his feet overlarge, near knocked the box over as he got a paper out. "Tessie," Mr. Summers said. She hesitated for a minute, looking around defiantly and then set her lips and went up to the box. She snatched a paper out and held it behind her.

"Bill," Mr. Summers said, and Bill Hutchinson reached into the box and felt around, bringing his hand out at last with the slip of paper in it.

The crowd was quiet. A girl whispered, "I hope it's not Nancy," and the sound of the whisper reached the edges of the crowd.

"It's not the way it used to be." Old Man Warner said clearly. "People ain't the way they used to be." "All right," Mr. Summers said. "Open the papers. Harry, you open little Dave's."

Mr. Graves opened the slip of paper and there was a general sigh through the crowd as he held it up and everyone could see that it was blank. Nancy and Bill. Jr. opened theirs at the same time, and both beamed and laughed, turning around to the crowd and holding their slips of paper above their heads.

"Tessie," Mr. Summers said. There was a pause, and then Mr. Summers looked at Bill Hutchinson, and Bill unfolded his paper and showed it. It was blank.

"It's Tessie," Mr. Summers said, and his voice was hushed. "Show us her paper. Bill."

Bill Hutchinson went over to his wife and forced the slip of paper out of her hand. It had a black spot on it, the black spot Mr. Summers had made the night before with the heavy pencil in the coal company office. Bill Hutchinson held it up, and there was a stir in the crowd.

"All right, folks." Mr. Summers said. "Let's finish quickly."

Although the villagers had forgotten the ritual and lost the original black box, they still remembered to use stones. The pile of stones the boys had made earlier was ready; there were stones on the ground with the blowing scraps of paper that had come out of the box. Delacroix selected a stone so large she had to pick it up with both hands and turned to Mrs. Dunbar. "Come on," she said. "Hurry up."

Mr. Dunbar had small stones in both hands, and she said, gasping for breath, "I can't run at all. You'll have to go ahead and I'll catch up with you."

The children had stones already. And someone gave little Davy Hutchinson few pebbles. Tessie Hutchinson was in the center of a cleared space by now, and she held her hands out desperately as the villagers moved in on her. "It isn't fair," she said. A stone hit her on the side of the head.

Old Man Warner was saying, "Come on, come on, everyone." Steve Adams was in the front of the crowd of villagers, with Mrs. Graves beside him.

"It isn't fair, it isn't right," Mrs. Hutchinson screamed, and then they were upon her.

THE MOST DANGEROUS GAME
Richard Connell

"Off there to the right—somewhere—is a large island," said Whitney. "It's rather a mystery—"

"What island is it?" Rainsford asked.

"The old charts call it 'Ship-Trap Island,'" Whitney replied. "A suggestive name, isn't it? Sailors have a curious dread of the place. I don't know why. Some superstition—"

"Can't see it," remarked Rainsford, trying to peer through the dank tropical night that was palpable as it pressed its thick warm blackness in upon the yacht.

"You've good eyes," said Whitney, with a laugh, "and I've seen you pick off a moose moving in the brown fall bush at four hundred yards, but even you can't see four miles or so through a moonless Caribbean night."

"Nor four yards," admitted Rainsford. "Ugh! It's like moist black velvet."

"It will be light in Rio," promised Whitney. "We should make it in a few days. I hope the jaguar guns have come from Purdey's. We should have some good hunting up the Amazon. Great sport, hunting."

"The best sport in the world," agreed Rainsford.

"For the hunter," amended Whitney. "Not for the jaguar."

"Don't talk rot, Whitney," said Rainsford. "You're a big-game hunter, not a philosopher. Who cares how a jaguar feels?"

"Perhaps the jaguar does," observed Whitney.

"Bah! They've no understanding."

"Even so, I rather think they understand one thing—fear. The fear of pain and the fear of death."

"Nonsense," laughed Rainsford. "This hot weather is making you soft, Whitney. Be a realist. The world is made up of two classes—the hunters and the huntees. Luckily, you and I are the hunters. Do you think we've passed that island yet?"

"I can't tell in the dark. I hope so."

"Why?" asked Rainsford.

"The place has a reputation—a bad one."

"Cannibals?" suggested Rainsford.

"Hardly. Even cannibals wouldn't live in such a God-forsaken place. But it's gotten into sailor lore, somehow. Didn't you notice that the crew's nerves seemed a bit jumpy to-day?"

"They were a bit strange, now you mention it. Even Captain Nielsen—"

"Yes, even that tough-minded old Swede, who'd go up to the devil himself and ask him for a light. Those fishy blue eyes held a look I never saw there before. All I could get out of him was: 'This place has an evil name among seafaring men, sir.' Then he said to me, very gravely: 'Don't you feel anything?'—as if the air about us was actually poisonous. Now, you mustn't laugh when I tell you this—I did feel something like a sudden chill."

"There was no breeze. The sea was as flat as a plate-glass window. We were drawing near the island then. What I felt was a—a mental chill; a sort of sudden dread."

"Pure imagination," said Rainsford. "One superstitious sailor can taint the whole ship's company with his fear."

"Maybe. But sometimes I think sailors have an extra sense that tells them when they are in danger. Sometimes I think evil is a tangible thing—with wave lengths, just as sound and light have. An evil place can, so to speak, broadcast vibrations of evil. Anyhow, I'm glad we're getting out of this zone. Well, I think I'll turn in now, Rainsford."

"I'm not sleepy," said Rainsford. "I'm going to smoke another pipe on the after deck."

"Good night, then, Rainsford. See you at breakfast."

"Right. Good night, Whitney."

There was no sound in the night as Rainsford sat there, but the muffled throb of the engine that drove the yacht swiftly through the darkness, and the swish and ripple of the wash of the propeller.

Rainsford, reclining in a steamer chair, indolently puffed on his favorite brier. The sensuous drowsiness of the night was on him.

"It's so dark," he thought, "that I could sleep without closing my eyes; the night would be my eyelids—"

An abrupt sound startled him. Off to the right he heard it, and his ears, expert in such matters, could not be mistaken. Again he heard the sound, and again. Somewhere, off in the blackness, some one had fired a gun three times.

Rainsford sprang up and moved quickly to the rail, mystified. He strained his eyes in the direction from which the reports had come, but it was like trying to see through a blanket. He leaped upon the rail and balanced himself there, to get greater elevation; his pipe, striking a rope, was knocked from his mouth. He lunged for it; a short, hoarse cry came from his lips as he realized he had reached too far and had lost his balance. The cry was pinched off short as the blood-warm waters of the Caribbean Sea closed over his head.

He struggled up to the surface and tried to cry out, but the wash from the speeding yacht slapped him in the face and the salt water in his open mouth made him gag and strangle. Desperately he struck out with strong strokes after the receding lights of the yacht, but he stopped before he had swum fifty feet. A certain cool-headedness had come to him; it was not the first time he had been in a tight place. There was a chance that his cries could be heard by some one aboard the yacht, but that chance was slender, and grew more slender as the yacht raced on. He wrestled himself out of his clothes, and shouted with all his power. The lights of the yacht became faint and ever-vanishing fireflies; then they were blotted out entirely by the night.

Rainsford remembered the shots. They had come from the right, and doggedly he swam in that direction, swimming with slow, deliberate strokes, conserving his strength. For a seemingly endless time he fought the sea. He began to count his strokes; he could do possibly a hundred more and then—

Rainsford heard a sound. It came out of the darkness, a high screaming sound, the sound of an animal in an extremity of anguish and terror.

He did not recognize the animal that made the sound; he did not try to; with fresh vitality he swam toward the sound. He heard it again; then it was cut short by another noise, crisp, staccato.

"Pistol shot," muttered Rainsford, swimming on.

Ten minutes of determined effort brought another sound to his ears—the most welcome he had ever heard—the muttering and growling of the sea breaking on a rocky shore. He was almost on the rocks before he saw them; on a night less calm he would have been shattered against them. With his remaining strength he dragged himself from the swirling waters. Jagged crags appeared to jut into the opaqueness, he forced himself upward, hand over hand. Gasping, his hands raw, he reached a flat place at the top. Dense jungle came down to the very edge of the cliffs. What perils that tangle of trees and underbrush might hold for him did not concern Rainsford just then. All he knew was that he was safe from his enemy, the sea, and that utter weariness was on him. He flung himself down at the jungle edge and tumbled headlong into the deepest sleep of his life.

When he opened his eyes he knew from the position of the sun that it was late in the afternoon. Sleep had given him new vigor; a sharp hunger was picking at him. He looked about him, almost cheerfully.

"Where there are pistol shots, there are men. Where there are men, there is food," he thought. But what kind of men, he wondered, in so forbidding a place? An unbroken front of snarled and ragged jungle fringed the shore.

He saw no sign of a trail through the closely knit web of weeds and trees; it was easier to go along the shore, and Rainsford floundered along by the water. Not far from where he had landed, he stopped.

Some wounded thing by the evidence a large animal, had thrashed about in the underbrush; the jungle weeds were crushed down and the moss was lacerated; one patch of weeds was stained crimson. A small, glittering object not far away caught Rainsford's eye and he picked it up. It was an empty cartridge.

"A twenty-two," he remarked. "That's odd. It must have been a fairly large animal too. The hunter had his nerve with him to tackle it with a light gun. It's clear that the brute put up a fight. I suppose the first three shots I heard was when the hunter flushed his quarry and wounded it. The last shot was when he trailed it here and finished it."

He examined the ground closely and found what he had hoped to find—the print of hunting boots. They pointed along the cliff in the direction he had been going. Eagerly he hurried along, now slipping on a rotten log or a loose stone, but making headway; night was beginning to settle down on the island.

Bleak darkness was blacking out the sea and jungle when Rainsford sighted the lights. He came upon them as he turned a crook in the coast line, and his first thought was that he had come upon a village, for there were many lights. But as he forged along he saw to his great astonishment that all the lights were in one enormous building—a lofty structure with pointed towers plunging upward into the gloom. His eyes made out the shadowy outlines of a palatial château; it was set on a high bluff, and on three sides of it cliffs dived down to where the sea licked greedy lips in the shadows.

"Mirage," thought Rainsford. But it was no mirage, he found, when he opened the tall spiked iron gate. The stone steps were real enough; the massive door with a leering gargoyle for a knocker was real enough; yet about it all hung an air of unreality.

He lifted the knocker, and it creaked up stiffly, as if it had never before been used. He let it fall, and it startled him with its booming loudness. He thought he heard steps within; the door remained closed. Again Rainsford lifted the heavy knocker, and let it fall. The door opened then, opened as suddenly as if it were on a spring, and Rainsford stood blinking in the river of glaring gold light that poured out. The first thing Rainsford's eyes discerned was the largest man Rainsford had ever seen—a gigantic creature, solidly made and black-bearded to the waist. In his hand the man held a long-barreled revolver, and he was pointing it straight at Rainsford's heart.

Out of the snarl of beard two small eyes regarded Rainsford.

"Don't be alarmed," said Rainsford, with a smile which he hoped was disarming. "I'm no robber. I fell off a yacht. My name is Sanger Rainsford of New York City."

The menacing look in the eyes did not change. The revolver pointed as rigidly as if the giant were a statue. He gave no sign that he understood Rainsford's words, or that he had even heard them. He was dressed in uniform, a black uniform trimmed with gray astrakhan.

"I'm Sanger Rainsford of New York," Rainsford began again. "I fell off a yacht. I am hungry."

The man's only answer was to raise with his thumb the hammer of his revolver. Then Rainsford saw the man's free hand go to his forehead in a military salute, and he saw him click his heels together and stand at attention. Another man was coming down the broad marble steps, an erect, slender man in evening clothes. He advanced to Rainsford and held out his hand.

In a cultivated voice marked by a slight accent that gave it added precision and deliberateness, he said: "It is a very great pleasure and honor to welcome Mr. Sanger Rainsford, the celebrated hunter, to my home."

Automatically Rainsford shook the man's hand.

"I've read your book about hunting snow leopards in Tibet, you see," explained the man. "I am General Zaroff."

Rainsford's first impression was that the man was singularly handsome; his second was that there was an original, almost bizarre quality about the general's face. He was a tall man past middle age, for his hair was a vivid white; but his thick eyebrows and pointed military mustache were as black as the night from which Rainsford had come. His eyes, too, were black and very bright. He had high cheek bones, a sharp-cut nose, a spare, dark face, the face of a man used to giving orders, the face of an aristocrat. Turning to the giant in uniform, the general made a sign. The giant put away his pistol, saluted, withdrew.

"Ivan is an incredibly strong fellow," remarked the general, "but he has the misfortune to be deaf and dumb. A simple fellow, but, I'm afraid, like all his race, a bit of a savage."

"Is he Russian?"

"He is a Cossack,"[1] said the general, and his smile showed red lips and pointed teeth. "So am I."

"Come," he said, "we shouldn't be chatting here. We can talk later. Now you want clothes, food, rest. You shall have them. This is a most restful spot."

Ivan had reappeared, and the general spoke to him with lips that moved but gave forth no sound.

---

[1] From the southern part of European Russia, the Cossacks were known as exceptionally fine horsemen and light cavalrymen and, under the Czars, were feared for their ruthless raids.

"Follow Ivan, if you please, Mr. Rainsford," said the general. "I was about to have my dinner when you came. I'll wait for you. You'll find that my clothes will fit you, I think."

It was to a huge, beam-ceilinged bedroom with a canopied bed big enough for six men that Rainsford followed the silent giant. Ivan laid out an evening suit, and Rainsford, as he put it on, noticed that it came from a London tailor who ordinarily cut and sewed for none below the rank of duke.

The dining room to which Ivan conducted him was in many ways remarkable. There was a medieval magnificence about it; it suggested a baronial hall of feudal times with its oaken panels, its high ceiling, its vast refectory table where twoscore men could sit down to eat. About the hall were the mounted heads of many animals—lions, tigers, elephants, moose, bears; larger or more perfect specimens Rainsford had never seen. At the great table the general was sitting, alone.

"You'll have a cocktail, Mr. Rainsford," he suggested. The cocktail was surpassingly good; and, Rainsford noted, the table appointments were of the finest—the linen, the crystal, the silver, the china.

They were eating borsch, the rich, red soup with whipped cream so dear to Russian palates. Half apologetically General Zaroff said: "We do our best to preserve the amenities of civilization here. Please forgive any lapses. We are well off the beaten track, you know. Do you think the champagne has suffered from its long ocean trip?"

"Not in the least," declared Rainsford. He was finding the general a most thoughtful and affable host, a true cosmopolite. But there was one small trait of the general's that made Rainsford uncomfortable.

Whenever he looked up from his plate he found the general studying him, appraising him narrowly.

"Perhaps," said General Zaroff, "you were surprised that I recognized your name. You see, I read all books on hunting published in English, French, and Russian. I have but one passion in my life, Mr. Rainsford, and it is the hunt."

"You have some wonderful heads here," said Rainsford as he ate a particularly well cooked filet mignon. "That Cape buffalo[2] is the largest I ever saw."

---

[2]Big, quick, intelligent, when separated from the herd, a rogue, one of the most dangerous African game animals.

"Oh, that fellow. Yes, he was a monster."

"Did he charge you?"

"Hurled me against a tree," said the general. "Fractured my skull. But I got the brute."

"I've always thought," said Rainsford, "that the Cape buffalo is the most dangerous of all big game."

For a moment the general did not reply; he was smiling his curious red-lipped smile. Then he said slowly: "No. You are wrong, sir. The Cape buffalo is not the most dangerous big game." He sipped his wine. "Here in my preserve on this island," he said in the same slow tone, "I hunt more dangerous game."

Rainsford expressed his surprise. "Is there big game on this island?"

The general nodded. "The biggest."

"Really?"

"Oh, it isn't here naturally, of course. I have to stock the island."

"What have you imported, general?" Rainsford asked. "Tigers?"

The general smiled. "No," he said. "Hunting tigers ceased to interest me some years ago. I exhausted their possibilities, you see. No thrill left in tigers, no real danger. I live for danger, Mr. Rainsford."

The general took from his pocket a gold cigarette case and offered his guest a long black cigarette with a silver tip; it was perfumed and gave off a smell like incense.

"We will have some capital hunting, you and I," said the general. "I shall be most glad to have your society."

"But what game—" began Rainsford.

"I'll tell you," said the general. "You will be amused, I know. I think I may say, in all modesty, that I have done a rare thing. I have invented a new sensation. May I pour you another glass of port, Mr. Rainsford?"

"Thank you, general."

The general filled both glasses, and said: "God makes some men poets. Some He makes kings, some beggars. Me He made a hunter. My hand was made for the trigger, my father said. He was a very rich man with a quarter of a million acres in the Crimea, and he was an ardent sportsman. When I was only five years old he gave me a little gun, specially made in Moscow for me, to shoot sparrows with. When I shot some of his prize turkeys with it, he did not punish me; he complimented me on my marksmanship. I killed my first bear in the Caucasus when I was ten. My whole life has been one prolonged hunt. I went into the army—it was expected of noblemen's sons—and for a time commanded a division of Cossack cavalry, but my real interest was always the hunt. I have hunted every kind of game in every land. It would be impossible for me to tell you how many animals I have killed."

The general puffed at his cigarette.

"After the debacle in Russia[3] I left the country, for it was imprudent for an officer of the Czar to stay there. Many noble Russians lost everything. I, luckily, had invested heavily in American securities, so I shall never have to open a tea room in Monte Carlo or drive a taxi in Paris. Naturally, I continued to hunt—grizzlies in your Rockies, crocodiles in the Ganges, rhinoceroses in East Africa. It was in Africa that the Cape buffalo hit me and laid me up for six months. As soon as I recovered I started for the Amazon to hunt jaguars, for I had heard they were unusually cunning. They weren't." The Cossack sighed. "They were no match at all for a hunter with his wits about him, and a high-powered rifle. I was bitterly disappointed. I was lying in my tent with a splitting headache one night when a terrible thought pushed its way into my mind. Hunting was beginning to bore me! And hunting, remember, had been my life. I have heard that in America business men often go to pieces when they give up the business that has been their life."

"Yes, that's so," said Rainsford.

The general smiled. "I had no wish to go to pieces," he said. "I must do something. Now, mine is an analytical mind, Mr. Rainsford. Doubtless that is why I enjoy the problems of the chase."

"No doubt, General Zaroff."

"So," continued the general, "I asked myself why the hunt no longer fascinated me. You are much younger than I am, Mr. Rainsford, and have not hunted as much, but you perhaps can guess the answer."

"What was it?"

---

[3]The revolution of 1917 which overthrew the Czar and prepared the way for communist rule.

"Simply this: hunting had ceased to be what you call 'a sporting proposition.' It had become too easy. I always got my quarry. Always. There is no greater bore than perfection."

The general lit a fresh cigarette.

"No animal had a chance with me any more. That is no boast; it is a mathematical certainty. The animal had nothing but his legs and his instinct. Instinct is no match for reason. When I thought of this it was a tragic moment for me, I can tell you."

Rainsford leaned across the table, absorbed in what his host was saying.

"It came to me as an inspiration what I must do," the general went on.

"And that was?"

The general smiled the quiet smile of one who has faced an obstacle and surmounted it with success. "I had to invent a new animal to hunt," he said.

"A new animal? You're joking."

"Not at all," said the general. "I never joke about hunting. I needed a new animal. I found one. So I bought this island, built this house, and here I do my hunting. The island is perfect for my purposes—there are jungles with a maze of trails in them, hills, swamps—"

"But the animal, General Zaroff?"

"Oh," said the general, "it supplies me with the most exciting hunting in the world. No other hunting compares with it for an instant. Every day I hunt, and I never grow bored now, for I have a quarry with which I can match my wits."

Rainsford's bewilderment showed in his face.

"I wanted the ideal animal to hunt," explained the general. "So I said: 'What are the attributes of an ideal quarry?' And the answer was, of course: 'it must have courage, cunning, and, above all, it must be able to reason.'"

"But no animal can reason," objected Rainsford.

"My dear fellow," said the general, "there is one that can."

"But you can't mean—" gasped Rainsford.

"And why not?"

"I can't believe you are serious, General Zaroff. This is a grisly joke."

"Why should I not be serious? I am speaking of hunting."

"Hunting? Good God, General Zaroff, what you speak of is murder."

The general laughed with entire good nature. He regarded Rainsford quizzically. "I refuse to believe that so modern and civilized a young man as you seem to be harbors romantic ideas about the value of human life. Surely your experiences in the war—"

"Did not make me condone cold-blooded murder," finished Rainsford stiffly.

Laughter shook the general. "How extraordinarily droll you are!" he said. "One does not expect nowadays to find a young man of the educated class, even in America, with such a naive, and, if I may say so, mid-Victorian point of view. It's like finding a snuffbox in a limousine. Ah, well, doubtless you had Puritan ancestors. So many Americans appear to have had. I'll wager you'll forget your notions when you go hunting with me. You've a genuine new thrill in store for you, Mr. Rainsford."

"Thank you, I'm a hunter, not a murderer."

"Dear me," said the general, quite unruffled, "again that unpleasant word. But I think I can show you that your scruples are quite ill founded."

"Yes?"

"Life is for the strong, to be lived by the strong, and, if need be, taken by the strong. The weak of the world were put here to give the strong pleasure. I am strong. Why should I not use my gift? If I wish to hunt, why should I not? I hunt the scum of the earth—sailors from tramp ships—lascars, blacks, Chinese, whites, mongrels—a thoroughbred horse or hound is worth more than a score of them."

"But they are men," said Rainsford hotly.

"Precisely," said the general. "That is why I use them. It gives me pleasure. They can reason, after a fashion. So they are dangerous."

"But where do you get them?"

The general's left eyelid fluttered down in a wink. "This island is called Ship Trap," he answered. "Sometimes an angry god of the high seas sends them to me. Sometimes, when Providence is not so kind, I help Providence a bit. Come to the window with me."

Rainsford went to the window and looked out toward the sea.

"Watch! Out there!" exclaimed the general, pointing into the night. Rainsford's eyes saw only blackness, and then, as the general pressed a button, far out to sea Rainsford saw the flash of lights.

The general chuckled. "They indicate a channel," he said, "where there's none: giant rocks with razor edges crouch like a sea monster with wide-open jaws. They can crush a ship as easily as I crush this nut." He dropped a walnut on the hardwood floor and brought his heel grinding down on it. "Oh, yes," he said, casually, as if in answer to a question, "I have electricity. We try to be civilized here."

"Civilized? And you shoot down men?"

A trace of anger was in the general's black eyes, but it was there for but a second, and he said, in his most pleasant manner: "Dear me, what a righteous young man you are! I assure you I do not do the thing you suggest. That would be barbarous. I treat these visitors with every consideration. They get plenty of good food and exercise. They get into splendid physical condition. You shall see for yourself tomorrow."

"What do you mean?"

"We'll visit my training school," smiled the general. "It's in the cellar. I have about a dozen pupils down there now. They're from the Spanish bark San Lucar that had the bad luck to go on the rocks out there. A very inferior lot, I regret to say. Poor specimens and more accustomed to the deck than to the jungle."

He raised his hand, and Ivan, who served as waiter, brought thick Turkish coffee. Rainsford, with an effort, held his tongue in check.

"It's a game, you see," pursued the general blandly. "I suggest to one of them that we go hunting. I give him a supply of food and an excellent hunting knife. I give him three hours' start. I am to follow, armed only with a pistol of the smallest caliber and range. If my quarry eludes me for three whole days, he wins the game. If I find him"—the general smiled—"he loses."

"Suppose he refuses to be hunted?"

"Oh," said the general, "I give him his option, of course. He need not play that game if he doesn't wish to. If he does not wish to hunt, I turn him over to Ivan. Ivan once had the honor of serving as official knouter to the Great White Czar, and he has his own ideas of sport. Invariably, Mr. Rainsford, invariably they choose the hunt."

"And if they win?"

The smile on the general's face widened. "To date I have not lost," he said.

Then he added, hastily: "I don't wish you to think me a braggart, Mr. Rainsford. Many of them afford only the most elementary sort of problem. Occasionally I strike a tartar. One almost did win. I eventually had to use the dogs."

"The dogs?"

"This way, please. I'll show you."

The general steered Rainsford to a window. The lights from the windows sent a flickering illumination that made grotesque patterns on the courtyard below, and Rainsford could see moving about there a dozen or so huge black shapes; as they turned toward him, their eyes glittered greenly.

"A rather good lot, I think," observed the general. "They are let out at seven every night. If anyone should try to get into my house—or out of it—something extremely regrettable would occur to him." He hummed a snatch of song from the Folies Bergère.[4]

"And now," said the general, "I want to show you my new collection of heads. Will you come with me to the library?"

"I hope," said Rainsford, "that you will excuse me tonight, General Zaroff. I'm really not feeling at all well."

"Ah, indeed?" the general inquired solicitously. "Well, I suppose that's only natural, after your long swim. You need a good, restful night's sleep. Tomorrow you'll feel like a new man, I'll wager. Then we'll hunt, eh? I've one rather promising prospect—"

Rainsford was hurrying from the room.

"Sorry you can't go with me tonight," called the general.

"I expect rather fair sport—a big, strong black. He looks resourceful—Well, good night, Mr. Rainsford; I hope you have a good night's rest."

The bed was good, and the pajamas of the softest silk, and he was tired in every fiber of his being, but nevertheless Rainsford could not quiet his brain with the opiate of sleep. He lay, eyes wide open. Once he thought he heard stealthy steps in the corridor outside his room. He sought to throw open the door; it would not open.

---

[4]Paris theatre and music hall which in 1918 reestablished itself as the scene for revues, spectaculars, etc.

He went to the window and looked out. His room was high up in one of the towers. The lights of the château were out now, and it was dark and silent, but there was a fragment of sallow moon, and by its wan light he could see, dimly, the courtyard; there, weaving in and out in the pattern of shadow, were black, noiseless forms; the hounds heard him at the window and looked up, expectantly, with their green eyes. Rainsford went back to the bed and lay down. By many methods he tried to put himself to sleep. He had achieved a doze when, just as morning began to come, he heard, far off in the jungle, the faint report of a pistol.

General Zaroff did not appear until luncheon. He was dressed faultlessly in the tweeds of a country squire. He was solicitous about the state of Rainsford's health.

"As for me," sighed the general, "I do not feel so well. I am worried, Mr. Rainsford. Last night I detected traces of my old complaint."

To Rainsford's questioning glance the general said: "Ennui. Boredom." Then, taking a second helping of Crêpes Suzette, the general explained: "The hunting was not good last night. The fellow lost his head. He made a straight trail that offered no problems at all. That's the trouble with these sailors; they have dull brains to begin with, and they do not know how to get about in the woods. They do excessively stupid and obvious things. It's most annoying. Will you have another glass of Chablis, Mr. Rainsford?"

"General," said Rainsford firmly, "I wish to leave this island at once."

The general raised his thickets of eyebrows; he seemed hurt. "But, my dear fellow," the general protested, "you've only just come. You've had no hunting."

"I wish to go today," said Rainsford. He saw the dead black eyes of the general on him, studying him. General Zaroff's face suddenly brightened.

He filled Rainsford's glass with venerable Chablis from a dusty bottle.

"Tonight," said the general, "we will hunt—you and I."

Rainsford shook his head. "No, general," he said. "I will not hunt."

The general shrugged his shoulders and delicately ate a hot-house grape. "As you wish, my friend," he said. "The choice rests entirely with you. But may I not venture to suggest that you will find my idea of sport more diverting than Ivan's?"

He nodded toward the corner to where the giant stood, scowling, his thick arms crossed on his hogshead of chest.

"You don't mean—" cried Rainsford.

"My dear fellow," said the general, "have I not told you I always mean what I say about hunting? This is really an inspiration. I drink to a foeman worthy of my steel—at last."

The general raised his glass, but Rainsford sat staring at him.

"You'll find this game worth playing," the general said enthusiastically. "Your brain against mine. Your woodcraft against mine. Your strength and stamina against mine. Outdoor chess! And the stake is not without value, eh?"

"And if I win—" began Rainsford huskily.

"I'll cheerfully acknowledge myself defeated if I do not find you by midnight of the third day," said General Zaroff. "My sloop will place you on the mainland near a town."

The general read what Rainsford was thinking.

"Oh, you can trust me," said the Cossack. "I will give you my word as a gentleman and a sportsman. Of course you, in turn, must agree to say nothing of your visit here."

"I'll agree to nothing of the kind," said Rainsford.

"Oh," said the general, "in that case—But why discuss that now? Three days hence we can discuss it over a bottle of Veuve Cliquot,[5] unless—"

The general sipped his wine.

Then a businesslike air animated him. "Ivan," he said to Rainsford, "will supply you with hunting clothes, food, a knife. I suggest you wear moccasins; they leave a poorer trail. I suggest too that you avoid the big swamp in the southeast corner of the island. We call it Death Swamp. There's quicksand there. One foolish fellow tried it. The deplorable part of it was that Lazarus followed him. You can imagine my feelings, Mr. Rainsford. I loved Lazarus; he was the finest hound in my pack. Well, I must beg you to excuse me now. I always take a siesta after lunch. You'll hardly have time for a nap, I fear. You'll want to start, no doubt. I shall not follow till

---

[5]A fine, champagne; Chablis is a very dry white Burgundy table wine; Chambertin is a highly esteemed red Burgundy wine.

dusk. Hunting at night is so much more exciting than by day, don't you think? Au revoir, Mr. Rainsford, au revoir."

General Zaroff, with a deep, courtly bow, strolled from the room.

From another door came Ivan. Under one arm he carried khaki hunting clothes, a haversack of food, a leather sheath containing a long-bladed hunting knife; his right hand rested on a cocked revolver thrust in the crimson sash about his waist . . .

Rainsford had fought his way through the bush for two hours. "I must keep my nerve. I must keep my nerve," he said through tight teeth.

He had not been entirely clear-headed when the château gates snapped shut behind him. His whole idea at first was to put distance between himself and General Zaroff, and, to this end, he had plunged along, spurred on by the sharp rowels of something very like panic. Now he had got a grip on himself, had stopped, and was taking stock of himself and the situation.

He saw that straight flight was futile; inevitably it would bring him face to face with the sea. He was in a picture with a frame of water, and his operations, clearly, must take place within that frame.

"I'll give him a trail to follow," muttered Rainsford, and he struck off from the rude paths he had been following into the trackless wilderness. He executed a series of intricate loops; he doubled on his trail again and again, recalling all the lore of the fox hunt, and all the dodges of the fox. Night found him leg-weary, with hands and face lashed by the branches, on a thickly wooded ridge. He knew it would be insane to blunder on through the dark, even if he had the strength. His need for rest was imperative and he thought: "I have played the fox, now I must play the cat of the fable."[6] A big tree with a thick trunk and outspread branches was nearby, and, taking care to leave not the slightest mark, he climbed up into the crotch, and stretching out on one of the broad limbs, after a fashion, rested. Rest brought him new confidence and almost a feeling of security. Even so zealous a hunter as General Zaroff

---

[6]The fox boasts of his many tricks to elude the hounds; the cat knows only one—to climb the nearest tree—but that is worth more than all of the fox's tricks.

could not trace him there, he told himself; only the devil himself could follow that complicated trail through the jungle after dark. But, perhaps, the general was a devil—

An apprehensive night crawled slowly by like a wounded snake, and sleep did not visit Rainsford, although the silence of a dead world was on the jungle. Toward morning when a dingy gray was varnishing the sky, the cry of some startled bird focused Rainsford's attention in that direction.

Something was coming through the bush, coming slowly, carefully, coming by the same winding way Rainsford had come. He flattened himself down on the limb, and through a screen of leaves almost as thick as tapestry, he watched. The thing that was approaching was a man.

It was General Zaroff. He made his way along with his eyes fixed in utmost concentration on the ground before him. He paused, almost beneath the tree, dropped to his knees and studied the ground. Rainsford's impulse was to hurl himself down like a panther, but he saw the general's right hand held something metallic—a small automatic pistol.

The hunter shook his head several times, as if he were puzzled. Then he straightened up and took from his case one of his black cigarettes; its pungent incense-like smoke floated up to Rainsford's nostrils.

Rainsford held his breath. The general's eyes had left the ground and were traveling inch by inch up the tree. Rainsford froze there, every muscle tensed for a spring. But the sharp eyes of the hunter stopped before they reached the limb where Rainsford lay; a smile spread over his brown face. Very deliberately he blew a smoke ring into the air; then he turned his back on the tree and walked carelessly away, back along the trail he had come. The swish of the underbrush against his hunting boots grew fainter and fainter.

The pent-up air burst hotly from Rainsford's lungs. His first thought made him feel sick and numb. The general could follow a trail through the woods at night; he could follow an extremely difficult trail; he must have uncanny powers; only by the merest chance had the Cossack failed to see his quarry.

Rainsford's second thought was even more terrible. It sent a shudder of cold horror through his whole being. Why had the general smiled? Why had he turned back?

Rainsford did not want to believe what his reason told him was true, but the truth was as evident as the sun that had by now pushed through the morning mists. The general was playing with him! The general was saving him for another day's sport! The Cossack was the cat; he was the mouse. Then it was that Rainsford knew the full meaning of terror.

"I will not lose my nerve. I will not."

He slid down from the tree, and struck off again into the woods. His face was set and he forced the machinery of his mind to function. Three hundred yards from his hiding place he stopped where a huge dead tree leaned precariously on a smaller, living one. Throwing off his sack of food, Rainsford took his knife from its sheath and began to work with all his energy.

The job was finished at last, and he threw himself down behind a fallen log a hundred feet away. He did not have to wait long. The cat was coming again to play with the mouse.

Following the trail with the sureness of a bloodhound, came General Zaroff. Nothing escaped those searching black eyes, no crushed blade of grass, no bent twig, no mark, no matter how faint, in the moss. So intent was the Cossack on his stalking that he was upon the thing Rainsford had made before he saw it. His foot touched the protruding bough that was the trigger. Even as he touched it, the general sensed his danger and leaped back with the agility of an ape. But he was not quite quick enough; the dead tree, delicately adjusted to rest on the cut living one, crashed down and struck the general a glancing blow on the shoulder as it fell; but for his alertness, he must have been smashed beneath it. He staggered, but he did not fall; nor did he drop his revolver. He stood there, rubbing his injured shoulder, and Rainsford, with fear again gripping his heart, heard the general's mocking laugh ring through the jungle.

"Rainsford," called the general, "if you are within the sound of my voice, as I suppose you are, let me congratulate you. Not many men know how to make a Malay man-catcher. Luckily, for me, I too have hunted in Malacca. You are proving interesting, Mr. Rainsford. I am going now to have my wound dressed; it's only a slight one. But I shall be back. I shall be back."

When the general, nursing his bruised shoulder, had gone, Rainsford took up his flight again. It was flight now, a desperate, hopeless flight, that carried him on for some hours. Dusk came, then darkness, and still he pressed on. The ground grew softer under his moccasins; the vegetation grew ranker, denser; insects bit him savagely. Then, as he stepped forward, his foot sank into the ooze. He tried to wrench it back, but the muck sucked viciously at his foot as if it were a giant leech. With a violent effort, he tore loose. He knew where he was now. Death Swamp and its quicksand.

His hands were tight closed as if his nerve were something tangible that some one in the darkness was trying to tear from his grip. The softness of the earth had given him an idea. He stepped back from the quicksand a dozen feet or so, and, like some huge prehistoric beaver, he began to dig.

Rainsford had dug himself in in France[7] when a second's delay meant death. That had been a placid pastime compared to his digging now. The pit grew deeper; when it was above his shoulders, he climbed out and from some hard saplings cut stakes and sharpened them to a fine point. These stakes he planted in the bottom of the pit with the points sticking up. With flying fingers he wove a rough carpet of weeds and branches and with it he covered the mouth of the pit. Then, wet with sweat and aching with tiredness, he crouched behind the stump of a lightning-charred tree.

He knew his pursuer was coming; he heard the padding sound of feet on the soft earth, and the night breeze brought him the perfume of the general's cigarette. It seemed to Rainsford that the general was coming with unusual swiftness; he was not feeling his way along, foot by foot. Rainsford, crouching there, could not see the general, nor could he see the pit. He lived a year in a minute. Then he felt an impulse to cry aloud with joy, for he heard the sharp crackle of the breaking branches as the cover of the pit gave way; he heard the sharp scream of pain as the pointed stakes found their mark. He leaped up from his place of concealment. Then he cowered back. Three feet from the pit a man was standing, with an electric torch in his hand.

"You've done well, Rainsford," the voice of the general called. "Your Burmese tiger pit has claimed one of my best dogs. Again

---

[7]During World War I he had quickly dug a hole or trench to shelter himself from exploding shells, bullets, etc.

you score. I think, Mr. Rainsford, I'll see what you can do against my whole pack. I'm going home for a rest now. Thank you for a most amusing evening."

At daybreak Rainsford, lying near the swamp, was awakened by the sound that made him know that he had new things to learn about fear. It was a distant sound, faint and wavering, but he knew it. It was the baying of a pack of hounds.

Rainsford knew he could do one of two things. He could stay where he was and wait. That was suicide. He could flee. That was postponing the inevitable. For a moment he stood there, thinking. An idea that held a wild chance came to him, and, tightening his belt, he headed away from the swamp.

The baying of the hounds drew nearer, then still nearer, nearer, ever nearer. On a ridge Rainsford climbed a tree. Down a watercourse, not a quarter of a mile away, he could see the bush moving. Straining his eyes, he saw the lean figure of General Zaroff; just ahead of him Rainsford made out another figure whose wide shoulders surged through the tall jungle weeds; it was the giant Ivan, and he seemed pulled forward by some unseen force; Rainsford knew that Ivan must be holding the pack in leash.

They would be on him any minute now. His mind worked frantically. He thought of a native trick he had learned in Uganda. He slid down the tree. He caught hold of a springy young sapling and to it he fastened his hunting knife, with the blade pointing down the trail; with a bit of wild grapevine he tied back the sapling. Then he ran for his life. The hounds raised their voices as they hit the fresh scent. Rainsford knew now how an animal at bay feels.

He had to stop to get his breath. The baying of the hounds stopped abruptly, and Rainsford's heart stopped too. They must have reached the knife.

He shinnied excitedly up a tree and looked back. His pursuers had stopped. But the hope that was in Rainsford's brain when he climbed died, for he saw in the shallow valley that General Zaroff was still on his feet. But Ivan was not. The knife, driven by the recoil of the springing tree, had not wholly failed.

"Nerve, nerve, nerve!" he panted, as he dashed along. A blue gap showed between the trees dead ahead. Ever nearer drew the hounds. Rainsford forced himself on toward that gap. He reached it. It was the shore of the sea. Across a cove he could see the gloomy gray stone of the château. Twenty feet below him the sea rumbled and hissed. Rainsford hesitated. He heard the hounds. Then he leaped far out into the sea . . .

When the general and his pack reached the place by the sea, the Cossack stopped. For some minutes he stood regarding the blue-green expanse of water. He shrugged his shoulders. Then he sat down, took a drink of brandy from a silver flask, lit a perfumed cigarette, and hummed a bit from Madame Butterfly.

General Zaroff had an exceedingly good dinner in his great paneled dining hall that evening. With it he had a bottle of Pol Roger and half a bottle of Chambertin. Two slight annoyances kept him from perfect enjoyment. One was the thought that it would be difficult to replace Ivan; the other was that his quarry had escaped him; of course the American hadn't played the game—so thought the general as he tasted his after-dinner liqueur. In his library he read, to soothe himself, from the works of Marcus Aurelius. At ten he went up to his bedroom. He was deliciously tired, he said to himself, as he locked himself in. There was a little moonlight, so, before turning on his light, he went to the window and looked down at the courtyard. He could see the great hounds, and he called: "Better luck another time," to them. Then he switched on the light.

A man, who had been hiding in the curtains of the bed, was standing there.

"Rainsford!" screamed the general. "How in God's name did you get here?"

"Swam," said Rainsford. "I found it quicker than walking through the jungle."

The general sucked in his breath and smiled. "I congratulate you," he said. "You have won the game."

Rainsford did not smile. "I am still a beast at bay," he said, in a low, hoarse voice. "Get ready, General Zaroff."

The general made one of his deepest bows. "I see," he said. "Splendid! One of us is to furnish a repast for the hounds. The other will sleep in this very excellent bed. On guard, Rainsford . . ."

He had never slept in a better bed, Rainsford decided.

THE MOTHS
Helena María Viramontes

I was fourteen years old when Abuelita requested my help. And it seemed only fair. Abuelita had pulled me through the rages of scarlet fever by placing, removing, and replacing potato slices on my temples; she had seen me through several whippings, an arm broken by a dare jump off Tío Enrique's toolshed, puberty, and my first lie. Really, I told Amá, it was only fair.

Not that I was her favorite granddaughter or anything special. I wasn't even pretty or nice like my older sisters and I just couldn't do the girl things they could do. My hands were too big to handle the fineries of crocheting or embroidery and I always pricked my fingers or knotted my colored threads time and time again while my sisters laughed and called me Bull Hands with their cute water-like voices. So I began keeping a piece of jagged brick in my sock to bash my sisters or anyone who called me Bull Hands. Once, while we all sat in the bedroom, I hit Teresa on the forehead, right above her eyebrow, and she ran to Amá with her mouth open, her hand over her eye while blood seeped between her fingers. I was used to the whippings by then.

I wasn't respectful either. I even went so far as to doubt the power of Abuelita's slices, the slices she said absorbed my fever. "You're still alive, aren't you?" Abuelita snapped back, her pasty gray eye beaming at me and burning holes in my suspicions. Regretful that I had let secret questions drop out of my mouth, I couldn't look into her eyes. My hands began to fan out, grow like a liar's nose until they hung by my side like low weights. Abuelita made a balm out of dried moth wings and Vicks and rubbed my hands, shaped them back to size, and it was the strangest feeling. Like bones melting. Like sun shining through the darkness of your eyelids. I didn't mind helping Abuelita after that, so Amá would always send me over to her.

In the early afternoon Amá would push her hair back, hand me my sweater and shoes, and tell me to go to Mama Luna's. This was to avoid another fight and another whipping, I knew. I would deliver one last direct shot on Marisela's arm and jump out of our house, the slam of the screen door burying her cries of anger, and I'd gladly go help Abuelita plant her wild lilies or jasmine or heliotrope or cilantro or hierbabuena in red Hills Brothers coffee cans. Abuelita would wait for me at the top step of her porch, holding a hammer and nail and empty coffee cans. And although we hardly spoke, hardly looked at each other as we worked over root transplants, I always felt her gray eye on me. It made me feel, in a strange sort of way, safe and guarded and not alone. Like God was supposed to make you feel.

On Abuelita's porch, I would puncture holes in the bottom of the coffee cans with a nail and a precise hit of a hammer. This completed, my job was to fill them with red clay mud from beneath her rosebushes, packing it softly, then making a perfect hole, four fingers round, to nest a sprouting avocado pit, or the spidery sweet potatoes that Abuelita rooted in mayonnaise jars with toothpicks and daily water, or prickly chayotes that produced vines that twisted and wound all over her porch pillars, crawling to the roof, up and over the roof, and down the other side, making her small brick house look like it was cradled within the vines that grew pear-shaped squashes ready for the pick, ready to be steamed with onions and cheese and butter. The roots would burst out of the rusted coffee cans and search for a place to connect. I would then feed the seedlings with water.

But this was a different kind of help, Amá said, because Abuelita was dying. Looking into her gray eye, then into her brown one, the doctor said it was just a matter of days. And so it seemed only fair that these hands she had melted and formed found use in rubbing her caving body with alcohol and marijuana, rubbing her arms and legs, turning her face to the window so that she could watch the bird of paradise blooming or smell the scent of clove in the air. I toweled her face frequently and held her hand for hours. Her gray wiry hair hung over the mattress. For as long as I could remember, she'd kept her long hair in braids. Her mouth was vacant, and when she slept her eyelids never closed all the way. Up close, you could see her gray eye beaming out the window, staring hard as if to remember everything. I never kissed her. I left the window open when I went to the market.

Across the street from Jay's Market there was a chapel. I never knew its denomination, but I went in just the same to search for candles. There were none, so I sat down on one of the pews. After I cleaned my fingernails, I looked up at the high ceiling. I had forgotten the vastness of these places, the coolness of the marble pillars and the frozen statues with blank eyes. I was alone. I knew why I had never returned.

That was one of Apá's biggest complaints. He would pound his hands on the table, rocking the sugar dish or spilling a cup of coffee, and scream that if I didn't go to mass every Sunday to save my goddamn sinning soul, then I had no reason to go out of the house, period. *Punto final.* He would grab my arm and dig his nails into me to make sure I understood the importance of catechism. Did he make himself clear? Then he strategically directed his anger at Amá for her lousy ways of bringing up daughters, being disrespectful and unbelieving, and my older sisters would pull me aside and tell me if I didn't get to mass right this minute, they were all going to kick the holy shit out of me. Why am I so selfish? Can't you see what it's doing to Amá, you idiot? So I would wash my feet and stuff them in my black Easter shoes that shone with Vaseline, grab a missal and veil, and wave goodbye to Amá.

I would walk slowly down Lorena to First to Evergreen, counting the cracks on the cement. On Evergreen I would turn left and walk to Abuelita's. I liked her porch because it was shielded by the vines of the chayotes and I could get a good look at the people and car traffic on Evergreen without them knowing. I would jump up the porch steps, knock on the screen door as I wiped my feet, and call, Abuelita? Mi Abuelita? As I opened the door and stuck my head in, I would catch the gagging scent of toasting chile on the *placa.* When I entered the *sala,* she would greet me from the kitchen, wringing her hands in her apron. I'd sit at the corner of the table to keep from being in her way. The chiles made my eyes water. Am I crying? No, Mama Luna, I'm sure not crying. I don't like going to mass, but my eyes watered anyway, the tears dropping on the tablecloth like candle wax. Abuelita lifted the burnt chiles from the fire and sprinkled water on them until the skins began to separate. Placing them in front of me, she turned to check the menudo. I peeled the skins off and put the flimsy, limp-looking green and yellow chiles in the *molcajete* and began to crush and crush and twist and crush the heart out of the tomato, the clove of garlic, the stupid chiles that made me cry, crushed them until they turned into liquid under my bull hand. With a wooden spoon, I scraped hard to destroy the guilt, and my tears were gone. I put the bowl of chile next to a vase filled with freshly cut roses. Abuelita touched my hand and pointed to the bowl of menudo that steamed in front of me. I spooned some chile into the menudo and rolled a corn tortilla thin with the palms of my hands. As I ate, a fine Sunday breeze entered the kitchen and a rose petal calmly feathered down to the table.

I left the chapel without blessing myself and walked to Jay's. Most of the time Jay didn't have much of anything. The tomatoes were always soft and the cans of Campbell soup had rust spots on them. There was dust on the tops of cereal boxes. I picked up what I needed: rubbing alcohol, five cans of chicken broth, a big bottle of Pine Sol. At first Jay got mad because I thought I had forgotten the money. But it was there all the time, in my back pocket.

When I returned from the market, I heard Amá crying in Abuelita's kitchen. She looked up at me with puffy eyes. I placed the bags of groceries on the table and began putting the cans of soup away. Amá sobbed quietly. I never kissed her. After a while, I patted her on the back for comfort. Finally: "?Y mi Amá?" she asked in a whisper, then choked again and cried into her apron.

Abuelita fell off the bed twice yesterday, I said, knowing that I shouldn't have said it and wondering why I wanted to say it because it only made Amá cry harder. I guess I became angry and just so tired of the quarrels and beatings and unanswered prayers and my hands just there hanging helplessly by my side. Amá looked at me again, confused, angry, and her eyes were filled with sorrow. I went outside and sat on the porch swing and watched the people pass. I sat there until she left. I dozed off repeating the words to myself like rosary prayers: when do you stop giving when do you start giving when do you . . . and when my hands fell from my lap, I awoke to catch them. The sun was setting, an orange glow, and I knew Abuelita was hungry.

There comes a time when the sun is defiant. Just about the time when moods change, inevitable seasons of a day, transitions from one color to another, that hour or minute or second when the sun is finally defeated, finally sinks into the realization that it cannot, with all its power to heal or burn, exist forever, there comes an illumination where the sun and earth meet, a final burst of burning red-orange fury reminding us that although endings are inevitable, they are necessary for rebirths, and when that time came, just when I switched on the light in the kitchen to open Abuelita's can of soup, it was probably then that she died.

The room smelled of Pine Sol and vomit, and Abuelita had defecated the remains of her cancerous stomach. She had turned to the window and tried to speak, but her mouth remained open and speechless. I heard you, Abuelita, I said, stroking her cheek, I heard you. I opened the windows of the house and let the soup simmer and overboil on the stove. I turned the stove off and poured the soup down the sink. From the cabinet I got a tin basin, filled it with lukewarm water, and carried it carefully to the room. I went to the linen closet and took out some modest bleached white towels. With the sacredness of a priest preparing his vestments, I unfolded the towels one by one on my shoulders. I removed the sheets and blankets from her bed and peeled off her thick flannel nightgown. I toweled her puzzled face, stretching out the wrinkles, removing the coils of her neck, toweled her shoulders and breasts. Then I changed the water. I returned to towel the creases of her stretch-marked stomach, her sporadic vaginal hairs, and her sagging thighs. I removed the lint from between her toes and noticed a mapped birthmark on the fold of her buttock. The scars on her back, which were as thin as the lifelines on the palms of her hands, made me realize how little I really knew of Abuelita. I covered her with a thin blanket and went into the bathroom. I washed my hands, turned on the tub faucets, and watched the water pour into the tub with vitality and steam. When it was full, I turned off the water and undressed. Then, I went to get Abuelita.

She was not as heavy as I thought, and when I carried her in my arms, her body fell into a V, and yet my legs were tired, shaky, and I felt as if the distance between the bedroom and bathroom was miles and years away. Amá, where are you?

I stepped into the bathtub, one leg first, then the other. I bent my knees to descend into the water, slowly, so I wouldn't scald her skin. There, there, Abuelita, I said, cradling her, smoothing her as we descended, I heard you. Her hair fell back and spread across the water like eagle's wings. The water in the tub overflowed and poured onto the tile of the floor. Then the moths came. Small, gray ones that came from her soul and out through her mouth fluttering to light, circling the single dull light bulb of the bathroom. Dying is lonely and I wanted to go to where the moths were, stay with her and plant chayotes whose vines would crawl up her fingers and into the clouds; I wanted to rest my head on her chest with her stroking my hair, telling me about the moths that lay within the soul and slowly eat the spirit up; I wanted to return to the waters of the womb with her so that we would never be alone again. I wanted. I wanted my Amá. I removed a few strands of hair from Abuelita's face and held her small light head within the hollow of my neck. The bathroom was filled with moths, and for the first time in a long time I cried, rocking us, crying for her, for me, for Amá, the sobs emerging from the depths of anguish, the misery of feeling half born, sobbing until finally the sobs rippled into circles and circles of sadness and relief. There, there, I said to Abuelita, rocking us gently, there, there.

THE POSSIBILITY OF EVIL
Shirley Jackson

Miss Adela Strangeworth came daintily along Main Street on her way to the grocery. The sun was shining, the air was fresh and clear after the night's heavy rain, and everything in Miss Strangeworth's little town looked washed and bright. Miss Strangeworth took deep breaths and thought that there was nothing in the world like a fragrant summer day.

She knew everyone in town, of course; she was fond of telling strangers—tourists who sometimes passed through the town and stopped to admire Miss Strangeworth's roses—that she had never spent more than a day outside this town in all her long life. She was seventy-one, Miss Strangeworth told the tourists, with a pretty little dimple showing by her lip, and she sometimes found herself thinking that the town belonged to her. "My grandfather built the first house on Pleasant Street," she would say, opening her blue eyes wide with the wonder of it. "This house, right here. My family has lived here for better than a hundred years. My grandmother planted these roses, and my mother tended them, just as I do. I've watched my town grow; I can remember when Mr. Lewis, Senior, opened the grocery store, and the year the river flooded out the shanties on the low road, and the excitement when some young folks wanted to move the park over to the space in front of where the new post office is today. They wanted to put up a statue of Ethan Allen." Miss Strangeworth would frown a little and sound stern, "But it should have been a statue of my grandfather. There wouldn't have been a town here at all if it hadn't been for my grandfather and the lumber mill."

Miss Strangeworth never gave away any of her roses, although the tourists often asked. The roses belonged on Pleasant Street, and it bothered Miss Strangeworth to think of people wanting to carry them away, to take them into strange towns and down strange streets When the new minister came, and the ladies were gathering flowers to decorate the church, Miss Strangeworth sent over a great basket of gladioli; when she picked the roses at all, she set them in bowls and vases around the inside of the house her grandfather had built.

Walking down Main Street on a summer morning, Miss Strangeworth had to stop every minute or so to say good morning to someone or to ask after someone's health. When she came into the grocery, half a dozen people turned away from the shelves and the counters to wave at her or call out good morning.

"And good morning to you, too, Mr. Lewis," Miss Strangeworth said at last. The Lewis family had been in the town almost as long as the Strangeworths; but the day young Lewis left high school and went to work in the grocery, Miss Strangeworth had stopped calling him Tommy and started calling him Mr. Lewis, and he had stopped calling her Addie and started calling her Miss Strangeworth. They had been in high school together, and had gone to picnics together, and to high-school dances and basketball games; but now Mr. Lewis was behind the counter in the grocery, and Miss Strangeworth was living alone in the Strangeworth house on Pleasant Street.

"Good morning," Mr. Lewis said, and added politely, "Lovely day."

"It is a very nice day," Miss Strangeworth said, as though she had only just decided that it would do after all. "I would like a chop, please, Mr. Lewis, a small, lean veal chop. Are those strawberries from Arthur Parker's garden? They're early this year."

"He brought them in this morning," Mr. Lewis said.

"I shall have a box," Miss Strangeworth said. Mr. Lewis looked worried, she thought, and for a minute she hesitated, but then she decide surely he could not be worried over the strawberries. He looked very tired indeed. He was usually so chipper, Miss Strangeworth thought, and almost commented, but it was far too personal a subject to be introduced to Mr. Lewis, the grocer, so she only said, "And a can of cat food and, I think, a tomato."

Silently, Mr. Lewis assembled her order on the counter, and waited.

Miss Strangeworth looked at him curiously and then said, "It's Tuesday, Mr. Lewis. You forgot to remind me."

"Did I? Sorry."

"Imagine your forgetting that I always buy my tea on Tuesday," Miss Strangeworth said gently. "A quarter pound of tea, please, Mr. Lewis."

"Is that all, Miss Strangeworth?"

"Yes, thank you, Mr. Lewis. Such a lovely day, isn't it?"

"Lovely," Mr. Lewis said.

Miss Strangeworth moved slightly to make room for Mrs. Harper at the counter. "Morning, Adela," Mrs. Harper said, and Miss Strangeworth said, "Good morning, Martha."

"Lovely day," Mrs. Harper said, and Miss Strangeworth said, "Yes lovely," and Mr. Lewis, under Mrs. Harper's glance, nodded.

"Ran out of sugar for my cake frosting," Mrs. Harper explained.

Her hand shook slightly as she opened her pocketbook. Miss Strangeworth wondered, glancing at her quickly, if she had been taking proper care of herself. Martha Harper was not as young as she used to be, Miss Strangeworth thought. She probably could use a good strong tonic.

"Martha," she said, "you don't look well."

"I'm perfectly all right," Mrs. Harper said shortly. She handed her money to Mr. Lewis, took her change and her sugar, and went out without speaking again. Looking after her, Miss Strangeworth shook her head slightly. Martha definitely did not look well.

Carrying her little bag of groceries, Miss Strangeworth came out of the store into the bright sunlight and stopped to smile down on the Crane baby. Don and Helen Crane were really the two most infatuated young parents she had ever known, she thought indulgently, looking at the delicately embroidered baby cap and the lace-edged carriage cover.

"That little girl is going to grow up expecting luxury all her life," she said to Helen Crane.

Helen laughed. "That's the way we want her to feel," she said. "Like a princess."

"A princess can see a lot of trouble sometimes," Miss Strangeworth said dryly. "How old is Her Highness now?"

"Six months next Tuesday," Helen Crane said, looking down with rapt wonder at her child. "I've been worrying, though, about her. Don't you think she ought to move around more? Try to sit up, for instance?"

"For plain and fancy worrying," Miss Strangeworth said, amused, "give me a new mother every time."

"She just seems slow," Helen Crane said.

"Nonsense. All babies are different. Some of them develop much more quickly than others."

"That's what my mother says." Helen Crane laughed, looking a little bit ashamed.

"I suppose you've got young Don all upset about the fact that his daughter is already six months old and hasn't yet begun to learn to dance?"

"I haven't mentioned it to him. I suppose she's just so precious that I worry about her all the time."

"Well, apologize to her right now," Miss Strangeworth said. "She is probably worrying about why you keep jumping around all the time." Smiling to herself and shaking her old head, she went on down the sunny street, stopping once to ask little Billy Moore why he wasn't out riding in his daddy's shiny new car, and talking for a few minutes outside the library with Miss Chandler, the librarian, about the new novels to be ordered and paid for by the annual library appropriation. Miss Chandler seemed absent-minded and very much as though she were thinking about something else. Miss Strangeworth noticed that Miss Chandler had not taken much trouble with her hair that morning, and sighed. Miss Strangeworth hated sloppiness.

Many people seemed disturbed recently, Miss Strangeworth thought. Only yesterday the Stewarts' fifteen-year-old Linda had run crying down her own front walk and all the way to school, not caring who saw her. People around town thought she might have had a fight with the Harris boy, but they showed up together at the soda shop after school as usual, both of them looking grim and bleak. Trouble at home, people concluded, and sighed over the problems of trying to raise kids right these days.

From halfway down the block Miss Strangeworth could catch the heavy scent of her roses, and she moved a little more quickly. The perfume of roses meant home, and home meant the Strangeworth House on Pleasant Street. Miss Strangeworth stopped at her own front gate, as she always did, and looked with deep pleasure at her house, with the red and pink and white roses massed along the narrow lawn, and the ramblers going up along the porch; and the neat, the unbelievable trim lines of the house itself, with its slimness and its washed white look. Every window sparkled, every curtain hung stiff and straight, and even the stones of the front walk were swept and clear. People around town wondered how old Miss Strangeworth managed to keep the house looking the way it did, and there was a legend about a tourist once mistaking it for the local museum and going all through the place without finding out about his mistake. But the town was proud of Miss Strangeworth and her roses and her house. They had all grown together.

Miss Strangeworth went up her front steps, unlocked her front door with her key, and went into the kitchen to put away her groceries. She debated about having a cup of tea and then decided that it was too close to midday dinnertime; she would not have the appetite for her little chop if she had tea now. Instead she went into the light, lovely sitting room, which still glowed from the hands of her mother and her grandmother, who had covered the chairs with bright chintz and hung the curtains. All the furniture was spare and shining, and the round hooked rugs on the floor had been the work of Miss Strangeworth's grandmother and her mother. Miss Strangeworth had put a bowl of her red roses on the low table before the window, and the room was full of their scent.

Miss Strangeworth went to the narrow desk in the corner and unlocked it with her key. She never knew when she might feel like writing letters, so she kept her notepaper inside and the desk locked. Miss Strangeworth's usual stationery was heavy and cream-colored, with STRANGEWORTH HOUSE engraved across the top, but, when she felt like writing her other letters, Miss Strangeworth used a pad of various-colored paper bought from the local newspaper shop. It was almost a town joke, that colored paper, layered in pink and green and blue and yellow; everyone in town bought it and used it for odd, informal notes and shopping lists. It was usual to remark, upon receiving a note written on a blue page, that so-and-so would be needing a new pad soon; here she was, down to the blue already. Everyone used the matching envelopes for tucking away recipes, or keeping odd little things in, or even to hold cookies in the school lunch boxes. Mr. Lewis sometimes gave them to the children for carrying home penny candy.

Although Miss Strangeworth's desk held a trimmed quill pen which had belonged to her grandfather, and a gold-frosted fountain pen which had belonged to her father, Miss Strangeworth always used a dull stub of pencil when she wrote her letters, and she printed them in a childish block print. After thinking for a minute, although she had been phasing the letter in the back of her mind all the way home, she wrote on a pink sheet: DIDN'T YOU EVER SEE AN IDIOT CHILD BEFORE? SOME PEOPLE JUST SHOULDN'T HAVE CHILDREN SHOULD THEY?

She was pleased with the letter. She was fond of doing things exactly right. When she made a mistake, as she sometimes did, or when the letters were not spaced nicely on the page, she had to take the discarded page to the kitchen stove and burn it at once. Miss Strangeworth never delayed when things had to be done.

After thinking for a minute, she decided that she would like to write another letter, perhaps to go to Mrs. Harper, to follow up the ones she had already mailed. She selected a green sheet this time and wrote quickly: HAVE YOU FOUND OUT YET WHAT THEY WERE ALL LAUGHING ABOUT AFTER YOU LEFT THE BRIDGE CLUB ON THURSDAY? OR IS THE WIFE REALLY ALWAYS THE LAST ONE TO KNOW?

Miss Strangeworth never concerned herself with facts; her letters all dealt with the more negotiable stuff of suspicion. Mr. Lewis would never have imagined for a minute that his grandson might be lifting petty cash from the store register if he had not had one of Miss Strangeworth's letters. Miss Chandler, the librarian, and Linda Stewart's parents would have gone unsuspectingly ahead with their lives, never aware of possible evil lurking nearby, if Miss Strangeworth had not sent letters opening their eyes. Miss Strangeworth would have been genuinely shocked if there had been anything between Linda Stewart and the Harris boy, but, as long as evil existed unchecked in the world, it was Miss Strangeworth's duty to keep her town alert to it. It was far more sensible for Miss Chandler to wonder what Mr. Shelley's first wife had really died of than to take a chance on not knowing. There were so many wicked people in the world and only one Strangeworth left in the town. Besides, Miss Strangeworth liked writing her letters.

She addressed an envelope to Don Crane after a moment's thought, wondering curiously if he would show the letter to his wife, and using a pink envelope to match the pink paper. Then she addressed a second envelope, green, to Mrs. Harper. Then an idea came to her and she selected a blue sheet and wrote: YOU NEVER KNOW ABOUT DOCTORS. REMEMBER THAT THEY'RE ONLY HUMAN AND NEED MONEY LIKE THE REST OF US. SUPPOSE THE KNIFE SLIPPED ACCIDENTALLY. WOULD DR. BURNS GET HIS FEE AND A LITTLE EXTRA FROM THAT NEPHEW OF YOURS?

She addressed the blue envelope to old Mrs. Foster, who was having an operation next month. She had thought of writing one more letter, to the head of the school board, asking how a chemistry teacher like Billy Moore's father could afford a new convertible, but, all at once, she was tired of writing letters. The three she had done would do for one day. She could write more tomorrow; it was not as though they all had to be done at once.

She had been writing her letters sometimes two or three every day for a week, sometimes no more than one in a month—for the past year. She never got any answers, of course, because she never signed her name. If she had been asked, she would have said that her name, Adela Strangeworth, a name honored in the town for so many years, did not belong on such trash. The town where she lived had to be kept clean and sweet, but people everywhere were lustful and evil and degraded, and needed to be watched; the world was so large, and there was only one Strangeworth left in it. Miss Strangeworth sighed, locked her desk, and put the letters into her big black leather pocketbook, to be mailed when she took her evening walk.

She broiled her little chop nicely, and had a sliced tomato and a good cup of tea ready when she sat down to her midday dinner at the table in her dining room, which could be opened to seat twenty-two, with a second table, if necessary, in the hall. Sitting in the warm sunlight that came through the tall windows of the dining room, seeing her roses massed outside, handling the heavy, old silverware and the fine translucent china, Miss Strangeworth was pleased; she would not have cared to be doing anything else. People must live graciously, after all, she thought, and sipped her tea. Afterward, when her plate and cup and saucer were washed and dried and put back onto the shelves where they belonged, and her silverware was back in the mahogany silver chest, Miss Strangeworth went up the graceful staircase and into her bedroom, which was the front room overlooking the roses, and had been her mother's and her grandmother's. Their Crown Derby dresser set and furs had been kept here, their fans and silver-backed brushes and their own bowls of roses; Miss Strangeworth kept a bowl of white roses on the bed table.

She drew the shades, took the rose satin spread from the bed, slipped out of her dress and her shoes, and lay down tiredly. She knew that no doorbell or phone would ring; no one in town would dare to disturb Miss Strangeworth during her afternoon nap. She slept, deep in the rich smell of roses.

After her nap she worked in her garden for a little while, sparing herself because of the heat; then she came in to her supper. She ate asparagus from her own garden, with sweet-butter sauce and a soft-boiled egg, and, while she had her supper, she listened to a late-evening news broadcast and then to a program of classical music on her small radio. After her dishes were done and her kitchen set in order, she took up her hat—Miss Strangeworth's hats were proverbial in the town; people believed that she had inherited them from her mother and her grandmother—and, locking the front door of her house behind her, set off on her evening walk, pocketbook under her arm. She nodded to Linda Stewart's father, who was washing his car in the pleasantly cool evening. She thought that he looked troubled.

There was only one place in town where she could mail her letters, and that was the new post office, shiny with red brick and silver letters. Although Miss Strangeworth had never given the matter any particular thought, she had always made a point of mailing her letters very secretly; it would, of course, not have been very wise to let anyone see her mail them. Consequently, she timed her walk so she could reach the post office just as darkness was starting to dim the outlines of the trees and the shapes of people's faces, although no one could ever mistake Miss Strangeworth, with her dainty walk and her rustling skirts.

There was always a group of young people around the post office, the very youngest roller-skating upon its driveway, which went all the way around the building and was the only smooth road in town; and the slighter older ones already knowing how to gather in small groups and chatter and laugh and make great, excited plans for going across the street to the soda shop in a minute or two. Miss Strangeworth had never had any self-consciousness ارتشاك before the children. She did not feel that any of them were staring at her unduly or longing to laugh at her; it would have been most reprehensible for their parents to permit their children to mock Miss Strangeworth of Pleasant Street. Most of the children stood back respectfully as Miss Strangeworth passed, silenced briefly in her presence, and some of the older children greeted her, saying soberly, "Hello, Miss Strangeworth."

Miss Strangeworth smiled at them and quickly went on. It had been a long time since she had known the name of every child in town. The mail slot was in the door of the post office. The children stood away as Miss Strangeworth approached it, seemingly surprised anyone should want to use the post office after it had been officially closed up for the night and turned over to the children. Miss Strangeworth stood by the door, opening her black pocketbook to take out the letters, and heard a voice which she knew at once to be Linda Stewart's. Poor little Linda was crying again, and Miss Strangeworth listened carefully. This was, after all, her town, and these were her people; if one of them was in trouble, she ought to know about it.

"I can't tell you, Dave," Linda was saying—so she was talking to the Harris boy, as Miss Strangeworth had supposed—"I just can't. It's just nasty."

"But why won't your father let me come around any more? What on earth did I do?"

"I can't tell you. I just wouldn't tell you for anything. You've got to have a dirty, dirty mind for things like that."

"But something's happened. You've been crying and crying, and your father is all upset. Why can't I know about it, too? Aren't I like one of the family?"

"Not any more, Dave, not any more. You're not to come near our house again, my father said so. He said he'd horsewhip you.

That's all I can tell you: You're not to come near our house any
more."

"But I didn't do anything."

"Just the same, my father said . . ."

Miss Strangeworth sighed and turned away. There was so
much evil in people. Even in a charming little town like this one,
there was still so much evil in people.

She slipped her letters into the slot, and two of them fell inside. The third caught on the edge and fell outside, onto the ground
at Miss Strangeworth's feet. She did not notice it because she was
wondering whether a letter to the Harris boy's father might not
be of some service in wiping out this potential badness. Wearily
Miss Strangeworth turned to go home to her quiet bed in her lovely
house, and never heard the Harris boy calling to her to say that she
had dropped something.

"Old lady Strangeworth's getting deaf," he said, looking after
her and holding in his hand the letter he had picked up.

"Well, who cares?" Linda said. "Who cares any more, anyway?"

"It's for Don Crane," the Harris boy said, "this letter. She
dropped a letter addressed to Don Crane. Might as well take it on
over. We pass his house anyway." He laughed. "Maybe it's got a
check or something in it and he'd be just as glad to get it tonight
instead of tomorrow."

"Catch old lady Strangeworth sending anybody a check,"
Linda said. "Throw it in the post office. Why do anyone a favor?"
She sniffled. "Doesn't seem to me anybody around here cares
about us," she said. "Why should we care about them?"

"I'll take it over anyway," the Harris boy said. "Maybe it's
good news for them. Maybe they need something happy tonight,
too. Like us."

Sadly, holding hands, they wandered off down the dark street,
the Harris boy carrying Miss Strangeworth's pink envelope in his
hand.

Miss Strangeworth awakened the next morning with a feeling
of intense happiness and, for a minute wondered why, and then remembered that this morning three people would open her letters.
Harsh, perhaps, at first, but wickedness was never easily banished,

and a clean heart was a scoured heart. She washed her soft old face and brushed her teeth, still sound in spite of her seventy-one years, and dressed herself carefully in her sweet, soft clothes and buttoned shoes. Then, coming downstairs and reflecting that perhaps a little waffle would be agreeable for breakfast in the sunny dining room, she found the mail on the hall floor and bent to pick it up.

A bill, the morning paper, a letter in a green envelope that looked oddly familiar. Miss Strangeworth stood perfectly still for a minute, looking down at the green envelope with the penciled printing, and thought: It looks like one of my letters. Was one of my letters sent back? No, because no one would know where to send it. How did this get here?

Miss Strangeworth was a Strangeworth of Pleasant Street. Her hand did not shake as she opened the envelope and unfolded the sheet of green paper inside. She began to cry silently for the wickedness of the world when she read the words: LOOK OUT AT WHAT USED TO BE YOUR ROSES.

THE SECRET LIFE OF WALTER MITTY

James Thurber

This story is a superb example of the use of the limited omniscient point of view. The contrast of Mitty's thoughts, his daydreaming, with his humdrum everyday life creates the humor and irony of this story; without this contrast, the story has no meaning. As you read, pay close attention to the following:

The relationship between the central idea and the point of view is critical. If a different point of view were used, more than likely the central idea would be lost.

The connection between the narrative voice and the language of that voice; the point of view is what makes that connection.

When you finish, ask yourself how the story would change if a different point of view were used. In fact, the point of view in the story is inconsistent, it is entirely from Mitty's point of view that we see it, but he shifts back and forth from the "real" world to that of his fantasies. Why is that necessary?

"We're going through!" The Commander's voice was like thin ice breaking. He wore his full-dress uniform, with the heavily braided white cap pulled down rakishly over one cold gray eye. "We can't make it, sir. It's spoiling for a hurricane, if you ask me." "I'm not asking you, Lieutenant Berg," said the Commander. "Throw on the power lights! Rev her up to 8,500! We're going through!" The pounding of the cylinders increased: ta-pocketa-pocketa-pocketa-pocketa-pocketa. The Commander stared at the ice forming on the pilot window. He walked over and twisted a row of complicated dials. "Switch on No. 8 auxiliary!" he shouted. "Switch on No. 8

auxiliary!" repeated Lieutenant Berg. "Full strength in No. 3 turret!" shouted the Commander. "Full strength in No. 3 turret!" The crew, bending to their various tasks in the huge, hurtling eight-engined Navy hydroplane, looked at each other and grinned. "The Old Man'll get us through," they said to one another. "The Old Man ain't afraid of Hell!" . . .

"Not so fast! You're driving too fast!" said Mrs. Mitty. "What are you driving so fast for?" 3rd

"Hmm?" said Walter Mitty. He looked at his wife, in the seat beside him, with shocked astonishment. She seemed grossly unfamiliar, like a strange woman who had yelled at him in a crowd. "You were up to fifty-five," she said. "You know I don't like to go more than forty. You were up to fifty-five." Walter Mitty drove on toward Waterbury in silence, the roaring of the SN202 through the worst storm in twenty years of Navy flying fading in the remote, intimate airways of his mind. "You're tensed up again," said Mrs. Mitty. "It's one of your days. I wish you'd let Dr. Renshaw look you over."

Walter Mitty stopped the car in front of the building where his wife went to have her hair done. "Remember to get those overshoes while I'm having my hair done," she said. "I don't need overshoes," said Mitty. She put her mirror back into her bag. "We've been all through that," she said, getting out of the car. "You're not a young man any longer." He raced the engine a little. "Why don't you wear your gloves? Have you lost your gloves?" Walter Mitty reached in a pocket and brought out the gloves. He put them on, but after she had turned and gone into the building and he had driven on to a red light, he took them off again. "Pick it up, brother!" snapped a cop as the light changed, and Mitty hastily pulled on his gloves and lurched ahead. He drove around the streets aimlessly for a time, and then he drove past the hospital on his way to the parking lot.

. . . "It's the millionaire banker, Wellington McMillan," said the pretty nurse. "Yes?" said Walter Mitty, removing his gloves slowly. "Who has the case?" "Dr. Renshaw and Dr. Benbow, but there are two specialists here, Dr. Remington from New York and Mr. Pritchard-Mitford from London. He flew over." A door opened down a long, cool corridor and Dr. Renshaw came out. He looked distraught and haggard. "Hello, Mitty," he said. "We're having the devil's own time with McMillan, the millionaire banker and close personal friend of Roosevelt. Obstreosis of the ductal tract. Tertiary. Wish you'd take a look at him."

"Glad to," said Mitty.

In the operating room there were whispered introductions: "Dr. Remington, Dr. Mitty. Mr. Pritchard-Mitford, Dr. Mitty."

"I've read your book on streptothricosis," said Pritchard-Mitford, shaking hands. "A brilliant performance, sir."

"Thank you," said Walter Mitty.

"Didn't know you were in the States, Mitty," grumbled Remington. "Coals to Newcastle, bringing Mitford and me up here for a tertiary."

"You are very kind," said Mitty. A huge, complicated machine, connected to the operating table, with many tubes and wires, began at this moment to go pocketa-pocketa-pocketa.

"The new anesthetizer is giving away!" shouted an intern. "There is no one in the East who knows how to fix it!" "Quiet, man!" said Mitty, in a low, cool voice. He sprang to the machine, which was now going pocketa-pocketa-queep-pocketa-queep. He began fingering delicately a row of glistening dials: "Give me a fountain pen!" he snapped. Someone handed him a fountain pen. He pulled a faulty piston out of the machine and inserted the pen in its place. "That will hold for ten minutes," he said. "Get on with the operation." A nurse hurried over and whispered to Renshaw, and Mitty saw the man turn pale. "Coreopsis has set in," said Renshaw nervously. "If you would take over, Mitty?" Mitty looked at him and at the craven figure of Benbow, who drank, and at the grave uncertain faces of the two great specialists. "If you wish," he said. They slipped a white gown on him; he adjusted a mask and drew on thin gloves; nurses handed him shining . . .

"Back it up, Mac! Look out for that Buick!" Walter Mitty jammed on the brakes. "Wrong lane, Mac," said the parking-lot attendant, looking at Mitty closely. "Gee. Yeh," muttered Mitty. He began cautiously to back out of the lane marked "Exit Only." "Leave her sit there," said the attendant: "I'll put her away."

Mitty got out of the car. "Hey, better leave the key." "Oh," said Mitty, handing the man the ignition key. The attendant vaulted into the car, backed it up with insolent skill, and put it where it belonged.

They're so damn cocky, thought Walter Mitty, walking along Main Street; they think they know everything. Once he had tried to take his chains off, outside New Milford, and he had got them wound around the axles. A man had had to come out in a wrecking car and unwind them, a young, grinning garageman. Since then Mrs. Mitty always made him drive to a garage to have the chains taken off. The next time, he thought, I'll wear my right arm in a sling; they won't grin at me then. I'll have my right arm in a sling and they'll see I couldn't possibly take the chains off myself. He kicked at the slush on the sidewalk. "Overshoes," he said to himself, and he began looking for a shoe store.

When he came out into the street again, with the overshoes in a box under his arm, Walter Mitty began to wonder what the other thing was his wife had told him to get. She had told him, twice, before they set out from their house for Waterbury. In a way he hated these weekly trips to town—he was always getting something wrong. Kleenex, he thought, Squibb's, razor blades? No. Toothpaste, toothbrush, bicarbonate, carborundum, initiative and referendum? He gave it up. But she would remember it. "Where's the what's-its-name?" she would ask. "Don't tell me you forgot the what's-its-name." A newsboy went by shouting something about the Waterbury trial.

. . . "Perhaps this will refresh your memory." The District Attorney suddenly thrust a heavy automatic at the quiet figure on the witness stand. "Have you ever seen this before?" Walter Mitty took the gun and examined it expertly. "This is my Webley-Vickers 50.80," he said calmly. An excited buzz ran around the courtroom. The Judge rapped for order. "You are a crack shot with any sort of firearms, I believe?" said the District Attorney, insinuatingly. "Objection!" shouted Mitty's attorney. "We have shown that the defendant could not have fired the shot. We have shown that he wore his right arm in a sling on the night of the fourteenth of July." Walter Mitty raised his hand briefly and the bickering attorneys were stilled. "With any known make of gun," he said evenly, "I could have killed Gregory Fitzhurst at three hundred feet with my left hand." Pandemonium broke loose in the courtroom. A woman's scream rose above the bedlam and suddenly a lovely, dark-haired girl was in Walter Mitty's arms. The District Attorney struck at her savagely. Without rising from his chair, Mitty let the man have it on the point of the chin. "You miserable cur!"

"Puppy biscuit," said Walter Mitty. He stopped walking and the buildings of Waterbury rose up out of the misty courtroom and surrounded him again. A woman who was passing laughed. "He said 'Puppy biscuit,'" she said to her companion. "That man said 'Puppy biscuit' to himself." Walter Mitty hurried on. He went into an A & P, not the first one he came to but a smaller one farther up the street. "I want some biscuit for small, young dogs," he said to the clerk. "Any special brand, sir?" The greatest pistol shot in the world thought a moment. "It says 'Puppies Bark for It' on the box," said Walter Mitty.

His wife would be through at the hairdresser's in fifteen minutes, Mitty saw in looking at his watch, unless they had trouble drying it; sometimes they had trouble drying it. She didn't like to get to the hotel first; she would want him to be there waiting for her as usual. He found a big leather chair in the lobby, facing a window, and he put the overshoes and the puppy biscuit on the floor beside it. He picked up an old copy of Liberty and sank down into the chair. "Can Germany Conquer the World Through the Air?" Walter Mitty looked at the pictures of bombing planes and of ruined streets.

. . . "The cannonading has got the wind up in young Raleigh, sir," said the sergeant. Captain Mitty looked up at him through tousled hair. "Get him to bed," he said wearily. "With the others. I'll fly alone." "But you can't sir," said the sergeant anxiously. "It takes two men to handle that bomber and the Archies are pounding hell out of the air. Von Richtman's circus is between here and Saulier." "Somebody's got to get that ammunition dump," said Mitty. "I'm going over. Spot of brandy?" He poured a drink for the sergeant and one for himself. War thundered and whined around the dugout and battered at the door. There was a rending of wood and splinters flew through the room. "A bit of a near thing," said Captain Mitty carelessly. "The box barrage is closing in," said the sergeant. "We only live once, Sergeant," said Mitty, with his faint, fleeting smile. "Or do we?" He poured another brandy and tossed it off. "I never see a man could hold his brandy like you, sir," said the sergeant. "Begging your pardon, sir." Captain Mitty stood up and strapped on his huge Webley-Vickers automatic. "It's forty kilometers through hell, sir," said the sergeant. Mitty finished one last brandy. "After all," he said softly, "what isn't?" The pounding of the cannon increased; there was the rat-tat-tatting of machine guns, and from somewhere came the menacing pocketa-pocketa-pocketa of the new flame-throwers. Walter Mitty walked to the door of the dugout humming "Auprés de Ma Blonde." He turned and waved to the sergeant. "Cheerio!" he said. . . .

Something struck his shoulder. "I've been looking all over this hotel for you," said Mrs. Mitty. "Why do you have to hide in this old chair? How did you expect me to find you?"

"Things close in," said Walter Mitty vaguely.

"What?" Mrs. Mitty said. "Did you get the what's-its-name? The puppy biscuit? What's in that box?"

"Overshoes," said Mitty.

"Couldn't you have put them on in the store?"

"I was thinking," said Walter Mitty. "Does it ever occur to you that I am sometimes thinking?" She looked at him. "I'm going to take your temperature when I get you home," she said.

They went out through the revolving doors that made a faintly derisive whistling sound when you pushed them. It was two blocks to the parking lot. At the drugstore on the corner she said, "Wait here for me. I forgot something. I won't be a minute." She was more than a minute.

Walter Mitty lighted a cigarette. It began to rain, rain with sleet in it. He stood up against the wall of the drugstore, smoking. . . . He put his shoulders back and his heels together. "To hell with the handkerchief," said Walter Mitty scornfully. He took one last drag on his cigarette and snapped it away. Then, with that faint, fleeting smile playing about his lips, he faced the firing squad; erect and motionless, proud and disdainful, Walter Mitty, the Undefeated, inscrutable to the last.

THE STAR
Arthur C. Clarke

Even popular or escape fiction may have a thematic basis; it may make a comment about some aspect of the human condition. Although escapist literature (like the following science fiction story) is written primarily for entertainment, it can also broaden our own awareness of ourselves and our lives. The best stories achieve a balance between enlightenment and entertainment, skillfully blending the theme and the elements.

"The Star" makes a strong statement about human nature by blending literary elements like character, setting, and conflict with an entertaining narrative. Although the story is set in the future, Clarke's realistic characters still behave like people you may know. But their behavior is spurred by an event that is both familiar and puzzling.

As you read, keep in mind that the main character in this story is a Jesuit monk, a member of the Society of Jesus (a Catholic religious order founded by Ignatius Loyola in 1534). Jesuits devote their lives to missionary and educational work and are also known as the intellectuals of the church. The story makes a reference to a painting by Paul Rubens (1577–1640), a Flemish artist who painted a well-known picture of Loyola. And the story mentions two Latin phrases. The first, AD MAJOREM DEI GLORIUM, *means "For the greater glory of God." The second is the* Exercitia Spiritualia, *which means "Spiritual Exercises," a book written by Loyola, which the Jesuits use for guidance.*

Everything that happens in this story—the actions and words of the characters, the setting, the slow-but-sure progress to the surprise ending—points to a central idea which is a statement about the relationship we each have to God; it's a concern that is as old as human nature itself.

It is three thousand light years to the Vatican. Once, I believed that space could have no power over faith, just as I believed that the heavens declared the glory of God's handiwork. Now I have seen that handiwork, and my faith is sorely troubled. I stare at the crucifix that hangs on the cabin wall above the Mark VI Computer, and for the first time in my life I wonder if it is no more than an empty symbol.

I have told no one yet, but the truth cannot be concealed. The facts are there for all to read, recorded on the countless miles of magnetic tape and the thousands of photographs we are carrying back to Earth. Other scientists can interpret them as easily as I can, and I am not one who would condone that tampering with the truth which often gave my order a bad name in the olden days.

The crew are already sufficiently depressed: I wonder how they will take this ultimate irony. Few of them have any religious faith, yet they will not relish using this final weapon in their campaign against me—that private, good-natured, but fundamentally serious, war which lasted all the way from Earth. It amused them to have a Jesuit as chief astrophysicist: Dr. Chandler, for instance, could never get over it. (Why are medical men such notorious atheists?) Sometimes he would meet me on the observation deck, where the lights are always low so that the stars shine with undiminished glory. He would come up to me in the gloom and stand staring out of the great oval port, while the heavens crawled slowly around us as the ship turned end over end with the residual spin we had never bothered to correct.

"Well, Father," he would say at last, "it goes on forever and forever, and perhaps Something made it. But how you can believe that Something has a special interest in us and our miserable little world—that just beats me." Then the argument would start, while the stars and nebulae would swing around us in silent, endless arcs beyond the flawlessly clear plastic of the observation port.

It was, I think, the apparent incongruity of my position that caused most amusement to the crew. In vain I would point to my three papers in the Astrophysical Journal, my five in the Monthly Notices of the Royal Astronomical Society. I would remind them that my order has long been famous for its scientific works. We may be few now, but ever since the eighteenth century we have made contributions to astronomy and geophysics out of all proportion to our numbers. Will my report on the Phoenix Nebula end our thousand years of history? It will end, I fear, much more than that.

I do not know who gave the nebula its name, which seems to me a very bad one. If it contains a prophecy, it is one that cannot be verified for several billion years. Even the word nebula is misleading: this is a far smaller object than those stupendous clouds of mist— the stuff of unborn stars—that are scattered throughout the length of the Milky Way. On the cosmic scale, indeed, the Phoenix Nebula is a tiny thing—a tenuous shell of gas surrounding a single star.

Or what is left of a star . . .

The Rubens engraving of Loyola seems to mock me as it hangs there above the spectrophotometer tracings. What would you, Father, have made of this knowledge that has come into my keeping, so far from the little world that was all the universe you knew? Would your faith have risen to the challenge, as mine has failed to do?

You gaze into the distance, Father, but I have traveled a distance beyond any that you could have imagined when you founded our order a thousand years ago. No other survey ship has been so far from Earth: we are at the very frontiers of the explored universe. We set out to reach the Phoenix Nebula, we succeeded, and we are homeward bound with our burden of knowledge. I wish I could lift that burden from my shoulders, but I call to you in vain across the centuries and the light years that lie between us.

On the book you are holding the words are plain to read. AD MAJOREM DEI GLORIAM, the message runs, but it is a message I can no longer believe. Would you still believe it, if you could see what we have found?

We knew, of course, what the Phoenix Nebula was. Every year, in our galaxy alone, more than a hundred stars explode, blazing for a few hours or days with thousands of times their normal brilliance before they sink back into death and obscurity. Such are the ordinary novae—the commonplace disasters of the universe. I have recorded the spectrograms and light curves of dozens since I started working at the Lunar Observatory.

But three or four times in every thousand years occurs something beside which even a nova pales into total insignificance.

When a star becomes a supernova, it may for a little while outshine all the massed suns of the galaxy. The Chinese astronomers watched this happen in A.D. 1054, not knowing what it was they saw. Five centuries later, in 1572, a supernova blazed in Cassiopeia so brilliantly that it was visible in the daylight sky. There have been three more in the thousand years that have passed since then.

Our mission was to visit the remnants of such a catastrophe, to reconstruct the events that led up to it, and, if possible, to learn its cause. We came slowly in through the concentric shells of gas that had been blasted out six thousand years before, yet were expanding still. They were immensely hot, radiating even now with a fierce violet light, but were far too tenuous to do us any damage. When the star had exploded, its outer layers had been driven upward with such speed that they had escaped completely from its gravitational field. Now they formed a hollow shell large enough to engulf a thousand solar systems, and at its center burned the tiny, fantastic object which the star had now become—a White Dwarf, smaller than the Earth, yet weighing a million times as much.

The glowing gas shells were all around us, banishing the normal night of interstellar space. We were flying into the center of a cosmic bomb that had detonated millennia ago and whose incandescent fragments were still hurtling apart. The immense scale of the explosion, and the fact that the debris already covered a volume of space many billions of miles across, robbed the scene of any visible movement. It would take decades before the unaided eye could detect any motion in these tortured wisps and eddies of gas, yet the sense of turbulent expansion was overwhelming.

We had checked our primary drive hours before, and were drifting slowly toward the fierce little star ahead. Once it had been a sun like our own, but it had squandered in a few hours the energy that should have kept it shining for a million years. Now it was a shrunken miser, hoarding its resources as if trying to make amends for its prodigal youth.

No one seriously expected to find planets. If there had been any before the explosion, they would have been boiled into puffs of vapor, and their substance lost in the greater wreckage of the star itself. But we made the automatic search, as we always do when approaching an unknown sun, and presently we found a single small world circling the star at an immense distance. It must have been the Pluto of this vanished solar system, orbiting on the frontiers of the night. Too far from the central sun ever to have known life, its remoteness had saved it from the fate of all its lost companions.

The passing fires had seared its rocks and burned away the mantle of frozen gas that must have covered it in the days before the disaster. We landed, and we found the Vault.

Its builders had made sure that we would. The monolithic marker that stood above the entrance was now a fused stump, but even the first long-range photographs told us that here was the work of intelligence. A little later we detected the continent-wide pattern of radioactivity that had been buried in the rock. Even if the pylon above the Vault had been destroyed, this would have remained, an immovable and all but eternal beacon calling to the stars. Our ship fell toward this gigantic bull's-eye like an arrow into its target.

The pylon must have been a mile high when it was built, but now it looked like a candle that had melted down into a puddle of wax. It took us a week to drill through the fused rock, since we did not have the proper tools for a task like this. We were astronomers, not archaeologists, but we could improvise. Our original purpose was forgotten: this lonely monument, reared with such labor at the greatest possible distance from the doomed sun, could have only one meaning. A civilization that knew it was about to die had made its last bid for immortality.

It will take us generations to examine all the treasures that were placed in the Vault. They had plenty of time to prepare, for their sun must have given its first warnings many years before the final detonation. Everything that they wished to preserve, all the fruit of their genius, they brought here to this distant world in the days before the end, hoping that some other race would find it and that they would not be utterly forgotten. Would we have done as well, or would we have been too lost in our own misery to give thought to a future we could never see or share?

If only they had had a little more time! They could travel freely enough between the planets of their own sun, but they had not yet learned to cross the interstellar gulfs, and the nearest solar system was a hundred light-years away. Yet even had they possessed the secret of the Transfinite Drive, no more than a few millions could have been saved. Perhaps it was better thus.

Even if they had not been so disturbingly human as their sculpture shows, we could not have helped admiring them and grieving for their fate. They left thousands of visual records and the machines for projecting them, together with elaborate pictorial instructions from which it will not be difficult to learn their written language. We have examined many of these records, and brought to life for the first time in six thousand years the warmth and beauty of a civilization that in many ways must have been superior to our own. Perhaps they only showed us the best, and one can hardly blame them. But their words were very lovely, and their cities were built with a grace that matches anything of man's. We have watched them at work and play, and listened to their musical speech sounding across the centuries. One scene is still before my eyes—a group of children on a beach of strange blue sand, playing in the waves as children play on Earth. Curious whiplike trees line the shore, and some very large animal is wading in the shadows yet attracting no attention at all.

And sinking into the sea, still warm and friendly and life-giving, is the sun that will soon turn traitor and obliterate all this innocent happiness.

Perhaps if we had not been so far from home and so vulnerable to loneliness, we should not have been so deeply moved. Many of us had seen the ruins of ancient civilizations on other worlds, but they had never affected us so profoundly. This tragedy was unique. It is one thing for a race to fail and die, as nations and cultures have done on Earth. But to be destroyed so completely in the full flower of its achievement, leaving no survivors—how could that be reconciled with the mercy of God?

My colleagues have asked me that, and I have given what answers I can. Perhaps you could have done better, Father Loyola, but I have found nothing in the *Exercitia Spiritualia* that helps me here. They were not an evil people: I do not know what gods they worshiped, if indeed they worshiped any. But I have looked back at them across the centuries, and have watched while the loveliness they used their last strength to preserve was brought forth again into the light of their shrunken sun. They could have taught us much: why were they destroyed?

I know the answers that my colleagues will give when they get back to Earth. They will say that the universe has no purpose and no plan, that since a hundred suns explode every year in our galaxy, at this very moment some race is dying in the depths of space. Whether that race has done good or evil during its lifetime will make no difference in the end: there is no divine justice, for there is no God.

Yet, of course, what we have seen proves nothing of the sort. Anyone who argues thus is being swayed by emotion, not logic. God has no need to justify His actions to man. He who built the universe can destroy it when He chooses. It is arrogance—it is perilously near blasphemy—for us to say what He may or may not do.

This I could have accepted, hard though it is to look upon whole worlds and peoples thrown into the furnace. But there comes a point when even the deepest faith must falter, and now, as I look at the calculations lying before me, I know I have reached that point at last.

We could not tell, before we reached the nebula, how long ago the explosion took place. Now, from the astronomical evidence and the record in the rocks of that one surviving planet, I have been able to date it very exactly. I know in what year the light of this colossal conflagration reached our Earth. I know how brilliantly the supernova whose corpse now dwindles behind our speeding ship once shone in terrestrial skies. I know how it must have blazed low in the east before sunrise, like a beacon in that oriental dawn.

There can be no reasonable doubt: the ancient mystery is solved at last. Yet, oh God, there were so many stars you could have used. What was the need to give these people to the fire, that the symbol of their passing might shine above Bethlehem?

THE STORY OF AN HOUR
Kate Chopin

Knowing that Mrs. Mallard was afflicted with a heart trouble, great care was taken to break to her as gently as possible the news of her husband's death.

It was her sister Josephine who told her, in broken sentences; veiled hints that revealed in half concealing.

Her husband's friend Richards was there, too, near her. It was he who had been in the newspaper office when intelligence of the railroad disaster was received, with Brently Mallard's name leading the list of "killed." He had only taken the time to assure himself of its truth by a second telegram, and had hastened to forestall any less careful, less tender friend in bearing the sad message.

She did not hear the story as many women have heard the same, with a paralyzed inability to accept its significance. She wept at once, with sudden, wild abandonment, in her sister's arms. When the storm of grief had spent itself she went away to her room alone. She would have no one follow her.

There stood, facing the open window, a comfortable, roomy armchair. Into this she sank, pressed down by a physical exhaustion that haunted her body and seemed to reach into her soul.

She could see in the open square before her house the tops of trees that were all aquiver with the new spring life. The delicious breath of rain was in the air. In the street below a peddler was crying his wares. The notes of a distant song which some one was singing reached her faintly, and countless sparrows were twittering in the eaves.

There were patches of blue sky showing here and there through the clouds that had met and piled one above the other in the west facing her window.

She sat with her head thrown back upon the cushion of the chair, quite motionless, except when a sob came up into her throat and shook her, as a child who has cried itself to sleep continues to sob in its dreams.

She was young, with a fair, calm face, whose lines bespoke repression and even a certain strength. But now there was a dull stare in her eyes, whose gaze was fixed away off yonder on one of those patches of blue sky. It was not a glance of reflection, but rather indicated a suspension of intelligent thought.

There was something coming to her and she was waiting for it, fearfully. What was it? She did not know; it was too subtle and elusive to name. But she felt it, creeping out of the sky, reaching toward her through the sounds, the scents, the color that filled the air.

Now her bosom rose and fell tumultuously. She was beginning to recognize this thing that was approaching to possess her, and she was striving to beat it back with her will—as powerless as her two white slender hands would have been.

When she abandoned herself a little whispered word escaped her slightly parted lips. She said it over and over under her breath: "free, free, free!" The vacant stare and the look of terror that had followed it went from her eyes. They stayed keen and bright. Her pulses beat fast, and the coursing blood warmed and relaxed every inch of her body.

She did not stop to ask if it were or were not a monstrous joy that held her. A clear and exalted perception enabled her to dismiss the suggestion as trivial.

She knew that she would weep again when she saw the kind, tender hands folded in death; the face that had never looked save with love upon her, fixed and gray and dead. But she saw beyond that bitter moment a long procession of years to come that would belong to her absolutely. And she opened and spread her arms out to them in welcome.

There would be no one to live for during those coming years; she would live for herself. There would be no powerful will bending hers in that blind persistence with which men and women believe they have a right to impose a private will upon a fellow-creature. A kind intention or a cruel intention made the act seem no less a crime as she looked upon it in that brief moment of illumination.

Plot her rising emotion.

And yet she had loved him—sometimes. Often she had not. What did it matter! What could love, the unsolved mystery, count for in face of this possession of self-assertion which she suddenly recognized as the strongest impulse of her being!

"Free! Body and soul free!" she kept whispering.

Josephine was kneeling before the closed door with her lips to the keyhole, imploring for admission.

"Louise, open the door! I beg; open the door—you will make yourself ill. What are you doing Louise? For heaven's sake open the door."

"Go away. I am not making myself ill." No; she was drinking in a very elixir of life through that open window.

Her fancy was running riot along those days ahead of her. Spring days, and summer days, and all sorts of days that would be her own. She breathed a quick prayer that life might be long. It was only yesterday she had thought with a shudder that life might be long.

She arose at length and opened the door to her sister's importunities. There was a feverish triumph in her eyes, and she carried herself unwittingly like a goddess of Victory. She clasped her sister's waist, and together they descended the stairs. Richards stood waiting for them at the bottom.

Someone was opening the front door with a latchkey. It was Brently Mallard who entered, a little travel-stained, composedly carrying his grip-sack and umbrella. He had been far from the scene of accident, and did not even know there had been one. He stood amazed at Josephine's piercing cry; at Richards' quick motion to screen him from the view of his wife.

But Richards was too late.

When the doctors came they said she had died of heart disease—of joy that kills.

Bcz her → diy
freedom
was fal

But the doctor says, she died Bcz she happy for coming back her husband.

CI : people cant Live w/o freedom.
extrem disaponmnt of loosing freedom can killed

THE TRUSTY
Ron Rash

They had been moving up the road a week without seeing another farmhouse, and the nearest well, at least the nearest the owner would let Sinkler use, was half a mile back. What had been a trusty sluff job was now as onerous as swinging a Kaiser blade or shoveling out ditches. As soon as he'd hauled the buckers back to the cage truck it was time to go again. He asked Vickery if someone could spell him, and the bull guard said that Sinkler could always strap on a pair of leg irons and grab a handle. "Bolick just killed a rattlesnake in them weeds yonder," the bull guard said. "I bet he'd square a trade with you." When Sinkler asked if come morning he could walk ahead to search for another well, Vickery's lips tightened, but he nodded.

The next day, Sinkler took the metal buckets and walked until he found a farmhouse. It was no closer than the other, even a bit farther, but worth padding the hoof a few extra steps. The well he'd been using belonged to a hunchbacked widow. The woman who appeared in this doorway wore her hair in a similar tight bun and draped herself in the same sort of flour-cloth dress, but she looked to be in her mid-twenties, like Sinkler. Two weeks would pass before they got beyond this farmhouse, perhaps another two weeks before the next well. Plenty of time to quench a different kind of thirst. As he entered the yard, the woman looked past the barn to a field where a man and his draft horse were plowing. The woman gave a brisk whistle and the farmer paused and looked their way. Sinkler stopped, but did not set the buckets down.

"What you want," the woman said, not so much a question as a demand.

"Water," Sinkler answered. "We've got a chain gang working on the road."

354

"I'd have reckoned you to bring water with you."

"Not enough for ten men all day."

The woman looked out at the field again. Her husband watched but did not unloop the rein from around his neck. The woman stepped onto the six nailed-together planks that looked more like a raft than a porch. Firewood was stacked on one side, and closer to the door an axe leaned between a shovel and a hoe. She let her eyes settle on the axe long enough to make sure he noticed it. Sinkler saw now that she was younger than he'd thought, maybe eighteen, at most twenty, more girl than woman.

"How come you not to have chains on you?"

"I'm a trusty," Sinkler said, smiling. "A prisoner, but one that can be trusted."

"And all you want is water?"

Sinkler thought of several possible answers.

"That's what they sent me for."

"I don't reckon there to be any money in it for us?" the girl asked.

"No, just gratitude from a bunch of thirsty men, and especially me for not having to haul it so far."

"I'll have to ask my man," she said. "Stay here in my yard."

For a moment he thought she might take the axe with her. As she walked into the field, Sinkler studied the house, which was no bigger than a fishing shack. The dwelling appeared to have been built in the previous century. The door opened with a latch, not a knob, and no glass filled the window frames. Sinkler stepped closer to the entrance and saw two ladder-back chairs, a small table set on a puncheon floor. Sinkler wondered if these apple-knockers had heard they were supposed to be getting a new deal.

"You can use the well," the girl said when she returned, "but he said you need to forget one of them pails here next time you come asking for water."

Worth it, he figured, even if Vickery took the money out of Sinkler's own pocket, especially with no sign of another farmhouse. It would be a half-dollar at most, easily made up with one slick deal in a poker game. He nodded and went to the well, sent the rusty bucket down into the dark. The girl went up on the porch but didn't go inside.

"What you in prison for?"

"Thinking a bank manager wouldn't notice his teller slipping a few bills in his pocket."

"Whereabouts?"

"Raleigh."

I ain't never been past Asheville," the girl said. "How long you in for?"

"Five years. I've done sixteen months."

Sinkler raised the bucket, water leaking from the bottom as he transferred its contents. The girl stayed on the porch, making sure that all he took was water.

"You lived here long?"

"Me and Chet been here a year," the girl said. "I grew up across the ridge yonder."

"You two live alone, do you?"

"We do," the girl said, "but there's a shotgun just inside the door and I know how to bead it."

"I'm sure you do," Sinkler said. "You mind telling me your name, just so I'll know what to call you?"

"Lucy Sorrels."

He waited to see if she'd ask his.

"Mine's Sinkler," he said when she didn't.

He filled the second bucket but made no move to leave, instead looking around at the trees and mountains as if just noticing them. Then he smiled and gave a slight nod.

"Must be lonely being out so far from everything," Sinkler said. "At least, I would think so."

"And I'd think them men to be getting thirsty," Lucy Sorrels said.

"Probably," he agreed, surprised at the smarts she showed in turning his words back on him. "But I'll return soon to brighten your morning."

"When you planning to leave one of them pails?" she asked.

"End of the day."

She nodded and turned and went into the shack.

"The rope broke," he told Vickery as the prisoners piled into the truck at quitting time.

The guard looked not so much skeptical as aggrieved that Sinkler thought him fool enough to believe it. Vickery answered that if Sinkler thought he'd lightened his load he was mistaken.

It'd be easy enough to find another bucket, maybe one that could hold an extra gallon. Sinkler shrugged and lifted himself into the cage truck, found a place on the metal bench among the sweating convicts. He'd won over the other guards with cigarettes and small loans, that and his mush talk, but not Vickery, who'd argued that making Sinkler a trusty would only give him a head start when he tried to escape.

The bull guard was right about that. Sinkler had more than fifty dollars in poker winnings now, plenty enough cash to get him across the Mississippi to where he could finally shed himself of the whole damn region. He'd grown up in Montgomery, but when the law got too interested in his comings and goings he'd gone north to Knoxville and then went to Memphis, before recrossing Tennessee on his way to Raleigh. Sinkler's talents had led him to establishments his sleight of hand needed no deck of cards. A decent suit, clean fingernails, and buffed shoes, and he could walk into a business and be greeted as a solid citizen. Tell a story about being in town because of an ailing mother, and you were the cat's pajamas. They'd take the Help Wanted sign out of the window and pretty much replace it with Help Yourself. Sinkler remembered the afternoon in Memphis when he'd stood by the river after grifting a clothing store of forty dollars in two months. Keep heading west or turn back east—that was the choice. He'd flipped a silver dollar to decide, a rare moment when he'd trusted his life purely to luck.

This time he'd cross the river, start in Kansas City or Saint Louis. He'd work the stores and cafes and newsstands and anywhere else with a till or a cash register. Except for a bank. Crooked as bankers were, Sinkler should have realized how quickly they'd recognize him as one of their own. No, he'd not make that mistake again.

That night, when the stockade lights were snuffed, he lay in his bunk and thought about Lucy Sorrels. Eighteen months, a year and a half, had passed since he'd been with a woman. After that long, almost any female would make the sap rise. There was nothing about her face to hold a man's attention, but curves tightened the right parts of her dress. Nice legs, too. Each trip to the well, he had tried to make small talk.

Lucy Sorrels had given him the icy mitts, but he had a mouth to warm her up. It was only on the last haul that the husband had come in from his field. He'd barely responded to Sinkler's "how do you do's and much obliged." He looked to be around forty, and Sinkler suspected that part of his terseness was due to the presence of a younger man around his wife. After a few moments, the farmer had nodded at the pail in Sinkler's left hand. "You'll be leaving that right?" When Sinkler said yes, the husband told Lucy to switch it with the leaky well bucket, then walked into the barn.

Two days passed before Lucy asked if he'd ever thought of trying to escape.

"Of course," Sinkler answered. "Have you?"

She looked at him in a way he could not read.

"How come you ain't done it, then? They let you roam near anywhere you want, and you ain't got shackles."

"Maybe I enjoy the free room and board," Sinkler answered. He turned a thumb toward his stripes. "Nice duds, too. They even let you change them out every Sunday. "

"I don't think I could stand it," Lucy Sorrels said. "Being locked up so long and knowing I had nigh on three years."

He checked her lips for the slightest upward curve of a smile, but it wasn't there.

"Yeah," Sinkler said, taking a step closer. "You don't seem the sort to stand being locked up. I'd think a young gal pretty as you would want to see more of the world."

"How come you ain't done it?" she asked again, and brushed some loose wisps of hair behind her ear.

"Maybe the same reason as you," Sinkler said. "Out here in the boonies you can't exactly get whisked away to another place. I haven't seen more than a couple of cars and trucks on this road, and those driving them know there's prisoners about. They wouldn't be fool enough to pick up a stranger. Haven't seen a lot of train tracks crossing the road, either."

"Anybody ever try?" Lucy asked.

"Yeah, two weeks ago. Fellow ran that morning and the bloodhounds had him grabbing sky by dark. All he got for his trouble was a bunch of tick bites and briar scratches. That and another year added to his sentence."

For the first time since she'd gone to fetch her husband, Lucy stepped off the porch and put some distance between her and the door. The shotgun and axe, too, which meant that she was starting to trust him at least a little. She stood in the yard and looked up at an eave, where black insects hovered around clots of dried mud.

"Them dirt daubers is a nuisance," Lucy said. "I knock their nests down and they build them back the next day."

"I'd guess them to be about the only thing that wants to stay around here, don't you think?"

"You've got a saucy way of talking," she said.

"You don't seem to mind it too much," Sinkler answered, and nodded toward the field. "An older fellow like that usually keeps a close eye on a pretty young wife, but he must be the trusting sort, or is it he just figures he's got you corralled in?"

He lifted the full buckets and stepped close enough to the barn not to be seen from the field. "You don't have to stand so far from me, Lucy Sorrels. I don't bite."

She didn't move toward him, but she didn't go back to the porch, either.

"If you was to escape, where would you go?"

"Might depend on who was going with me," Sinkler answered. "What kind of place would you like to visit?"

"Like you'd just up and take me along. I'd likely that about as much as them daubers flying me out of here."

"No, I'd need to get to know my traveling partner better," Sinkler said. "Make sure she really cared about me. That way she wouldn't take a notion to turn me in."

"You mean for the reward money?"

Sinkler laughed.

You've got to be a high cloud to have a reward put on you, darling. They'd not even bother to put my mug in a post office, which is fine by me. Buy my train ticket and I'd be across the Mississippi in two days. Matter of fact, I've got money enough saved up to buy two tickets."

"Enough for two tickets?" Lucy asked.

"I do indeed."

"Why come you to think a person would turn you in if there ain't no reward?"

"Bad conscience—which is why I've got to be sure my travelling partner doesn't have one." Sinkler smiled. "Like I said, you don't have to stand so far away. We could even step into the barn for a few minutes."

Lucy looked toward the field and let her gaze linger long enough that he thought she just might do it.

"I have chores to get done," she said and went into the shack.

Sinkler headed back down the road, thinking things out. By the time he set the sloshing buckets beside the prison truck, he'd figured a way to get Lucy Sorrels' dress raised with more than just sweet talk. He'd tell her there was an extra set of truck keys in a guard's front desk and that he'd steal them, and wait until the guards were distracted to jump in and drive away. She'd know beforehand and be in the woods down the road. They'd go to Asheville and get the first train. It was a damn good story, one Sinkler himself might have believed if he didn't know that all the extra truck keys were locked inside a thousand-pound Mosler safe.

When he entered the yard the next morning, Lucy came to the well but stayed on the opposite side. Like a skittish dog, Sinkler thought, and imagined holding out a pack of gum or a candy bar to bring her the rest of the way. She wore the same dress as always, but her hair was unpinned and fell across her shoulders. It was blonder and curlier than he'd supposed. Set free for him, Sinkler knew. A cool, steady breeze gave the air an early-autumn feel, and helped round the curves beneath the muslin.

"Your hair being down like that—it looks good," he said. "I bet that's the way you wear it to bed."

She didn't blush. Sinkler worked the crank and the well bucket descended into the earth. Once both his buckets were filled, he explained his plan.

"There's an easier way," Lucy said. "One where you don't need the truck, not even a road."

"I never figured you to be the know-all on prison escapes."

"There's a trail on the yon side of that ridge," Lucy said, nodding past the field. "You can follow it all the way to Asheville."

"Asheville's at least thirty miles from here."

"That's by the road. It's no more than eight if you cut through the gap. You just got to know the right trails."

"Which I don't."

"I do," she said. "I've done it in three hours easy."

For a few moments, Sinkler didn't say anything. It was as though the key he'd been imagining had suddenly appeared in his hand. He left the buckets where they were and stepped closer to the barn. When he gestured Lucy closer, she came. He settled an arm around her waist and felt her yield to him. Her lips opened to his and she did not resist when his free hand cupped a breast. To touch a woman after so long made him feather-legged. A bead of sweat trickled down his brow as she pressed her body closer and settled a hand on his thigh. Only when Sinkler tried to lead her into the barn did Lucy resist.

"He can't see us from down there."

"It ain't just that," Lucy said. "My bleed time's started."

Sinkler felt so rabbity that he told her he didn't care.

"There'd be a mess and he'd know the why of it."

He felt frustration simmer into anger. He tried to step away, but Lucy pulled him back, pressed her face into his chest.

"If we was far away it wouldn't matter. I hate it here. He cusses me near every day and won't let me go nowhere. When he gets drunk, he'll load his shotgun and swear he's going to shoot me."

She let go of him slowly. The only sound was a clucking chicken and the breeze tinking the well bucket against the narrow stone wellhead.

"All you and me have to do is get on the train in Asheville," Lucy said," and not him nor the law can catch us. I know where he keeps his money. I'll get it if you ain't got enough."

He met her eyes, then looked past her. The sun was higher now, angled in over the mountaintops, and the new well bucket winked silver as it swayed. Sinkler lifted his gaze to the cloudless sky. It would be another hot, dry, miserable day and he'd be out in it. At quitting time he'd go back and wash up with water dingy enough to clog a strainer, eat what would gag a hog, then at nine o'clock set his head on a grimy pillow. Three and a half more years. Sinkler studied the ridgeline, found the gap that would lead to Asheville.

"I've got money," he told Lucy. "It's the getting to where I can spend it that's been the problem."

That night, as he lay in his bunk, Sinkler pondered the plan. An hour would pass before anyone would start looking for him, and even then they'd search first along the road. As far out as the prisoners were working, it'd take at least four hours to get the bloodhounds on his trail, and by the time the dogs tracked him to Asheville he'd be on a train. It could be months, or never, until such a chance came again. But the suddenness of the opportunity unsettled him. He would take a couple of days, think it out. The grit in the gears would be Lucy. Giving her the slop in Asheville would be nigh impossible, so he'd be with her until the next stop, probably Knoxville or Raleigh. Which could be all for the better. A hotel room and a bottle of bootleg whiskey and they'd have them a high old time. He could sneak out early morning while she slept. If she took what her husband had hidden, she'd have enough for a new start, and another reason not to drop a dime and phone the police.

Of course, many another convict would simply wait until trail's end, then let a good sixed rock take care of it, lift what money she had, and be on his way. Travelling with a girl that young was a risk. She might say or do something to make a bluecoat suspicious. Or, waking up to find him gone, put the law on him just for spite.

The next morning, the men loaded up and drove to where they'd quit the day before. They weren't far from the farmhouse now, only a few hundred yards. As he carried the buckets up the road, Sinkler realized that if Lucy knew the trail, then the husband did, too. The guards would see the farmer in the field and tell him who they were looking for. How long after that would he find out that she was gone? It might be just minutes before the husband went to check. But only if the guards were looking in that direction. He could tell Vickery this well was low and the farmer wouldn't let him use it anymore, so he had to go back down the road to the widow's. He could walk in that direction and then cut into the woods and circle back.

Sinkler was already drawing water when Lucy came out. Primping for him, he knew, her hair unpinned and freshly combed, curtaining a necklace with a heart shaped locket. She smelled good, too, a bright clean smell, like honeysuckle. In the distance, the husband was strapped to his horse, the tandem trudging endlessly across the field. From what Sinkler had seen, the man worked as hard as the road crews and had about as much to show for it. Twenty years older and too much of a gink to realize what Lucy understood at eighteen. Sinkler stepped closer to the barn and she raised her mouth to his, found his tongue with her tongue.

"I been thirsting for that all last night and this morning." Lucy said when she broke off the kiss. "That's what it's like—a thirsting. Chet ain't never been able to staunch it, but you can."

She laid her head against his chest and held him tight. Feeling the desperation of her embrace, Sinkler knew that she'd risk her life to help him get away, help them get away. But a girl her age could turn quick as a weathervane, He set his hands on her shoulders and gently but firmly pushed her back enough to meet her eyes.

"You ain't just playing some make believe with me, because if you are it's time to quit playing."

"I'll leave this second if you got need to," Lucy said. "I'll go get his money right now. I counted it this morning when he left. It's near seven dollars. That's enough, ain't it, at least to get us tickets?"

"You've never rode a train, have you?" Sinkler asked.

"No."

"It costs more than that."

"How much more?"

"Closer to five each," Sinkler said, "just to get to Knoxville or Raleigh."

For a few moments she said nothing, then she touched the locket.

"This is a pass-me-down from my momma. It's pure silver and we could sell it."

Sinkler slipped a hand under the locket, inspected it with the feigned attentiveness of a jeweler.

"And all this time I thought you had a heart of gold, Lucy Sorrels," Sinkler said and smiled as he let the locket slide off his palm. "No, darling. You keep it around your pretty neck. I got plenty for tickets, and maybe something extra for a shiny bracelet to go with that necklace."

"Then I want to go tomorrow," Lucy said, and moved closer to him, "My bleed time is near over."

Sinkler smelled the honeysuckle and desire swamped him. He tried to clear his mind and come up with reasons to delay, but none came.

"We'll leave in the morning," Sinkler said.

"All right," She said, touching him a moment longer before removing her hand.

Sinkler nodded. "We'll travel light."

"I don't mind that," Lucy said. "It ain't like I got piddling anyway."

"Can you get me one of his shirts and some pants?"

Lucy nodded.

"Don't pack any of it until tomorrow morning when he's in the field," Sinkler said.

"Where are we going?" she asked. "I mean for good?"

"Where do you want to go?

"I was notioning California. They say it's like Paradise out there."

"That'll do me just fine," Sinkler said, then grinned. "That's just where an angel like you belongs."

The next morning, he told Vickery that the Sorrels' well was going dry and he'd have to backtrack to the other one. That'll be almost a mile jaunt for you," Vickery said, and shook his head in mock sympathy. Sinkler walked until he was out of sight. He found himself a marker, a big oak with a trunk cracked by lightning, then stepped over the ditch and entered the woods. He set the buckets by a rotting stump, close enough to the oak tree to be easily found if something went wrong. Because Sinkler knew that, when it came time to lay down or fold, Lucy might still think twice about leaving her folks or trusting someone she'd hardly known two weeks, and a convict at that. Or the husband might notice a little thing like Lucy not gathering eggs or putting a kettle on for supper, things Sinkler should have warned her to do.

Sinkler stayed close to the road, and soon heard the clink of leg chains and the rasp of shovels gathering dirt. Glimpses of black-and-white caught his eye as he made his way past. The sounds of the chain gang faded, and not long after that the trees thinned, the barn's gray planking filling the gaps. Sinkler did not enter the yard. Lucy stood just inside the farmhouse door. He studied the shack for any hint that the farmer had found out. But all was as it had been, clothing pinned on the wire between two trees, cracked corn spilled on the ground for the chickens, the axe still on the porch beside the hoe. He angled around the barn until he could see the field. The farmer was there, hitched to the horse and plow. Sinkler called her name and Lucy stepped out on the porch. She wore the same muslin dress and carried a knotted bedsheet in her hand. When she got to the woods, Lucy opened the bedsheet and removed a shirt and what was little more than two slaps of tied leather.

"Go over by the well and put these brogans on, "Lucy said. "It's a way to fool them hounds."

"We need to get going," Sinkler said.

"It'll just take a minute."

He did what she asked, checking the field to make sure that the farmer wasn't looking in their direction.

"Keep your shoes in your hand," Lucy said, and walked toward Sinkler with the shirt.

When she was close, Lucy got on her knees and rubbed the shirt cloth over the ground, all the way to Sinkler's feet.

"Walk over to the other side of the barn, "she told him, scrubbing the ground as she followed.

She motioned him to stay put and retrieved the bedsheet.

"This way," she said and led him down the slated ground and into the woods.

"You expect me to wear these all the way to Asheville?" Sinkler said after the flapping leather almost tripped him.

"No, just up to the ridge."

They stayed in the woods and along the field's far edge and then climbed the ridge. At the top Sinkler took off the brogans and looked back through the trees and saw the square of plowed soil, now no bigger than a barn door. The farmer was still there.

Lucy untied the bedsheet and handed him the pants and shirt. He took off the stripes and hid them behind a tree. Briefly, Sinkler thought about taking a little longer before he dressed, suggesting to Lucy that the bedsheet might have another use. Just a few more hours, he reminded himself, you'll be safe for sure and rolling with her in a big soft bed. The chambray shirt wasn't a bad fit, but the denim pants hung loose on his hips. Every few steps, Sinkler had to hitch them back up. The bedsheet held nothing more and Lucy stuffed it in a rock crevice.

"You bring that money?" he asked.

"You claimed us not to need it," Lucy said, a harshness in her voice he'd not heard before. "You weren't trifling with me about having money for the train tickets, were you?"

"No, darling, and plenty enough to buy you that bracelet and a real dress instead of that flour sack you got on. Stick with me and you'll ride the cushions."

They moved down the ridge through a thicket of rhododendron, the ground so aslant that in a couple of places he'd have tumbled if he hadn't watched how Lucy did it, front foot sideways and leaning backward. At the bottom, the trail forked. Lucy nodded to the left. The land continued downhill, then curved and leveled out. After a while, the path snaked in the undergrowth and Sinkler knew that without Lucy he'd be completely lost. You're doing as much for her as she for you, he reminded himself, and thought again about what another convict might do, what he'd known all along he couldn't do. When others had brought derringers or Arkansas toothpicks to card games, Sinkler had come empty-handed; either one could take its owner straight to the morgue or the prison. He'd always made a show of slapping his pockets and opening his coat at such gatherings. "I'll not hurt anything but a fellow's wallet," he'd say. Men had been killed twice in his presence, but he'd never had a weapon aimed in his direction.

Near another ridge, they crossed a creek that was little more than a spring seep. They followed the ridge awhile, and then the trail widened and they moved back downhill and up again. Each rise and fall of the land looked like what had come before. The mountain air was thin, and if Sinkler hadn't been hauling water the distances he had he wouldn't have had the spunk to keep going. They went on, the trees shading them from the sun, but even so he grew thirsty and kept hoping they'd come to a stream he could drink from. There was no stream, but they finally came to another spring seep.

"I've got to have some water," he said.

Sinkler kneeled beside the creek. The water was so shallow that he had to lean over and steady himself with one hand, cupping the other to get a dozen leaky palmfuls in his mouth. He stood and brushed the damp sand off his hand and his knees. The woods were completely silent, no murmur of wind, not a bird singing.

The trees cut out much of the sky, but he could tell that the sun was starting to slip behind the mountains. Fewer dapples of light were on the forest floor, more shadows. Soon the prisoners would be heading back, one man fewer. Come suppertime, the gangs would be spooning beans off a tin plate while Sinkler sat in a dining car eating steak with silverware. By then, the warden would have chewed out Vickery's skinny ass but good, maybe even fired him. The other guards, the ones he'd duped even more, would be explaining why they'd recommended making Sinkler a trusty in the first place.

When the trail narrowed again, a branch snagged Lucy's sleeve and ripped the grayed muslin. She surprised him with her profanity as she examined the torn cloth.

"I'd not think a sweet little gal like you to know words like that."

She glared at him and Sinkler raised his hands, palms out.

"Just teasing you a bit, darling. You should have brought another dress. I know I told you to pack light, but light didn't mean bring nothing."

"Maybe I ain't got another damn dress," Lucy said.

"But you will, and soon, and like I said, it'll be a spiffy one."

"If I do," Lucy said, "I'll use this piece of shit for nothing but scrub rags."

She let go of the cloth. The branch had scratched her neck and she touched it with her finger, confirmed that it wasn't bleeding. Had the locket been around her neck, the chain might have snapped, but it was in her pocket. Or so he assumed. If she'd forgotten it in the haste of packing, now didn't seem the time to bring it up.

As they continued their descent, he thought again about what would happen once they were safely free. He was starting to see a roughness about Lucy that her youth and country ways had masked. Perhaps he could take her with him beyond the first stop. He'd worked with a whore in Atlanta once, let her go in and distract a clerk while he took whatever they could fence. The whore hadn't been as young and innocent seeming as Lucy. Even Lucy's plainness would be an advantage—harder to describe her to the law. Maybe tonight in the hotel room she'd give him another reason to let her tag along awhile.

The trail curved and then went uphill. Surely for the last time, he figured, and told himself he'd be damn glad to be back in a place where a man didn't have to be half goat to get somewhere. Sinkler searched through the branches and leaves for a brick smokestack, the glint of a train rail. They were both breathing harder now, and even Lucy was looking tuckered.

Up ahead, another seep crossed the path and Sinkler paused. "I'm going to sip me some more water."

"We're almost there," Lucy said.

He heard it then, the rasping plunge of metal into dirt. The rhododendron was too thick to see through. Whatever it was, it meant they were indeed near civilization.

I guess we are," he said, but Lucy had already gone ahead.

As Sinkler hitched the sagging pants up yet again, he decided that the first thing he'd do after buying the tickets was find a clothing store or gooseberry a clothesline. He didn't want to look like a damn hobo. Even in town, they might have to walk a ways for water, so Sinkler kneeled. Someone whistled near the ridge and the rasping stopped. As he pressed his palm into the sand, he saw that a handprint was already there beside it, his handprint. Sinkler studied it awhile, than slowly rocked back until his buttocks touched his shoe heels. He stared at the two star-shaped indentations, water slowly filling the new one.

No one would hear the shot, he knew. And, in a few weeks, when autumn came and the trees started to shed, the upturned earth would be completely obscured. Leaves rustled as someone approached. The footsteps paused, and Sinkler heard the soft click of a safety being released. The leaves rustled again, but he was too worn out to run. They'd want the clothes as well as the money, he told himself, and there was no reason to prolong any of it. His trembling fingers clasped the shirt's top button, pushed it through the slit in the chambray.

THE WAY UP TO HEAVEN
Roald Dahl

["The Way Up to Heaven" by Roald Dahl from *Kiss Kiss*, 1954. Reprinted by permission of David Higham Associates Limited.]

All her life, Mrs. Foster had had an almost pathological fear of missing a train, a plane, a boat, or even a theatre curtain. In other respects, she was not a particularly nervous woman, but the mere thought of being late on occasions like these would throw her into such a state of nerves that she would begin to twitch. It was nothing much—just a tiny vellicating muscle in the corner of the left eye, like a secret wink—but the annoying thing was that it refused to disappear until an hour or so after the train or plane or whatever it was had been safely caught.

It was really extraordinary how in certain people a simple apprehension about a thing like catching a train can grow into a serious obsession. At least half an hour before it was time to leave the house for the station, Mrs. Foster would step out of the elevator all ready to go, with hat and coat and gloves, and then, being quite unable to sit down, she would flutter and fidget about from room to room until her husband, who must have been well aware of her state, finally emerged from his privacy and suggested in a cool dry voice that perhaps they had better be going now, had they not?

Mr. Foster may possibly have had a right to be irritated by this foolishness of his wife's, but he could have had no excuse for increasing her misery by keeping her waiting unnecessarily. Mind you, it is by no means certain that this is what he did, yet whenever they were to go somewhere, his timing was so accurate—just a minute or two late, you understand—and his manner so bland that it was hard to believe he wasn't purposely inflicting a nasty private little torture of his own on the unhappy lady. And one thing he must have known—that she would never dare to call out and tell him to hurry. He had disciplined her too well for that. He must also have known that if he was prepared to wait even beyond the last moment of safety, he could drive her nearly into hysterics. On one or two special occasions in the later years of their married life, it seemed almost as though he had *wanted* to miss the train simply in order to intensify the poor woman's suffering.

Assuming (though one cannot be sure) that the husband was guilty, what made his attitude doubly unreasonable was the fact that, with the exception of this one small irrepressible foible, Mrs. Foster was and always had been a good and loving wife. For over thirty years, she had served him loyally and well. There was no doubt about this. Even she, a very modest woman, was aware of it, and although she had for years refused to let herself believe that Mr. Foster would ever consciously torment her, there had been times recently when she had caught herself beginning to wonder. Mr. Eugene Foster, who was nearly seventy years old, lived with his wife in a large six story house in New York City, on East Sixty-second Street, and they had four servants. It was a gloomy place, and few people came to visit them. But on this particular morning in January, the house had come alive and there was a great deal of bustling about. One maid was distributing bundles of dust sheets to every room, while another was draping them over the furniture. The butler was bringing down suitcases and putting them in the hall. The cook kept popping up from the kitchen to have a word with the butler, and Mrs. Foster herself, in an old-fashioned fur coat and with a black hat on the top of her head, was flying from room to room and pretending to supervise these operations. Actually, she was thinking of nothing at all except that she was going to miss her plane if her husband didn't come out of his study soon and get ready.

"What time is it, Walker?" she said to the butler as she passed him.

"It's ten minutes past nine, Madam."

"And has the car come?"

"Yes, Madam, it's waiting. I'm just going to put the luggage in now."

"It takes an hour to get to Idlewild," she said. "My plane leaves at eleven. I have to be there half an hour beforehand for the formalities. 1 shall be late. I just know I'm going to be late."

"I think you have plenty of time, Madam," the butler said kindly. "I warned Mr. Foster that you must leave at nine-fifteen. There's still another five minutes."

"Yes, Walker, I know, I know. But get the luggage in quickly, will you please?"

She began walking up and down the hall, and whenever the butler came by, she asked him the time. This, she kept telling herself, was the one plane she must not miss. It had taken months to persuade her husband to allow her to go. If she missed it, he might easily decide that she should cancel the whole thing. And the trouble was that he insisted on coming to the airport to see her off.

"Dear God," she said aloud, "I'm going to miss it. I know, I know, I *know* I'm going to miss it." The little muscle beside the left eye was twitching madly now. The eyes themselves were very close to tears.

"What time is it, Walker?"

"It's eighteen minutes past, Madam."

"Now I really will miss it!" she cried. "Oh, I wish he would come!"

This was an important journey for Mrs. Foster. She was going all alone to Paris to visit her daughter, her only child, who was married to a Frenchman. Mrs. Foster didn't care much for the Frenchman, but she was fond of her daughter, and, more than that, she had developed a great yearning to set eyes on her three grandchildren. She knew them only from the many photographs that she had received and that she kept putting up all over the house. They were beautiful, these children. She doted on them, and each time a new picture arrived she would carry it away and sit with it for a long time, staring at it lovingly and searching the small faces for signs of that old satisfying blood likeness that meant so much. And now, lately, she had come more and more to feel that she did not really wish to live out her days in a place where she could not be near these children, and have them visit her, and take them out for walks, and buy them presents, and watch them grow. She knew, of course, that it was wrong and in a way disloyal to have thoughts like these while her husband was still alive. She knew also that although he was no longer active in his many enterprises, he would never consent to leave New York and live in Paris. It was a miracle that he had ever agreed to let her fly over there alone for six weeks to visit them. But, oh, how she wished she could live there always, and be close to them!

"Walker, what time is it?"

"Twenty-two minutes past, Madam."

As he spoke, a door opened and Mr. Foster came into the hall. He stood for a moment, looking intently at his wife, and she looked back at him—at this diminutive but still quite dapper old man with the huge bearded face that bore such an astonishing resemblance to those old photographs of Andrew Carnegie.

"Well," he said, "I suppose perhaps we'd better get going fairly soon if you want to catch that plane."

"Yes, dear—*yes*! Everything's ready. The car's waiting."

"That's good," he said. With his head over to one side, he was watching her closely. He had a peculiar way of cocking the head and then moving it in a series of small, rapid jerks. Because of this and because he was clasping his hands up high in front of him, near the chest, he was somehow like a squirrel standing there—a quick clever old squirrel from the Park.

"Here's Walker with your coat, dear. Put it on."

"I'll be with you in a moment," he said. "I'm just going to wash my hands."

She waited for him, and the tall butler stood beside her, holding the coat and the hat.

"Walker, will I miss it?"

"No, Madam," the butler said. "I think you'll make it all right."

Then Mr. Foster appeared again, and the butler helped him on with his coat. Mrs. Foster hurried outside and got into the hired Cadillac. Her husband came after her, but he walked down the steps of the house slowly, pausing halfway to observe the sky and to sniff the cold morning air.

"It looks a bit foggy," he said as he sat down beside her in the car. "And it's always worse out there at the airport. I shouldn't be surprised if the flight's cancelled already."

"Don't say that, dear—*please*."

They didn't speak again until the car had crossed over the river to Long Island.

"I arranged everything with the servants," Mr. Foster said. "They're all going off today. I gave them half-pay for six weeks and told Walker I'd send him a telegram when we wanted them back."

"Yes," she said. "He told me."

"I'll move into the club tonight. It'll be a nice change staying at the club."

"Yes, dear. I'll write to you."

"I'll call in at the house occasionally to see that everything's all right and to pick up the mail."

"But don't you really think Walker should stay there all the time to look after things?" she asked meekly.

"Nonsense. It's quite unnecessary. And anyway, I'd have to pay him full wages."

"Oh yes," she said. "Of course."

"What's more, you never know what people get up to when they're left alone in a house," Mr. Foster announced, and with that he took out a cigar and, after snipping off the end with a silver cutter, lit it with a gold lighter.

She sat still in the car with her hands clasped together tight under the rug.

"Will you write to me?" she asked.

"I'll see," he said. "But I doubt it. You know I don't hold with letter-writing unless there's something specific to say."

"Yes, dear, I know. So don't you bother."

They drove on, along Queen's Boulevard, and as they approached the flat marshland on which Idlewild is built, the fog began to thicken and the car had to slow down.

"Oh dear!" cried Mrs. Foster. "I'm *sure* I'm going to miss it now! What time is it?"

"Stop fussing," the old man said. "It doesn't matter anyway. It's bound to be cancelled now. They never fly in this sort of weather. I don't know why you bothered to come out."

She couldn't be sure, but it seemed to her that there was suddenly a new note in his voice, and she turned to look at him. It was difficult to observe any change in his expression under all that hair. The mouth was what counted. She wished, as she had so often before, that she could see the mouth clearly. The eyes never showed anything except when he was in a rage.

"Of course," he went on, "if by any chance it *does* go, then I agree with you—you'll be certain to miss it now. Why don't you resign yourself to that?"

She turned away and peered through the window at the fog. It seemed to be getting thicker as they went along, and now she could only just make out the edge of the road and the margin of grassland beyond it. She knew that her husband was still looking at her. She glanced at him again, and this time she noticed with a kind of horror that he was staring intently at the little place in the corner of her left eye where she could feel the muscle twitching.

"Won't you?" he said.

"Won't I what?"

"Be sure to miss it now if it goes. We can't drive fast in this muck."

He didn't speak to her any more after that. The car crawled on and on. The driver had a yellow lamp directed on to the edge of the road, and this helped him to keep going. Other lights, some white and some yellow, kept coming out of the fog towards them, and there was an especially bright one that followed close behind them all the time.

Suddenly, the driver stopped the car.

"There!" Mr. Foster cried. "We're stuck. I knew it."

"No, sir," the driver said, turning round. "I've made it. This is the airport."

Without a word, Mrs. Foster jumped out and hurried through the main entrance into the building. There was a mass of people inside, mostly disconsolate passengers standing around the ticket counters. She pushed her way through and spoke to the clerk.

"Yes," he said. "Your flight is temporarily postponed. But please don't go away.

"We're expecting the weather to clear any moment."

She went back to her husband who was still sitting in the car and told him the news. "But don't you wait, dear," she said. "There's no sense in that."

"I won't," he answered. "So long as the driver can get me back. Can you get me back, driver?"

"I think so," the man said.

"Is the luggage out?"

"Yes, sir."

"Good-bye, dear," Mrs. Foster said, leaning into the car and giving her husband a small kiss on the coarse grey fur of his cheek.

"Good-bye," he answered. "Have a good trip."

The car drove off, and Mrs. Foster was left alone.

The rest of the day was a sort of nightmare for her. She sat for hour after hour on a bench, as close to the airline counter as possible, and every thirty minutes or so she could get up and ask the clerk if the situation had changed. She always received the same reply—that she must continue to wait, because the fog might blow away at any moment. It wasn't until after six in the evening that the loudspeakers finally announced that the flight had been postponed until eleven o'clock the next morning.

Mrs. Foster didn't quite know what to do when she heard this news. She stayed sitting on her bench for at least another half-hour, wondering, in a tired, hazy sort of way, where she might go to spend the night. She hated to leave the airport. She didn't wish to see her husband. She was terrified that in one way or another he would eventually manage to prevent her from getting to France. She would have liked to remain just where she was, sitting on the bench the whole night through. That would be the safest. But she was already exhausted, and it didn't take her long to realize that this was a ridiculous thing for an elderly lady to do. So in the end she went to a phone and called the house.

Her husband, who was on the point of leaving for the club, answered it himself. She told him the news, and asked whether the servants were still there.

"They've all gone," he said.

"In that case, dear, I'll just get myself a room somewhere for the night. And don't you bother yourself about it at all."

"That would be foolish," he said. "You've got a large house here at your disposal. Use it."

"But, dear, it's *empty*."

"Then I'll stay with you myself."

"There's no food in the house. There's nothing."

"Then eat before you come in. Don't be so stupid, woman. Everything you do, you seem to want to make a fuss about it."

"Yes," she said. "I'm sorry. I'll get myself a sandwich here, and then I'll come on in."

Outside, the fog had cleared a little, but it was still a long, slow drive in the taxi, and she didn't arrive back at the house on Sixty-second Street until fairly late.

Her husband emerged from his study when he heard her coming in. "Well," he said, standing by the study door, "how was Paris?"

"We leave at eleven in the morning," she answered. "It's definite."

"You mean if the fog clears."

"It's clearing now. There's a wind coming up."

"You look tired," he said. "You must have had an anxious day."

"It wasn't very comfortable. I think I'll go straight to bed."

"I've ordered a car for the morning." he said. "Nine o'clock."

"Oh, thank you, dear. And I certainly hope you're not going to bother to come all the way to see me off."

"No," he said slowly. "I don't think I will. But there's no reason why you shouldn't drop me at the club on your way."

She looked at him, and at that moment he seemed to be standing a long way off from her, beyond some borderline. He was suddenly so small and far away that she couldn't be sure what he was doing, or what he was thinking, or even what he was.

"The club is downtown," she said. "It isn't on the way to the airport."

"But you'll have plenty of time, my dear. Don't you want to drop me at the club?"

"Oh, yes—of course."

"That's good. Then I'll see you in the morning at nine."

She went up to her bedroom on the second floor, and she was so exhausted from her day that she fell asleep soon after she lay down.

Next morning, Mrs. Foster was up early, and by eight-thirty she was downstairs and ready to leave.

Shortly after nine, her husband appeared. "Did you make any coffee?" he asked.

"No, dear. I thought you'd get a nice breakfast at the club. The car is here. It's been waiting. I'm all ready to go."

They were standing in the hall—they always seemed to be meeting in the hall nowadays—she with her hat and coat and purse, he in a curiously cut Edwardian jacket with high lapels.

"Your luggage?"

"It's at the airport."

"Ah yes," he said. "Of course. And if you're going to take me to the club first, I suppose we'd better get going fairly soon, hadn't we?"

"Yes!" she cried. "Oh, yes—*please!*"

"I'm just going to get a few cigars. I'll be right with you. You get in the car."

She turned and went out to where the chauffeur was standing, and he opened the car door for her as she approached.

"What time is it?" she asked him.

"About nine-fifteen."

Mr. Foster came out five minutes later, and watching him as he walked slowly down the steps, she noticed that his legs were like goat's legs in those narrow stovepipe trousers that he wore. As on the day before, he paused half-way down to sniff the air and to examine the sky. The weather was still not quite clear, but there was a wisp of sun coming through the mist.

"Perhaps you'll be lucky this time," he said as he settled himself beside her in the car.

"Hurry, please," she said to the chauffer. "Don't bother about the rug. I'll arrange the rug. Please get going. I'm late."

The man went back to his seat behind the wheel and started the engine.

"*Just* a moment!" Mr. Foster said suddenly. "Hold it a moment, chauffeur, will you?"

"What is it, dear?" She saw him searching the pockets of his overcoat.

"I had a little present I wanted you to take to Ellen," he said. "Now, where on earth is it? I'm sure I had it in my hand as I came down."

"I never saw you carrying anything. What sort of present?"

"A little box wrapped up in white paper. I forgot to give it to you yesterday. I don't want to forget it today."

"A little box!" Mrs. Foster cried. "I never saw any little box!" She began hunting frantically in the back of the car.

Her husband continued searching through the pockets of his coat. Then he unbuttoned the coat and felt around in his jacket. "Confound it," he said, "I must've left it in my bedroom. I won't be a moment."

"Oh, *please!*" she cried. "We haven't got time! Please leave it! You can mail it. It's only one of those silly combs anyway. You're always giving her combs."

"And what's wrong with combs, may I ask?" he said, furious that she should have forgotten herself for once.

"Nothing, dear, I'm sure. But . . ."

"Stay here!" he commanded. "I'm going to get it."

"Be quick, dear! Oh, *please* be quick!"

She sat still, waiting and waiting.

"Chauffeur, what time is it?"

The man had a wristwatch, which he consulted. "I make it nearly nine-thirty."

"Can we get to the airport in an hour?"

"Just about."

At this point, Mrs. Foster suddenly spotted a corner of something white wedged down in the crack of the seat on the side where her husband had been sitting. She reached over and pulled out a small paper-wrapped box, and at the same time she couldn't help noticing that it was wedged down firm and deep, as though with the help of a pushing hand.

"Here it is!" she cried. "I've found it! Oh dear, and now he'll be up there forever searching for it! Chauffeur, quickly—run in and call him down, will you please?"

The chauffeur, a man with a small rebellious Irish mouth, didn't care very much for any of this, but he climbed out of the car and went up the steps to the front door of the house. Then he turned and came back. "Door's locked," he announced. "You got a key?"

"Yes—wait a minute." She began hunting madly in her purse. The little face was screwed up tight with anxiety, the lips pushed outward like a spout.

"Here it is! No—I'll go myself. It'll be quicker. I know where he'll be."

She hurried out of the car and up the steps to the front door, holding the key in one hand. She slid the key into the keyhole and was about to turn it—and then she stopped. Her head came up, and she stood there absolutely motionless, her whole body arrested right in the middle of all this hurry to turn the key and get into the house, and she waited—five, six, seven, eight, nine, ten seconds, she waited. The way she was standing there, with her head in the air and the body so tense, it seemed as though she were listening for the repetition of some sound that she had heard a moment before from a place far away inside the house.

Yes—quite obviously she was listening. Her whole attitude was a *listening* one. She appeared actually to be moving one of her ears closer and closer to the door. Now it was right up against the door, and for still another few seconds she remained in that position, head up, ear to door, hand on key, about to enter but not entering, trying instead, or so it seemed, to hear and to analyze these sounds that were coming faintly from this place deep within the house.

Then, all at once, she sprang to life again. She withdrew the key from the door and came running back down the steps.

"It's too late!" she cried to the chauffeur. "I can't wait for him, I simply can't. I'll miss the plane. Hurry now, driver, hurry! To the airport!"

The chauffeur, had he been watching her closely, might have noticed that her face had turned absolutely white and that the whole expression had suddenly altered. There was no longer that rather soft and silly look. A peculiar hardness had settled itself upon the features. The little mouth, usually so flabby, was now tight and thin, the eyes were bright, and the voice, when she spoke, carried a new note of authority.

"Hurry, driver, hurry!"

"Isn't your husband traveling with you?" the man asked, astonished.

"Certainly not! I was only going to drop him at the club. It won't matter. He'll understand. He'll get a cab. Don't sit there talking, man. *Get going*! I've got a plane to catch for Paris!"

With Mrs. Foster urging him from the back seat, the man drove fast all the way, and she caught her plane with a few minutes to spare. Soon she was high up over the Atlantic, reclining comfortably in her airplane chair, listening to the hum of the motors, heading for Paris at last. The new mood was still with her. She felt remarkably strong and, in a queer sort of way, wonderful. She was a trifle breathless with it all, but this was more from pure astonishment at what she had done than anything else, and as the plane flew farther and farther away from New York and East Sixty-second Street, a great sense of calmness began to settle upon her.

By the time she reached Paris, she was just as strong and cool and calm as she could wish.

She met her grandchildren, and they were even more beautiful in the flesh than in their photographs. They were like angels, she told herself, so beautiful they were. And every day she took them for walks, and fed them cakes, and bought them presents, and told them charming stories.

Once a week, on Tuesdays, she wrote a letter to her husband a nice, chatty letter—full of news and gossip, which always ended with the words Now be sure to take your meals regularly, dear, although this is something I'm afraid you may not be doing when I'm not with you.'

When the six weeks were up, everybody was sad that she had to return to America, to her husband. Everybody, that is, except her. Surprisingly, she didn't seem to mind as much as one might have expected, and when she kissed them all good-bye, there was something in her manner and in the things she said that appeared to hint at the possibility of a return in the not too distant future.

However, like the faithful wife she was, she did not overstay her time. Exactly six weeks after she had arrived, she sent a cable to her husband and caught the plane back to New York.

Arriving at Idlewild, Mrs. Foster was interested to observe that there was no car to meet her. It is possible that she might even have been a little amused. But she was extremely calm and did not over tip the porter who helped her into a taxi with her baggage.

New York was colder than Paris, and there were lumps of dirty snow lying in the gutters of the streets. The taxi drew up before the house on Sixty-second Street, and Mrs. Foster persuaded the driver to carry her two large cases to the top of the steps. Then she paid him off and rang the bell. She waited, but there was no answer. Just to make sure, she rang again, and she could hear it tinkling shrilly far away in the pantry, at the back of the house. But still no one came.

So she took out her own key and opened the door herself.

The first thing she saw as she entered was a great pile of mail lying on the floor where it had fallen after being slipped through the letter box. The place was dark and cold. A dust sheet was still draped over the grandfather clock. In spite of the cold, the atmosphere was peculiarly oppressive, and there was a faint and curious odor in the air that she had never smelled before.

She walked quickly across the hall and disappeared for a moment around the corner to the left, at the back. There was something deliberate and purposeful about this action; she had the air of a woman who is off to investigate a rumor or to confirm a suspicion. And when she returned a few seconds later, there was a little glimmer of satisfaction on her face.

She paused in the center of the hall, as though wondering what to do next. Then, suddenly, she turned and went across into her husband's study. On the desk she found his address book, and after hunting through it for a while she picked up the phone and dialed a number.

"Hello," she said. "Listen—this is Nine East Sixty-second Street. . . . Yes, that's right. Could you send someone round as soon as possible, do you think? Yes, it seems to be stuck between the second and third floors. At least, that's where the indicator's pointing. . . . Right away? Oh, that's very kind of you. You see, my legs aren't any too good for walking up a lot of stairs. Thank you so much. Good-bye."

She replaced the receiver and sat there at her husband's desk, patiently waiting for the man who would be coming soon to repair the elevator.

THIS IS WHAT IT MEANS TO SAY PHOENIX, ARIZONA
Sherman Alexie

Just after Victor lost his job at the BIA, he also found out that his father had died of a heart attack in Phoenix, Arizona. Victor hadn't seen his father in a few years, only talked to him on the telephone once or twice, but there still was a genetic pain, which was soon to be pain as real and immediate as a broken bone.

Victor didn't have any money. Who does have money on a reservation, except the cigarette and fireworks salespeople? His father had a savings account waiting to be claimed, but Victor needed to find a way to get to Phoenix. Victor's mother was just as poor as he was, and the rest of his family didn't have any use at all for him. So Victor called the Tribal Council.

"Listen," Victor said. "My father just died. I need some money to get to Phoenix to make arrangements."

"Now, Victor," the council said. "You know we're having a difficult time financially."

"But I thought the council had special funds set aside for stuff like this."

"Now, Victor, we do have some money available for the proper return of tribal members' bodies. But I don't think we have enough to bring your father all the way back from Phoenix."

"Well," Victor said. "It ain't going to cost all that much. He had to be cremated. Things were kind of ugly. He died of a heart attack in his trailer and nobody found him for a week. It was really hot, too. You get the picture."

"Now, Victor, we're sorry for your loss and the circumstances. But we can really only afford to give you one hundred dollars."

"That's not even enough for a plane ticket."

"Well, you might consider driving down to Phoenix."

"I don't have a car. Besides, I was going to drive my father's pickup back up here."

"Now, Victor," the council said. "We're sure there is somebody who could drive you to Phoenix. Or is there somebody who could lend you the rest of the money?"

"You know there ain't nobody around with that kind of money."

"Well, we're sorry, Victor, but that's the best we can do."

Victor accepted the Tribal Council's offer. What else could he do? So he signed the proper papers, picked up his check, and walked over to the Trading Post to cash it.

While Victor stood in line, he watched Thomas Builds-the-Fire standing near the magazine rack, talking to himself. Like he always did. Thomas was a storyteller that nobody wanted to listen to. That's like being a dentist in a town where everybody has false teeth.

Victor and Thomas Builds-the-Fire were the same age, had grown up and played in the dirt together. Ever since Victor could remember, it was Thomas who always had something to say.

Once, when they were seven years old, when Victor's father still lived with the family, Thomas closed his eyes and told Victor this story: "Your father's heart is weak. He is afraid of his own family. He is afraid of you. Late at night he sits in the dark. Watches the television until there's nothing but that white noise. Sometimes he feels like he wants to buy a motorcycle and ride away. He wants to run and hide. He doesn't want to be found."

Thomas Builds-the-Fire had known that Victor's father was going to leave, knew it before anyone. Now Victor stood in the Trading Post with a one-hundred-dollar check in his hand, wondering if Thomas knew that Victor's father was dead, if he knew what was going to happen next.

Just then Thomas looked at Victor, smiled, and walked over to him.

"Victor, I'm sorry about your father," Thomas said.

"How did you know about it?" Victor asked.

"I heard it on the wind. I heard it from the birds. I felt it in the sunlight. Also, your mother was just in here crying."

"Oh," Victor said and looked around the Trading Post. All the other Indians stared, surprised that Victor was even talking to Thomas. Nobody talked to Thomas because he told the same damn stories over and over again. Victor was embarrassed, but he thought that Thomas might be able to help him. Victor felt a sudden need for tradition.

"I can lend you the money you need," Thomas said suddenly. "But you have to take me with you."

"I can't take your money," Victor said. "I mean, I haven't hardly talked to you in years. We're not really friends anymore."

"I didn't say we were friends. I said you had to take me with you."

"Let me think about it."

Victor went home with his one hundred dollars and sat at the kitchen table. He held his head in his hands and thought about Thomas Builds-the-Fire, remembered little details, tears and scars, the bicycle they shared for a summer, so many stories.

Thomas Builds-the-Fire sat on the bicycle, waited in Victor's yard. He was ten years old and skinny. His hair was dirty because it was the Fourth of July.

"Victor," Thomas yelled. "Hurry up. We're going to miss the fireworks."

After a few minutes, Victor ran out of his house, jumped the porch railing, and landed gracefully on the sidewalk.

"And the judges award him a 9.95, the highest score of the summer," Thomas said, clapped, laughed.

"That was perfect, cousin," Victor said. "And it's my. turn to ride the bike."

Thomas gave up the bike and they headed for the fairgrounds. It was nearly dark and the fireworks were about to start.

"You know," Thomas said. "It's strange how us Indians celebrate the Fourth of July. It ain't like it was our independence everybody was fighting for."

"You think about things too much," Victor said. "It's just supposed to be fun. Maybe junior will be there."

"Which Junior? Everybody on this reservation is named junior."

And they both laughed.

The fireworks were small, hardly more than a few bottle rockets and a fountain. But it was enough for two Indian boys. Years later, they would need much more.

Afterwards, sitting in the dark, fighting off mosquitoes, Victor turned to Thomas Builds-the-Fire.

"Hey," Victor said. "Tell me a story."

Thomas closed his eyes and told this story: "There were these two Indian boys who wanted to be warriors. But it was too late to be warriors in the old way. All the horses were gone. So the two Indian boys stole a car and drove to the city. They parked the stolen car in front of the police station and then hitchhiked back home to the reservation. When they got back, all their friends cheered and their parents' eyes shone with pride. You were very brave, everybody said to the two Indian boys. Very brave."

"Ya-hey," Victor said. "That's a good one. I wish I could be a warrior."

"Me, too," Thomas said.

They went home together in the dark, Thomas on the bike now, Victor on foot. They walked through shadows and light from streetlamps.

"We've come a long ways," Thomas said. "We have outdoor lighting."

"All I need is the stars," Victor said. "And besides, you still think about things too much."

They separated then, each headed for home, both laughing all the way.

Victor sat at his kitchen table. He counted his one hundred dollars again and again. He knew he needed more to make it to Phoenix and back. He knew he needed Thomas Builds-the-Fire. So he put his money in his wallet and opened the front door to find Thomas on the porch.

"Ya-hey, Victor," Thomas said. "I knew you'd call me."

Thomas walked into the living room and sat down on Victor's favorite chair.

"I've got some money saved up," Thomas said. "It's enough to get us down there, but you have to get us back."

"I've got this hundred dollars," Victor said. "And my dad had a savings account I'm going to claim."

"How much in your dad's account?"

"Enough. A few hundred."

"Sounds good. When we leaving?"

*   *   *

When they were fifteen and had long since stopped being friends, Victor and Thomas got into a fistfight. That is Victor was really drunk and beat Thomas up for no reason at all. All the other Indian boys stood around and watched it happen. Junior was there and so were Lester, Seymour, and a lot of others. The beating might have gone on until Thomas was dead if Norma Many Horses hadn't come along and stopped it.

"Hey, you boys," Norma yelled and jumped out of her car.

"Leave him alone."

If it had been someone else, even another man, the Indian boys would've just ignored the warnings. But Norma was a warrior. She was powerful. She could have picked up any two of the boys and smashed their skulls together. But worse than that, she would have dragged them all over to some tipi and made them listen to some elder tell a dusty old story.

The Indian boys scattered, and Norma walked over to Thomas and picked him up.

"Hey, little man, are you okay?" she asked.

Thomas gave her a thumbs up.

"Why they always picking on you?"

Thomas shook his head, closed his eyes, but no stories came to him, no words or music. He just wanted to go home, to lie in his bed and let his dreams tell his stories for him.

Thomas Builds-the-Fire and Victor sat next to each other in the airplane, coach section. A tiny white woman had the window seat. She was busy twisting her body into pretzels. She was flexible.

"I have to ask," Thomas said, and Victor closed his eyes in embarrassment.

"Don't," Victor said.

"Excuse me, miss," Thomas asked. "Are you a gymnast or something?"

"There's no something about it," she said. "I was first alternate on the 1980 Olympic team."

"Really?" Thomas asked.

"Really."

"I mean, you used to be a world-class athlete?" Thomas asked.

"My husband still thinks I am."

Thomas Builds-the-Fire smiled. She was a mental gymnast, too. She pulled her leg straight up against her body so that she could've kissed her kneecap.

"I wish I could do that," Thomas said.

Victor was ready to jump out of the plane. Thomas, that crazy Indian storyteller with ratty old braids and broken teeth, was flirting with a beautiful Olympic gymnast. Nobody back home on the reservation would ever believe it.

"Well," the gymnast said. "It's easy. Try it."

Thomas grabbed at his leg and tried to pull it up into the same position as the gymnast. He couldn't even come close, which made Victor and the gymnast laugh.

"Hey," she asked. "You two are Indian, right?"

"Full-blood," Victor said.

"Not me," Thomas said. "I'm half magician on my mother's side and half clown on my father's."

They all laughed.

"What are your names?" she asked.

"Victor and Thomas."

"Mine is Cathy. Pleased to meet you all."

The three of them talked for the duration of the flight. Cathy the gymnast complained about the government, how they screwed the 1980 Olympic team by boycotting.

"Sounds like you all got a lot in common with Indians," Thomas said.

Nobody laughed.

After the plane landed in Phoenix and they had all found their way to the terminal, Cathy the gymnast smiled and waved good-bye.

"She was really nice," Thomas said.

"Yeah, but everybody talks to everybody on airplanes," Victor said. "It's too bad we can't always be that way."

"You always used to tell me I think too much," Thomas said. "Now it sounds like you do."

"Maybe I caught it from you."

"Yeah."

Thomas and Victor rode in a taxi to the trailer where Victor's father died.

"Listen," Victor said as they stopped in front of the trailer. "I never told you I was sorry for beating you up that time."

"Oh, it was nothing. We were just kids and you were drunk."

"Yeah, but I'm still sorry."

"That's all right."

Victor paid for the taxi and the two of them stood in the hot Phoenix summer. They could smell the trailer.

"This ain't going to be nice," Victor said. "You don't have to go in."

"You're going to need help."

Victor walked to the front door and opened it. The stink rolled out and made them both gag. Victor's father had lain in that trailer for a week in hundred-degree temperatures before anyone found him. And the only reason anyone found him was because of the smell. They needed dental records to identify him. That's exactly what the coroner said. They needed dental records.

"Oh, man," Victor said. "I don't know if I can do this."

"Well, then don't."

"But there might be something valuable in there."

"I thought his money was in the bank."

"It is. I was talking about pictures and letters and stuff like that."

"Oh," Thomas said as he held his breath and followed Victor into the trailer.

*   *   *

When Victor was twelve, he stepped into an underground wasp nest. His foot was caught in the hole, and no matter how hard he struggled, Victor couldn't pull free. He might have died there, stung a thousand times, if Thomas Builds-the-Fire had not come by.

"Run," Thomas yelled and pulled Victor's foot from the hole. They ran then, hard as they ever had, faster than Billy Mills, faster than Jim Thorpe, faster than the wasps could fly.

Victor and Thomas ran until they couldn't breathe, ran until it was cold and dark outside, ran until they were lost and it took hours to find their way home. All the way back, Victor counted his stings.

"Seven," Victor said. "My lucky number."

Victor didn't find much to keep in the trailer. Only a photo album and a stereo. Everything else had that smell stuck in it or was useless anyway.

"I guess this is all," Victor said. "It ain't much."

"Better than nothing," Thomas said.

"Yeah, and I do have the pickup."

"Yeah," Thomas said. "It's in good shape."

"Dad was good about that stuff."

"Yeah, I remember your dad."

"Really?" Victor asked. "What do you remember?"

Thomas Builds-the-Fire closed his eyes and told this story: "I remember when I had this dream that told me to go to Spokane, to stand by the Falls in the middle of the city and wait for a sign. I knew I had to go there but I didn't have a car. Didn't have a license. I was only thirteen. So I walked all the way, took me all day, and I finally made it to the Falls. I stood there for an hour waiting. Then your dad came walking up. What the hell are you doing here? he asked me. I said, Waiting for a vision. Then your father said, All you're going to get here is mugged. So he drove me over to Denny's, bought me dinner, and then drove me home to the reservation. For a long time I was mad because I thought my dreams had lied to me. But they didn't. Your dad was my vision. Take care of each other is what my dreams were saying. Take care of each other."

Victor was quiet for a long time. He searched his mind for memories of his father, found the good ones, found a few bad ones, added it all up, and smiled.

"My father never told me about finding you in Spokane," Victor said.

"He said he wouldn't tell anybody. Didn't want me to get in trouble. But he said I had to watch out for you as part of the deal."

"Really?"

"Really. Your father said you would need the help. He was right."

"That's why you came down here with me, isn't it?" Victor asked.

"I came because of your father."

Victor and Thomas climbed into the pickup, drove over to the bank, and claimed the three hundred dollars in the savings account.

Thomas Builds-the-Fire could fly.

Once, he jumped off the roof of the tribal school and flapped his arms like a crazy eagle. And he flew. For a second, he hovered, suspended above all the other Indian boys who were too smart or too scared to jump.

"He's flying," junior yelled, and Seymour was busy looking for the trick wires or mirrors. But it was real. As real as the dirt when Thomas lost altitude and crashed to the ground.

He broke his arm in two places.

"He broke his wing," Victor chanted, and the other Indian boys joined in, made it a tribal song.

"He broke his wing, he broke his wing, he broke his wing," all the Indian boys chanted as they ran off, flapping their wings, wishing they could fly, too. They hated Thomas for his courage, his brief moment as a bird. Everybody has dreams about flying. Thomas flew.

One of his dreams came true for just a second, just enough to make it real.

Victor's father, his ashes, fit in one wooden box with enough left over to fill a cardboard box.

"He always was a big man," Thomas said.

Victor carried part of his father and Thomas carried the rest out to the pickup. They set him down carefully behind the seats, put a cowboy hat on the wooden box and a Dodgers cap on the cardboard box. That's the way it was supposed to be.

"Ready to head back home," Victor asked.

"It's going to be a long drive."

"Yeah, take a couple days, maybe."

"We can take turns," Thomas said.

"Okay," Victor said, but they didn't take turns. Victor drove for sixteen hours straight north, made it halfway up Nevada toward home before he finally pulled over.

"Hey, Thomas," Victor said. "You got to drive for a while."

"Okay."

Thomas Builds-the-Fire slid behind the wheel and started off down the road. All through Nevada, Thomas and Victor had been amazed at the lack of animal life, at the absence of water, of movement.

"Where is everything?" Victor had asked more than once.

Now when Thomas was finally driving they saw the first animal, maybe the only animal in Nevada. It was a long-eared jackrabbit.

"Look," Victor yelled. "It's alive."

Thomas and Victor were busy congratulating themselves on their discovery when the jackrabbit darted out into the road and under the wheels of the pickup.

"Stop the goddamn car," Victor yelled, and Thomas did stop, backed the pickup to the dead jackrabbit.

"Oh, man, he's dead," Victor said as he looked at the squashed animal.

"Really dead."

"The only thing alive in this whole state and we just killed it."

"I don't know," Thomas said. "I think it was suicide."

Victor looked around the desert, sniffed the air, felt the emptiness and loneliness, and nodded his head.

"Yeah," Victor said. "It had to be suicide."

"I can't believe this," Thomas said. "You drive for a thousand miles and there ain't even any bugs smashed on the windshield. I drive for ten seconds and kill the only living thing in Nevada."

Yeah," Victor said. "Maybe I should drive."

"Maybe you should."

Thomas Builds-the-Fire walked through the corridors of the tribal school by himself. Nobody wanted to be anywhere near him because of all those stories. Story after story.

Thomas closed his eyes and this story came to him: "We are all given one thing by which our lives are measured, one determination. Mine are the stories which can change or not change the world. It doesn't matter which as long as I continue to tell the stories. My father, he died on Okinawa in World War II, died fighting for this country, which had tried to kill him for years. My mother, she died giving birth to me, died while I was still inside her. She pushed me out into the world with her last breath. I have no brothers or sisters. I have only my stories which came to me before I even had the words to speak. I learned a thousand stories before I took my first thousand steps. They are all I have. It's all I can do."

Thomas Builds-the-Fire told his stories to all those who would stop and listen. He kept telling them long after people had stopped listening.

Victor and Thomas made it back to the reservation just as the sun was rising. It was the beginning of a new day on earth, but the same old shit on the reservation.

"Good morning," Thomas said.

"Good morning."

The tribe was waking up, ready for work, eating breakfast, reading the newspaper, just like everybody else does. Willene LeBret was out in her garden wearing a bathrobe. She waved when Thomas and Victor drove by.

"Crazy Indians made it," she said to herself and went back to her roses.

Victor stopped the pickup in front of Thomas Builds-the-Fire's HUD house. They both yawned, stretched a little, shook dust from their bodies.

"I'm tired," Victor said.

"Of everything," Thomas added.

They both searched for words to end the journey. Victor needed to thank Thomas for his help, for the money, and make the promise to pay it all back.

"Don't worry about the money," Thomas said. "It don't make any difference anyhow."

"Probably not, enit?"

"Nope."

Victor knew that Thomas would remain the crazy storyteller who talked to dogs and cars, who listened to the wind and pine trees. Victor knew that he couldn't really be friends with Thomas, even after all that had happened. It was cruel but it was real. As real as the ashes, as Victor's father, sitting behind the seats.

"I know how it is," Thomas said. "I know you ain't going to treat me any better than you did before. I know your friends would give you too much shit about it."

Victor was ashamed of himself. Whatever happened to the tribal ties, the sense of community? The only real thing he shared with anybody was a bottle and broken dreams. He owed Thomas something, anything.

"Listen," Victor said and handed Thomas the cardboard box which contained half of his father. "I want you to have this."

Thomas took the ashes and smiled, closed his eyes, and told this story: "I'm going to travel to Spokane Falls one last time and toss these ashes into the water. And your father will rise like a salmon, leap over the bridge, over me, and find his way home. It will be beautiful. His teeth will shine like silver, like a rainbow. He will rise, Victor, he will rise."

Victor smiled.

"I was planning on doing the same thing with my half," Victor said. "But I didn't imagine my father looking anything like a salmon. I thought it'd be like cleaning the attic or something. Like letting things go after they've stopped having any use."

"Nothing stops, cousin," Thomas said. "Nothing stops."

Thomas Builds-the-Fire got out of the pickup and walked up his driveway. Victor started the pickup and began the drive home.

"Wait," Thomas yelled suddenly from his porch. "I just got to ask one favor."

Victor stopped the pickup, leaned out the window, and shouted back. "What do you want?"

"Just one time when I'm telling a story somewhere, why don't you stop and listen?" Thomas asked.

"Just once?"

"Just once."

Victor waved his arms to let Thomas know that the deal was good. It was a fair trade, and that was all Victor had ever wanted from his whole life. So Victor drove his father's pickup toward home while Thomas went into his house, closed the door behind him, and heard a new story come to him in the silence afterwards.

TO BUILD A FIRE
Jack London

The day had dawned cold and gray when the man turned aside from the main Yukon trail. He climbed the high earth-bank where a little-traveled trail led east through the pine forest. It was a high bank, and he paused to breathe at the top. He excused the act to himself by looking at his watch. It was nine o'clock in the morning. There was no sun or promise of sun, although there was not a cloud in the sky. It was a clear day. However, there seemed to be an indescribable darkness over the face of things. That was because the sun was absent from the sky. This fact did not worry the man. He was not alarmed by the lack of sun. It had been days since he had seen the sun.

The man looked along the way he had come. The Yukon lay a mile wide and hidden under three feet of ice. On top of this ice were as many feet of snow. It was all pure white. North and south, as far as his eye could see, it was unbroken white. The one thing that relieved the whiteness was a thin dark line that curved from the pine-covered island to the south. It curved into the north, where it disappeared behind another pine-covered island. This dark line was the trail—the main trail. It led south 500 miles to the Chilcoot Pass, and salt water. It led north 75 miles to Dawson, and still farther on to the north a thousand miles to Nulato, and finally to St. Michael, on Bering Sea, a thousand miles and half a thousand more.

But all this—the distant trail, no sun in the sky, the great cold, and the strangeness of it all—had no effect on the man. It was not because he was long familiar with it. He was a newcomer in the land, and this was his first winter. The trouble with him was that he was not able to imagine. He was quick and alert in the things of life, but only in the things, and not in the significances. Fifty degrees below zero meant 80 degrees of frost. Such facts told him that it was cold and uncomfortable, and that was all. It did not lead him to consider his weaknesses as a creature affected by temperature. Nor did he think about man's general weakness, able to live only within narrow limits of heat and cold. From there, it did not lead him to thoughts of heaven and the meaning of a man's life. 50 degrees below zero meant a bite of frost that hurt and that must be guarded against by the use of mittens, ear coverings, warm moccasins, and thick socks. 50 degrees below zero was to him nothing more than 50 degrees below zero. That it should be more important than that was a thought that never entered his head.

As he turned to go, he forced some water from his mouth as an experiment. There was a sudden noise that surprised him. He tried it again. And again, in the air, before they could fall to the snow, the drops of water became ice that broke with a noise. He knew that at 50 below zero water from the mouth made a noise when it hit the snow. But this had done that in the air. Undoubtedly it was colder than 50 below. But exactly how much colder he did not know. But the temperature did not matter. He was headed for the old camp on Henderson Creek, where the boys were already. They had come across the mountain from the Indian Creek country. He had taken the long trail to look at the possibility of floating logs from the islands in the Yukon down the river when the ice melted. He would be in camp by six o'clock that evening. It would be a little after dark, but the boys would be there, a fire would be burning, and a hot supper would be ready. As he thought of lunch, he pressed his hand against the package under his jacket. It was also under his shirt, wrapped in a handkerchief, and lying for warmth against the naked skin. Otherwise, the bread would freeze. He smiled contentedly to himself as he thought of those pieces of bread, each of which enclosed a generous portion of fried bacon.

He plunged among the big pine trees. The trail was not well marked here. Several inches of snow had fallen since the last sled had passed. He was glad he was without a sled. Actually, he carried nothing but the lunch wrapped in the handkerchief. He was surprised, however, at the cold. It certainly was cold, he decided, as he rubbed his nose and face with his mittened hand. He had a good growth of hair on his face, but that did not protect his nose or the upper part of his face from the frosty air.

Following at the man's heels was a big native dog. It was a wolf dog, gray-coated and not noticeably different from its brother, the wild wolf. The animal was worried by the great cold. It knew that this was no time for traveling. Its own feeling was closer to the truth than the man's judgment. In reality, it was not merely colder than 50 below zero; it was colder than 60 below, than 70 below. It was 75 below zero. Because the freezing point is 32 above zero, it meant that there were 107 degrees of frost. The dog did not know anything about temperatures. Possibly in its brain there was no understanding of a condition of very cold, such as was in the man's brain. But the animal sensed the danger. Its ear made it question eagerly every movement of the man as if expecting him to go into camp or to seek shelter somewhere and build a fire. The dog had learned about fire, and it wanted fire. Otherwise, it would dig itself into the snow and find shelter from the cold air.

The frozen moistness of its breathing had settled on its fur in a fine powder of frost. The hair on the man's face was similarly frosted, but more solidly. It took the form of ice and increased with every warm, moist breath from his mouth. Also, the man had tobacco in his mouth. The ice held his lips so tightly together that he could not empty the juice from his mouth. The result was a long piece of yellow ice hanging from his lips. If he fell down it would break, like glass, into many pieces. He expected the ice formed by the tobacco juice, having been out twice before when it was very cold. But it had not been as cold as this, he knew. He continued through the level forest for several miles. Then he went down a bank to the frozen path of a small stream.

This was Henderson Creek and he knew he was ten miles from where the stream divided. He looked at his watch. It was ten o'clock. He was traveling at the rate of four miles an hour. Thus, he figured that he would arrive where the stream divided at half-past twelve. He decided he would eat his lunch when he arrived there.

The dog followed again at his heels, with its tail hanging low, as the man started to walk along the frozen stream. The old sled trail could be seen, but a dozen inches of snow covered the marks of the last sleds. In a month no man had traveled up or down that silent creek. The man went steadily ahead. He was not much of a thinker. At that moment he had nothing to think about except that he would eat lunch at the stream's divide and that at six o'clock he would be in camp with the boys. There was nobody to talk to; and, had there been, speech would not have been possible because of the ice around his mouth. Once in a while the thought repeated itself that it was very cold and that he had never experienced such cold.

As he walked along he rubbed his face and nose with the back of his mittened hand. He did this without thinking, frequently changing hands. But, with all his rubbing, the instant he stopped, his face and nose became numb. His face would surely be frozen. He knew that and he was sorry that he had not worn the sort of nose guard Bud wore when it was cold. Such a guard passed across the nose and covered the entire face. But it did not matter much, he decided. What was a little frost? A bit painful, that was all. It was never serious.

Empty as the man's mind was of thoughts, he was most observant. He noticed the changes in the creek, the curves and the bends. And always he noted where he placed his feet. Once, coming around a bend, he moved suddenly to the side, like a frightened horse. He curved away from the place where he had been walking and retraced his steps several feet along the trail. He knew the creek was frozen to the bottom. No creek could contain water in that winter. But he knew also that there were streams of water that came out from the hillsides and ran along under the snow and on top of the ice of the creek. He knew that even in the coldest weather these streams were never frozen, and he also knew their danger. They hid pools of water under the snow that might be three inches deep, or three feet. Sometimes a skin of ice half an inch thick covered them, and in turn was covered by the snow. Sometimes there was both water and thin ice, and when a man broke through he could get very wet. That was why he had jumped away so suddenly. He had felt the ice move under his feet. He had also heard the noise of the snow-covered ice skin breaking. And to get his feet wet in such a temperature meant trouble and danger. At the very least it meant delay, because he would be forced to stop and build a fire. Only under its protection could he bare his feet while he dried his socks and moccasins. He stood and studied the creek bottom and its banks. He decided that the flowing stream of water came from the right side. He thought a while, rubbing his nose and face. Then he walked to the left. He stepped carefully and tested the ice at each step. Once away from the danger, he continued at his four-mile pace.

During the next two hours he came to several similar dangers. Usually the snow above the pools had a sunken appearance. However, once again he came near to falling through the ice. Once, sensing danger, he made the dog go ahead. The dog did not want to go. It hesitated until the man pushed it forward. Then it went quickly across the white, unbroken surface. Suddenly it fell through the ice, but climbed out on the other side, which was firm. It had wet its feet and legs. Almost immediately the water on them turned to ice. The dog made quick efforts to get the ice off its legs. Then it lay down in the snow and began to bite out the ice that had formed between the toes. The animal knew enough to do this. To permit the ice to remain would mean sore feet. It did not know this. It merely obeyed the commands that arose from the deepest part of its being. But the man knew these things, having learned them from experience. He removed the mitten from his right hand and helped the dog tear out the pieces of ice. He did not bare his fingers more than a minute, and was surprised to find that they were numb. It certainly was cold. He pulled on the mitten quickly and beat the hand across his breast.

At twelve o'clock the day was at its brightest. Yet the sun did not appear in the sky. At half-past twelve, on the minute, he arrived at the divide of the creek. He was pleased at his rate of speed. If he continued, he would certainly be with the boys by six o'clock that evening. He unbuttoned his jacket and shirt and pulled forth his lunch. The action took no more than a quarter of a minute, yet in that brief moment the numbness touched his bare fingers. He did not put the mitten on, but instead, struck the fingers against his leg. Then he sat down on a snow-covered log to eat. The pain that followed the striking of his fingers against his leg ceased so quickly that he was frightened. He had not had time to take a bite of his lunch. He struck the fingers repeatedly and returned them to the mitten. Then he bared the other hand for the purpose of eating. He tried to take a mouthful, but the ice around his mouth prevented him. Then he knew what was wrong. He had forgotten to build a fire and warm himself. He laughed at his own foolishness. As he laughed, he noted the numbness in his bare fingers. Also, he noted that the feeling which had first come to his toes when he sat down was already passing away. He wondered whether the toes were warm or whether they were numb. He moved them inside the moccasins and decided that they were numb.

He pulled the mitten on hurriedly and stood up. He was somwhat frightened. He stamped forcefully until the feeling returned to his feet. It certainly was cold, was his thought. That man from Sulphur Creek had spoken the truth when telling how cold it sometimes got in this country. And he had laughed at him at the time! That showed one must not be too sure of things. There was no mistake about it, it was cold. He walked a few steps, stamping his feet and waving his arms, until reassured by the returning warmth. Then he took some matches and proceeded to make a fire. In the bushes, the high water had left a supply of sticks. From here he got wood for his fire. Working carefully from a small beginning, he soon had a roaring fire. Bending over the fire, he first melted the ice from his face. With the protection of the fire's warmth he ate his lunch. For the moment, the cold had been forced away. The dog took comfort in the fire, lying at full length close enough for warmth and far enough away to escape being singed.

When the man had finished eating, he filled his pipe with tobacco and had a comfortable time with a smoke. Then he pulled on his mittens, settled his cap firmly about his ears, and started along the creek trail toward the left. The dog was sorry to leave and looked toward the fire. This man did not know cold. Possibly none of his ancestors had known cold, real cold. But the dog knew and all of its family knew. And it knew that it was not good to walk outside in such fearful cold. It was the time to lie in a hole in the snow and to wait for this awful cold to stop. There was no real bond between the dog and the man. The one was the slave of the other. The dog made no effort to indicate its fears to the man. It was not concerned with the well-being of the man. It was for its own sake that it looked toward the fire. But the man whistled, and spoke to it with the sound of the whip in his voice. So the dog started walking close to the man's heels and followed him along the trail.

The man put more tobacco in his mouth and started a new growth of amber ice on his face. Again his moist breath quickly powdered the hair on his face with white. He looked around him. There did not seem to be so many pools of water under the snow on the left side of Henderson Creek, and for half an hour the man saw no signs of any. And then it happened. At a place where there were no signs, the man broke through. It was not deep. He was wet to the knees before he got out of the water to the firm snow.

He was angry and cursed his luck aloud. He had hoped to get into camp with the boys at six o'clock, and this would delay him an hour. Now he would have to build a fire and dry his moccasins and socks. This was most important at that low temperature. He knew that much. So he turned aside to the bank, which he climbed. On top, under several small pine trees, he found some firewood which had been carried there by the high water of last year. There were some sticks, but also larger branches, and some dry grasses. He threw several large branches on top of the snow. This served for a foundation and prevented the young flame from dying in the wet snow. He made a flame by touching a match to a small piece of tree bark that he took from his pocket. This burned even better than paper. Placing it on the foundation, he fed the young flame with pieces of dry grass and with the smallest dry sticks.

He worked slowly and carefully, realizing his danger. Gradually, as the flame grew stronger, he increased the size of the sticks with which he fed it. He sat in the snow, pulling the sticks from the bushes under the trees and feeding them directly to the flame. He knew he must not fail. When it is 75 below zero, a man must not fail in his first attempt to build a fire. This is especially true if his feet are wet. If his feet are dry, and he fails, he can run along the trail for half a mile to keep his blood moving. But the blood in wet and freezing feet cannot be kept moving by running when it is 75 degrees below. No matter how fast he runs, the wet feet will freeze even harder.

All this the man knew. The old man on Sulphur Creek had told him about it, and now he was grateful for the advice. Already all feeling had gone from his feet. To build the fire he had been forced to remove his mittens, and the fingers had quickly become numb. His pace of four miles an hour had kept his heart pushing the blood to all parts of his body. But the instant he stopped, the action of the heart slowed down. He now received the full force of the cold. The blood of his body drew back from it. The blood was alive, like the dog. Like the dog, it wanted to hide and seek cover, away from the fearful cold. As long as he walked four miles an hour, the blood rose to the surface. But now it sank down into the lowest depths of his body. His feet and hands were the first to feel its absence. His wet feet froze first. His bare fingers were numb, although they had not yet begun to freeze. Nose and face were already freezing, while the skin of all his body became cold as it lost its blood.

But he was safe. Toes and nose and face would be only touched by the frost, because the fire was beginning to burn with strength. He was feeding it with sticks the size of his finger. In another minute he would be able to feed it with larger branches. Then he could remove his wet moccasins and socks. While they dried, he could keep his naked feet warm by the fire, rubbing them first with snow. The fire was a success. He was safe. He remembered the advice of the old man on Sulphur Creek, and smiled. The man had been very serious when he said that no man should travel alone in that country after 50 below zero. Well, here he was; he had had the accident; he was alone; and he had saved himself. Those old men were rather womanish, he thought. All a man must do was to keep his head, and he was all right. Any man who was a man could travel alone. But it was surprising, the rapidity with which his face and nose were freezing. And he had not thought his fingers could lose their feeling in so short a time. Without feeling they were, because he found it very difficult to make them move together to grasp a stick. They seemed far from his body and from him. When he touched a stick, he had to look to see whether or not he was holding it.

All of which mattered little. There was the fire, promising life with every dancing flame. He started to untie his moccasins. They were coated with ice. The thick socks were like iron almost to the knees. The moccasin's strings were like ropes of steel. For a moment he pulled them with his unfeeling fingers. Then, realizing the foolishness of it, he grasped his knife.

But before he could cut the strings, it happened. It was his own fault, or instead, his mistake. He should not have built the fire under the pine tree. He should have built it in an open space. But it had been easier to pull the sticks from the bushes and drop them directly on the fire. Now the tree under which he had done this carried a weight of snow on its branches. No wind had been blowing for weeks and each branch was heavy with snow. Each time he pulled a stick he shook the tree slightly. There had been just enough movement to cause the awful thing to happen. High up in the tree one branch dropped its load of snow. This fell on the branches beneath. This process continued, spreading through the whole tree. The snow fell without warning upon the man and the fire, and the fire was dead. Where it had burned was a pile of fresh snow.

The man was shocked. It was like hearing his own judgment of death. For a moment he sat and stared at the spot where the fire had been. Then he grew very calm. Perhaps the old man on Sulphur Creek was right. If he had a companion on the trail he would be in no danger now. The companion could have built the fire. Now, he must build the fire again, and this second time he must not fail. Even if he succeeded, he would be likely to lose some toes. His feet must be badly frozen by now, and there would be some time before the second fire was ready.

Such were his thoughts, but he did not sit and think them. He was busy all the time they were passing through his mind. He made a new foundation for a fire, this time in the open space, where no tree would be above it. Next, he gathered dry grasses and tiny sticks. He could not bring his fingers together to pull them out of the ground, but he was able to gather them by the handful. In this way he also got many pieces that were undesirable, but it was the best he could do. He worked carefully, even collecting an armful of the larger branches to be used later when the fire gathered strength. And all the while the dog sat and watched him. There was an anxious look in its eyes, because it depended upon him as the fire provider, and the fire was slow in coming.

When all was ready, the man reached in his pocket for the second piece of tree bark. He knew the bark was there, although he could not feel it with his fingers. He tried again and again, but he could not grasp it. And all the time, in his mind, he knew that each instant his feet were freezing. This thought alarmed him, but he fought against it and kept calm. He pulled on his mittens with his teeth, and began swinging his arms. Then he beat his hands with all his strength against his sides. He did this while he was sitting down. Then he stood up to do it. All the while the dog sat in the snow, its tail curled warmly over its feet and its sharp wolf ears bent forward as it looked at the man. And the man, as he waved his arms and hands, looked with longing at the creature that was warm and secure in the covering provided by nature.

After a time, he began to notice some feeling in his beaten fingers. The feeling grew stronger until it became very painful, but the man welcomed the pain. He pulled the mitten from his right hand and grasped the tree bark from his pocket. The bare fingers were quickly numb again. Next, he brought out his pack of matches. But the awful cold had already driven the life out of his fingers. In his effort to separate one match from the others, the whole pack fell in the snow. He tried to pick it out of the snow, but failed. The dead fingers could neither touch nor hold. Now he was very careful. He drove the thought of his freezing feet, and nose, and face, from his mind. He devoted his whole soul to picking up the matches. He followed the movement of his fingers with his eyes, using his sense of sight instead of that of touch. When he saw his fingers on each side of the pack, he closed them. That is, he willed to close them, because the fingers did not obey. He put the mitten on the right hand again, and beat it fiercely against his knee. Then, with both mittened hands, he lifted up the pack of matches, along with much snow, to the front of his jacket. But he had gained nothing.

After some struggling he managed to get the pack between his mittened hands. In this manner he carried it to his mouth. The ice broke as he opened his mouth with a fierce effort. He used his upper teeth to rub across the pack in order to separate a single match. He succeeded in getting one, which he dropped on his jacket. His condition was no better. He could not pick up the match. Then he thought how he might do it. He picked up the match in his teeth and drew it across his leg. Twenty times he did this before he succeeded in lighting it. As it flamed he held it with his teeth to the tree bark. But the burning smell went up his nose, causing him to cough. The match fell into the snow and the flame died.

The old-timer on Sulphur Creek was right, he thought in the moment of controlled despair that followed. After 50 below zero, a man should travel with a companion. He beat his hands, but failed to produce any feeling in them. Suddenly he bared both hands, removing the mittens with his teeth. He caught the whole pack of matches between his hands. His arm muscles were not frozen and he was able to press the hands tightly against the matches. Then he drew the whole pack along his leg. It burst into flame, 70 matches at once! There was no wind to blow them out. He kept his head to one side to escape the burning smell, and held the flaming pack to the tree bark. As he so held it, he noticed some feeling in his hand. His flesh was burning. He could smell it. The feeling developed into pain. He continued to endure it. He held the flame of the matches to the bark that would not light readily because his own burning hands were taking most of the flame.

Finally, when he could endure no more, he pulled his hands apart. The flaming matches fell into the snow, but the tree bark was burning. He began laying dry grasses and the tiniest sticks on the flame. He could not choose carefully because they must be pieces that could be lifted between his hands. Small pieces of green grass stayed on the sticks, and he bit them off as well as he could with his teeth. He treated the flame carefully. It meant life, and it must not cease. The blood had left the surface of his body and he now began to shake from the cold. A large piece of a wet plant fell on the little fire. He tried to push it out with his fingers. His shaking body made him push it too far and he scattered the little fire over a wide space. He tried to push the burning grasses and sticks together again. Even with the strong effort that he made, his trembling fingers would not obey and the sticks were hopelessly scattered. Each stick smoked a little and died. The fire provider had failed. As he looked about him, his eyes noticed the dog sitting across the ruins of the fire from him. It was making uneasy movements, slightly lifting one foot and then the other.

The sight of the dog put a wild idea into his head. He remembered the story of the man, caught in a storm, who killed an animal and sheltered himself inside the dead body and thus was saved. He would kill the dog and bury his hands in the warm body until feeling returned to them. Then he could build another fire. He spoke to the dog, calling it to him. But in his voice was a strange note of fear that frightened the animal. It had never known the man to speak in such a tone before. Something was wrong and it sensed danger. It knew not what danger, but somewhere in its brain arose a fear of the man. It flattened its ears at the sound of the man's voice; its uneasy movements and the liftings of its feet became more noticeable. But it would not come to the man. He got down on his hands and knees and went toward the dog. But this unusual position again excited fear and the animal moved away.

The man sat in the snow for a moment and struggled for calmness. Then he pulled on his mittens, using his teeth, and then stood on his feet. He glanced down to assure himself that he was really standing, because lack of feeling in his feet gave him no relation to the earth. His position, however, removed the fear from the dog's mind. When he commanded the dog with his usual voice, the dog obeyed and came to him. As it came within his reach, the man lost control. His arms stretched out to hold the dog and he experienced real surprise when he discovered that his hands could not grasp. There was neither bend nor feeling in the fingers. He had forgotten for the moment that they were frozen and that they were freezing more and more. All this happened quickly and before the animal could escape, he encircled its body with his arms. He sat down in the snow, and in this fashion held the dog, while it barked and struggled.

But it was all he could do: hold its body encircled in his arms and sit there. He realized that he could not kill the dog. There was no way to do it. With his frozen hands he could neither draw nor hold his knife. Nor could he grasp the dog around the throat. He freed it and it dashed wildly away, still barking. It stopped 40 feet away and observed him curiously, with ears sharply bent forward.

The man looked down at his hands to locate them and found them hanging on the ends of his arms. He thought it curious that it was necessary to use his eyes to discover where his hands were. He began waving his arms, beating the mittened hands against his sides. He did this for five minutes. His heart produced enough blood to stop his shaking. But no feeling was created in his hands.

A certain fear of death came upon him. He realized that it was no longer a mere problem of freezing his fingers and toes, or of losing his hands and feet. Now it was a problem of life and death with the circumstances against him. The fear made him lose control of himself and he turned and ran along the creek bed on the old trail. The dog joined him and followed closely behind. The man ran blindly in fear such as he had never known in his life. Slowly, as he struggled through the snow, he began to see things again—the banks of the creek, the bare trees, and the sky. The running made him feel better. He did not shake any more. Maybe, if he continued to run, his feet would stop freezing. Maybe if he ran far enough, he would find the camp and the boys. Without doubt, he would lose some fingers and toes and some of his face. But the boys would take care of him and save the rest of him when he got there. And at the same time, there was another thought in his mind that said he would never get to the camp and the boys. It told him that it was too many miles away, that the freezing had too great a start and that he would soon be dead. He pushed this thought to the back of his mind and refused to consider it. Sometimes it came forward and demanded to be heard. But he pushed it away and tried to think of other things.

It seemed strange to him that he could run on feet so frozen that he could not feel them when they struck the earth and took the weight of his body. He seemed to be flying along above the surface and to have no connection with the earth. His idea of running until he arrived at the camp and the boys presented one problem: he lacked the endurance. Several times he caught himself as he was falling. Finally, he dropped to the ground, unable to stop his fall. When he tried to rise, he failed. He must sit and rest, he decided. Next time he would merely walk and keep going. As he sat and regained his breath, he noted that he was feeling warm and comfortable. He was not shaking, and it even seemed that a warm glow had come to his body. And yet, when he touched his nose or face, there was no feeling. Running would not bring life to them. Nor would it help his hands and feet. Then the thought came to him that the frozen portions of his body must be increasing. He tried to keep this thought out of his mind and to forget it. He knew that such thoughts caused a feeling of fright in him and he was afraid of such feelings. But the thought returned and continued, until he could picture his body totally frozen. This was too much, and again he ran wildly along the trail. Once he slowed to a walk, but the thought that the freezing of his body was increasing made him run again.

And all the time the dog ran with him, at his heels. When he fell a second time, the dog curled its tail over its feet and sat in front of him, facing him, curiously eager. The warmth and security of the animal angered him. He cursed it until it flattened its ears. This time the shaking because of the cold began more quickly. He was losing his battle with the frost. It was moving into his body from all sides. This thought drove him forward. But he ran no more than 100 feet, when he fell head first. It was his last moment of fear. When he had recovered his breath and his control, he sat and thought about meeting death with dignity. However, the idea did not come to him in exactly this manner. His idea was that he had been acting like a fool. He had been running around like a chicken with its head cut off. He was certain to freeze in his present circumstances, and he should accept it calmly. With this newfound peace of mind came the first sleepiness. A good idea, he thought, to sleep his way to death. Freezing was not as bad as people thought. There were many worse ways to die.

He pictured the boys finding his body the next day. Suddenly he saw himself with them, coming along the trail and looking for himself. And, still with them, he came around a turn in the trail and found himself lying in the snow. He did not belong with himself any more. Even then he was outside of himself, standing with the boys and looking at himself in the snow. It certainly was cold, was his thought. When he returned to the United States he could tell the folks what real cold was. His mind went from this to the thought of the old man of Sulphur Creek. He could see him quite clearly, warm and comfortable, and smoking a pipe.

"You were right, old fellow. You were right," he murmured to the old man of Sulphur Creek.

Then the man dropped into what seemed to him the most comfortable and satisfying sleep he had ever known. The dog sat facing him and waiting. The brief day ended in a long evening. There were no signs of a fire to be made. Never in the dog's experience had it known a man to sit like that in the snow and make no fire. As the evening grew darker, its eager longing for the fire mastered it. With much lifting of its feet, it cried softly. Then it flattened its ears, expecting the man's curse. But the man remained silent. Later, the dog howled loudly. And still later it moved close to the man and caught the smell of death. This made the animal back away. A little longer it delayed, howling under the stars that leaped and danced and shone brightly in the cold sky. Then it turned and ran along the trail toward the camp it knew, where there were the other food providers and fire providers.

YOLANDA
Oscar Casares

When I can't sleep at night I think of Yolanda Castro. She was a woman who lived next door to us one summer when I was growing up. I've never told Maggie about her because it's not something she'd appreciate knowing. Trust me. Tonight, like most nights, she fell asleep before I was even done brushing my teeth. And now all I can hear are little snores. Sometimes she even talks to herself, shouts out other people's names, and then in the morning says she can't remember any of it. Either way, I let her go on sleeping. She's over on her side of the bed. It's right where she ought to be. This thing with Yolanda doesn't really concern her.

I was only twelve years old when Frank and Yolanda Castro moved into the beige house with green trim. Frank pulled up on our street in a U-Haul he'd driven all the way from California to Texas. I remember it being a different neighborhood back then. Everybody knew everybody, and people left their doors unlocked at night. You didn't worry about people stealing shit you didn't lock up. I'm talking about more than twenty years ago now. I'm talking about before some drunk spent all afternoon in one of the cantinas on Fourteenth Street, then drove his car straight into the Rivas front yard and ran over the Baby Jesus that was still lying in the manger because Lonny Rivas was too *flojo* to put it away a month after Christmas, and then the guy tried to run, but fell down, asleep, in our yard, and when the cops were handcuffing him all he could say was *ma-ri-juan-a*, which even then, at the age of fifteen, I knew wasn't a good thing to say when you were being arrested. This was before Pete Zuniga was riding his brand-new ten-speed from Western Auto and, next to the Friendship Garden, saw a white dude who'd been knifed a couple of dozen times and was

409

floating in the green water of the resaca. Before some crazy woman hired a curandera to put a spell on her daughter's ex-boyfriend, which really meant hiring a couple of hit men from Matamoros to do a drive-by. Before the cops ever had to show up at El Disco de Oro Tortillería. Like holding up a 7-Eleven was getting old, right? You know, when you could sit at the Brownsville Coffee Shop #1 and not worry about getting it in the back while you ate your menudo. When you didn't have to put an alarm *and* the Club on your car so it wouldn't end up in Reynosa. Before my father had to put iron bars on the windows and doors because some future convict from the junior high was always breaking into the house. And before my father had to put a fence in the front because, in his words, I'm sick and tired of all those damn dogs making poo in my yard. I guess what I'm trying to say is, things were different back then.

Frank Castro was an older man, in his fifties by that point, and Yolanda couldn't have been more than thirty, if that. My mother got along with Yolanda okay and even helped her get a job at the HEB store where she had worked since before I was born. You could say that was where the problems started, because Frank Castro didn't want his wife working at HEB, or any other place for that matter. You have no business being in that grocery store, I heard him yell one night when I was trying to fall asleep. I could hear almost everything Frank yelled that summer. Our houses were only a few yards apart, and my window was the closest to the action. My father's bougainvillaeas were the dividing line between the two properties. I heard Yolanda beg Frank to please let her take the job. I heard Frank yell something in Spanish about how no woman in his family had ever worked behind a cosmetics counter, selling lipstick. I heard her promise she'd only work part-time, and she'd quit if they ever scheduled her on nights or weekends. I heard her tell him how much she loved him and how she'd never take a job that would keep them apart. Francisco, tú eres mi vida, she said to him. I heard him get real quiet. Then I heard Frank and Yolanda Castro making love. I didn't know what making love sounded like back then, but I can tell you now that's what it was.

If you saw what Yolanda looked like, you might not have blamed Frank for not wanting her to leave the house. It also wouldn't have been a big mystery to you how she went into the store applying for a job in the meat department and ended up getting one in cosmetics. The only girl I'd ever seen that even came close to being as beautiful as Yolanda was in a *Playboy* I found under my parents' bed the summer before. The girl in the magazine had the same long black hair, light brown skin, and green eyes that Yolanda did, only she was sitting bareback on an Appaloosa.

The thing I remember most about Frank was his huge forearms. They were like Popeye's, except with a lot more black and gray hair mixed in. But the hair on his arms was just the beginning. There wasn't a time I saw the guy that he didn't look like he could've used a good shave. And it didn't help that his thick eyebrows were connected into one long eyebrow that stretched across the bottom of his forehead like a piece of electrical tape. He was average size, but he looked short and squatty when he stood next to Yolanda. Frank was a mechanic at the airport and, according to my father, probably made good money. I was with my father the first time he met Frank. He always made it a point to meet any new neighbors and then come back to the house and give a full report to my mother, who would later meet the neighbors herself and say he was exaggerating about how shifty so-and-so's eyes were or how rich he thought another neighbor might be because he had one of those new foreign cars in the driveway, un carro extranjero, a Toyota or a Honda. Frank was beginning to mow his front yard when we walked up. My father introduced me as his boy, and I shook our neighbor's sweaty hand. I've lived thirty-six years on this earth and never shaken hands with a bear, but I have a good idea that it wouldn't be much different from shaking Frank Castro's hand. Even his fingers needed a haircut. Frank stood there answering a couple of my father's questions about whether he liked the neighborhood (he liked it) and how long he had lived in California before moving back to Texas (ten years—he held up both hands to show us exactly how many). Suddenly, my father nodded and said we had to go. He turned around and walked off, then looked over his shoulder and yelled at me to hurry up. This whole time, Frank had not shut off his mower. My father was forced to stand there and shout over the sound of the engine. The report on Frank wasn't pretty when we got back to the house. From that point on, my father would only refer to him as El Burro.

It wasn't just my father. Nobody liked Frank. He had this thing about his yard where he didn't want anybody getting near it. We found this out one day when Lonny and I were throwing the football around in the street. Lonny was showing off and he threw the ball over my head, way over, and it landed in Frank's yard. When I was getting the ball, Frank opened the front door and yelled something about it being private property. Then he went over, turned on the hose, and started watering his yard and half the street in front of his yard. He did this every afternoon from that day on. The hose with a spray gun in his right hand, and a Schlitz tallboy in his left. Lonny thought we should steal the hose when Frank wasn't home, or maybe poke a few holes in it, just to teach the fucker a lesson. One Saturday morning we even saw him turn the hose on some Jehovahs who were walking up the street towards his house. A skinny man wearing a tie and short-sleeve shirt kept trying to give him a pamphlet, but Frank wasn't listening.

My mother gave Yolanda a ride to work every day. In the after-noons, Yolanda got off work early enough to be waiting for Frank to pull up in his car and drive her back to the house. My mother told us at home that Yolanda had asked Frank to teach her how to drive when they first got married but that Frank had said she was his princesa now and any place she needed to go, he'd take her. One morning, when both my mother and Yolanda had the day off, my mother asked her if she wanted to learn how to drive. They drove out by the port, and my mother pulled over so Yolanda could take the wheel. I was hanging out at the Jiffy-Mart, down the street, when I saw Yolanda driving my mother's car. Yolanda honked the horn, and they both waved at me as they turned the corner.

That night—like a lot of nights that summer—I listened to Frank and Yolanda Castro. What they said went something like this:

"I can show you."

"I don't wanna see."

"Why not?"

"Because you have *no* business driving a car around town."

"But this way you don't have to pick me up every day. You can come straight home, and I'll be here already, waiting."

"I don't care. I'm talking about you learning to drive."

"Frank, it's nothing."

"You don't even have a car. What do you want with a license?"

"I can buy one."

"With what?"

"I've been getting bonuses. The companies give us a little extra if we sell more of their makeup."

"Is that right?"

"It isn't that much, Frank."

"And then?"

"Well, maybe I can buy a used one."

"It's because of that store."

"What's wrong with the store?"

"It's putting ideas in your head."

"Frank, what ideas?"

"Ideas! Is there some place I haven't taken you?"

"No."

"Well, then?"

"Francisco."

"Don't 'Francisco' me."

"Baby . . ."

"¡Qué no!"

They were beginning to remind me of one of my mother's novelas, which she was probably watching in the living room at that very moment. Things like that usually made me want to laugh—and I did a little, into my pillow, but it was only because I couldn't believe I was actually hearing it, and I could see Frank Castro pounding me into the ground with his big forearms if he ever found out.

"No! I said."

"I'm not Trini."

"I never said . . ."

"Then stop treating me like her. ¿No sabes qué tanto te quiero, Francisco?"

It got quiet for a while after that. Then there was the sound of something hitting the floor, the sound of two bodies dropping

on a bed with springs that had seen better days (and nights), the
sound of Yolanda saying, *Ay, Diosito*, over and over and over
again—just like my tía Hilda did the day her son, my cousin Rudy,
almost drowned in the swimming pool at the Civic Center—then
the sound of the bed springs making their own crazy music, and
the sound of what I imagine a bear is like when he's trying to make
little bears.

Yolanda kept getting a ride to work with my mother, and Frank
kept bringing her home in the afternoons. My mother had offered
to drive Yolanda to the DPS office and let her borrow our car for
the driving part of the test, but Yolanda said she'd changed her
mind and didn't want to talk about it. I heard my mother telling my
father what she'd said, and they agreed it probably had something
to do with Frank. El Burro, my father let out when they didn't have
anything else to say.

It was the Fourth of July when I got sick that summer. I
remember my mother wouldn't let me go outside with Lonny. He
kept yelling at me from the street that night to stop being a baby
and come out of the house so I could pop some firecrackers. We'd
been talking all week about shooting some bottle rockets in the
direction of Frank's house. It didn't feel like anything at first, just
a fever, but the next morning we knew it was the chicken pox. My
mother had to miss a few days of work, staying home with me until
I got over the worst part. After that, Yolanda volunteered to come
look in on me when she wasn't working. But I told my mother I
didn't want her coming over when I still looked like those dead
people in that *Night of the Living Dead* movie. My mother said
Yolanda would understand I was sick, and if she didn't, that's
what I'd get for watching those kinds of movies. So for about a
week she came over in the mornings and we watched *The Price Is
Right* together. Yolanda was great at guessing the prices of things,
and she said it was from working in a grocery store and having
a good memory. I told her I thought she should go on the show.
She laughed and said she probably wouldn't win anything, since
she'd be too nervous. What I meant to say was that she should go
on the show and be one of the girls who stands next to the car,
smiling. She was prettier than any of them, but I never told her
that, because I got embarrassed whenever I thought about saying it.

If Yolanda came over in the afternoon, we'd watch *General Hospital* together. She said she'd been watching it for years. There wasn't anything else on at that hour, so I didn't really care. Once, she brought over some lime sherbet, and we played Chinese checkers in my room until she had to get home to Frank Castro. Each time she left she'd reach down and give me a little kiss on the cheek, and each time her hair smelled like a different fruit. Sometimes like a pear, sometimes like a strawberry, sometimes like an apple. The strawberry was my favorite.

*   *   *

This was about the time when Frank said that from now on, he would take Yolanda to work in the morning—no matter how out of the way it was for him, or the fact that he and my mother were always pulling out of the driveway at the same time. A week or two went by, and then my mother told my father that Frank had started showing up at the store in the middle of the day, usually during his lunch hour, but sometimes also at two or three in the afternoon. He wouldn't talk to Yolanda, but instead just hung out by the magazine rack, pretending to read a wrestling magazine. Yolanda tried to ignore him. My mother said she had talked to her in the break room, but Yolanda kept saying it was nothing, that Frank's hours had changed at the airport.

There was one Saturday when he was off from work, and as usual, he spent it in his front yard, sitting in a green lawn chair, drinking tallboys. He had turned on the sprinkler and was watching his grass and half the street get a good watering. Lonny and I were throwing the football around. Frank sat in that stupid chair all afternoon. He only went in to grab another beer and, I guess, take a piss. Each time he got up and turned around, we shot him the finger.

That night, I heard Frank's voice loud and clear. He wanted answers. Something about a phone number. Something about a customer he'd seen Yolanda talking to a couple of days earlier. Did she think he was blind? What the hell was so funny when the two of them were talking? How many times? he wanted to know. ¡Desgraciado! Where? Goddammit! he wanted to know. What game show? ¡El sanavabiche! Something shattered against the wall and then a few seconds later Yolanda screamed. I sat up. I didn't know if I could form words if I had to. What the hell were you doing listening anyway? they would ask me. There was another scream and then the sound of the back door slamming. I looked out my window and saw Frank Castro chase Yolanda into their backyard. She was wearing a nightgown that came down to her knees. Frank had on the same khakis and muscle shirt he'd worn that afternoon. He only ran a few feet down from the back steps before his head hit the clothesline, and he fell to the ground, hard. Yolanda didn't turn to look back and ran around the right side of their house. I thought she'd gone back inside to call the police. Then I heard footsteps and a tapping on my window. It was Yolanda whispering, Open it, open it.

I didn't say anything for a long time. Yolanda had climbed in and let down the blinds. We were lying on the bed, facing the window. She was behind me, holding me tight. I finally asked her if she wanted a glass of water or some Kool-Aid. I made it myself, I told her. It's the orange kind, I said. I didn't know what else to talk about. She said no, and then she told me to be quiet. I kept thinking, This has to be a dream and any minute now my mother's going to walk in and tell me the barbacoa is sitting on the table and to come eat because we're going to eleven o'clock mass and don't even think about putting on those blue jeans with the patches in the knees ¿me entiendes? But that wasn't happening, and something told me then that no matter what happened after tonight, this was something I'd never forget. There would always be a time *before* Yolanda crawled into my bed and a time *after*. As she held me, I could feel her heart beating. Then I felt her chiches pressed against my back. And even though I couldn't see them, I knew they were perfect like the rest of her. I knew that they'd fit right in the palms of my hands, if only I had enough guts to turn around. Just turn around, that's all I had to do. I thought back to when she was tapping on the window, and I was sure she wasn't wearing a bra. I was sure there was nothing but Yolanda underneath her nightgown. I could have sworn I'd seen even more. I'd been close to a woman's body before. But this wasn't like when my tía Gloria came into town and couldn't believe how much I'd grown, and then she squeezed me so hard my head got lost in her huge and heavily perfumed chiches. And it wasn't anything like the Sears catalog where the girls had a tiny rose at the top of their panties. No, this was Yolanda and she was in my bed, pressed up against my back, like it was the only place in the world for us to be.

I could go on and tell you the rest of the details—how I never turned around and always regretted it, how we stayed there and listened to Frank crying in his backyard, how Lonny's dad finally called the cops on his ass, how Yolanda had a cousin pick her up the next morning, how she ended up leaving Frank for a man who worked for one of the shampoo companies, how it didn't matter because she'd also been seeing an assistant manager and would be having his baby soon enough, and how it really didn't matter because the assistant manager was already married and wasn't about to leave his wife and kids, and how, actually, none of it mattered because she'd been taking money out of the register and was about to be caught—but that's not the part of the story I like to remember.

In that bed of mine, the one with the Dallas Cowboy pillows and covers, Yolanda and I were safe. We were safe from Frank Castro and safe from anybody else that might try to hurt us. And it was safe for me to fall asleep in Yolanda's arms, with her warm, beautiful body pressed against mine, and dream that we were riding off to some faraway place on an Appaloosa.